THE
SIERRA CLUB
GUIDE TO
THE
NATURAL AREAS
OF OREGON
AND WASHINGTON

THE SIERRA CLUB GUIDES
TO THE NATURAL AREAS OF THE UNITED STATES

The Natural Areas of California

The Natural Areas of Oregon and Washington

THE
SIERRA CLUB
GUIDE TO
THE
NATURAL AREAS
OF OREGON
AND WASHINGTON

JOHN PERRY

AND

JANE GREVERUS PERRY

SIERRA CLUB BOOKS   SAN FRANCISCO

The Sierra Club, founded in 1892 by John Muir, has devoted itself to the study and protection of the earth's scenic and ecological resources—mountains, wetlands, woodlands, wild shores and rivers, deserts and plains. The publishing program of the Sierra Club offers books to the public as a nonprofit educational service in the hope that they may enlarge the public's understanding of the Club's basic concerns. The point of view expressed in each book, however, does not necessarily represent that of the Club. The Sierra Club has some fifty chapters coast to coast, in Canada, Hawaii, and Alaska. For information about how you may participate in its programs to preserve wilderness and the quality of life, please address inquiries to Sierra Club, 530 Bush Street, San Francisco, CA 94108.

Library of Congress Cataloging in Publication Data

Perry, John, 1914–
The Sierra Club guide to the natural areas of
Oregon and Washington.

Includes bibliographical references and index.
1. Outdoor recreation—Washington (State)—Guide-books.
2. Natural history—Washington (State) 3. Natural areas
—Washington (State)—Guide-books. 4. Washington (State)
—Description and travel—1981– —Guide-books.
5. Outdoor recreation—Oregon—Guide-books. 6. Natural
history—Oregon. 7. Natural areas—Oregon—Guide-books.
8. Oregon—Description and travel—1981– —Guide-books.
I. Perry, Jane Greverus. II. Title.
GV191.42.W2P47 1983   917.97   82-16937
ISBN 0-87156-334-7

Cover design by Gael Towey Dillon
Book design concept by Lilly Langotsky
Illustrations by Nancy Warner
Printed in the United States of America
10 9 8 7 6 5 4 3

CONTENTS

INTRODUCTION

This is a guide to the quiet places, where plants grow, birds sing, and the signs of man are few.

Western friends warned that the quiet places have been overrun. One must make reservations weeks ahead to enter a wilderness. Beach parking is full by midmorning. Noisy off-road vehicles have driven off wildlife and hikers.

Certainly the western landscape has been much changed since we first saw it 50 years ago. The forests are a giant patchwork, great openings formed by clear-cutting. Some trails have been trampled into muddy ditches. Many hillsides show the scars of ORV's. "Campground full" signs are common.

Yet we had no difficulty finding quiet places. In the last phase of our research, we traveled 11,500 miles in these two states, camping every night in our motor home or in a tent beside a trail. On most nights we were alone or with few neighbors.

People congregate. Most seem to prefer the developed recreation sites, the publicized trails. Most come at certain seasons. Those who seek solitude can find it, often nearby. One night we had a 17-mile-long river canyon all to ourselves, on another a splendid valley dotted by small lakes.

In the East, less than 10% of the land is publicly owned. Most federal and state parks, forests, and wildlife areas occupy land that was once private. Much of it was abused and abandoned, surrendered in lieu of tax payment or sold for a few dollars per acre. Today most eastern states are paying high prices for remaining fragments of wetlands and undeveloped coast.

More than half of Oregon and almost a third of Washington remain in federal ownership, and both states also have extensive landholdings. Most of these public lands are in the mountains and deserts, although Oregon has kept much of its seacoast in public ownership.

HOW WE SELECTED SITES

We use the term "natural area" broadly, generically. A few specialists have objected. They have appropriated the term and devised narrow definitions. "Federal Research Natural Areas," for example, are "lands on which various natural features are preserved in an undisturbed state solely for research and educational purposes."

We look for places where a visitor can enjoy nature. Most such places are not pristine. Some have been logged, farmed, mined, or otherwise disturbed, but the healing processes of nature are at work. Most wildlife refuges are not "natural," since their ponds and marshes are maintained by dikes and crops are planted to support waterfowl. Without such places few waterfowl would travel the flyways. When tens of thousands of geese and ducks endorse these places, they're good enough for us.

Large National Forests and National Parks were automatic selections. We studied smaller sites more critically. We would not include a State Park planned for intensive recreation. If, in addition to a developed area, it also had a few hundred roadless acres of interest to hikers and birders, we would consider it.

In studying a small site, we considered its setting. A small seaside park may provide access to a dozen miles of uncluttered ocean beach. A park with little more than a campground may be a wilderness trailhead. A site that is intolerably crowded on the Fourth of July may offer splendid solitude in December.

THE PUBLIC DOMAIN

When we had screened every National Park, National Forest, and National Wildlife Refuge, we had 16 million acres left over, what remains of the original public domain. Because of the different terms negotiated when these two states entered the Union, all but 310,000 acres of this is in Oregon. It sprawls over the landscape, sometimes in huge, solid blocks, sometimes in a checkerboard of 1-mi. squares, alternating with state and private land. It includes mountains, deserts, plains, canyons, rivers, lakes, and wetlands.

Its boundaries are not marked. It is not divided into neat packages, like parks and forests. We could not write a single entry for, say, the 15.7 million acres of public domain in Oregon. We looked for outstanding features, such as a mountain or canyon, then studied the surrounding area. Finally, we fixed arbitrary boundaries enclosing areas that seemed to fit together.

BLM was then engaged in a prodigious task mandated by Congress: identifying each roadless area of 5,000 or more acres, then gathering data to judge its suitability for wilderness status. This data and other documents in BLM District files were invaluable to us, as were our many talks with BLM specialists. We knew where to look when our field work began.

Our entries for BLM sites have local names and unmarked boundaries. The visitor will find no signs, no gates, and—except at a few recreation sites—no facilities. Only by chance will a BLM staff member be present. It is almost as unlikely that he will encounter other visitors.

These millions of acres are yours to enjoy. Here you can drive, hike, backpack, ride horseback, and camp almost anywhere, hunt and fish subject to state laws. Except in a few developed recreation areas, you are unlikely to meet other visitors.

Much of this land has been leased, usually for grazing, and some has been fenced by cattlemen. This does not shut you out. Where public land is fenced and gated, you have the right to enter—and close the gate behind you.

How do you know you are on public land? In some areas, private and public lands are intermixed. Our entries are for areas with few private inholdings. If you have doubts or concerns, visit the BLM District Office.

What if a rancher tells you to get off his place? Go quietly. You could have strayed onto private land. But some ranchers have used the public land for so long they consider it their own. Perhaps previous visitors have misbehaved. However, such confrontations are rare even on private land. Should you have one, the BLM office would like to know about it.

OTHER PUBLIC LANDS

We reluctantly decided to omit county and regional parks. Inquiries convinced us that few could supply the data we needed. Some, we were advised, would refuse our request, holding that their parks are for local taxpayers, not outsiders. At best, a large task would have a small yield.

We have included no military reservations. Some of these are large, and many permit limited public use. However, the limits are usually strict, and they often change from day to day. The base nearest our home has a special number one calls to hear whether visitors are permitted today. Most public use of these reservations is by hunters and fishermen, but if there is one near you, inquire. Some reservations have naturalists or wildlife managers who can tell you what's there and who may even offer a guided tour.

PRIVATE LANDS

Some of the largest private holdings are those of timber companies. In the past some companies permitted or invited public use. We wrote to the largest and asked if this was still the case. Only two replied. Both asked that we not mention their lands. Neither answered our question.

Off the record, company officials said, "We allow public use, but we don't want publicity. If many more people come, we'll have to close the gates. And we must be able to close them at any time, without notice, for operating reasons."

A state wildlife official confirmed this. Most timber company lands are used by hunters and fishermen, he said, and sometimes by hikers. Some owners require permits. A few charge fees. He advised prospective visitors to inquire at the nearest federal or state forestry office. Our advice: Forget it, unless you have a special interest in an area.

HOW WE GATHERED INFORMATION

Other guidebooks offer information about National Parks, National Forests, and National Wildlife Refuges. We know of no book in print that describes the state lands of the region, nor is there a guide to the public domain.

Roughly a third of the information assembled here is available somewhere in print: leaflets, booklets, maps, technical reports, species checklists, and various official documents. We gathered over a thousand items.

Another third is in the files of state and federal agencies, much of it in district and local offices. When our friends imagined we were hiking on mountain trails, we were often combing through hundreds of file drawers.

The final third we could obtain only by questionnaire, interview, and observation. The response to our 8-page questionnaire was unbelievably good. Our talks with managers and specialists filled many notebooks. Our own field notes went into a cassette recorder as we hiked or drove.

Have we visited every site? Many, not all. We have been frequent visitors to this region since 1929. We planned our 11,500-mile itinerary to visit sites we hadn't seen before.

Gathering so much information at first hand would require several lifetimes. Just compiling a decent bird list for one site would require monthly visits for a year. We had to rely on what others had observed over past years.

Good data is available for most National Parks, Forests, and Refuges, and BLM has greatly expanded its data on the public domain. Most state agencies have far less, so we went to their local managers. Few are professionals, but they have the outdoorsman's knowledge of nature. Their information was uneven. One could tell us more about local plants than about wildlife. Another knew all the local mammals but only a few birds. Most mentioned the larger, more colorful species; few nonprofessionals could tell us about mice, shrews, bats, or sparrows.

The method does not assure scientific accuracy. We checked what we could, deleted some obvious errors, deleted some improbables. Errors doubtless remain.

CHECKING

Every entry was sent to the site or to its district or state headquarters. Response was again excellent: 100% for major sites, well over 95% for smaller ones. Entries came back with corrections and additions. Most of this data was checked in late 1980 or early 1981.

WHAT'S NOT IN THE ENTRIES

Entries do not include information about:

Picnic grounds. One can picnic almost anywhere.

Campground facilities. Excellent directories are published.

Cabins, inns, lodges. We could not distinguish among lodgings on public land, lodgings on private inholdings, and lodgings just outside.

Restaurants and snack bars presented the same difficulty. Also, many close when crowds are absent.

Playgrounds, golf courses, etc.

Admission fees. Many parks charge fees. They change from year to year. Toll booths are often closed when visitors are few.

Rock climbing, rockhounding, spelunking, and scuba diving are too specialized for a general guide.

CHANGES

These are hard times for the public lands. For years budgets failed to keep pace with increasing public use. Now federal and state agency budgets have been cut, in some cases savagely. The permanent damage thus inflicted on precious natural resources is of deep concern to us, but beyond the scope of this book. Readers will encounter many reductions in opportunities and services:

- Publications may be out of print. Others, once free, will be sold.
- Campfire programs, guided walks, and other interpretive programs may be curtailed.
- Some campgrounds may be closed, others operated for shorter seasons. Facilities may be reduced. Broken or vandalized equipment may not be replaced.
- Some wildlife refuges may be closed, perhaps seasonally or on certain days. Visitors may be restricted to smaller portions of refuges.
- Maintenance of hiking trails may be reduced.
- Snow plowing may be discontinued on some park roads.

HOW TO USE THIS BOOK

Each state is divided into zones. Zone boundaries follow county lines, with minor exceptions. A map showing these zones appears at the beginning of each state section, together with an alphabetical list of all sites within that state.

At the beginning of each zone section is a zone map on which sites are spotted, with key numbers. Sites are listed in numerical order.

- If you plan to visit an area, find the corresponding zone and see what other sites in the zone would interest you.
- If you plan to visit—say—a National Park, locate its key number on the zone map and see what other sites are nearby.
- Entries are arranged alphabetically within zones. Information in entries is presented in a standard sequence.

SITE NAME

Parks are for people. Most parks have formal entrances. Most parks are closed to logging and hunting. Most parks have developed recreation sites. Parks have more facilities, more supervision, more rules, and more visitors than forests or refuges.

Forests are for trees and water. National Forests are managed for wood, water, wildlife, and recreation, although critics charge imbalance. Timber is often harvested on the more humid western slopes, vegetation maintained in semiarid areas. Hunting and fishing in National Forests are governed by state law. Recreation has a high priority in many National Forests. While there are campgrounds, one can make camp almost anywhere.

Wildlife management areas, state operated, are for birds and beasts, fishes included. In the past, most visits were by hunters and fishermen, whose license fees supported the state systems. Now visits by "nonconsumptive users," such as hikers and birdwatchers, are welcomed, especially outside hunting season.

National Wildlife Refuges are also for birds and beasts, but many have visitor facilities: auto tour routes, exhibits, information centers. Hunting is usually permitted, though often restricted to certain parts of the refuge and with special rules.

Public domain lands, managed by BLM, have many uses, including grazing, mining, forestry, and geothermal development. Most areas are open to public use. Large areas are far from any paved roads, and access often requires 4-wheel drive or a sturdy pickup truck. In the many roadless areas, travel is by foot or horseback. Most BLM lands are arid or semiarid.

Multiple Use Areas are peculiar to Washington and described in the state preface.

ADMINISTERING AGENCY

Entries name the agencies with management responsibility, not parent departments. Addresses of state agency headquarters appear in state prefaces, those of federal regional offices in this main preface.

ACREAGE

Many National Forests and some other sites have "inholdings," privately owned land within their boundaries. If these are significant, the entry gives both the acreage within the boundaries and the acreage of publicly owned land.

HOW TO GET THERE

Routings begin from points easily found on ordinary highway maps. For large sites, the route is one most visitors use.

Don't rely on written directions. You need maps. When a routing leaves the main routes shown on your map, make local inquiries. You'll hear about road conditions and perhaps learn more about the area.

Both states have thousands of miles of unpaved roads, many of them not shown on highway maps. National Forest maps show the Forest roads. The public domain has BLM-maintained roads and "ways," vehicle tracks not officially recognized or maintained as roads. Visit the BLM District Office before venturing far on these backcountry routes.

OPEN HOURS

Most National Parks are open 24 hours. Many State Parks are closed at night, though campers may be able to leave or enter. National Wildlife Refuges and many state wildlife management areas are closed at night. Forests don't have gates.

SYMBOLS

Symbols tell at a glance if a site offers camping, swimming, etc. Most symbols have obvious meanings:

 Without the pack, this means "hiking," with it, "backpacking." The entry for a small site carries the backpacking symbol if it serves as trailhead.

 In addition to canoeable waters, this symbol is also used for white water requiring rafts.

 Used for ski touring, usually includes snowshoeing.

 We used this sightseeing symbol in our *Guide to the Natural Areas of the Eastern United States* to indicate places of special scenic value. It doesn't appear here because of its wide application in the West. Almost every natural area is worth seeing.

In many cases, the symbols correspond to items in the "Activities" part of the entry. If there is no useful information to report, the symbol stands alone.

DESCRIPTION

Each site is briefly characterized: terrain, main physical features, climate, vegetation, wildlife. Subheads such as *"Plants"* and *"Birds"* do not appear in all entries, usually because no one has studied these areas.

Even if complete flora and fauna lists were available, reproducing them would require a library rather than a volume. Using whatever data we could gather, we have made selections of species, attempting to characterize the principal plant and animal communities. In some cases this has seemed best achieved by listing the most common species. In others it seemed useful to mention rarities.

Comprehensive mammal lists were less often available than bird lists. Information on reptiles and amphibians was scarce.

In entries, the singular is used to signify single species. Plurals signify more than one species. Example: ". . . mountain bluebird, woodpeckers . . ."

Note: Authorities often decree changes in common names. "Myrtle warbler" and "Audubon's warbler" have become "yellow-rumped warbler." But "Traill's flycatcher" has been split into "willow flycatcher" and "alder flycatcher." Most species checklists supplied to us include some of the old names. Our purpose has been to use the names most readers now use.

FEATURES

Noted first are wilderness areas, primitive areas, and other large and noteworthy portions of sites.

For several years all federal land-managing agencies have, at the direction of Congress, been identifying and studying roadless areas of 5,000 or more acres and recommending those that meet the criteria for wilderness designation. Final designation is by Congress. Wilderness areas are closed to virtually all entry except by visitors on foot or horseback.

We gathered our data while this process was going on, and while Secretary of the Interior Watt was proposing some highly controversial curtailments in the wilderness scheme. Although the decision by Congress determines the future of an area, it does not transform it. Thus we have not been limited by pending congressional decisions but have based our choices on what sites are today.

This portion of entries also mentions other noteworthy site features, such as waterfalls, canyons, major rivers, and caverns. It also mentions the principal recreation sites.

Because our concern is with natural areas, we give little or no attention to forts and other historical features.

INTERPRETATION

Here we note visitor centers, museums, nature trails, campfire programs, guided hikes, and other naturalist programs.

ACTIVITIES

Camping: Entries note numbers of sites, seasons of operation, and whether reservations are required. (Reservation requirements and systems change from year to year.)

Camping in parks is limited to campgrounds.

One can camp almost anywhere in National Forests. Along some heavily traveled routes, camping is restricted to campgrounds. In some Forest areas, camping is prohibited during periods of high fire danger.

One can camp almost anywhere on the public domain.

Most National Wildlife Refuges prohibit camping. Some state wildlife areas permit it. In some cases, hunters are allowed to park RV's overnight in parking areas.

Can one "camp"—park an RV overnight—in highway rest stops or roadside pullouts? In Oregon, only where posted. In Washington, except where posted. If there is any enforcement, it's on major highways and near congested areas.

Hiking, backpacking: The backpacking symbol is used where hiking with trailside camping is permitted and attractive. It is used for some small sites that serve as trailheads.

Trails in parks are more likely to be marked and maintained than trails in forests, although many National Forests have extensive trail systems. National Parks and Forests often have connecting trails.

Over most of the public domain, you're on your own, although there are numerous unmapped trails and tracks.

If you plan a backcountry trip, visit the nearest Ranger Station or BLM District Office for useful advice on routes, trail conditions, and whether many hikers are on the trail. You may be shown trail maps, even photographs of your destination.

We haven't tried to list all available trail guides. More appear each year, and many are available only locally.

The hiking season in the high country is relatively short, though it varies from place to place and year to year. Some of the National Parks and National Forests publish trail bulletins. From October into July, it's advisable to get the current bulletin or call the nearest Ranger Station before undertaking a long hike. Snow and ice are not the only problems. The melt and runoff create hazards. The June 21 Trail Report from North Cascades National Park begins:

Stream crossings continue to be hazardous and difficult . . . shouldn't be attempted unless hikers are sure of their safety . . . Use a good sturdy stick or rope, and unfasten the waistband on your backpack.

Mud is an obstacle until the ground dries, and until then trail crews won't come in to clear away downed trees and repair washouts.

While the high country is splendid, the Northwest offers delightful trails in every season. Winter is the best time to explore desert canyons. The lower slopes and valleys are at their best in spring and fall.

Hunting: Except for the parks, portions of some wildlife refuges, and recreation areas, public lands are generally open to hunting. State regulations apply everywhere, as do federal regulations on migratory species. Wildlife management areas often have special rules limiting the number of hunters or permitting hunting only on certain days.

Fishing: Entries report whether fishing is possible and name the principal species. In some National Parks, stocking has been discontinued, in keeping with the policy of maintaining near-natural conditions.

Swimming: We report what we were told. Swimming from many Pacific beaches is said to be cold, rough, and dangerous. In some State Parks, swimming is permitted only when lifeguards are present. Responses from forests and BLM sites often failed to mention swimming even though lakes and rivers are present. Management is permissive: Swim where you wish, at your own risk.

Boating: The symbol is not used for bodies of water smaller than 100 acres.

Canoeing, kayaking, drift boating, rafting: It seemed impractical to have symbols for each, although each is the choice for certain streams. Usually the text makes the distinction.

Horse riding: The symbol is used where pack trips and other trail riding were reported. Horses can be ridden in many other places: on any suitable trail in a National Forest, for example, or anywhere on BLM land. If horse rentals were said to be available, this is noted in text, but the reader is warned that such enterprises come and go.

Skiing: Downhill ski areas are mentioned when they are on public land. Many ski areas are concessioner-operated.

Ski touring: Usually one can ski cross-country wherever there's enough snow. We note where this was reported as a popular activity.

Snowmobiling: Noted where reported. Many National and State Parks restrict or prohibit snowmobiles. They are banned in wilderness areas.

RULES AND REGULATIONS

All sites have them. Parks have the most.

Pets: In parks, the general rule is that pets must be leashed. They are often prohibited on trails and beaches and in buildings.

Refuges and wildlife areas generally require that dogs be leashed, except while used in hunting.

Some sites ban pets altogether, and entries note this.

CAUTIONS

Some site managers thought you should be warned—about ocean currents, summer thunderstorms, rattlesnakes. We report their warnings. But keep in mind that other managers didn't mention similar hazards.

PUBLICATIONS

Entries list publications issued by sites or about sites. If a site has a descriptive leaflet, you may be able to have it sent to you, but fewer and fewer sites have sufficient manpower to respond to such requests. Most leaflets, species checklists, nature trail guides, etc., are available only on site.

National Forests will send maps by mail. In 1981 the price was increased to $1.

"Checklist available" usually means copies can be obtained. Not always. At some sites supplies were exhausted, but we were allowed to study file copies.

REFERENCES

These are publications pertaining to a site offered by commercial publishers or natural history associations.

Publications pertaining to an entire state are listed in the state preface. Those pertaining to the entire region are listed below.

AGENCY OFFICES AND PUBLICATIONS

Federal

U. S. Forest Service
Pacific Northwest Region
319 SW Pine St.
Portland, OR 97208
(503) 221-2971

Publications Include:
Franklin, Jerry F., and D. T. Dyrness. *Natural Vegetation of Oregon and Washington.* Washington, 1973.
(U.S. Government Printing Office Stock Number 0101-00329. 417 pp.)
Stalking the Wilderness Experience
Your Wilderness Trip
The Wilderness Traveler
Wild and Scenic Rivers
Discover Birding in the National Forests
Wildlife for Tomorrow
National Forest Campground Directory
Backpacking in the National Forests
Backpacking
Horse Sense on Backcountry Trips
Resorts and Packers on the National Forests
Winter Travel in the National Forests
Snow Avalanche
Winter Recreation Safety Guide

National Park Service
Pacific Northwest Regional Office
1424 Fourth Ave.
Seattle, WA 98101
(206) 442-5565

Publications Include:
Camping in the National Park System
Backcountry Travel in the National Park System
National Recreation Trails

U. S. Fish and Wildlife Service
Pacific Region
500 NE Multnomah St.
Portland, OR 97232
(503) 231-6121

Bureau of Land Management
U. S. Dept. of the Interior

Washington, DC 20240
(202) 343-1000.
(Oregon HQ listed in State Preface;
includes Washington.)

Publications Include:
BLM Facts, Oregon and Washington
Camping on the Public Lands
Desert Dangers

REFERENCES

General

Frome, Michael. *Rand McNally National Park Guide.* Chicago, New York, San Francisco: Rand McNally. Annual editions.

Hilts, Len. *Rand McNally National Forest Guide.* Chicago, New York, San Francisco: Rand McNally, 1976.

Landi, Val. *The Bantam Great Outdoors Guide to the United States and Canada.* New York: Bantam Books, 1978.

Riley, Laura and William. *Guide to the National Wildlife Refuges.* Garden City, NY: Anchor Press/Doubleday, 1979.

Sutton, Ann and Myron. *Wilderness Areas of North America.* New York: Funk & Wagnalls, 1974.

Tilden, Freeman. *The National Parks.* New York: Alfred A. Knopf, 1976.

Harris, Stephen L. *Fire and Ice: The Cascade Volcanoes.* Seattle: The Mountaineers.

Plants

Taylor. *Mountain Wildflowers of the Pacific Northwest.* Portland: Binford & Mort.

Horn, Elizabeth L. *Wildflowers I: The Cascades.* Beaverton, OR: Touchstone Press.

Valum, Rolf, and Ronald J. Taylor. *Wildflowers II: Sagebrush Country.* Beaverton, OR: Touchstone Press.

Mammals

Larrison, Earl J. *Mammals of the Northwest.* Seattle: Seattle Audubon Society, 1952.

Camping

Rand McNally Campground and Trailer Park Guide. New York, Chicago, San Francisco: Rand McNally. Annual editions.

Woodall's. Highland Park, IL: Woodall Publishing Co. Annual editions.

Hiking, backpacking

Meves, Eric. *Guide to Backpacking in the United States.* New York: Collier, 1977.

Green, David. *A Pacific Crest Odyssey.* Berkeley: Wilderness Press, 1979.
The Pacific Crest Trail. Washington: The National Geographic Society, 1973.
Schaffer, Jeffrey, and Bev and Fred Hartline. *The Pacific Crest Trail, Volume 2, Oregon and Washington.* Berkeley: Wilderness Press, 1979 (3rd ed.).
Fish, Byron. *60 Unbeaten Paths—Washington, Oregon, and Idaho.* Seattle: Superior Publishing Co.
Hart, John. *Hiking the Bigfoot Country.* San Francisco: Sierra Club Books.
Spring, Ira, and Harvey Manning. *102 Hikes in the Alpine Lakes: South Cascades and Olympics.* Seattle: The Mountaineers.

Boating
Calhoun, Bruce. *Northwest Passages.* Ventura, CA: Western Marine Enterprises.
Schaffer, Ann. *Canoeing Western Waterways: The Coastal States.* New York: Harper and Row, 1977.

Skiing
Prater, Gene. *Ski and Snowshoe Routes in the Cascades.* Seattle: The Mountaineers.

OREGON

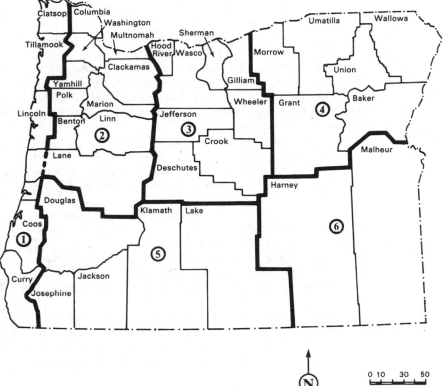

Clatsop Columbia
Washington
Tillamook Multnomah Sherman
Hood Umatilla Wallowa
River Wasco
Yamhill Morrow
Polk Clackamas Union
Lincoln Marion Gilliam
Benton Linn Jefferson Wheeler Grant Baker
② ③ ④
Lane Crook
Deschutes Malheur
Douglas Harney
Klamath Lake
Coos ⑥
①
⑤
Curry Jackson
Josephine

N

0 10   30   50

scale   miles

OREGON

Oregon's principal geographic features are conspicuous: the Pacific Ocean on the W, the Columbia River Gorge on the N. Three principal mountain ranges dominate the skyline: the Coast Range near the sea, the Cascade Mountains about 75 mi. to the E, and the Blue Mountains in the NE corner, extending SW. The SE portion of the state is high desert.

Between the ocean and the Coast Range is a narrow marine shelf, seldom more than 4 mi. wide. The Coast itself, sometimes rocky, sometimes sandy, is largely owned by the state. The Coast Range is not high, generally 2,000–3,000 ft. in the N, 3,000–4,000 ft. in the S, but it intercepts moist sea air, producing some of the heaviest annual rainfalls in the nation.

Most of the state's population lives in the fertile Willamette Valley, between the Coast Range and the Cascades. The Cascade Range has an average height of 5,000 ft., a few peaks rising over 10,000; Mt. Hood, highest in the state, reaches 11,245 ft. Near the California border, the two ranges merge, forming the rugged Rogue River Mountains.

The two ranges have successively stripped much of the moisture from E-moving air masses. The E two-thirds of the state is relatively dry. Only high mountains, such as the Steens, catch much precipitation.

The Blue Mountains extend SW to the valleys of the John Day and Deschutes rivers in central Oregon. Part of the chain extends SE to the Snake River Valley, at the Idaho border; in the NE a separate branch is called the Wallowa Mountains.

The Columbia Basin, on the Oregon side of the Columbia River from the Cascades to the Wallowas, is the state's major wheat-producing region. The SE, a vast area bounded by the Cascades on the W, the Blue Mountains on the N, is dry, some sections receiving as little as 8 in. of precipitation per year, most of this in the winter months.

Most of the mountainous and desert areas are public land. Indeed, 53% of the state's land area is in federal ownership. The 14 National Forests include over 12 million acres, more than a third of the federal land. Most of the rest is high desert, part of the public domain.

The state is endowed with exceptional natural diversity, from sealevel to snowcapped mountains, from rain forest to desert. Often there are dramatic contrasts: mountains rising steeply from the sea, flatlands terminating in near-vertical escarpments, waterfowl congregating in wetlands surrounded by miles of desert.

It is not pristine. Of the state's 30 million forested acres, less than 5% are closed to logging. Elsewhere only scattered old-growth stands remain, and their days are numbered. Clear-cutting is standard practice, and many forest landscapes are patchworks in shades of brown and green. Chronic overgrazing has inflicted costly damage on grasslands. The great Columbia River is now a succession of impoundments.

Even so, much of Oregon still resembles what the early settlers saw, and one can still see the ruts made by their wagon wheels. Large areas are true wilderness, roadless, uninhabited, isolated. On foot or horseback, or in a pickup or four-wheel-drive vehicle, one can leave the paved roads, strike out cross-country, and travel for miles in solitude.

FEDERAL AND STATE AGENCIES

FEDERAL AGENCIES
U.S. Forest Service
Pacific Northwest Region
P.O. Box 3623
Portland, OR 97208
(503) 221-2971

The Siuslaw National Forest occupies the central portion of the Coast Range. In several places it includes Pacific shoreline, notably the extensive Oregon Dunes National Recreation Area. The Siskiyou National Forest is in the SW corner of the state, near but not touching the Coast, extending E along the California border to meet a part of the Rogue River National Forest.

Seven National Forests—Mt. Hood, Willamette, Deschutes, Umpqua, Winema, Fremont, and Rogue River—form a huge block of land in the Cascade Range, from the Columbia River to California. In the NE, the Wallowa-Whitman, Umatilla, and Ochoco National Forests are not so solid a mass, but their several large blocks occupy much of the Blue Mountains. The Wallowa-Whitman includes the Oregon side of the Hells Canyon National Recreation Area.

PUBLICATIONS
Pacific Crest National Scenic Trail—Oregon (brochure, maps).
Wilderness permit information and application form.
Resorts and Packers in the National Forests.
Horse Sense on Backcountry Pack Trips.
Hints for Hunters.
Campground Directory (booklet, maps).
List of Recreation, Wilderness, and Special Area maps for sale.
Hall, Frederick C. *Plant Communities of the Blue Mountains in Eastern Oregon and Southeastern Washington.* 1973. 62 pp., illus. (Descriptive of Malheur, Ochoco, Umatilla, and Wallowa-Whitman National Forests.)

South Cascades Snow Trails (map, information).
Oregon Marked Cross-Country Ski Trails (leaflet).
Willamette Pass Ski Tours (leaflet).
Jackson-Klamath Winter Trails (maps).
Northwest Ski (list of commercial ski areas).

U.S. National Park Service
Pacific Northwest Regional Office
1424 Fourth Ave.
Seattle, WA 98101
(206) 442-5565

Crater Lake is Oregon's only National Park. It has National Forests on all four sides. Oregon Caves National Monument is within the Siskiyou National Forest. The John Day Fossil Beds National Monument has three separate units in N central Oregon.

U.S. Bureau of Land Management
729 NE Oregon St.
Portland, OR 97208
(503) 234-4001

The BLM manages the public domain, almost 16 million acres in Oregon, 1/4 of the state's land area. BLM lands constitute most of the state's SE quarter, with arms extending NW beyond Bend, Redmond, and Prineville, and NE beyond the Oxbow Dam on the Snake River. Smaller but interesting tracts are in the valleys of the lower Deschutes and John Day rivers. Most of this land is high desert.

Much BLM land is scattered through the Willamette Valley in a checkerboard pattern, more in the S than in the N. Most of this is forest land managed for timber production. The BLM maintains a number of pleasant campsites here, but we found few tracts suitable for entries.

We had often driven across SE Oregon, aware of little more than endless expanses of sagebrush, a monotonous landscape we felt no impulse to explore on foot. We should have remembered that road builders choose the easiest routes, avoiding deep canyons, steep cliffs, lakes, marshes, and other obstacles. The most interesting terrain is well off the main roads.

As in other states with BLM lands, our task was to identify sites with noteworthy qualities. The public domain does not come in discrete packages like parks and refuges. We had first to find an interesting central feature, such as a mountain, butte, escarpment, canyon, lava flow, or marsh, then fix arbitrary boundaries defining the area one might explore from a single base or access route. We relied heavily on data gathered by BLM for its wilderness inventory. The names attached to these sites are those used in the inventory. They have local meanings, but don't expect to find many of them on maps.

Nor do they appear on road signs. These sites are not like parks. They have no visitor facilities, no resident personnel. In most cases you won't know you're there unless you have studied a BLM map, had local advice, or recognized a landmark.

Are they worth exploring? The desert is a harsh environment, but many people find it fascinating. We do. A small but growing number of outdoorsmen are backpacking in canyons, camping with pickup trucks, studying desert flora. Part of the fascination is knowing that not much has changed here since the first settlers came.

Before going far off main roads, a visit to the nearest BLM District Office is advisable. Each has a recreation specialist as well as specialists in wildlife, plant life, and geology. They're glad to help you choose a route, tell you what to expect, warn of any current problems, show you their maps.

DISTRICTS

*Baker District, P.O. Box 987, Baker, OR 97814; (503) 523-6391. *Burns District, 74 South Alvord St., Burns, OR 97720; (503) 573-2071. Coos Bay District, 333 S. Fourth St., Coos Bay, OR 97420; (503) 269-5880. Eugene District, 1255 Pearl St., Eugene, OR 97401; (503) 687-6650. *Lakeview District, 1000 Ninth St. S., Lakeview, OR 97630; (503) 947-2177. Medford District, 310 W. Sixth St., Medford, OR 97501; (503) 779-2351. *Prineville District, 185 E. Fourth St., Prineville, OR 97754; (503) 447-4115. Roseburg District, 777 NW Garden Valley Blvd., Roseburg, OR 97470; (503) 672-4491. Salem District, 3550 Liberty Road S., Salem, OR 97302; (503) 399-5646. *Vale District, 365 A St. W., Vale, OR 97918; (503) 473-3144.

PUBLICATIONS

BLM Recreation Guide for Oregon. (Map showing all federal lands, BLM campgrounds, other features.)

Maps of Central Vale District, Siuslaw, Baker District, Upper Willamette.

The Bureau of Land Management in Oregon and Washington. Information pages.

Central Oregon Rockhound Guide (map).

Recreation Access. (Pamphlet explaining public rights on public lands.)

Foot Trails, Salem District.

Birds of the Medford District.

U.S. Fish and Wildlife Service
Pacific Region
500 NE Multnomah St.
Portland, OR 97232
(503) 231-6121

---

*Most entries for BLM sites are within these Districts.

The Malheur National Wildlife Refuge in SE Oregon is one of the nation's principal nesting, feeding, and resting areas for waterfowl. Another channel of the Pacific Flyway comes through the Klamath marshes, three important fragments of which are units of the Klamath Basin Refuges. (Other units are in California.) The largest federal refuge is for upland species: the Hart Mountain National Antelope Range, not far N of the Charles Sheldon Antelope Range in Nevada. Smaller but important federal refuges are in the Columbia River, the Willamette Valley, and on the Coast.

STATE AGENCIES
Oregon State Highway Division
101 State Highway Building
Salem, OR 97310

PUBLICATIONS
Highway map.
Oregon Boating Guide.
Willamette River Recreation Guide.

Oregon Parks and Recreation Division
Transportation Building
Salem, OR 97310
(503) 378-6305

Oregon has more than 235 state parks, plus state-owned areas destined to become parks. Yet the entire state park system occupies only 92,000 acres. The system is a unit of the Department of Transportation, and many of the "parks" are small but attractive roadside rest areas.

One of Oregon's great achievements is the chain of parks, beach-access points, overlooks, and other state lands beside the sea. No other state has had the foresight and political courage to keep so much of its seacoast in public ownership. True, much of the land just above the beach is open to development. Also, more than 2/5 of the beaches are open to off-road vehicles, and the ORV groups are demanding more. The popular beaches are often crowded. But one can find long, quiet stretches where storm and tide have erased all sign of prior visits.

We judged 56 parks suitable for entries. More than half are on the Coast, offering or giving access to extensive open beaches. Gathering data on the parks wasn't easy. State headquarters could offer little information, and only a few of the local managers could speak with authority about their plants and animals. Nor could most of them supply descriptive leaflets, fauna and flora checklists, or trail maps.

The parks have 54 campgrounds with 5,686 sites. Campground opening and closing dates are announced each year; those in the entries are approximate. All parks are open all year, but only 11 campgrounds have no closed season. Reservations are accepted for 13 of the campgrounds. Visitors without reservations get whatever is left. The application form (in the following list) tells which parks have reservation systems.

Primitive hiker-biker camps are available at 20 coastal parks.

PUBLICATIONS
Oregon Parks (map and list).
Oregon Climates (leaflet).
Campsite reservation application and information.
Your Pet in Oregon State Parks.

Oregon Forestry Department
2600 State St.
Salem, OR 97310
(503) 378-2560

This department manages more than 785,000 acres of state-owned forests. 670,000 acres are in 5 State Forests, the balance scattered in smaller tracts. Most of this land was logged over or burned before coming into state owner-ship in the 1930s. Under better management, the forests have come back, providing improved wildlife habitat and recreation opportunities. But multi-ple use is not the prevailing doctrine; the mandate is to produce and harvest for revenue. Other forest values are secondary. Even so, we looked at the five State Forests and include all as entries.

PUBLICATIONS
State Forestry in Oregon (leaflet).
Oregon Trees and Forests (leaflet).
Big Tree Hunter's Guide (leaflet, list of species champions).

Oregon Fish and Wildlife Commission
Department of Fish & Wildlife
506 S.W. Mill St.
Portland, OR 97208
(503) 229-5551

Management of state-owned game lands is for benefits to wildlife, hunters, and fishermen. However, most areas are open to hikers and other noncon-sumptive users. We selected the sites where visits outside hunting season could be interesting.

PUBLICATIONS
The Department has many publications pertaining to hunting and fishing.

REFERENCES
This list is not a comprehensive bibliography. A number of the named publishers specialize regionally; most will send lists.

GENERAL

Ferguson, Denzel and Nancy. *Oregon's Great Basin Country*. Burns, OR: Gail Graphics, 1978.

Mainwaring, William L. *Exploring Oregon's Central and Southern Cascades*. Salem, OR: Westridge Press, 1979.

Mainwaring, William L. *Exploring the Oregon Coast*. Salem, OR: Westridge Press.

Schwartz, Susan. *Cascade Companion*. Seattle: Pacific Search Press, 1976.

Wellborn, Sherry (ed.). *Oregon Coast Range Wilderness*. Siuslaw Task Force, P.O. Box 863, Corvallis, OR 97330.

WILDLIFE

Ramsey, Fred L. *Birding Oregon*. Audubon Society of Corvallis, Corvallis, OR 97330.

Spring, Bob and Ira. *Oregon Wildlife Areas*. Seattle: Superior Publishing, 1978.

HIKING

The following are a few of the many trail guides. More are published each year, some available only locally.

Bucy, David E. M., and Mary C. McCauley, *A Hiker's Guide to the Oregon Coast Trail*. State Parks and Recreation Branch, Salem, OR.

Hayes, Bruce. *Unobscured Horizons, Untravelled Trails*. Portland: Bruce Hayes, 1979. (Available from Oregon High Desert Study Group, P.O. Box 25, St. Paul, OR 97137.)

Lowe, Don and Roberta. *60 Hiking Trails, Central Oregon Cascades*. Beaverton, OR: Touchstone Press.

Lowe, Don and Roberta. *62 Hiking Trails, Northern Oregon Cascades*. Beaverton, OR: Touchstone Press.

Lowe, Don and Roberta. *Hiking the Columbia Gorge*. Beaverton, OR: Touchstone Press.

PACK TRIPS

Official Oregon Guides and Packers Directory. Oregon Guides and Packers, Inc., Lake Oswego, OR 97034.

BOATING

Garrin, John. *Oregon River Tours*. Portland: Binford and Mort.

Schwind, Dick. *West Coast River Touring: Rogue River and the South*. Beaverton, OR: Touchstone Press.

SKIING

A General Guide to Central Oregon Cross-country Skiing. Bend Chapter, Oregon Nordic Club, Bend, OR 97701.

Prater, Gene. *Snow Trails: Ski and Snowshoe Routes in the Cascades*. Seattle: The Mountaineers.

Newman, Doug, and Sharrard, Sally. *Oregon Ski Tours.* Beaverton, OR: Touchstone Press.

ROCKHOUNDING

Central Oregon Rockhound Guide. Map available from Forest Service, BLM, and Prineville-Crook County Chamber of Commerce, Prineville, OR 97754.

Oregon Rocks, Fossils, Minerals. State Department of Transportation, Salem, OR 97310.

McMullen, Dean. *Oregon Underfoot.* Beaverton, OR: Touchstone Press.

ZONE 1

Note: This is a long, narrow zone with many small sites. Rather than clutter the map with numbers, we have used brackets to divide the zone into three parts. The zone preface lists sites in this zone in geographic sequence, N to S.

Sites 1–16	WA boundary to Lincoln City
Sites 17–39	Lincoln City to Bandon
Sites 40–54	Bandon to CA boundary

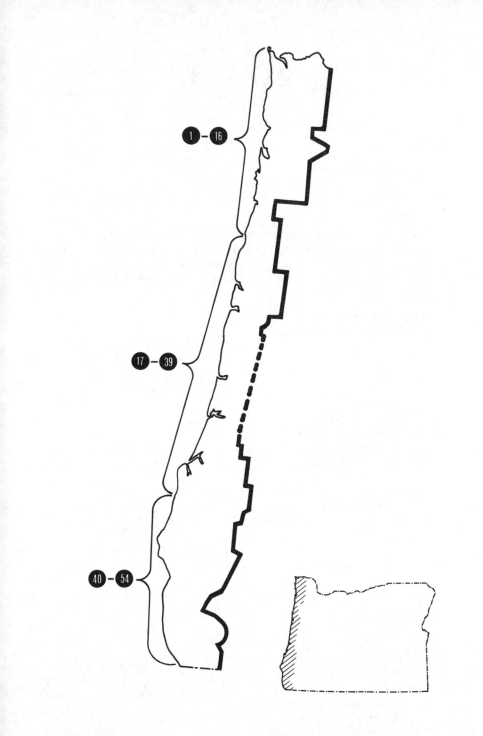

ZONE 1

Includes these counties:

Clatsop	Lane (W portion only)	Coos
Tillamook	Douglas (W portion only)	Curry
Lincoln		

In OR zone 1, many parks are arranged along the N-S Coast Road. It seems useful to provide a special listing of these, in linear order. Sites are listed from N to S, in three sections. Sites in the left column have ocean frontage. Those in the right column are inland but can be reached conveniently from the Coast Road.

Washington boundary to Lincoln City

1. Fort Stevens State Park

    2. Clatsop State Forest
    3. Jewell Meadows Wildlife Area
    4. Tillamook State Forest
    5. Saddle Mountain State Park

6. Ecola State Park
7. Hug Point State Park
8. Oswald West State Park
9. Nehalem Bay State Park
10. Cape Meares National Wildlife Refuge
11. Cape Meares State Park
12. Three Arch Rocks National Wildlife Refuge
13. Cape Lookout State Park

    14. Siuslaw National Forest

15. Cape Kiwanda State Park
16. Nestucca Spit State Park

Lincoln City to Bandon

17. Fogarty Creek State Park
18. Boiler Bay Wayside
19. Otter Crest Wayside
20. Devil's Punchbowl State Park
21. Beverly Beach State Park

22. Agate Beach Wayside
23. South Beach State Park
24. Ona Beach State Park
25. Seal Rock Wayside
26. Beachside State Park
27. Neptune State Park
28. Carl G. Washburne
    Memorial State Park
29. Devil's Elbow State Park
30. Darlingtonia Wayside
31. Oregon Dunes National
    Recreation Area
32. Jessie M. Honeyman
    Memorial State Park

33. Elliott State Forest

34. Umpqua Lighthouse
    State Park

35. William M. Tugman State Park

36. Sunset Bay State Park
37. Shore Acres State Park
38. Cape Arago State Park
39. Bullards Beach State
    Park

Bandon to California boundary
40. Bandon Ocean Wayside
41. Bandon State Park
42. Cherry Creek Research
    Natural Area
43. New River
44. Floras Lake State Park
45. Cape Blanco State Park
46. Humbug Mountain State
    Park

47. Rogue Wild and Scenic River
48. Siskiyou National Forest

49. Cape Sebastian State
    Park
50. Pistol River State Park
51. Samuel H. Boardman
    State Park
52. Harris Beach State Park

53. Loeb State Park
54. Azalea State Park

The Coast Range parallels the ocean shore from N to S, never far inland. Elevations are 2,000–3,000 ft. in the N, 3,000–4,000 ft. in the S, with occasional peaks 1,000–1,500 ft. higher. This range, intercepting the E flow of moist air from the ocean, produces heavy rainfalls, in places well over 100 in. per year.

At some points along the Coast, mountains rise directly from the sea and rocky promontories extend beyond the general shoreline. Elsewhere a marine terrace extends inland for 1/2 mi. to 4 mi. Most beaches are broad and sandy. Often they are backed by dunes, some low, others a few hundred feet high. And often an area of small trees, brush, and wildflowers lies back of the dunes; here, too, are a number of freshwater lakes and marshes.

Ample moisture and fine soils combine to make the forests of the Coast Range among the world's most productive. Western hemlock, Sitka spruce, western redcedar, and Douglas-fir are the most prominent species. Clearcutting, the prevailing logging method, has seriously marred the coastal landscape. Great brown patches show where logging was fairly recent. Cultivation of even-aged stands of single species replaces brown patches with shades of green.

US 101 is the Coast Highway except for a few intervals where local roads are closer to the ocean. Inevitably, sections of it have become congested and cluttered with the garish commercialism that defaces many seaside communities. These sections are usually near the ends of routes from the E.

More such development is occurring, but many segments of US 101 are still breathtakingly scenic. At times the highway is notched into towering cliffs, far above the sea. A few miles later it may run just back of low outer dunes or beside an estuary. Now and then it passes through forest, and one can occasionally glimpse the sea through the trees.

One seldom drives more than a few miles without seeing a place to park and walk to the seaside. Although the road was not planned as a scenic route, overlooks are numerous. Indeed, it seems that wherever the view is splendid there's a place to stop and park.

Because of the almost unbroken chain of beaches, we include as entries a number of State Parks that are not in themselves natural areas, sites we would not include if they stood alone. We have omitted a number of State Waysides, smaller State Parks, and county and municipal beaches, either because they are within developed areas or they seem less interesting.

Motor vehicles are allowed to drive on the beach, a policy that doubtless seemed innocent when first adopted, but each year adds more noise, trash, and hazards. Not all beaches are motorways. The official state highway map shows where vehicles are prohibited altogether and where they are prohibited at certain times. Although the Oregon Dunes National Recreation Area is federal, its beaches are state controlled, and vehicles are allowed on most of them.

Islands are scattered along the Coast, some just bits of rock rising above the waves, others a few acres in size. Many have odd shapes: spires, haystacks, arches. Many are included in the Oregon Islands National Wildlife Refuge. We have not made this refuge an entry, because its elements, most of them very small, extend over 290 mi., and landing is prohibited. Together with other islands, promontories, and cliffs, they provide safe nesting and resting areas for countless gulls, terns, cormorants, puffins, guillemots, and other seabirds, as well as haven for seals and sea lions. During their migrations, gray whales are commonly seen from many vantage points on shore. Jetties, sand spits, mudflats, and salt marshes attract great numbers of shorebirds and waterfowl.

The sea-tempered climate is equable; seldom is it uncomfortably hot or cold. However, rain and fog are frequent from late October to mid-May. Half of the very large annual precipitation falls from December through February, most of the rest in spring and fall. Coastal summers are clear and cool.

One can expect the more popular sites to be crowded on summer weekends. As the rising price of gasoline deterred many vacationers from long-distance travel, Oregonians rejoiced that they could enjoy their own parks again. Not all sites are crowded. We had no difficulty finding quiet places on a midsummer visit. The busiest parks are, of course, those with the most campsites; those which accept reservations have done so in self-defense.

Such is the appeal of beaches that most visitors ignore the coastal forests. Yet these forests, because of the ample moisture, are quite unlike forests E of the mountains. Although only a few fragments of the original forest remain, these are well worth visiting. The 1-mi. trail through the rain forest at Cape Meares offers a memorable experience. Two National Forests and three State Forests are in this coastal zone. Timber is harvested in all of them, but there are areas where trees have grown to respectable size and are not yet scheduled for cutting.

Hiking, backpacking: The Oregon Coast Trail is not completed. We were advised that it can be hiked from the Columbia River to Tillamook Bay, 64 mi. of the projected 370 mi. A number of our entries S of Tillamook include the statement "On the Oregon Coast Trail." Most of these sites have primitive hiker-biker camps. Many beaches S of Tillamook can be hiked, for a total of 214 miles, but the segments are not yet linked.

A Coast Range Trail is being planned by a private hiking association. Also planned are several trails across the Coast Range.

Swimming: An official publication noted "swimming" at a certain State Park. Responding to our questionnaire, the local manager said "no swimming." It's a judgment call. Swimming is forbidden on few beaches but inadvisable on many. The water is cold. Strong currents and tricky waves are common. Here and there are sheltered coves where the water is quiet and a few degrees warmer. Many people splash in the surf, in shallow areas; few venture into deep water for actual swimming.

Boating: Entries note which sites have ramps, whether on rivers or freshwater lakes. *A Guide to Oregon Boating Facilities* (see state introduction) lists 273 available ramps, fuel docks, moorings, etc., along the Coast.

AGATE BEACH WAYSIDE
Oregon Parks and Recreation Division
18 acres.

1 mi. N of Newport off US 101.

Beach access 1 mi. S of Yaquina Head. Viewpoint. Short trails. Usually a broad sandy beach. Agate hunting is significant when wave action exposes the gravel bed below the sand.

Birds: Nesting common murre and Brandt's cormorant at nearby Yaquina Head Refuge. Species often seen include surfbird, rhinoceros auklet, tufted puffin, pigeon guillemot, loons.

AZALEA STATE PARK
Oregon Parks and Recreation Division
36 acres.

On US 101 at Brookings, 6 mi. N of CA border.

Five varieties of wild azaleas bloom here Apr.–June. Some plants 20 ft. high, over 300 years old.

BANDON OCEAN WAYSIDE
Oregon Parks and Recreation Division
15 acres.

1/2 mi. S of Bandon off US 101.

Beach access. Sand dunes. Viewpoint: numerous tall, slender offshore rocks. A massive offshore rock that displays a profile resembling a head is known locally as "Face Rock."

BANDON STATE PARK
Oregon Parks and Recreation Division
879 acres.

From Bandon, 4 mi. S on US 101. Right 1 mi. on Bradley Lake Rd.

Beach access. Entrance road crosses vegetated dunes. Large and small off-shore rocks to N, extensive stretch of broad sand beach to S. A small creek cuts through the N end, a popular wading area for children.

BEACHSIDE STATE PARK
Oregon Parks and Recreation Division
17 acres.

On US 101, 4 mi. S of Waldport.

1/2 mi. of hard sand beach. Partially wooded site: shore pine and spruce, salal in understory.

Camping: 80 sites. Apr.–Nov. Reservations.

HEADQUARTERS: P.O. Box 1350, Newport, OR 97365; (503) 563-3023.

BEVERLY BEACH STATE PARK
Oregon Parks and Recreation Division
130 acres.

On US 101, 7 mi. N of Newport.

Large, heavily used campground on E side of Coast Highway. Passage under highway to wide sand beach, partly sheltered by headlands, backed by fossil-bearing cliffs.

INTERPRETATION: *Nature trail. Evening slide programs.*

ACTIVITIES
  Camping: 278 sites. All year. Reservations.
  Hiking, backpacking: Primitive hiker-biker camp. Hiking on beach. Segment of Oregon Coast Trail (see state introduction).

HEADQUARTERS: Star Route North, Box 684, Newport, OR 97365; (503) 265-7655.

BOILER BAY WAYSIDE
Oregon Parks and Recreation Division
33 acres.

From Newport, 15 mi. N on US 101.

Rocky coast; waves sending spray high. Blowhole on promontory has waterspout in storms, sometimes at high tide. Viewpoint.

BULLARDS BEACH STATE PARK
Oregon Parks and Recreation Division
1,226 acres.

1 mi. N of Bandon on US 101.

Attractive, popular park on the ocean and Coquille River. Entrance road passes among vegetated dunes, past campground, along river, to parking area near jetty and old lighthouse. Area back of foredunes is grassy, many wildflowers, some groves of shore pine. 4 mi. of wide sand beach. 3 mi. of river frontage.
  Birds: Surfbird, oystercatcher, turnstone, other shorebirds often seen on jetty, which is open to foot traffic. Good birding along river's mudflats.

ACTIVITIES
  Camping: 192 sites. All year.
  Hiking, backpacking: Primitive hiker-biker camp. Pleasant hiking along beach and river, back of dunes.
  Boating: Ramp on river.
  Horse riding: Designated area for parking and unloading horse trailers.

HEADQUARTERS: Box 25, Bandon, OR 97411; (503) 347-2209.

CAPE ARAGO STATE PARK; SHORE ACRES STATE PARK; SUNSET BAY STATE PARK
Oregon Parks and Recreation Division
Total 1,272 acres.

SW of Coos Bay on Cape Arago Highway; Cape Arago State Park is about 14 mi. from Coos Bay.

Closely related parks, not quite adjacent. Much of the land was part of an estate including fine botanic gardens, now maintained at Shore Acres. Cape Arago projects 1/2 mi. into the sea, with rocky cliffs up to 100 ft.

Sunset Bay State Park, 395 acres. A small bay almost entirely enclosed by precipitous sandstone cliffs. Conifers growing to the edge of the bluffs. Small rock islands at the bay's opening. Sheltered from wind and wave. Wide sand beach. Water usually warmer than at the open beaches outside.

Shore Acres State Park, 743 acres, is 1 mi. beyond Sunset Bay. The former owner employed talented landscape designers, imported many varieties of exotic plants. The state now maintains the gardens. The shoreline features huge sandstone slabs, so tilted that breaking waves send spray high into the air.

Cape Arago State Park, 134 acres, 2 mi. beyond Shore Acres, is a small, neatly kept day-use area offering fine views of the scenic Coast. Steller sea lions often seen. Sand beaches N and S of Cape, not suitable for swimming. Tidepools.

Birds: Many shorebirds, including occasional rarities. Some nesting species on the cliffs. Seen from the headlands: red-necked grebe, red-throated loon, pigeon guillemot, rhinoceros auklet, shearwaters, tufted puffin, scoter, gulls and terns. Many passerine species at Shore Acres.

ACTIVITIES
Camping: At Sunset Bay. 137 sites. Mid-Apr.–Oct. Reservations.
Hiking, backpacking: On the Oregon Coast Trail. Primitive hiker-biker camp at Cape Arago. Trail links the three units.
Swimming: At Sunset Bay.

Pets are prohibited at Shore Acres.

HEADQUARTERS: Sunset Bay State Park, 13030 Cape Arago Highway, Coos Bay, OR 97420; (503) 888-4902.

CAPE BLANCO STATE PARK
Oregon Parks and Recreation Division
1,880 acres.

From Port Orford, 9 mi. N on US 101, then left to Park.

Cape is most westerly point in Oregon. Cape road crosses low-lying meadows and marshes, then climbs to park, 200 ft. above sealevel. Site of historic lighthouse. Sweeping views of Coast to N and S. Park is largely forested, Sitka spruce and alder. 2 1/2 mi. frontage on Sixes River. Road and trails down to ocean beaches. Offshore rocks. Many wildflowers, including yellowhead, yellow coneflower, coral bells, yellow sand verbena, northern dune tansy.

Birds: Lighthouse area offers opportunity to observe migrating warblers in fall. Noted on visit: flicker, tree and cliff swallows, goldfinch, robin, cormorant, gulls.

ACTIVITIES

Camping: 58 sites, mid-Apr.–Nov.
Hiking, backpacking: Primitive hiker-biker camp. Beach hiking.
Fishing: River: chinook, cutthroat, steelhead.

HEADQUARTERS: P.O. Box 299, Sixes, OR 97476; (503) 332-2971.

CAPE KIWANDA STATE PARK
Oregon Parks and Recreation Division
185 acres.

From Pacific City, 3 mi. N on Sand Lake–Pacific City Rd.

Cape Kiwanda juts seaward about 1,500 ft. Rugged sandstone headland up to 220 ft. above the sea. 1 1/2 mi. of ocean beach. Some areas of sand dunes. Site is 80% forested: shore pine, Douglas-fir, Sitka spruce, western hemlock. Rhododendron, wildflowers on the Three Capes Scenic Drive, linking Capes Meares, Lookout, and Kiwanda.

Boating: Ramp. Dory fishing fleet launches here.

CAPE LOOKOUT STATE PARK
Oregon Parks and Recreation Division
1,974 acres.

12 mi. SW of Tillamook, on Three Capes Scenic Drive.

Basalt headland extends 2 mi. into the ocean; ridge 800 ft. above sealevel. S face has nearly vertical cliffs. Lower N face is indented with coves. From the base of the headland, Netarts Sand Spit extends 5 mi. to N, enclosing Netarts Bay. Marshes fringe the bay. Beach along the spit is broad, sandy.

Plants: Coastal rain forest; annual rainfall about 90 in. Sitka spruce, western hemlock, western redcedar, with red alder along clearings. Understory of salal, box blueberry, salmonberry, Pacific wax myrtle. Forest groundcover includes swordfern, skunk cabbage, trillium, lily-of-the-valley, other wildflowers.

Birds: Over 150 species identified. Diverse habitats attract bay ducks, shorebirds, seabirds, passerines.

FEATURES

Netarts Sand Spit: one of the least developed sand spit–estuary sites in OR. N third is dune system partially stabilized by vegetation. Middle third is a dense forest of Sitka spruce. S third partially forested with shore and maritime pines. Salt marshes along bay side. The N 3 mi. of the spit has been proposed for permanent preservation as a natural area.

Three Capes Scenic Drive links Capes Meares, Lookout, and Kiwanda.

INTERPRETATION: *Campfire programs,* June–Aug.

ACTIVITIES

Camping: 245 sites. All year. Reservations.

Hiking, backpacking: Primitive hiker-biker camp. 5-mi. trail from main campground to tip of Cape. Trailhead at midpoint, junction of park road and Scenic Drive. From here trail passes through mature rain forest, along ridge with fine views on both sides. A new trail, 2 mi. long, descends from the trailhead down the S side of the Cape. Beach hiking on Spit.

HEADQUARTERS: 13000 Whiskey Creek Rd. W., Tillamook, OR 97141; (503) 842-4981.

CAPE MEARES NATIONAL WILDLIFE REFUGE; THREE ARCH ROCKS NATIONAL WILDLIFE REFUGE
U.S. Fish and Wildlife Service
138 acres/17 acres.

Access to Cape Meares National Wildlife Refuge by foot trail from Cape Meares State Park. Three Arch Rocks, offshore, can be seen from the Cape.

Vertical sea cliffs, rocky outcroppings, rolling headlands. Largely forested with Sitka spruce and western hemlock, all old-growth. Refuge for colonial seabirds and other coastal species. Three Arch Rocks, offshore islands, is one of the continent's most populous bird colonies during the nesting season. Off limits but close to shore observation points. Large herd of northern sea lions.

Birds: Include double-crested, Brandt's, and pelagic cormorants; surfbird, black turnstone, common murre, tufted puffin, red and northern phalaropes, pigeon guillemot. Gulls include glaucous-winged, western, Thayer's, ring-billed, mew, Bonaparte's, Heermann's. Also peregrine falcon, pygmy owl, Vaux's swift, swallows, chickadees, thrushes, warblers.

Hiking: Trail through rain forest to lighthouse parking lot, about 1 mi., is exceptionally beautiful.

ADJACENT: Cape Meares State Park (see entry).

PUBLICATIONS
General information sheet.
Bird list.

HEADQUARTERS: c/o William L. Finley National Wildlife Refuge, Route 2, Box 208, Corvallis, OR 97330; (503) 757-7236.

CAPE MEARES STATE PARK
Oregon Parks and Recreation Division
233 acres.

10 mi. W of Tillamook, on Three Capes Scenic Drive, off US 101.

Promontory overlooking cliffs and offshore rocks with many nesting seabirds. Parking area, lighthouse, and several good viewpoints at the tip. "Octopus Tree," an exceptionally large, oddly branched spruce, diameter near base between 9 and 10 ft. On Three Capes Scenic Drive, linking Capes Meares, Lookout, and Kiwanda.

Hiking, backpacking: Primitive hiker-biker camp. Trail from park entrance to lighthouse, about 1 mi., through exceptionally fine rain forest. Also trail to beach, National Wildlife Refuge. Short section of Oregon Coast Trail.

ADJACENT: Capes Meares National Wildlife Refuge (see entry).

CAPE SEBASTIAN STATE PARK
Oregon Parks and Recreation Division
1,104 acres.

From Gold Beach, 7 mi. S on US 101.

The Cape is a precipitous headland 700 ft. above the sea. The Park is chiefly a fine viewpoint, vistas up and down the Coast, up to 50 mi. on clear days. Trails. Azalea, rhododendron, and ceanothus along the roadside. Sitka spruce forest covers a portion of the headland where a steep trail leads to the beach.

CARL G. WASHBURNE MEMORIAL STATE PARK
Oregon Parks and Recreation Division
1,209 acres.

14 mi. N of Florence on US 101.

2 mi. of ocean beach backed by dunes and large, rolling hills that are old dunes, now covered with vegetation, including fir, Sitka spruce, shore pine, cedar, hemlock. Prominent understory of evergreen huckleberry and rhododendron. Tidepools at base of rocky cliffs. Agates often found.

ACTIVITIES
Camping: 66 sites, mid-Apr.–Oct.
Hiking: Beach available well beyond site boundaries.

NEARBY: Siuslaw National Forest (see entry).

CHERRY CREEK RESEARCH NATURAL AREA
U.S. Bureau of Land Management
590 acres.

From Coquille on SR 42, turn N (just W of the Coquille High School) onto Fairview-McKinley Road. At Fairview, 9 mi. N, turn right onto Coos Bay Wagon Road. Go 7 mi. to Cherry Creek Park and turn left on Cherry Creek County Road. Proceed (road becomes BLM Cherry Creek Access Road) for 6 mi. to Big Tree Recreation Site, at edge of natural area. No roads or trails within natural area. Proceed across country on foot.

Complex ridge-and-valley topography bordering Cherry Creek. Lower and middle slopes moderate to steep; gentle to moderate along ridgetops. Elevations range from about 680 to about 1,480 ft.

Plants: Established for scientific research as a typical example of old-growth Douglas-fir and hemlock forest type. Average age of Douglas-fir over 300 years. Western hemlock somewhat younger. Redcedar and tan oak also present; bigleaf maple and California bay laurel common in streamside areas. Dense understory, mostly swordfern, with thickets of huckleberry, Oregon grape, rhododendron, vine maple.

Mammals: Elk, mule deer, black bear, mink, raccoon, ringtail, skunk, marten, weasel, snowshoe hare, many small rodents and bats.

No camping here or at the Big Tree Recreation Site.

HEADQUARTERS: Coos Bay District, Bureau of Land Management, 333 South Fourth Street, Coos Bay, OR 97420; (503) 269-5880.

CLATSOP STATE FOREST
Oregon Department of Forestry
154,000 acres.

E side of Clatsop County with small portions in Columbia County. SE of Astoria. Crossed by US 30, US 26, SR 202.

Forest land cut over and abandoned, now managed by the Department of Forestry under a mandate to produce revenue for the counties. Chiefly Douglas-fir and western hemlock. Mountainous terrain, rounded ridges, steep to moderate slopes. Highest point 3,020 ft. Annual precipitation about 90 in.

No campgrounds, long trails, or other recreation developments except as noted in Feature section. Managed for timber production, with concern for wildlife and water quality. Most recreational use is by hunters and fishermen. Hiking and sightseeing are increasing. The Forest has lakes, waterfalls, and streams in areas seldom visited outside hunting season. Vigorous wildlife population.

Worth exploring. A map is available and headquarters will advise where to go.

Plants: Principal tree species are Douglas-fir, western hemlock, Sitka spruce, western redcedar, noble and grand firs, red alder. Prominent in understory: swordfern, thimbleberry, salal, Oregon grape, salmonberry. Flowering species include red elderberry, devil's club, Indian thistle, red huckleberry, Oregon iris, white trillium, fireweed, Oregon anemone, paintbrush, penstemon, phlox.

Birds: 40 species recorded, including bald eagle, osprey, turkey vulture,

American kestrel, blue grouse, mountain quail, band-tailed pigeon, owl, rufous hummingbird, flycatchers, gray and Steller's jays, red-breasted nuthatch, western tanager, red crossbill.

Mammals: Include Roosevelt elk, mule deer, bobcat, spotted skunk, coyote, mountain beaver, Townsend chipmunk, chickaree, deer mouse, snowshoe hare, little brown myotis, big brown bat. Black bear present, seldom seen.

FEATURE: *Sunset Wayside Nature Study Area,* 48 mi. W of Portland on US
26. 1.3-mi. nature trail through mature and young forest areas, past meadows frequented by elk.

ACTIVITIES
Hiking: Service roads and fire trails.
Hunting: Deer, elk, bear.
Fishing: Trout, salmon, steelhead.
Swimming: No developed sites. Some streams have deep places.

NEARBY: Jewell Meadows Wildlife Area (see entry).

PUBLICATIONS
Forest leaflet.
Astoria District, Forestry Department, map, 1/2 in. = 1 mi.

HEADQUARTERS: Route 1, Box 950, Astoria, OR 97103; (503) 325-5451.

DARLINGTONIA STATE WAYSIDE
Oregon Parks and Recreation Division
18 acres.

From Florence, 5 mi. N on US 101.

Remarkable display of *Darlingtonia,* the insectivorous "cobra plant," so called because of its colorful cobralike hood. Boardwalk into the bog. Exhibit.

DEVIL'S ELBOW STATE PARK
Oregon Parks and Recreation Division
485 acres.

From Florence, 13 mi. N on US 101.

Bay with sandy beach. To N is rocky point with two huge rocks at tip. Trail to Heceta Head lighthouse and viewpoint.

ADJACENT: Carl G. Washburne Memorial State Park (see entry).

DEVIL'S PUNCHBOWL STATE PARK
Oregon Parks and Recreation Division
8 acres.

From Newport, 8 mi. N on US 101.

On a point of land. Viewpoint. Bowl-shaped rock formation has tunnel entrances from the sea through which waves thunder. Access to extensive sand beach. Marine gardens.

ECOLA STATE PARK
Oregon Parks and Recreation Division
1,299 acres.

From Cannon Beach, 2 mi. N on US 101.

Outstanding scenic area. 6 mi. of ocean frontage. Tillamook Head is a huge basalt promontory, spur of the Coast Range, highest point 1,200 ft. Large rocks offshore attract sea lions, seabirds. Annual precipitation about 82 in.

Plants: Upland area rolling to steep, largely forested. Some fine old-growth, immense Sitka spruce, western hemlock, with red alder, western redcedar. Understory: red huckleberry, salmonberry, red elderberry, swordfern, deerfern, ladyfern. Flowering plants include seaside tansy, lily-of-the-valley.

Birds: No list available, but diverse habitats attract good variety of sea, shore, and upland species.

Mammals: Include elk, mule deer, sea lion.

Reptiles and amphibians: Include northern alligator lizard, Pacific tree frog, western toad.

Hiking: On the Oregon Coast Trail.

ELLIOTT STATE FOREST
Oregon Department of Forestry
85,000 acres.

Umpqua River, E of Reedsport, is N boundary. From SR 38, secondary roads lead S into the Forest, notably Loon Lake and Scholfield roads.

Includes some of the steepest terrain in OR: deep canyons, knifelike ridges. Highest point: 2,097 ft. Although there are some disconnected tracts, most of the acreage is a solid block. Most of the forest was burned in 1868, but growing conditions are good and recovery was excellent. Public use has increased gradually; most visitors are those who prefer a primitive environment. We were told there is little hiking because of the steep terrain. However, more than 450 mi. of roads, most unpaved, some marginally maintained, offer some hiking opportunities. This is an active tree farm; drivers should be alert for log and rock trucks.

Plants: 90% of area in Douglas-fir. 60% is 80–100 years old, most of the rest under 25 years. Other species include red alder, hemlock, cedar, maple. Understory: swordfern, salal, evergreen and red huckleberries, rhododendron, Oregon grape. Flowering plants, limited under tree canopy, include trillium, sweet-scented bedstraw, oxalis.

Birds: No data. Common loon seen on Loon Lake.

Mammals: Roosevelt elk, black bear, mule deer.

FEATURES

10-mi scenic corridor along S bank of Lower Umpqua River.

Loon Lake, popular recreation area.

ACTIVITIES

Camping: BLM campground on Loon Lake. 30 sites. Memorial Day–Labor Day. Primitive camping elsewhere.

Fishing: Salmon, steelhead, in streams.

Boating: Dock, ramp, rentals at Loon Lake. Also boating on Umpqua River.

PUBLICATION: Forest leaflet. (Does not include map.)

HEADQUARTERS: Coos Management District, 300 Fifth St., Bay Park, Coos Bay, OR 97420; (503) 267-4136. (S of Coos Bay, off US 101, at top of Bunker Hill.)

FLORAS LAKE STATE PARK
Oregon Parks and Recreation Division
1,361 acres.

From Port Orford, N 10 mi. on US 101; follow signs to lake. Site is not well marked. Advised to park at airport, hike in.

Undeveloped site between lake and ocean. 1 mi. frontage on lake, 2 1/2 mi. on ocean. Vertical sandstone bluffs, over 200 ft. Forest of Sitka spruce, shore pine, western hemlock, with understory of salal, rhododendron, evergreen huckleberry.

FOGARTY CREEK STATE PARK
Oregon Parks and Recreation Division
142 acres.

From Depoe Bay, 2 mi. N on US 101.

Popular beach, wide and smooth. Fogarty Creek winds through. Wooded area back of beach: shore pine, alder, spruce.

FORT STEVENS STATE PARK
Oregon Parks and Recreation Division
3,763 acres.

From Astoria, 10 mi. W on US 101.

Attracts the most visitors of any OR state park, and parts of the site are highly developed. Historical area, but the site includes outstanding natural features.

Bounded on the N by the Columbia River, on the W by the ocean. Access to over 5 mi. of broad beach. 3 mi. of river frontage. Elevations to 100 ft. Includes Coffenbury Lake, about 1 mi. long, several smaller, shallow lakes. Narrow sand dune ridges, swampland, tidal marshes. W half of park consists of extensive sandflats that accreted after construction of the Columbia River jetties.

Plants: Botanists have identified 10 plant zones, from man-planted sand stabilization areas near the sea to native old-growth forest in the E interior. Foredunes have beach grass, seashore lupine, yellow sand verbena, sea lyme-grass, dune bluegrass. Shore pine planted back of dunes. Groundcovers of the stabilized sandflats include beach grasses, lupine, kinnikinick, salal, Scotch broom, twinberry. Ridge and swale vegetation is largely natural coastal forest: large red alder, Sitka spruce, shore pine, Douglas-fir, with western redcedar, hemlock, willow, Oregon crabapple, cascara, elderberry, salmonberry, ocean spray, huckleberry, blackberry, salal, swordfern.

Birds: Checklist on file. Trestle Bay tidal zone is a major stopover for migrating waterfowl. Nesting species include mallard, pintail, baldpate, teal, scaup, bufflehead. A few snowy plover nest on the beach. Clatsop Spit is known to birders as a place to spot rarities such as gyrfalcon, golden plover, sharp-tailed and buff-breasted sandpipers, Buller's shearwater. Spit is also a good area for migrating warblers.

Mammals: In the old-growth marshy spruce forest and lake areas, include mule deer, nutria, mink, beaver, raccoon, opossum, chickaree, chipmunk.

FEATURES

Historic area: gun batteries, building foundations, visitor center.

Columbia River Beach, via Jetty Road. About 1 mi. of frontage. Sightseeing.

Bay area, also via Jetty Road. Bay is about 2 mi. wide, much used by migrating waterfowl.

Fire Control Hill, reached by trail. Viewpoint.

Peter Iredale Beachfront, named for a wrecked ship. Miles of wide, sandy beaches.

Natural vegetation area at the S end of Coffenbury Lake.

ACTIVITIES

Camping: 603 sites. All year. Reservations.

Hiking, backpacking: Oregon Coast Trail begins here. Primitive hiker-biker camp. 8 mi. of trails within site.

Fishing: Salmon, flounder, bass, perch, ling cod, from jetty and N end of Spit. Fishing fair in the lakes.

Swimming: Lake, supervised mid-June to Labor Day. Surf swimming is inadvisable.

Boating: Ramps on Coffenbury, Crabapple, and Creep and Crawl lakes.

Bicycling: 7 mi. of bike trails.

Campground is generally full on peak holidays and late summer weekends.

PUBLICATIONS

Park leaflet with map.

Site map.

Bicycle and hiking trail map.

HEADQUARTERS: Hammond, OR 97121; (503) 861-1671.

HARRIS BEACH STATE PARK

Oregon Parks and Recreation Division

171 acres.

Near CA border. From Brookings, 2 mi. N on US 101.

Sandy beach with occasional rock outcroppings. Back of beach, land rises to moderately level bench, an ancient beach, about 160 ft. above sealevel. Offshore sea stacks and Goat Island, seabird rookery. Nature trail.

ACTIVITIES
Camping: 151 sites. All year. Reservations.
Hiking, backpacking: Primitive hiker-biker camp.

HEADQUARTERS: 1655 Highway 101, Brookings, OR 97415; (503) 469-2021.

HUG POINT STATE PARK
Oregon Parks and Recreation Division
131 acres.

From Cannon Beach, 4 mi. S on US 101.

Small, attractive, sheltered ocean beach.

HUMBUG MOUNTAIN STATE PARK
Oregon Parks and Recreation Division
1,842 acres.

From Port Orford, 6 mi. S on US 101.

On one of the most scenic sections of the Coast Road. Forested hills come down almost to the ocean's edge. At Humbug Mountain, the highway (traveling S) turns into Brush Creek Canyon and passes the mountain on the inland side. Mountain rises from the beach to 1,756 ft. Park has 4 mi. of ocean frontage; only 2 mi. are accessible, because of the steep bluffs.
Plants: Mountain slopes and canyon floor partially forested: Sitka spruce, western hemlock, Douglas-fir, alder, bigleaf maple. Virgin stand of Oregon myrtle.

ACTIVITIES
Camping: 106 sites. Mid-Apr. to Nov.
Hiking, backpacking: Primitive hiker-biker camp. 3-mi. trail to top of mountain. Beach hiking.
Fishing: Surf and creek.
Swimming: Surf. We saw people swimming in the creek.

HEADQUARTERS: Port Orford, OR 97465; (503) 332-6774.

JESSIE M. HONEYMAN MEMORIAL STATE PARK
Oregon Parks and Recreation Division
522 acres.
Within the Oregon Dunes National Recreation Area (see entry).

From Florence, 3 mi. S on US 101.

On both sides of US 101. Within the area of high dunes, but 2 mi. from the ocean beach. Frontage on Woahink and Cleawox lakes. One of the most popular parks; campground often crowded on weekends.

Plants: Some forested land on E, with fir, spruce, hemlock, cedar; understory of salal, rhododendron, huckleberry, thimbleberry, salmonberry. Park borders on a bog with insectivorous plants.

ACTIVITIES
Camping: 382 sites. All year. Reservations.
Hiking, backpacking: Primitive hiker-biker camp. Oregon Coast Trail passes through nearby Oregon Dunes National Recreation Area.
Swimming: Both lakes.
Boating: Both lakes. Ramps.
Fishing: In the lakes: lunker bass, crappie, bluegill, perch, catfish, trout.

PUBLICATION: Leaflet.

HEADQUARTERS: 84505 Highway 101, Florence, OR 97439; (503) 997-3851.

JEWELL MEADOWS WILDLIFE AREA
Oregon Department of Fish and Wildlife
1,123 acres.

From Portland, W on SR 26 to Jewell Junction, about 55 mi. Continue N on unmarked highway beside Nehalem River 9 mi. to Jewell. W 1 1/2 mi. on SR 202.

Three parcels of land and a privately owned buffer. Area is maintained to provide for wintering Roosevelt elk, habitat for elk and other wildlife. Hunting is prohibited. Elk can usually be seen Nov.–Apr., 75–200 animals, feeding and resting in the meadows. Other elk use the meadows along Beneke Creek.

When the elk move to higher ground for the summer, mule deer can often be seen early morning and evening.

Habitats on the area include mixed-age stands of conifers, hardwood forest of red alder and bigleaf maple, streamside trees and shrubs, abandoned orchards, grassy meadows, sedge wetlands, small ponds, clear streams. Wildflowers in Apr.–May. The Beneke Creek–Crawford Ridge loop is a pleasant, low-key, scenic drive on gravel roads.

NEARBY: Clatsop State Forest (see entry).

PUBLICATION: Folder with map.

HEADQUARTERS: Region 1, Department of Fish and Wildlife, Rt. 5, Box 325, Corvallis, OR 97330; (503) 757-4186.

LEWIS & CLARK NATIONAL WILDLIFE REFUGE
U.S. Fish and Wildlife Service
35,000 acres total; 8,313 acres of land.

Islands in the Columbia River E of Astoria. Access by private boat only.

Slow-moving river water has deposited silt in the estuary, forming marshy islands and sand bars. The Refuge, on the OR side of the main channel, includes 20 named islands and far more bars, mudflats, and tidal marshes. Most of the islands are flooded at high tides. Trees and shrubs on some of the higher islands upstream. The area, extending 15 mi. along the river, is the largest natural marsh in W Oregon, a major stopover for waterfowl on the Pacific Flyway.

Birds: In Feb. and Mar. some 3,000 whistling swan, 2,000 dusky Canada geese, and 50,000 ducks may be present, the ducks mostly mallard, pintail, wigeon, green-winged teal, with lesser number of scaup and canvasback. Bald eagle often seen. Many shorebirds on exposed flats.

Mammals: Beaver, muskrat, raccoon, mink, weasel. Deer and seal sometimes seen.

ACTIVITIES
Hunting: Waterfowl. Some portions may be closed. Inquire.
Fishing: Salmon, trout, sturgeon, warm-water game fish.
Boating: Those unfamiliar with this area should consult HQ before a visit. Some tidal channels are navigable only at high tide. HQ can also suggest launching points. Hunting leaflet says facilities are available at Aldrich Point and John Day Point.

PUBLICATIONS
Leaflet with map.
Bird checklist.
Hunting regulations.

HEADQUARTERS: P.O. Box 566, Cathlamet, WA 98612; (206) 795-3915.

LOEB STATE PARK
Oregon Parks and Recreation Division
320 acres.

From Brookings, 8 mi. NE on local road, along Chetco River.

In the Chetco River Canyon; 1/2 mi. of river frontage. Noted for a grove of virgin Oregon myrtle, a tree species with limited range. Also what is said to be the northernmost grove of Coast redwoods, diameters 5–8 ft.

ACTIVITIES
Camping: 53 sites, mid-Apr. to Oct.
Hiking, backpacking: Primitive hiker-biker camp. Trails in National Forest.

ADJACENT: Siskiyou National Forest (see entry).

HEADQUARTERS: c/o Harris Beach State Park, 1655 Highway 101, Brookings, OR 97415; (503) 469-2021.

NEHALEM BAY STATE PARK
Oregon Parks and Recreation Division
878 acres.

From Manzanita, 3 mi. S on US 101; right 1 1/2 mi. on entrance road.

Sand spit with dunes between Nehalem Bay and ocean. Entrance road passes among old dunes, fully vegetated, mostly shore pine with some Douglas-fir, spruce, hemlock, oak, none large. Then area of scrub with stunted shore pine, broom, gorse. 6 mi. of fine ocean beach.

ACTIVITIES

Camping: 292 sites. Mid-Apr. to Oct.

Hiking, backpacking: Primitive hiker-biker camp. On the Oregon Coast Trail.

Swimming: Sand beach on bay. Also surf.

Boating: Ramp on bay.

HEADQUARTERS: 8300 3rd St. Necarney, Nehalem, OR 97131; (503) 368-5943.

NEPTUNE STATE PARK
Oregon Parks and Recreation Division
302 acres.

From Yachats, 3 mi. S on US 101.

Scenic area. About 2 1/2 mi. of rugged, rocky ocean front. Terrain is rough. Salal, huckleberry, Sitka spruce. At N end is a deep, long fissure through which waves roll, breaking spectacularly.

NESTUCCA SPIT STATE PARK
Oregon Parks and Recreation Division
484 acres.

Just W of Pacific City.

Stabilized sand spit. 2 1/4 mi. of ocean frontage, 3 mi. on the estuary. Some shore pine with Scotch broom, beach grass. Tideflats. For shore- and seabirds, this offers as good birding as better-known sites to N and S.

Boating: Ramp on estuary of Nestucca River.

NEW RIVER
U.S. Bureau of Land Management
About 600 acres.

Between Bandon and Floras Lake State Parks. Only legal access is along the beach.

Designated an "Area of Critical Environmental Concern"—meaning a largely pristine habitat. Isolated 3-mi.-long sand beach. New River flows N, parallel with Coast, for several miles. From late spring to early fall, a sand bar blocks all stream outlets between the two State Parks. From late fall to early spring, the New River breaches one or more outlets, but one can usually find a place to wade across. E of the river are marshes, bogs, and partially stabilized sand dunes with European beach grass and shore pines. Waterfowl winter in the area. Many shorebirds nest in spring and summer.

ACTIVITIES

Camping: In 1981 the BLM permitted beach camping but was considering limitation to designated sites. Check BLM office or adjoining State Park.

Hiking: About 14 mi. of lightly traveled beach.

Fishing: Surf. Winter steelhead in river.

HEADQUARTERS: Coos Bay District, BLM, 333 S. Fourth St., Coos Bay, OR, 97420; (503) 269-5880.

ONA BEACH STATE PARK
Oregon Parks and Recreation Division
237 acres.

From Newport, 8 mi. S on US 101.

Broad, sand ocean beach. Boat ramp on Beaver Creek. Wooded hillside on S.

OREGON DUNES NATIONAL RECREATION AREA
U.S. Forest Service
20,832 acres/32,348 acres within boundaries.
Within and part of Siuslaw National Forest (see entry).

From Siuslaw River on N to Coos River on S. Several access roads from US 101. Foot trails to beach from 3 campgrounds.

The area extends 40 mi. along the ocean. Up to 2 1/2 mi. wide. Largely W of US 101 but includes frontage on Siltcoos Lake, Tahkenitch Lake, and Umpqua River E of the highway. The most extensive sand dune area on the West Coast, dunes up to 300 ft. high moving slowly E in the prevailing wind, gradually burying trees, in places coming close to the highway.

Only 8 vehicle and foot access points in the 40 mi. The beach is state land, and motor vehicles are allowed on about half of it. In three large sections, the dunes and area back of the dunes are also open to ORV's.

A number of large and small lakes and some marshy areas have formed back of the dunes. The principal plant species are beach grass, spreading gradually over dunes, and shore pine back of the dunes.

About a third of the area within boundaries is privately owned. Much of the private land is along the highway.

Because each vehicle access route leads to an area open to ORV's, many visitors assume the entire area is an ORV playground. When we visited, many 4-wheel-drive vehicles and sand buggies were roaring about, discouraging anyone in search of quiet places. The fact is that large areas are closed to all vehicles. ORV operators have been quick to popularize the site. Backpackers are still infrequent. Solitude by the sea is still available.

Fauna: No species checklists are yet available. Many sea- and shorebirds are seen, especially at river mouths. Eagle, blue heron, osprey around the lakes. Mule deer, raccoon, and beaver are common.

FEATURES

North Dunes: The best backcountry for hikers is between the Siltcoos and Umpqua rivers. Less open sand, more natural diversity. Access from Siltcoos Rd., Carter Lake campground, or Tahkenitch campground.

Umpqua Dunes Scenic Area: 3,000 acres, from Umpqua Lighthouse to Tenmile Creek. Includes the largest dunes. Much of the area is open to foot traffic only. Access from Eel Creek campground or Umpqua Lighthouse State Park.

Honeyman Dunes: SW of Cleowax Lake. Access from Jessie M. Honeyman State Park.

South Jetty, Siuslaw River: Vehicle access to parking areas. Dunes closed to ORV's. Beach closed to vehicles May 1–Sept. 30. One of the good birding spots.

INTERPRETATION

Visitor center on US 101 at Reedsport. Exhibits, literature, information.

River of No Return nature trail, in Siltcoos area.

Evening programs, other interpretive activities are planned. Inquire.

ACTIVITIES

Camping: 14 campgrounds, over 330 sites. Some all year.

Hiking, backpacking: Part of the Oregon Coast Trail. Beach and dune camping permitted—thus far. No water. If you hike through the dunes to the beach, mark your route; vegetation back of dunes is often dense and trails may be hard to find. Quicksand is more of a problem for vehicles than for hikers, but one can sink hip-deep.

Fishing: Surf, jetties, lakes.

Swimming: Unsupervised. Strong undertows and riptides. Occasional large waves.

Boating: Ramps on the 8 largest lakes and on Siuslaw and Umpqua rivers.

ORV's must comply with state and federal regulations. Special equipment required.

Occasional high waves. Near the water, don't turn your back on the surf; avoid logs and piles of driftwood.

PUBLICATIONS
Park leaflet with map.
Guide for Hiking and Off Road Vehicles.

ADJACENT OR NEARBY: Jessie M. Honeyman Memorial State Park, Umpqua Lighthouse State Park, William M. Tugman State Park (see entries).

HEADQUARTERS: 855 Highway Ave., Reedsport, OR 97467; (503) 271-3611.

OSWALD WEST STATE PARK
Oregon Parks and Recreation Division
2,474 acres.

From Cannon Beach, 10 mi. S on US 101.

Oregon Coast Range meets the ocean here. Most of Neahkahnie Mountain (1,661 ft.) is within the Park. Scenic section of the Coast Highway, high above the sea, many overlooks. Numerous small streams. The largest, Short Sands Creek and Necarney Creek, converge and enter the sea at Short Sands Beach. Except for this small beach, the Coast has vertical basaltic cliffs rising as much as 700 ft. Rock promontories extend into the ocean; the largest is Cape Falcon.

Plants: Dense vegetation, in places resembling rain forest. Principal trees: western hemlock, western redcedar, Sitka spruce. Along Short Sand and Necarney creeks, exceptionally large old-growth hemlock and spruce. Understory of salal, red huckleberry, salmonberry, thimbleberry, blackberry, red elderberry. Wildflowers include lily-of-the-valley, trillium, monkeyflower, wood sorrel, skunk cabbage.

Birds: Most common: 8 gull species, shorebirds, Steller's jay, raven, crow, swallows, robin. Brown pelican in migration.

Mammals: Often seen: chickaree, Townsend chipmunk, brush rabbit. Present but seldom seen: striped and spotted skunks, raccoon, mule deer, Roosevelt elk. California sea lion rarely seen.

ACTIVITIES
Camping: 36 primitive walk-in sites. Mid-Mar. to Nov.
Hiking, backpacking: 15 mi. of trails within the Park. On the Oregon Coast Trail. Scenic trails: Cape Falcon, Neahkahnie Mountain. Trails from parking areas to beach. Camp only at campground.
Fishing: Some trout in streams. Perch and greenling in surf.
Swimming: Limited by cold water. Unsupervised.

HEADQUARTERS: 8300 Third St., Nehalem, OR 97131; (503) 368-5943.

OTTER CREST WAYSIDE
Oregon Parks and Recreation Division
1 acre.

From Newport, 10 mi. N on US 101.

On Cape Foulweather, a flat-topped rock bluff 453 ft. above the sea. Viewpoint. Shoreline here has steep rock cliffs.

PISTOL RIVER STATE PARK
Oregon Parks and Recreation Division
440 acres.

From Gold Beach, 11 mi. S on US 101.

Wide sand beach. Large sand dunes. At S end, a 160-ft. rock knoll; viewpoint. At N end, Pistol River.

ROGUE WILD AND SCENIC RIVER
U.S. Forest Service/U.S. Bureau of Land Management
84 mi.

From the mouth of the Applegate River, 6 mi. W of Grants Pass to Lobster Creek Bridge, about 12 mi. upstream from Gold Beach. A Forest road parallels the lower portion, a BLM road the upper. The middle portion is roadless.

Designated a Wild and Scenic River in 1968, with three zones: the "Wild" zone is free-flowing, accessible only by trail, with a primitive shoreline, clean water. "Scenic" sections have road access points. "Recreational" sections have some shoreline development. The 47 mi. above Marial are administered by the BLM, the 37 below Marial by the Siskiyou National Forest. Visitors can travel the 84 mi. by boat, the wild portion on foot. The foot trail is closed to vehicles and horses. The float trip requires special boats and skills.

The river flows from NW of Crater Lake National Park, passing through the Umpqua and Rogue River National Forests in its upper reaches. Float trips through the Wild and Scenic portion usually begin at sites between Grants Pass and Grave Creek. From here the river cuts through dissected plateaus exposing serpentine, greenstone, granite, sandstone, slate, and shale. Many rapids, riffles, and falls. The canyon is narrow in places. Between Grants Pass and the sea, the river drops almost 1,000 ft.

Plants: Vegetation in and above the canyon is diverse because of the varied terrain, soils, and microclimates. On the upper reaches, willow along the banks, Oregon ash and bigleaf maple in moist places, Pacific madrone, California black ash, and Oregon white oak on dry ridges. Downstream, western redcedar, Port Orford cedar, Pacific yew, canyon live oak, golden chinquapin, tan oak, Oregon myrtle, with stands of Douglas-fir, western hemlock, grand fir, sugar pine. Rarities include weeping spruce, knobcone pine, and pitcher plants in remote sites. Many side streams lined with rhododendron, azalea, Pacific dogwood, Oregon grape, salal, salmonberry. Many ferns.

Birds: Species likely to be seen in proper season include pied-billed grebe, mallard, wood duck, goshawk, Virginia and sora rails, common snipe, mourning dove, common nighthawk, acorn woodpecker, western wood pewee; violet-green, tree, rough-winged, and barn swallows; plain titmouse, common bushtit, white-breasted nuthatch, winter and Bewick's wrens, western bluebird, solitary vireo, yellow warbler, yellow-breasted chat, northern oriole, lazuli bunting, lesser goldfinch; savannah, lark, white-crowned, golden-crowned, fox, Lincoln's, and song sparrows.

Mammals: Deer, bear, otter, raccoon, mink, chickaree, ring-tail.

ACTIVITIES

Camping: 19 Forest Service, BLM, and county campgrounds. 1,315 sites. Only 6 of the campgrounds have road access. Also trailside camping. Seasons vary; generally May–Oct.

Hiking, backpacking: A 40-mi. trail follows the N bank from Grave Creek to Illahe. Intermediate road access at Marial. Most hikers take 5 days for the trip. The trail is not difficult, but ask about current conditions. No vehicles or horses. Bring water purification tablets.

Fishing: The Rogue is a famous fishing stream. Salmon, steelhead, cutthroat, rainbow, shad, and sturgeon.

Boating: Special Rogue-type drift boats are generally used. Also rubber rafts. The river is wild and treacherous. Professional river guides take parties on 3- to 5-day float trips. Only people with considerable wild river experience should attempt the run without a guide. They should obtain detailed information and travel in groups of two or more boats. Individual float permits are required, obtainable from Galice Ranger District, Siskiyou National Forest, P.O. Box 1034, Grants Pass, OR 97526; (503) 476-6918. Commercial jet boats make daily trips from Gold Beach to Agness and return.

ADJACENT: Wild Rogue Wilderness of Siskiyou National Forest.

PUBLICATION: *The Rogue River, Wild and Scenic.* Map, description, information.

HEADQUARTERS: BLM, Medford District, 3040 Biddle Rd., Medford, OR 97501; (503) 776-4174. BLM, Coos Bay District, 333 S. Fourth St., Coos Bay, OR 97420; (503) 269-5880. Siskiyou National Forest, P.O. Box 440, 1501 NW 6th St., Grants Pass, OR 97526; (503) 479-5301.

SADDLE MOUNTAIN STATE PARK
Oregon Parks and Recreation Division
2,882 acres.

15 mi. inland from the sea. From Necanicum Junction on US 26 (9 mi. E of Seaside on US 101), 7 mi. N on entrance road.

W portion relatively flat, with young trees and shrubs. Larger area is occupied by the steep cliffs and slopes of Saddle Mountain; three main peaks over 3,200 ft. Sweeping views from top include snowcapped mountains, miles of shoreline, mouth of Columbia River.

Plants: Because of unique botanical features, 1,900 acres of the Park has been recommended for preserve status. Most of the site is forested. Old-growth stands include some of the largest western hemlock in the Coast Range, a forest of Sitka spruce and hemlock, and some ancient Pacific silver fir. About 300 plant species have been identified; more are thought to be present. Those identified include several rare or endangered species, some occurring only here. Outstanding array of wildflowers includes nodding onion, Oregon lily, yellow fawn lily, false Solomon's seal, lily-of-the-valley, Oregon purple iris, wood buttercup, columbine, bleeding heart, wallflower, saxifrages, goatsbeard, cinquefoil, redwood sorrel, violets, starflower, pentstemons, paintbrush. Many of the plant species found here are difficult to identify because they differ from typical forms of the species, a consequence of the mountain's isolation.

Birds: Include turkey vulture, Cooper's and sharp-shinned hawks, blue and ruffed grouse, mountain quail, screech and great horned owls, Vaux's swift, kingfisher, flicker; pileated, hairy, and downy woodpeckers; western wood pewee, black-capped and chestnut-backed chickadees, varied and Swainson's thrushes, golden-crowned and ruby-crowned kinglets, western tanager, pine siskin. Warblers: orange-crowned, yellow, yellow-rumped, hermit, MacGillivray's, Wilson's.

Mammals: Presumed to include vagrant, dusty, and marsh shrews, shrewmole, coast mole, several bat species, brush rabbit, snowshoe hare, mountain beaver, chickaree, deer mouse, white-footed vole, coyote, black bear, raccoon, short-tailed and long-tailed weasels, mink, bobcat, elk, mule deer.

ACTIVITIES

Camping: 6 primitive sites. Spring opening depends on weather.

Hiking: 3-mi. trail to mountaintop. Last 1/2 mile is steep. Often windy, chilly at top.

HEADQUARTERS: c/o Fort Stevens State Park, Hammond, OR 97121; (503) 861-1671.

SAMUEL H. BOARDMAN STATE PARK
Oregon Parks and Recreation Division
1,473 acres.

From Brookings, N about 6 mi. on US 101. Park extends N 9 mi.

Rugged coastline: cliffs, crags, promontories, offshore rocks. Also sand beaches. Four areas developed for day use. Trails to beaches. Viewpoints. Seabirds and marine mammals often seen offshore. Offshore rocks include wave-carved arches and islands covered with spruce trees. House Rock, 400 ft. above the sea, offers view of the shoreline S for 25 mi. to Pt. St. George in CA. Vegetation includes azalea, rhododendron, ceanothus, hillsides of Oregon iris.

SEAL ROCK WAYSIDE
Oregon Parks and Recreation Division
8 acres.

From Newport, 10 mi. S on US 101.

One of the best places to see seals, sea lions, and seabirds. Rugged coast; many offshore rocks.

SHORE ACRES STATE PARK
See Cape Arago State Park.

SISKIYOU NATIONAL FOREST
U.S. Forest Service
1,093,542 acres/1,163,583 acres within boundaries.

SW Oregon; 39,688 acres in NW California. W of Grants Pass. Principal access routes from US 101, US 199, I-5.

Near the Coast, but no ocean frontage. Covers a major portion of the Siskiyou Mountain Range, which links the Cascade Mountains on the E and Coast Range on the NW. Includes a small section of the Coast Range. Grayback Mountain, 7,055 ft. elevation, is highest point. Area is mountainous, steep, rough, with short drainages. Crossed by Rogue River (see entry). Five rivers originate within the Forest. Timberlands, open grass and brush areas; large outcrops of serpentine.

Plants: Area has unique botanical diversity, mingling of species characteristic of regions to N, S, E, and W. Also many relict species. Principal trees: Douglas-fir, ponderosa and sugar pines, Port Orford cedar; white, noble, and Shasta firs. Some old-growth stands. Among the rare species: weeping spruce. Prominent in understory: madrone, California black oak, tan oak, manzanita, bigleaf maple, buckthorn. Estimated 2,000 species of flowering plants, but no checklist is available.

Birds: Checklist of over 150 species. Common species include great blue heron, mallard, wood duck, common merganser, turkey vulture, red-tailed hawk, blue grouse, California quail, spotted sandpiper, band-tailed pigeon; spotted, screech, great horned, and pygmy owls; rufous hummingbird, belted kingfisher, common flicker, western wood pewee, tree and cliff swallows, Steller's jay, chestnut-backed chickadee, common bushtit, red-breasted nuthatch; house, winter, and Bewick's wrens; robin, varied thrush, golden-crowned kinglet. Warblers include orange-crowned, yellow-rumped, MacGillivray's, Wilson's. Also western tanager, pine siskin, American goldfinch, rufous-sided towhee, and sparrows: savannah, white-crowned, golden-crowned, and song.

Mammals: Checklist available. Often seen: mule deer, Roosevelt elk, black bear, Townsend chipmunk, western gray squirrel. Others include shrews, moles, bats, snowshoe hare, brush rabbit, mountain beaver, beaver, California and golden-mantled ground squirrels, pocket gophers, several mouse species, porcupine, gray fox, coyote, marten, fisher, mink, weasels, skunks, mountain lion, bobcat.

Reptiles and amphibians: Include several salamander species, tree frog, western toad, northern red-legged and foothill yellow-legged frogs, fence and sagebrush lizards, alligator lizard, and snakes: rubber boa, ringneck, racer, gopher, garter, California and mountain kingsnakes, western rattlesnake, various garter snakes.

FEATURES

Kalmiopsis Wilderness, 179,862 acres, in S central region. Two principal access routes: (1) from US 199 near Kerby, Eight Dollar Mountain Road N across Illinois River, up to parking area on ridge above Onion Camp; (2) from Brookings on US 101, E and N on local road beside Chetco River, then up past Long Ridge and Quail Prairie lookout to Vulcan Peak area. Both routes normally can be traveled by cars in good condition. Also off Forest Road 3504, Illinois River Rd., about 10 mi. W of Selma. Includes most of Chetco River headwater basin. Harsh, rugged country; rocky, brushy, low elevation canyons; rushing streams. Area has special interest for botanists, both because of great variety of species and presence of rarities.

Wild Rogue Wilderness, 36,038 acres, including 8,971 acres of BLM land, in N central region. (See entry for Rogue Wild and Scenic River, zone 1.) Very steep terrain; essentially a canyon. The Wilderness serves chiefly as a buffer zone for the Wild River. Only a few trails, steep and short. Brush and cliffs make cross-country travel next to impossible.

Several *botanical areas* and *research natural areas* have been established. These are of interest primarily to specialists, not the general public. Those interested should inquire at headquarters or any Ranger District office.

INCLUDES: *Oregon Caves National Monument.* (See entry in zone 5.)

ACTIVITIES

Camping: 21 campgrounds; 383 sites. Last part of May to Labor Day. Some campgrounds are primitive: pit toilets, no water or water that requires boiling. Several nearby BLM campgrounds.

Hiking: Trail along Rogue River. (See Rogue Wild and Scenic River entry.) Forest map shows extensive trail system, including trails in Kalmiopsis Wilderness. Some hikers camp in the wilderness area, but demand has not been sufficient to require a permit system.

Hunting: Deer, elk, bear, grouse, quail, pigeon, dove.

Fishing: Rogue and others rivers are well known for excellent fishing: chinook, steelhead, coho, cutthroat.

Boating: See entry for Rogue Wild and Scenic River. Also, the Illinois River, for about 35 mi. above its junction with the Rogue, is attracting whitewater enthusiasts. Class IV and V rapids in a run between steep canyon walls rimmed by lush green forests and mountains. The river flows NW, just N of the Kalmiopsis Wilderness.

Horse riding: Outfitters in nearby communities provide pack and saddle stock, guides.

PUBLICATIONS
Forest map. $1.00.
Kalmiopsis Wilderness map. $1.00.
Wild Rogue Wilderness map. $1.00.

HEADQUARTERS: P.O. Box 440, 1501 N.W. 6th St., Grants Pass, OR 97526; (503) 479-5301.

RANGER DISTRICTS: Chetco R.D., P.O. Box 730, 446 Oak St., Brookings, OR 97415; (503) 469-2196. Galice R.D., Post Office Bldg., P.O. Box 1131, Grants Pass, OR 97526; (503) 476-6918. Gold Beach R.D., P.O. Box 548, 1225 S. Ellensburg, Gold Beach, OR 97444; (503) 247-6651. Illinois Valley R.D., P.O. Box 389, Highway 199, Cave Junction, OR 97523; (503) 592-2166. Powers R.D., Powers, OR 97466; (503) 439-3011.

SIUSLAW NATIONAL FOREST
U.S. Forest Service
625,485 acres/835,376 acres within boundaries.

On or near the Coast. N portion from Cape Lookout to Lincoln Beach. S portion from near Yaquina River to Coos Bay. Access from US 101, US 20, SRs 22, 18, 34, 126, 38.

43 mi. of ocean frontage, the only National Forest with much seacoast. The coastal part of the Forest has been designated the Oregon Dunes National Recreation Area. We have made it a separate entry.

As the preceding acreage figures indicate, the Forest has many inholdings. The largest solid blocks of Forest land are in the S. The N portion is more fragmented but has several blocks of significant size.

The Forest extends inland over the Coast Range. It includes two prominent peaks: Mt. Hebo in the N, 3,147 ft.; and Mary's Peak to the E, 4,097 ft., highest in the Coast Range, offering splendid vistas. Steep slopes, sharp ridges, deep-cut canyons, open areas, sheer rock faces, cascades, waterfalls. Climate is moist, an average of 90 in. of rain each year, mostly in the winter. Snowfall is rare except on the peaks.

Inland hiking opportunities are limited. Dense vegetation makes off-trail travel next to impossible. The *Hiking Trails* leaflet listed under Publications offers nothing longer than 3 1/2 mi. Trails lead into roadless areas, two of the areas proposed for wilderness status. A network of paved and gravel roads opens most of the other Forest areas to travel.

Plants: One of the leading timber-producing National Forests. Much of the

Forest is in the western hemlock zone, Douglas-fir the most prominent species following fire or logging. Near the Coast, dense stands of Douglas-fir, western hemlock, red alder, with lesser amounts of western redcedar and Sitka spruce. Noble and Pacific silver firs at high elevations. Thick undergrowth of salmonberry, vine maple, salal, Oregon grape, blackberry, ferns, many wildflowers. As a consequence of fires and logging, only fragments of old-growth forest remain. Conservationists are seeking to preserve these, despite opposition from timber interests.

Birds: Over 100 species recorded. The variety of habitats—ocean shoreline, estuaries, dunes, meadows, streams, and dense forest—offers good birding opportunities. Species noted include loons, gadwall, pintail, shoveler, canvasback, bufflehead, grebes, Canada goose, scoter, mergansers, surfbird, yellowlegs, golden and bald eagles, various hawks and owls, western tanager, pine siskin, mountain quail, Steller's jay, common bushtit.

Mammals: Include shrew-mole, bats, raccoon, weasels, mink, red and gray foxes, mountain beaver, brush rabbit, snowshoe hare, coyote, bobcat, mule deer, Roosevelt elk, otter, chickaree, black bear.

FEATURES

Cascade Head Scenic Area, 9,670 acres. Off US 101 S of Neskowin. In the N portion of the Forest. The first such area designated by Congress. Cascade Head is a 1,770-ft. promontory. About 2 1/2 mi. of ocean frontage, estuary, floodplain, river, forest. Cliffs and offshore islands have nesting seabird colonies, seals, sea lions. Rain forest. Trails.

No *wilderness areas* have yet been designated by Congress. Two have been proposed. Conservationists, notably the Siuslaw Task Force, have urged wilderness status for several areas:

Umpqua Spit wilderness, 2,370 acres, awaits congressional action. It includes part of the Umpqua Dunes Scenic Area noted in the Oregon Dunes National Recreation Area entry. Bare sand dunes; vegetation behind the outer dunes.

Drift Creek roadless area, 11,500 acres, NE of Waldport. Steep forested slopes, dense tree canopy, small meadows. Considerable old-growth timber. Several trails.

Mount Hebo area, 31,349 acres surrounding Mt. Hebo, E of Pacific City. Pockets of mature trees; some stands up to 70 years old. Includes headwaters of several rivers.

Oregon Coast wilderness, 14,929 acres, is a Siuslaw Task Force proposal. 17 mi. S of Waldport. Would include little-disturbed watersheds, fine vegetation, good wildlife populations. Elevations to 2,200 ft.

Wassen Creek area, another Task Force proposal, is unusual in that it would include BLM and private land as well as National Forest land. 19,000 acres. E of Reedsport, S of the Smith River. Steep slopes, deep-cut canyons, cliffs, cascades, falls. No trails.

INTERPRETATION

Cape Perpetua Visitor Center, on US 101 2 mi. S of Yachats. *Exhibits, film, information, publications.* 7 *nature trails.* Points of interest reached by trails include tidepools, Devil's Churn, Spouting Horns, Cape Cove Beach.

22-mi. self-guided auto tour begins at Devil's Churn.

Campfire programs at Tillicum Beach and Cape Perpetua campgrounds.

ACTIVITIES

Camping: 36 campgrounds, 802 sites (including 14 campgrounds, 330 sites, in Oregon Dunes National Recreation Area). Several open all year. Trailside camping permitted in most areas.

Hiking: Oregon Coast Trail (see entry for Oregon Dunes National Recreation Area). Inland areas have few hiking trails because of thick vegetation and steep terrain.

Hunting: Deer, elk, bear, grouse, quail, pigeon, dove.

Fishing: Surf, lakes, streams.

PUBLICATIONS

Forest map. $1.00.

Campground information leaflet.

Cape Perpetua Visitor Center leaflet.

Cape Perpetua.

Auto tour leaflet.

Selected Hiking Trails.

Cascade Head booklet.

REFERENCE: Wellborn, Sherry, ed. *Oregon Coast Range Wilderness.* 1980. Siuslaw Task Force, P.O. Box 863, Corvallis, OR 97330. $2.95.

HEADQUARTERS: P.O. Box 1148, Corvallis, OR 97330; (503) 757-4480.

RANGER DISTRICTS: Hebo R.D., State Highway 22, Hebo, OR 97122; (503) 392-3161. Mapleton R.D., State Highway 126, Mapleton, OR 97453; (503) 268-4473. Alsea R.D., State Highway 34, Alsea, OR 97324; (503) 487-5811. Waldport R.D., U.S. Highway 101, Waldport, OR 97394; (503) 563-3211. Oregon Dunes National Recreation Area, 855 Highway Ave., Reedsport, OR 97467; (503) 271-3611.

SOUTH BEACH STATE PARK

Oregon Parks and Recreation Division
433 acres.

From Newport, 2 mi. S on US 101.

About 1 mi. of broad, sandy beach backed by 20-ft. dunes partly stabilized by beach grass, small pines. Back of the dunes, dense growth of salal, box blueberry. Rhododendron, shore pine planted in developed area. About 40 acres of rhododendron, pine and spruce.

Nature trail, about 1/2 mi.

ACTIVITIES
  Camping: 257 sites. Mid-Apr. to Oct. Reservations.
  Hiking, backpacking: 4 mi. of beach, beyond Park limits. On Oregon Coast Trail. Hiker-biker primitive camp.
  Fishing: Surf. Sea bass, cod, perch.
  Swimming: Surf, unsupervised.

HEADQUARTERS: P.O. Box 1350, Newport, OR 97365; (503) 867-7451.

SUNSET BAY STATE PARK
See Cape Arago State Park.

THREE ARCH ROCKS NATIONAL WILDLIFE REFUGE
See Cape Meares National Wildlife Refuge.

TILLAMOOK STATE FOREST
Oregon Department of Forestry
363,000 acres.

NW Oregon, about 25 mi. W of Portland. Crossed by SR 6, Glenwood to Tillamook, and local road NE from Mohler.

Steep mountain slopes. Highest point about 3,000 ft. Some ridges extremely sharp. More rounded mountains and gentler slopes near the Coast. Steep river gradients and occasional waterfalls in upstream areas. Rivers: Nehalem, Salmonberry, Miami, Kilchis, Wilson, Tualatin, Trask. Numerous smaller streams. Precipitation as much as 130 in. per year.
  Site of the Tillamook Burn, fires in 1933, 1939, and 1945 that destroyed 356,000 acres. Much of the burned area was abandoned by private owners. A state bond issue financed a major reforestation program. Significant timber harvesting will resume in 1990.
  Plants: 95% of the area is forested, much in even-aged stands. Principal tree species: Douglas-fir, western hemlock. No old growth. Other species include

Sitka spruce, western redcedar, noble fir, red alder, bigleaf maple. Understory includes vine maple, swordfern, California hazel, red huckleberry, bracken fern, thimbleberry, salmonberry, salal, trailing blackberry, Oregon grape, snowberry, huckleberry. Flowering species include starflower, trillium, thick-leaf lotus, elderberry, oceanspray, foxglove. A number of plant species found on King Mountain occur only on a few isolated peaks in the Coast Range.

Birds: 71 species recorded; more probably present. Noted: bald eagle, hawks, grouse, rufous hummingbird, common flicker, woodpeckers, wood pewee, Steller's jay, golden-crowned kinglet, western tanager, pine siskin, rufous-sided towhee.

Mammals: Include Roosevelt elk, mule deer, coyote, beaver, mountain beaver, rabbit, wood rat, raccoon, black bear, mink.

INTERPRETATION: *Auto tour route,* self-guided, 25 mi., begins at Rogers Camp. Emphasis on aspects of reforestation.

ACTIVITIES
Camping: Inadequate funds have caused closure of campgrounds. Camp in any suitable place unless posted.
Hiking, backpacking: 24 mi. of trails. Hikers can travel the entire system or use any of four intermediate access points.
Hunting: Deer, elk, bear.
Fishing: Streams. Trout, salmon, steelhead.
Swimming: Informal. Pools in streams. Unsupervised.
Horse riding: Trail section from Camp Brown to Elk Creek Park. (Portions on roads with vehicle traffic.)

Rogers Camp is a center for motorcycling. Cycles permitted on designated trails nearby.

PUBLICATIONS
Forest leaflet (no map).
Tillamook Forest Trails, with trail map.
Auto tour guide.

HEADQUARTERS: (District Office) 4907 E. Third St., Tillamook, OR 97141; (503) 842-2545. (1 mi. E of Tillamook, E of county fairgrounds.) (Area Office) 801 Gales Creek Rd., Forest Grove, OR 97116; (503) 357-2191.

UMPQUA LIGHTHOUSE STATE PARK
Oregon Parks and Recreation Division
2,715 acres.

From Reedsport, 6 mi. S on US 101.

At mouth of the Umpqua River. 2 1/2 mi. of ocean beach, 1/2 mi. on Lake Marie. Sand dunes to 500 ft., said to be highest in the United States. Islands of dead trees show how dunes have been moving E. Old dunes now partially stabilized by vegetation. Rhododendrons prominent, especially at Lake Marie. Nearby is jetty at mouth of Winchester Bay.

ACTIVITIES
  Camping: 63 sites. Mid-Apr. to Oct.
  Hiking, backpacking: On Oregon Coast Trail. Primitive hiker-biker camp.
  Swimming: Lake and surf.

ADJACENT: Oregon Dunes National Recreation Area (see entry).

HEADQUARTERS: Box 94, Winchester Bay, OR 97467; (503) 271-4118.

WILLIAM M. TUGMAN STATE PARK
Oregon Parks and Recreation Division
560 acres.

From Coos Bay, 19 mi. N on US 101.

On the inland side of the Coast Road; no ocean frontage. On Eel Lake, scenic area, surrounded by low forested hills. 5 mi. of lake frontage.

ACTIVITIES
  Camping: 115 sites. Mid-Apr. to Oct.
  Fishing: Trout.
  Swimming: Lake. Unsupervised.
  Boating: Large paved ramp and trailer parking. Boat speed limit 10 mph.

ADJACENT: Oregon Dunes National Recreation Area (see entry).

HEADQUARTERS: c/o Umpqua Lighthouse State Park, P.O. Box 94, Winchester Bay, OR 97467; (503) 271-4118.

ZONE 2

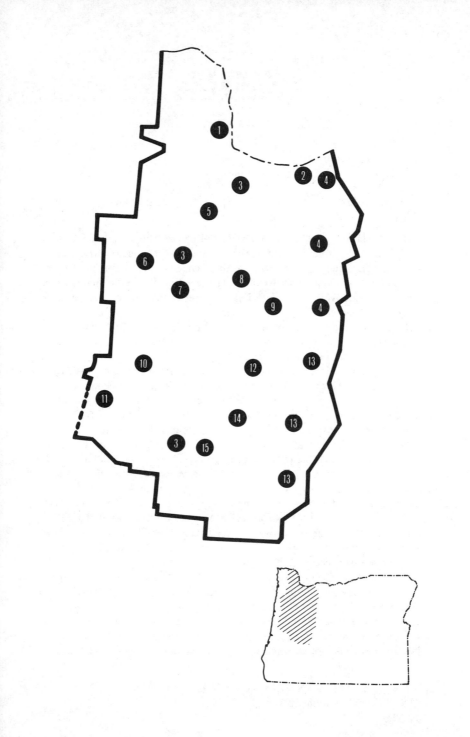

ZONE 2

Includes these counties:

Columbia	Clackamas	Linn
Washington	Marion	Lane (central and E
Multnomah	Polk	portions)
Yamhill	Benton	

The Willamette Valley lies between the Coast Range and the Cascade Mountains. This zone includes the valley and the W slope of the Cascades. It extends from the Columbia River to the Calapooya Mountains S of Eugene.

A majority of Oregonians live in this fertile valley. Soil and climate support a richly productive and diversified agriculture. Industry and commerce also concentrate here.

Before all this development, the valley supported large wildlife populations. Each spring and fall, vast numbers of waterfowl came through. Some spent the winter here, some were all-year residents. The flocks are smaller now, and their future depends in large measure on the few refuges that have been set aside.

As one might expect, the public parks near Portland, Salem, and other population centers are heavily used. Most of them could not be considered quiet natural areas. We have included several that still have relatively undisturbed portions, parks to be enjoyed chiefly midweek or off-season.

More than a dozen State Parks are strung along the Columbia River Gorge. The Gorge retains some of its original grandeur, but it is difficult to find a viewpoint that does not overlook busy highways, dams, locks, power plants, towns, and other shoreline structures. We did not think any of the parks suitable for an entry, but the Columbia River Gorge is described in summary.

Two National Forests include 97% of the acres in the entries that follow. Almost all of this Forest land is in the mountains to the E of the valley. These Forests are units of a huge block of National Forest land extending from the Columbia River to the California border.

Snow and rainfall are heavy on the W slopes. Many of the rivers flowing down from the mountains have been dammed, the U.S. Army Corps of Engineers being responsible for 10 of the principal impoundments. These reservoirs are much used for water-based recreation: water skiing, sailing, fishing, swimming, power boating. We have noted those that are within National Forests, not those surrounded by privately owned land.

ANKENY NATIONAL WILDLIFE REFUGE
U.S. Fish and Wildlife Service
2,796 acres.

From I-5, 10 mi. N of Albany, Talbot exit. Then 2 mi. W on Wintel Rd.

In the fertile Willamette Valley. Bottomlands near the confluence of the Santiam and Willamette rivers. One of three refuges in the Valley providing wintering grounds for the dusky Canada goose, a race with a restricted range. Feed crops are cultivated. Hedgerows of hawthorn, wild rose, ash, and berry species surround most fields. Several dense deciduous woods.

Several miles of paved county roads cross the Refuge, providing good viewing. The entire Refuge, including a 1 1/2-mi. trail through fields and woods, is open to foot travel Apr. 15–Nov. 1.

Birds: 193 species recorded. Chief waterfowl species: Canada goose, mallard, wigeon, pintail, green-winged teal. Also grebes, herons, hawks, quail, band-tailed pigeon, shorebirds, woodpeckers, many songbirds.

Mammals: Mule deer, red fox, opossum, nutria, raccoon, skunk, coyote.

Hunting: Waterfowl, dove, pheasant, quail. Special regulations.

Refuge is closed to all use mid-Jan. to Apr. 15. Closed to nonhunters Nov. 1–Apr. 15. Otherwise, open daylight hours.
Dogs must be leashed except when actively hunting.

PUBLICATIONS
Leaflet with map.
Bird, mammal, plant checklists.

HEADQUARTERS: 2301 Wintel Rd. S, Jefferson, OR 97352; (503) 327-2444.
Open weekdays, 7:30 A.M.–4 P.M.

BASKETT SLOUGH NATIONAL WILDLIFE REFUGE
U.S. Fish and Wildlife Service
2,492 acres.

12 mi. W of Salem. From intersection of SR 99W and SR 22, W 1 1/2 mi. on SR 22.

Near the center of fertile Willamette Valley. In open farm country near foothills of the Coast Range. An ancient lakebed surrounded by rolling, forested hills. One of three refuges in the Valley providing wintering grounds for the dusky Canada goose, a race with a restricted range. Feed crops are cultivated. General elevation about 200 ft.; Baskett Butte is 414 ft. Morgan Lake, 65 acres, is the primary feeding and resting area.

Birds: Seasonally common or abundant species include whistling swan, Canada goose, mallard, pintail, green-winged teal, wigeon, shoveler, wood duck. Also great blue heron, red-tailed hawk, marsh hawk, kestrel, ruffed grouse, California quail, pheasant, killdeer, snipe, greater yellowlegs, great horned owl, flicker, downy woodpecker, swallows, chickadees, jays, wrens, kinglets, cedar waxwing, several warblers.

Mammals: Common species include opossum, shrews, Townsend mole, little brown and big brown bats, raccoon, striped skunk, red fox, California ground squirrel, Townsend chipmunk, giant pocket gopher, deer mouse, nutria, brush rabbit, mule deer.

FEATURES: *Viewpoints*—waterfowl can be seen, fall and winter, from both sides of Coville and Smithfield county roads and parking areas on Coville.

ACTIVITIES

Hiking: Main trail, 3 mi.; closed Oct. 1–May 1 for benefit of wintering waterfowl. Baskett Butte trail, 1 mi., open all year.

Hunting: Waterfowl, upland game birds. Special regulations.

Dogs must be leashed except when actively hunting.

PUBLICATIONS
Leaflet with map.
Plant, bird, mammal checklists.

HEADQUARTERS: 10995 Highway 22, Dallas, OR 97338; (503) 623-2749. Open weekdays, 7:00 A.M.– 4:30 P.M.

BEN AND KAY DORRIS STATE PARK
Oregon Parks and Recreation Division
92 acres.

From Eugene, 31 mi. E on SR 126.

Forested site on McKenzie River. Boat ramp.

NEARBY: Willamette National Forest (see entry).

CASCADIA STATE PARK
Oregon Parks and Recreation Division
258 acres.

On US 20, 14 mi. E of Sweet Home.

Highway and South Santiam River Gorge bisect the site. River terrace and mountain slopes. Open meadows, old-growth timber stands. Much Pacific dogwood in the understory.

Camping: 26 primitive sites. Opening date determined by winter weather.

NEARBY: Willamette National Forest (see entry).

CHAMPOEG STATE PARK
Oregon Parks and Recreation Division
587 acres.

N of Salem. From I-5, Champoeg-Aurora exit, then 8 mi. W on River Road.

Wooded setting on the Willamette River. Although not an outstanding natural area, it has interest because of an arboretum and botanical garden featuring flora native to Oregon. Visitor center depicts aspects of Oregon history.

Camping: 48 sites. All year.

HEADQUARTERS: 7679 Champoeg Rd. NE, St. Paul, OR 97137; (503) 678-1251.

COLUMBIA RIVER GORGE
(See also zone 3 entry.)
Largely private ownership; some state and federal lands.

Along I-84 E of Portland.

The Gorge is a deep canyon between Washington and Oregon, a water route through the Cascade Mountains. Slopes rise steeply to 1,500 ft. and more, close to the river, with nearby mountains to 3,500 ft. The W portion, near Portland, has many spectacular waterfalls and sections of rain forest. Beyond the mountains, to the E, the Gorge opens on a landscape of oaks and grass-lands, blending into sagebrush desert.

This was one of the continent's most scenic areas. However, only scattered bits of shoreline remain in public ownership. Route I-84, close to the river, is Oregon's only E–W Interstate Highway and heavily traveled. The river's flow has been blocked by dams. Mining, industrial and commercial development, and suburban sprawl are invading the remaining natural areas. A Columbia Gorge National Scenic Area has been proposed in hopes of guiding rather than halting further development.

Many people enjoy driving the Scenic Highway, US 30, stopping for short walks to falls and overlooks. At Multnomah Falls one enters Mount Hood National Forest. For the next 27 mi. parking areas and trails lead up into the Forest.

ELIJAH BRISTOW STATE PARK
(formerly Dexter Dam State Park)
Oregon Parks and Recreation Division
797 acres.

15 mi. SE of Eugene on SR 58.

On both banks of the Middle Fork, Willamette River, just below Dexter Dam; at SE end of the Willamette Valley, close to the Cascade Range foothills. Scenic river shore forest, largely undeveloped; most of the site will remain in its natural condition. An area 3/4 mi. downstream from the dam has tall cottonwoods, some Douglas-fir, western redcedar. W side of river is an island, nesting for herons, osprey. Mainland portion has two backwater sloughs, greatest variety of trees in the park, active beaver. Bald eagle seen occasionally.

Plants: Tree species also include grand fir, western hemlock, western yew, incense cedar, western hazelnut, bigleaf maple, river willow. Shrubs include Oregon grape, salal, Scotch broom, blackberry, snowberry, poison oak. Wildflowers include trillium, wild strawberry, fringe cup, buttercup, larkspur, bleeding heart, lupine, purple iris, camas lily.

Birds: Include osprey, turkey vulture, red-tailed hawk, kestrel, mallard, pintail, wood duck, kingfisher, killdeer, great blue heron, rufous-sided towhee, scrub jay, solitary vireo, fox sparrow.

Mammals: Include mule deer, red fox, cottontail, beaver, muskrat, California ground squirrel, chickaree, pocket gopher.

Whitewater boating: Beginning of 208-mi. canoe trail down Willamette River Greenway (see entry). Park is located at river milepost 200.5 on the Middle Fork of the Willamette River.

NEARBY: Dexter Lake and Lookout Point Lake (U.S. Army Corps of Engineers); both within Willamette National Forest (see entry). Camping, fishing, swimming, boating.

HEADQUARTERS: 38259 Wheeler Rd., Dexter, OR 97431; (503) 726-8560.

MOUNT HOOD NATIONAL FOREST
U.S. Forest Service
1,060,253 acres.

From the Columbia River S. Crossed by US 26 and SR 35.

Many windows in Portland offer views of 11,235-ft. Mt. Hood. The Forest is one of the most popular resorts in the Northwest, summer and winter. Within the Forest boundaries are ski resorts, lodges, golf courses, restaurants, shops, private residences, and other developments. Half a million people a year come just to drive the main roads and see the sights. Cattle graze, timber is harvested, Christmas trees cut.

But visitors tend to congregate. It's a big Forest, and it's not difficult to find quiet places away from the main roads, trails where meetings with other hikers are infrequent.

The Forest straddles the Cascade Range. The area is mountainous, moderate to steep slopes, with over 4,500 mi. of streams, 161 lakes, 6 reservoirs. Snowfall is heavy in the high country. The skiing season begins in Nov. and ends about Apr., although one can still ski on the upper glaciers through the summer.

Over 3,000 miles of Forest roads, mostly unpaved, varying conditions. Most were built for logging access. A Forest map is necessary.

Plants: 85% of the area is forested. Principal tree species are Douglas-fir, western hemlock; Pacific silver, noble, and grand firs; ponderosa pine. Old-growth stands can be seen in several areas, notably Bagby Hot Springs and Bull of the Woods. Understory species include rhododendron, salal, Oregon grape, vine maple, huckleberry, bear grass, swordfern. Many wildflowers, but no list available. Reported above timberline: sulphur flower, penstemon, Jacob's ladder, arnica, Indian paintbrush, Cascade aster, yarrow.

Birds: Checklist of 132 species limited to Mt. Hood's S slope, a transition zone with 9,000-ft. altitude range. Species noted include pied-billed grebe, great blue and green herons, whistling swan, Canada and white-fronted geese, mallard, wood duck, Barrow's goldeneye, harlequin duck, hooded and common mergansers; sharp-shinned, Cooper's, and red-tailed hawks; golden and bald eagles, osprey, kestrel, spotted sandpiper, band-tailed pigeon, rock and mourning doves; barn, screech, and great horned owls. Also 7 woodpecker species, 8 flycatchers, 5 swallows, gray and Steller's jays; black-capped, mountain, and chestnut-backed chickadees; pygmy, red-breasted, and white-breasted nuthatches; water ouzel, 5 wrens, mountain bluebird, cedar waxwing.

Warblers include orange-crowned, Nashville, yellow, Audubon's, black-throated gray, Townsend's, hermit, MacGillivray's, Wilson's. Also purple, Cassin's, house, and gray-crowned rosy finches; red- and white-winged crossbills.

Mammals: No checklist available. Species reported include marmot, golden-mantled squirrel, pika, Townsend chipmunk, mule deer, shrew and coast moles; big brown, silver-haired, hoary, Townsend big-eared, and several other bats; snowshoe hare, red tree vole, porcupine, northern flying squirrel, deer mouse, chickaree, mountain lion, bobcat, marten, short-tailed and long-tailed weasels, spotted skunk, black bear.

FEATURES

Mount Jefferson Wilderness, 99,600 acres, dominated by 10,497-ft. Mt. Jefferson. Lowest point in the area is 3,000 ft. Five glaciers on the mountain. Alpine meadows, lakes seen only by hikers, many streams. Area is a volcanic plateau with several large, steep-sided extinct or dormant volcanos, small younger cones, lava flows. About 62% forested. More than 160 mi. of trails, including 36 mi. of the Pacific Crest Trail. Numerous lakes, about 60 offering opportunity for fishing. About 75 in. of precipitation annually, more than half as snow. Snowfall may begin in Oct., snow cover lasts into summer. The area includes portions of the Deschutes (zone 3) and Willamette (zone 2) National Forests (see entries).

Wilderness permit required. Special regulations govern use of horses.

Mount Hood Wilderness, 47,100 acres, includes the peak of Mt. Hood and slopes on the W, N, and E, extending W almost to Zigzag. About half alpine, high meadows with thin soil, fragile vegetation. *Wilderness permit required. Horses prohibited on many trails.*

Bull of the Woods roadless area, 10,200 acres. Numerous small lakes. Bull of the Woods peak, central portion of area, 5,523 ft. Timbered slopes and valleys.

Columbia roadless area, 40,900 acres, above the sheer cliffs of the Columbia River Gorge. Shown on some maps as "Columbia Gorge Recreation Area." Proposed for wilderness status. For about 28 mi. E of Multnomah Falls, the Forest boundary comes close to I-80 N and the river. Most of the land along the river is privately owned, and much of it has been developed. The Interstate is OR's principal W–E route. Along the route are many parking areas and trailheads. This is a popular hiking area, only a few miles from Portland on the Interstate, scenic, with mild winters. However, most hikers are day-trippers. With trail information, a backpacker should have little difficulty finding reasonable solitude in the backcountry.

The area has broad, flat ridgetops; deep, steep-sloped drainages; mountain peaks; lakes; waterfalls; cliffs; chasms. Elevations from 100 ft. near the river to 4,900 ft. on Mt. Defiance. Special bird and mammal lists for the Gorge have been prepared by the Skamania County Resource Agent and may be available from the Columbia Gorge Ranger District. A trail planning guide printed as part of the trails map (see below) lists 32 trails, from 0.6 to 21.1 mi. in length, with the elevation change for each. Loop trails range from 1.2 to 11.2 mi. The Pacific Crest Trail crosses the area.

Hikers should be aware that the Bull Run Watershed Management unit, on the SW of this area, is closed to public use, except for a segment of the Pacific Crest Trail.

Multnomah Falls, a major feature on the Gorge, was transferred to the Forest in 1943.

Salmon-Huckleberry area, 68,000 acres, SW of Mt. Hood, directly S of Zigzag. Forested slopes and ridges of the South Fork of the Salmon River and Mack Hall Creek. Salmon Butte, 4,877 ft., is landmark and viewpoint; reached by trail linking two Forest roads. Rain forest; dense stands of Douglas-fir, true firs, western redcedar, western hemlock, with dense understory. Hiking on moderate slopes. An 8,300-acre roadless portion of this area has been proposed for wilderness status.

Olallie Scenic Area, 10,798 acres, on the crest of the Cascade Range, adjoins Mount Jefferson Wilderness and Warm Springs Indian Reservation. Not classed as wilderness, but most of it is reached only by trail. Features include *Breitenbush Cascades,* river dropping 1,600 ft. in 0.8 mi. into a deep canyon; *Breitenbush Lake,* 60 acres, at 5,500 ft. elevation; *Olallie Meadow,* once a lake, now a marshy area slowly becoming forested; many wildflowers; *Olallie Butte,* 7,215 ft., highest cinder cone in the Cascade Range. *Olallie Lake,* 238 acres, is largest of several lakes in the area. More than 45 mi. of trails, including 15 mi. of Pacific Crest Trail. *Oregon Skyline Road, S-42, is scenic but primitive; not for trailers.*

Columbia River Scenic Highway, US 30, about 52 mi. from Wahkeena Falls to Mount Hood Loop Highway, SR 35. The National Forest boundary is close to the road and river. Indeed, a few small parcels are on the river but across railroad tracks. Many falls and other scenic features along the way. Parking areas and trailheads.

Combined with the *Mount Hood Loop* and US 26, this offers a 170-mi. auto tour from Portland. A leaflet describes features along the way and interesting side trips.

ACTIVITIES

Camping: 107 campgrounds; over 2,000 sites. Seasons vary with elevation and weather, some campgrounds opening Mar. and Apr., others not until July. Informal camping except where posted.

Hiking, backpacking: 1,170 mi. of established trails, plus many more mi. of little-used Forest roads. High country trails may not be open until July, but good hiking is available at lower altitudes. Wilderness hiking requires permit and observance of special rules. In addition to the maps listed under Publications, trail information sheets are available at HQ and Ranger Districts.

Hunting: Elk, deer, black bear, blue and ruffed grouse, quail, wild turkey.

Fishing: 1,500 mi. of trout streams, 277 mi. of salmon and steelhead streams. Also lake fishing.

Boating: Only 6 of the lakes and reservoirs exceed 100 acres. Ramps are indicated on 3. Boats with motors are prohibited on some lakes. Boats are used chiefly by fishermen.

Horse riding: Horse trails in all Ranger Districts. Outfitters may change from year to year; inquire.

Skiing: Several commercial ski areas operate within the Forest. HQ will supply leaflets.

Ski touring, snowmobiling: Winter sports map shows trails suitable for ski touring, snowmobiling, as well as closed routes.

PUBLICATIONS

Maps:
Forest. $1.00.
Mount Jefferson Wilderness. $1.00.
Mount Hood Wilderness. $1.00.
Forest Trails of the Columbia Gorge. $1.00.
Winter Sports.
Olallie Scenic Area.
Lakes of the Mount Hood National Forest.

Information pages:
Welcome Lakes.
Hideaway Lake.
Round Lake.
Big Slide Lake.
Mother Lode Lakes.
Pansy Lake.

Leaflets:
Lost Lake.
Multnomah Falls.
Forest Statistics.
Climbing Mt. Hood.
Camping Outside a Campground.
Bagby Hot Springs.
Timberline Wildlife.
Oregon Scenic Highway Drive; Mt. Hood Loop. Leaflet with map.
Rock Lakes Basin leaflet with map.
Birds of Mt. Hood's South Slope. Checklist.

Guides:
Columbia Gorge District Scenic Drive. (Mimeographed page.)
Eagle Creek Trail.
Salmon River–Hunchback Trail System.
Huckleberry Trail System.
Zigzag Mountain Trail System.
Mountain Meadows Loop Trail.
Veda Lake Trail.
Cool Creek Trail.
Salmon Butte Trail.
Castle Canyon Trail.
Flag Mountain Trail.
Day Hikes Around Mt. Hood.
Bull of the Woods leaflet with map.
Snow Machines, showing areas closed to snowmobiles, etc.
Horse Trails on the Zigzag District.
Wilderness permit information.
Leaflets issued by ski areas.

HEADQUARTERS: 19559 SE Division St., Gresham, OR 97030; (503) 667-0511.

RANGER DISTRICTS: Barlow R.D., Dufur, OR 97021; (503) 467-2291. Bear Springs R.D., Route 1, Box 65, Maupin, OR 97037; (503) 328-6211. Clackamas R.D., 61431 E. Highway 224, Estacada, OR 97023; (503) 630-4256. Columbia Gorge R.D., Route 3, Box 44A, Troutdale, OR 97060; (503) 695-2276. Hood River R.D., 6780 Highway 35, Mt. Hood, OR 97041; (503) 352-6002. Zigzag R.D., Zigzag, OR 97973; (503) 622-3191.

SANTIAM STATE FOREST
Oregon Department of Forestry
47,700 acres.

From Salem, SE on SR 22. Much of the Forest land is near the Santiam River between Mill City and Detroit Dam. Access is by unpaved Forest roads; advisable to consult map at HQ.

Gentle to very steep slopes on Willamette Valley side of the Cascade Mountains. Elevations from 830 to 4,725 ft. Climate is moist: about 75 in. of precipitation annually. Much of the Forest was logged off and abandoned before 1940. In 1951 fire destroyed 21,400 acres of prime timber. Timber was salvaged and the land reforested. The Forest is managed chiefly for timber production. North Santiam River is a whitewater stream. Several creeks, waterfalls.

Plants: 95% forested. No old-growth stands. Timber is harvested as it matures. Principal species: Douglas-fir, western hemlock, western redcedar at lower elevations; Douglas-fir, western hemlock, noble fir above. Red alder, bigleaf maple, black cottonwood along creeks. Understory of vine maple, salal, Oregon grape, swordfern, blackberry, thimbleberry. Flowering species include rhododendron, mountain ash, dogwood, salmonberry.

Birds: Common species include pileated woodpecker, nighthawk, junco, grosbeak, robin, bushtit, wood pewee, California quail, rufous hummingbird, common flicker, pine siskin.

Mammals: Mule deer, beaver, California ground squirrel, chickaree, snowshoe hare, chipmunk, mountain beaver, coyote. Elk, river otter, marten, bobcat, black bear.

INTERPRETATION: *Maples Wayside Nature Trail,* 35 mi. E of Salem on SR 22. Self-guiding, 1/4 mi.

ACTIVITIES
Camping: Scattered primitive sites.
Hiking: Only 2 mi. of established trails, to Shelburg Falls and Butte Creek Falls. Those interested in hiking elsewhere are advised to consult HQ.
Hunting: Deer, bear, elk.
Fishing: Trout, salmon, steelhead.
Whitewater boating: River is for experts only. Detailed information necessary.

NEARBY: Willamette National Forest (see entry).

PUBLICATIONS
Forest leaflet.
Nature trail guide.

HEADQUARTERS: 22965 North Fork Rd., SE, Lyons, OR 97358; (503) 859-2151.

SAUVIE ISLAND WILDLIFE AREA
Oregon Department of Fish and Wildlife
13,000 acres.

About 1 mi. N of Portland city line on US 30, turn E on Sauvie Island Bridge. Across bridge, left 2 mi. on Sauvie Island Rd. to HQ.
Open: 4 A.M.–10 P.M.

Large, irregularly shaped island in the Columbia River. S portion and several tracts in N portion are private land. Much of the N portion is low-lying, with lakes, channels, seasonal impoundments, marshes. Also oak-ash woodlands, grasslands, and cultivated fields. Embankment and sand beach along the Columbia River.

Chiefly for migrating and wintering waterfowl. About half of the area is open to hunting seasonally; the balance is wildlife refuge. Several roads lead to parking areas and trailheads. (See map available at HQ.) Some wildlife viewing is possible from autos, but limited during hunting season, when access by nonhunters is restricted.

Birds: Seasonally, large numbers of whistling swan, sandhill crane, mallard, pintail, wigeon, green-winged teal. In late November, flights of as many as 150,000 waterfowl can be seen. Other common species include great blue heron, Canada goose, cinnamon teal, shoveler, wood duck, bufflehead, ruddy duck, common merganser. Common birds of prey: turkey vulture, red-tailed hawk, marsh hawk, kestrel. Bald eagle late Nov. through the winter. California quail and pheasant both common. Also shorebirds: Virginia rail, sora, coot, killdeer, snipe, least sandpiper, western sandpiper. Also common flicker, hairy and downy woodpeckers, willow flycatcher, wood pewee, barn swallow, scrub jay, black-capped chickadee, bushtit, white-breasted nuthatch, Bewick's and long-billed marsh wrens, robin, varied thrush, kinglets. Warblers: orange-crowned, yellow, yellow-rumped, black-throated gray, common yellowthroat, Wilson's. Also crow, sparrows, finches, black-headed grosbeak, Bullock's oriole.

Mammals: Among those known or believed to be present are opossum, vagrant and Trowbridge shrews, Townsend and coast moles, little brown and big brown bats, brush rabbit, Townsend chipmunk, northern flying squirrel, California ground squirrel, beaver, nutria, muskrat, Camas pocket gopher, wood rat, voles, coyote, red fox, raccoon, striped skunk, mink, mule deer. Occasional Columbian white-tailed deer on N end of island.

FEATURES

Oak Island, with oak groves, offers access to Sturgeon Lake, largest body of water on the island. Fishing, swimming. Unimproved launching area for small boats. Closed to all entry except by permit during waterfowl hunting season.

Rentenaar Road, reached from Reeder Road on E side, is favored observation area to see late-afternoon flights of waterfowl in hunting season. Access to lower dike, foot route to McNary Lakes, Pete's Slough, other interior points, except in waterfowl hunting season.

Steelman Road, continuation of Sauvie Island Road, goes N to Crane Lake. From here, foot access to several points on W side of island. Closed except by permit in waterfowl hunting season.

Walton Beach, on Columbia River, on Reeder Road. Fishing, swimming.

ACTIVITIES

Hiking: On secondary roads, dikes, trails, Columbia River beach, etc. Much of the area is accessible only on foot or by small boat. Nonhunters are excluded from some areas in hunting season.

Hunting: Daily permit required. By permit, limited hunting for certain nongame species in the off-season.

Fishing: Chiefly warm-water species, primarily catfish, bass, crappie. Trout in Halderman Pond on Oak Island.

Swimming: Lake, river. No supervision.

Boating: Several launching sites. No hp limit on Sturgeon Lake. Many narrow channels are best explored by canoe; be alert for tide changes and swift tidal currents. Sturgeon Lake is extremely shallow in summer and affected by tides.

PUBLICATIONS

Leaflet with map.
Wildlife checklist.

HEADQUARTERS: Department of Fish and Wildlife, 506 SW Mill St., Portland, OR 97208; (503) 229-5403. Area manager, on the island: (503) 621-3488.

SILVER FALLS STATE PARK
Oregon Parks and Recreation Division
8,302 acres.

26 mi. E of Salem on SR 214.

OR's largest State Park, featuring 10 waterfalls, 5 over 100 ft. high. North and South Forks of Silver Creek cut deep gorges in the foothills of the Cascade Mountains. All of the falls are seen from within the canyon; moist microclimate, moss draped heavily on tree branches, deep moss on the ground, many ferns in forest understory.

The Park is well known and popular. South Falls day-use area is likely to be crowded on any fine weekend. However, the campground and picnic area are the places where people congregate. Canyon trails are likely to be uncrowded early and late in the day.

Plants: Heavily wooded, chiefly Douglas-fir and western hemlock. Some old-growth stands with large specimens. Understory includes salal, Oregon grape, vine maple, salmonberry, swordfern, maidenhair fern. Wildflowers include Klamath weed, forget-me-not, buttercup, wild ginger, foxglove, goatsbeard, coral bells, yellow monkeyflower, lily-of-the-valley, oxeye daisy, western starflower, western bleeding heart, spring beauty.

Birds: Species mentioned or noted are water ouzel, common flicker, white-crowned sparrow, California quail, downy woodpecker, wood pewee, black-capped chickadee, golden-crowned kinglet, Brewer's blackbird, rufous-sided towhee, dark-eyed junco.

Mammals: No data. Beaver are active in the Park.

FEATURES: *Silver Creek Canyon Trail,* 6 1/2-mi. circuit with optional shorter hikes. Canyon can be entered at several points, and trail has shorter loops. 10 waterfalls along the trail, highest 184 ft.

ACTIVITIES
Camping: 61 sites. Mid-Apr. to end of Oct.
Hiking: In addition to canyon trails, 12 mi. of trails in SE half of Park.
Swim: South Fork is dammed at day-use area, but water is only waist-deep.
Horse riding: Stable near entrance. Equestrian trails.

PUBLICATIONS
Leaflet with map. (May not be available.)
Map.
Canyon trail guide.

HEADQUARTERS: 20024 Silver Falls Highway, S.E., Sublimity, OR 97385; (503) 873-8681.

WILLAMETTE NATIONAL FOREST
U.S. Forest Service
1,675,157 acres.

Midway between Eugene and Bend, about 110 mi. N to S, 40 mi. wide. Crossed by US 20, SRs 22, 126, 58.

On the W slope of the Cascade Mountains. Largest National Forest in OR, together with adjacent Forests forming a block of over 9 million acres covering most of the OR Cascades.

Precipitation is heavy, from 50 to 120 in. a year, much as snow piling deep on the high slopes each winter. Moisture and favorable soils make this an outstanding timber-producing area. The runoff flows through over 1,500 mi. of rivers and streams, into 335 natural lakes and many reservoirs.

The Forest includes some of the highest country in the Cascades. Elevations range from 10,497 ft. at the top of Mt. Jefferson in the NE corner down to 935 ft. at the W edge. The steepest slopes are in the many deeply cut stream canyons.

Closeness to population centers and outstanding scenery have made the Willamette one of the most popular Forests. Many visitors come just to drive around one of the several scenic loops. Others congregate at the reservoirs just inside the W boundary. The several large wilderness areas and other roadless areas offer hikers and backpackers ample opportunities for solitude.

Plants: Densely forested, chiefly Douglas-fir, with noble fir, mountain hemlock, grand fir, and lodgepole pine at higher elevations. Although many variations occur, depending on the situations and histories of stands, a typical pattern has Douglas-fir as the dominant species, with associated western hemlock and western redcedar, the understory including Oregon grape, vine maple, salal, trailing blackberry, Pacific rhododendron, golden chinquapin. Typical herbs: Oregon oxalis, swordfern, white inside-out flower, twinflower, deerfoot vanillaleaf, evergreen violet, sweetscented bedstraw, western prince's pine, fairybells, deerfern. Nonforested areas include rock outcrops and scree slopes, mountain meadows, bogs.

Birds: Checklist available. Species reported include horned, western, and pied-billed grebes; great blue heron, common egret, Canada and white-fronted geese, mallard, pintail, green-winged and cinnamon teals, wigeon, shoveler, wood duck, common goldeneye, hooded merganser. Also goshawk; sharp-shinned, Cooper's, red-tailed, and rough-legged hawks; bald eagle, osprey, blue and ruffed grouse, California and mountain quail, band-tailed pigeon; barn, screech, great horned, spotted, and pygmy owls. Also rufous, Allen's, and calliope hummingbirds; common flicker and Williamson's sapsucker; pileated, Lewis's, hairy, downy, white-headed, black-backed three-toed and northern three-toed woodpeckers; black-capped, mountain, and chestnut-backed chickadees. Warblers include orange-crowned, Nashville, yellow, yellow-rumped, black-throated gray, Townsend's, MacGillivray's, Wilson's.

Mammals: No checklist available. Species reported include brush rabbit, snowshoe hare, mountain beaver, Townsend chipmunk, marmot, western gray squirrel, western pocket gopher, beaver, deer mouse, porcupine, coyote, red and gray foxes, black bear, raccoon, marten, fisher, long-tailed weasel, mink, wolverine, western spotted skunk, river otter, mountain lion, bobcat, Roosevelt elk, mule deer.

FEATURES

Mount Washington Wilderness, 46,655 acres, including 8,086 acres in the Deschutes National Forest. Rugged country topped by jagged peaks. Separated from Three Sisters Wilderness by SR 242. The 7,802-ft. mountain is a dissected volcano, the summit scraped bare by ice floes. Nearby is the "Black Wilderness," one of the largest lava sheets in the United States. Near the center, Belknap Crater, 6,872 ft., is a cinder and ash cone, source of much of the lava flow. The Pacific Crest Trail enters the area at McKenzie Pass, crosses part of the lava field, skirts Belknap Crater, and proceeds N on the W slopes of Mt. Washington to a region of dense forest and high lakes. A lower-altitude trail loops around 6,116-ft. Scott Mountain, passing near many small lakes. Hiking season begins June or July, depending on snow cover.

Three Sisters Wilderness, 245,302 acres, including 63,069 acres in the Deschutes National Forest. The Three Sisters are snowcapped high peaks. 14

glaciers. Volcanic landscape. Forests, alpine meadows, many lakes, water-falls. Separated from Mount Washington Wilderness by SR 242. Includes about 40 mi. of Pacific Crest Trail, plus a network of other trails. Area is usually accessible by July, snow remaining on some trails until Aug. Cool evenings; snow can fall in summer. Good trout fishing.

Mount Jefferson Wilderness, 100,208 acres, including 36,527 acres in the Deschutes and Mount Hood National Forests. Five glaciers on the 10,497-ft. mountain. Much of the high country is open and parklike, with scattered trees, scree slopes, patches of snow remaining through most of the summer. Lowest elevation is 3,000 ft. Most lakes and meadows are between 5,000 and 6,000 ft. About 150 lakes, most of them tiny, about 60 offering fishing. 36 mi. of the Pacific Crest Trail, more than 120 mi. of other trails.

Diamond Peak Wilderness, 36,637 acres, including 20,437 acres in the Deschutes National Forest. Area surrounds 8,744-ft. Diamond Peak, highest point in this area along the Cascade Crest. Boundaries are within 1 mi. of Odell, Summit, and Crescent lakes. Many smaller lakes within the area. About 50 mi. of trail, including a section of the Pacific Crest Trail. Bush-whacking is feasible with map and compass.

Wilderness permits are required for entry to the preceding areas.

Waldo Lake Recreation Area, 48,993 acres. A 6,700-acre lake, 6 mi. long, at 5,414 ft. elevation. The area lies between the Three Sisters and Diamond Peak Wilderness, just W of the Cascade Crest. Not a wilderness, because paved roads lead to developments on the E side, but the W and N shores are primitive, reached only on foot or by boat, and developments are set back from the E shore. Many miles of trails lead to countless small lakes, 286-ft. Salt Creek Falls, various peaks, and the Pacific Crest Trail. A 20-mi. loop trail circles Waldo Lake. Boating, but speed limited to 10 mph. Three camp-grounds, 208 sites.

McKenzie Pass on SR 242 offers an extraordinary vista of recent volcanic activity from Mt. Hood to the Three Sisters. Exhibits and leaflet at the Dee Wright Observatory. The pass is usually open July–Oct., otherwise closed by snow.

Scenic drives. 10 loop trips are described in a booklet listed under Publica-tions.

Detroit, Blue River, Cougar, and Hills Creek Lakes are U.S. Army Corps of Engineers lakes lying wholly or partially within the National Forest, on or near the W boundary. These and several Corps lakes nearby, outside the Forest, are popular recreation areas, chiefly water-based activities. The Forest Service has campgrounds at the lakes just named. The lakes are subject to considerable draw-down in dry weather.

INTERPRETATION

Lava River Interpretive Trail at McKenzie Pass on SR 242 W of Sisters. 1/2-mi. loop.

Evening programs are scheduled at some larger campgrounds in summer. Look for posted notices.

ACTIVITIES

Camping: 72 campgrounds, 1,600 sites. Seasonal openings range from Apr. 15 to July 1, closings from Sept. 15 to Nov. 30.

Hiking, backpacking: 1,200 mi. of trails, including trails in the wilderness areas and Waldo Lake Recreation Area. McKenzie River National Recreation Trail, 28 mi., follows the McKenzie River and SR 126 from Fish Lake, near US 20, S to McKenzie Bridge. Sections available from the road for short hikes. Fall Creek National Recreation Trail, 13 mi., begins just inside the Forest's W boundary, SE of Eugene, E of Fall Creek Lake, on Forest Road 18. Follows Fall Creek. Usually snow-free in winter. Suitable for short or overnight hikes.

Hunting: Deer, elk.

Fishing: Brook, rainbow, cutthroat trout.

Swimming: Chiefly at Waldo Lake and Corps of Engineers lakes.

Boating: Waldo Lake (10 mph limit) and Corps of Engineers lakes.

Canoeing: Whitewater canoeing, kayaking on McKenzie River.

Horse riding: Pack trips into wilderness areas. Pack and saddle stock, guide service, available at Stayton, OR.

Skiing: Willamette Ski Area. Dec.–Mar.

Ski touring: Trails S from Waldo Lake to Odell Lake and Crescent Lake in Deschutes National Forest, continuing to and into Crater Lake National Park.

ADJACENT OR NEARBY: Mount Hood National Forest (zone 2), Deschutes National Forest (zone 3), Umpqua National Forest (zone 5), Cascadia State Park (zone 2). See entries.

PUBLICATIONS

Forest map. $1.00.

Mount Washington Wilderness map. $1.00.

Mount Jefferson Wilderness map. $1.00.

Three Sisters Wilderness map. $1.00.

Diamond Peak Wilderness map.

Waldo Lake Recreation Area map.

Birds of the Willamette. Checklist.

Lakes of the Willamette National Forest.

McKenzie Pass folder.

The Forest by Road and Highway, auto tour booklet.

Willamette Trails, trail guide booklet.

McKenzie River National Recreation Trail folder.

Fall Creek National Recreation Trail folder.

Willamette Pass Ski Tours.

Santiam Pass Winter Recreation Area.

HEADQUARTERS: 210 E. 11th Ave., Eugene, OR 97401; (503) 687-6521.

RANGER DISTRICTS: Blue River R.D., Blue River, OR 97413; (503) 822-3317. Sweet Home R.D., 4431 Highway 20, Sweet Home, OR 97386; (503) 367-5168. Detroit R.D., Star Route, Box 320, Mill City, OR 97360; (503) 854-3366. McKenzie R.D., McKenzie Bridge, OR 97401; (503) 822-3381. Oakridge R.D., 46375 Highway 58, Westfir, OR 97492; (503) 782-2291. Rigdon R.D., 48458 Highway 58, Oakridge, OR 97463; (503) 782-2283. Lowell R.D., P.O. Box 325, Lowell, OR 97452; (503) 937-2129.

WILLAMETTE RIVER GREENWAY
Oregon Parks and Recreation Division
4,212 acres (state land).

From Cottage Grove Reservoir, near Cottage Grove, and Dexter Reservoir, near Dexter, to Multnomah Channel and Columbia River at Sauvie Island.

The Willamette River flows for over 200 mi. through the Willamette Valley. More than half the state's population lives within 10 miles of the river. Most lands bordering the river are privately owned. The river flows through towns and past factories, mills, warehouses, farms, and homes.

The Greenway Program is a cooperative state and local effort to maintain and enhance the remaining natural qualities of lands along the river. At intervals are state and local parks, river-access points, and other public sites.

Average river flow is 2–4 mph. Some upstream sections are swift and shallow, limiting use to rafts, canoes, and drift boats. Campgrounds are too infrequent to permit boat camping from end to end, but trips of a few days can be planned.

PUBLICATIONS:
Willamette River Recreation Guide.
16 maps.

HEADQUARTERS: Parks and Recreation Division, 525 Trade St. SE, Salem, OR 97310. For information: Oregon callers: 1-800-452-7813. Portland: 238-7491. Salem: 378-6500. Out of state: (503) 378-6500.

WILLIAM L. FINLEY NATIONAL WILDLIFE REFUGE
U.S. Fish and Wildlife Service
5,325 acres.

From Corvallis, 10 mi. S on SR 99W. W to entrance.
Open: Daylight hours.

Near the S end of the Willamette Valley. Mild, rainy winters provide good environment for waterfowl. Mostly cleared farmland in ryegrass and sudan grass. Hedgerows of rose and blackberry. Many man-made ponds and marshes; water levels down substantially in summer. Meandering creeks. Highest point: Pigeon Butte, 546 ft.

Best seen on foot. Two roads cross the site, which offer several viewpoints. Summer visits are least rewarding.

Plants: About 700 acres of woodland: Oregon oak, maple, fir. Thickets of Oregon ash. Many ferns, orchids, lilies in moist areas. In and around impoundments: cattail, bur-reed, pondweeds, arrowhead, water plantain. Great variety of grasses and sedges. Flowering species include buttercups, columbine, larkspur, Oregon grape, California poppy, bleeding heart, fringe cup, serviceberry, clovers, geraniums, hollyhocks, violets, starflower, forget-me-nots, daisy, thistles.

Birds: Entire population of dusky Canada goose winters in this region. Seasonally common and abundant species include great blue heron, whistling swan, Canada goose, mallard, pintail, green-winged teal, American wigeon, shoveler, wood duck, turkey vulture, red-tailed and marsh hawks, kestrel, California quail, pheasant, coot, killdeer, snipe, dunlin, band-tailed pigeon, mourning dove, great horned owl, rufous hummingbird, flicker, downy woodpecker, swallows, Steller's and scrub jays, black-capped chickadee, bushtit, nuthatches, brown creeper, long-billed marsh wren, robin, Swainson's and varied thrushes, kinglets, starling, orange-crowned and yellow-rumped warblers, common yellowthroat.

Mammals: Include opossum, shrews, little brown and big brown bats, raccoon, striped skunk, red fox, California ground squirrel, Townsend chipmunk, chickaree, giant pocket gopher, deer mouse, woodrats, gray-tailed vole, nutria, brush rabbit, mule deer.

INTERPRETATION

Trail of Discovery, self-guiding, passes several types of habitat.

Current information on bulletin boards and at self-guiding kiosks.

ACTIVITIES

Hiking: 10 mi. of trails. Cabell Marsh, Pigeon Butte, other points of interest reached only on foot.

Hunting: In designated area. Special rules. Inquire.

Fishing: Marginal. Cutthroat trout.

Much of the goose habitat is closed Nov. to mid-Apr.

PUBLICATIONS
  Refuge leaflet.
  Plant and wildlife checklists.
  Nature trail guide.
  Hunting information.

HEADQUARTERS: Route 2, Box 208, Corvallis, OR 97330; (503) 757-7236.

WINDY PEAK
Bureau of Land Management
4,500 acres.

From Junction City, N of Eugene, W on SR 36 to Deadwood. N about 5 mi. on Deadwood Creek Rd. Trailhead is opposite schoolhouse.

A roadless area on the E side of the Coast Range. Windy Peak is the highest point, 2,052 ft. The Siuslaw Task Force, a citizen conservation group, has urged inclusion of the area in an Oregon Coast Range Wilderness. (See their publication, so titled, in the Reference section of the Oregon Preface.) However, the area is part of the "O & C Lands" which were excluded from BLM's wilderness review. Further, BLM is legally mandated to manage these lands for timber production. When this entry was sent to BLM for review, we were advised that the area may be logged in the near future. It will not be difficult to see whether this has happened; the trail mentioned below is the centerline of a proposed logging road.

Plants: Vegetation is typical of the Central Coast Range. As a consequence of fires in the late 1800s, only a few pockets of virgin timber remain, but much of the timber is now about 100 years of age. Trees include western hemlock, Douglas-fir, with western redcedar. Dense stands of red alder and bigleaf maple in moist areas. Understory includes Pacific rhododendron, salal, bald-hip rose, thimbleberry, salmonberry, red huckleberry, evergreen huckleberry, vine maple, Pacific dogwood, hazelnut, bitter cherry, cascara, golden chinquapin. Wildflowers include prince's pine, foxglove, candyflower, star-flowered Solomon-plume, evergreen violet, Oregon oxalis, wild ginger, Pacific bleeding heart, fairy bells, fireweed, bead ruby, western trillium, Oregon iris.

Hiking: Volunteers have cleared and marked a 7-mi. trail. BLM notes that this trail crosses private as well as public land, is being used by local residents. The trail crosses the headwaters of several streams, passes some of the more mature timber stands, patches of rhododendron.

HEADQUARTERS: Bureau of Land Management, District Office, P.O. Box 10226, Eugene, OR 97440; (503) 687-6650.

ZONE 3

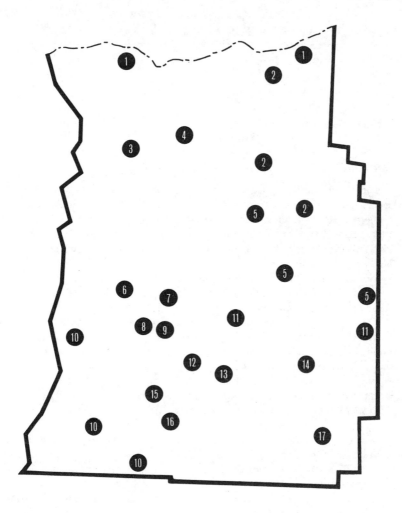
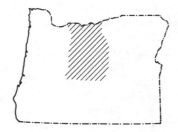

ZONE 3

Includes these counties:

Hood River	Gilliam	Crook
Wasco	Wheeler	Deschutes
Sherman	Jefferson	

The N zone boundary is the Columbia River. The Hood, Deschutes, and John Day rivers, flowing through the zone, empty into the Columbia, as do numerous lesser streams. The W boundary is the E slope of the Cascade Mountains. Part of Mt. Hood and a substantial portion of the Mount Hood National Forest are in zone 3, but the entry appears in zone 2, which has the larger portion.

The Blue Mountains intrude into the zone from the NE; this is the high country of the Ochoco National Forest, the E central part of the zone. S of these mountains begins the extensive high desert country.

Three National Forests within the zone include more than 2 million acres, by far the largest part of the public lands. Some relatively small tracts of public domain, lands administered by the Bureau of Land Management, are along the John Day and Deschutes rivers, still smaller tracts around Lake Billy Chinook, the White River, and lesser streams. Much of the high desert country in the SE part of the zone is public domain, partly as large blocks with many inholdings, partly as checkerboard.

Except in the mountains, rainfall is scanty in the zone: less than 14 in. per year at The Dalles, about 12 at Bend, less than 10 at Prineville, still less in the high desert. Wheat and other field crops are grown in the NE region, both with and without irrigation. Cattle ranching is somewhat more common in the central region.

The larger rivers of the zone have interesting possibilities. Several entries describe sections of the Crooked River: the N and S forks near the headwaters, a canyon S of Prineville, and a longer canyon downstream, partly within the Crooked River National Grassland. The John Day River attracts whitewater boaters in the spring, but its flow drops sharply in summer; then its canyon can be explored on foot. The Deschutes River has many aspects: fearsome white water, placid stretches, a large lake; it flows through grassy meadows and deep, rugged canyons.

The zone includes magnificent ponderosa forests, extensive stands of juniper, and sagebrush deserts. Wildlife varies with the habitats. Mule deer are common in several sectors; elk and pronghorn occur in some localities, in relatively small numbers. The zone has no extensive wetlands to attract vast numbers of waterfowl, but both residents and migrants can be seen on many lakes and streams.

About a dozen State Parks are along the Columbia River within this zone. They are mentioned, collectively, in the entry for Columbia River Gorge, but none met our criteria for natural areas. About a dozen State Parks are clustered in the region around Prineville and Bend. Of these, several are noted because of their scenic qualities or their proximity to natural areas.

In the high desert region, as explained in the state introduction, we have described a few places that have exceptional features.

BADLANDS
U.S. Bureau of Land Management
33,172 acres.

9 mi. E of Bend. N of US 20; S of Alfalfa. About 10 mi. E–W, 9 mi. N–S.

Many rolling hills with jagged dark reddish-brown and black basalt escarpments and outcroppings. Wind-blown sand has formed many small basins and valleys. Dense western juniper forest, including old stands, covers almost the entire area. Portions have been used for grazing, woodcutting, and bombing range; now reverting to natural state. 48 mi. of ways, most unused and reverting. Area proposed for wilderness designation. No roads or facilities.

Plants: Understory species include big sage, gray and green rabbitbrush, bitterbrush, Idaho fescue, bluebunch, wheatgrass, phlox, cheatgrass.

HEADQUARTERS: Prineville District, Bureau of Land Management, 185 E. Fourth St., P.O. Box 550, Prineville, OR 97754; (503) 447-4115.

COLUMBIA RIVER GORGE
(See also zone 2 entry.)

I-80N is close to the river from Bonneville to the zone boundary E of the intersection with SR 74.

The Gorge still has scenic qualities: forested hillsides, massive canyon walls, striking rock formations, waterfalls, valleys of tributary streams. Most of the hillsides are within the Mount Hood National Forest (see entry), and in places the Forest boundary is near the shore.

Bonneville Dam, The Dalles Dam, and John Day Dam have formed consecutive impoundments. Nowhere within this zone does the river flow free.

A narrow strip along the shore includes heavily traveled I-80N, railroad tracks, towns and cities, commercial and industrial establishments, and other visual clutter.

Trailheads at several points near I-80N exits give access to the Forest. Also near exits are a number of small State Parks, waysides, parking areas, and boat-launching facilities. Some have campgrounds. None met our criteria for entries. However, a trip through the Gorge can be pleasant.

PUBLICATIONS

Bonneville Lock and Dam, leaflet with information on parks and other facilities. Portland District, U.S. Army Corps of Engineers, P.O. Box 2946, Portland, OR 97208.

Forest Trails of the Columbia Gorge, map, Mount Hood National Forest, 2440 S.E. 195th, Portland, OR 97233.

Grauer, Jack, *Columbia River Gorge.* Jack Grauer, Box 692, Gresham, OR 97030, 1977. $2.00. (Includes topographic maps.)

CROOKED RIVER CANYON
U.S. Bureau of Land Management
13,586 acres.

From Prineville, 7 mi. S on SR 27.

The road first enters a steep-walled, narrow canyon: columnar basalt, cliffs, ledges, talus slopes. Here the river is swift and shallow, about 20 ft. wide. After 2 mi. the valley widens, the stream meandering through hayfields. 3 mi. further the canyon again narrows. The BLM land is on both sides of the river, the larger portion extending W about 6 mi. Above the canyon, the land is relatively flat, sloping downward to the W, with some low rolling hills, occasional outcroppings of brown basalt.

SR 27 is on the E side of the river, often close to the stream, occasionally climbing to points offering good views. Access to the W side is offered by primitive BLM and county roads not shown on highway maps. Inquire locally or at BLM's Prineville office. At the S end of the canyon, SR 27 crosses the dam impounding Prineville Reservoir.

Plants: A few large ponderosa along the river. Scattered clusters of juniper along the valley floor and slopes, with dense stands to the W. Big sage, bitterbrush, green rabbitbrush, native bunchgrass. In W portion, areas of crested wheatgrass seedings.

Fauna: No data. Observed: cottontail, jackrabbit, swallows, magpie, kingfisher, Brewer's blackbird.

ACTIVITIES

Camping: Primitive campgrounds are scattered along SR 27. Several, maintained by the BLM, have latrines, tables. Others are simply places where one can park beside the river. Another primitive campground is just beyond the dam, on the shore of the reservoir.

Hiking: The canyon is the most interesting portion of this site; side canyons and some moderate slopes offer opportunities. More than 10 mi. of ways in the W portion. Local advice says one can hike around the reservoir.

Boating: Light boats can be launched on the reservoir S of the dam. However, the access track is steep and rough with a near-hairpin turn. Anything larger than a rowboat should be launched at Prineville Reservoir State Park. The river is not suitable for canoeing, being shallow and rocky.

ADJACENT: Prineville Reservoir (see entry).

HEADQUARTERS: Prineville District, Bureau of Land Management, 185 E. Fourth St., P.O. Box 550, Prineville, OR 97754; (503) 447-4115.

CROOKED RIVER NATIONAL GRASSLAND
U.S. Forest Service
106,136 acres/151,138 acres within boundaries.

NW of Prineville. Largest block, irregular in shape, roughly a right triangle, mostly E of US 97, bisected by US 26, extending N from Jefferson County line. Other blocks around Lake Billy Chinook, extending SW around Crooked River Gorge and Deschutes River to Jefferson County line.

Land homesteaded around 1900. Included in submarginal farmlands acquired by government in 1930s. Now managed chiefly as grazing land. Elevations from about 2,200 ft. to 5,108 ft. In the largest block, much of the area is relatively flat, rising to high buttes in the S. Numerous intermittent streams. Haystack Reservoir, 180 acres, offers boating, fishing.

The land around Lake Billy Chinook has more interesting features. Round Butte Dam backed water up three principal streams—the Metolius, Deschutes, and Crooked rivers—forming a 4,000-acre lake consisting of three long, narrow arms in spectacular deep canyons. The Cove Palisades State Park (see entry) is a popular resort with marina, cafe, store, campgrounds, and other developments, mostly on the E side of the E arm. The access road W from Culver on US 97 descends into the canyon to the marina, with fine vistas, loops S along the shore, crosses one arm of the lake to The Peninsula, then another to the Lower Desert.

FEATURES

Deschutes River Gorge, scenic, winding river with rock walls 600 to 700 ft. tall. *Steelhead Falls* is in this canyon.

Alder Springs, called "an oasis in the high desert." Several springs feed into Squaw Creek.

Crooked River Gorge, an extension of the same gorge seen at Smith Rock State Park (see entry) and Peter Skene Ogden Scenic Wayside on US 97.

ACTIVITIES

Camping: Campground at Haystack Lake, 24 sites. Also camping at State Parks. Informal camping elsewhere on Forest Service land, unless posted.

Hiking: Primitive roads near and SW of Billy Chinook Lake. Bushwhacking feasible.

Swimming: Billy Chinook Lake.

Boating: Billy Chinook Lake and Haystack Reservoir.

The National Grassland is administered by the Ochoco National Forest.

PUBLICATION: Forest map. $1.00. Includes Ochoco National Forest.

HEADQUARTERS: Prineville, OR 97754; (503) 447-4120.

CROOKED RIVER, NORTH FORK
U.S. Bureau of Land Management
11,080 acres.

E of Prineville, on S boundary of Ochoco National Forest (see entry). No easy access and roads are not signed, but a Forest Road is nearby. Consult the BLM's Prineville Office or Ochoco National Forest HQ.

Narrow canyon up to 900 ft. deep winds S from National Forest boundary. Almost vertical basalt walls. Steep hills W of canyon; basalt flows to E. Many side canyons. Upper Falls is near the Forest boundary on private land, Lower Falls 11 mi. downstream. Upper Falls, unique in this desert country, drops 15–20 ft. into a pool.

Plants: Ponderosa pine forest at upper end of canyon, juniper-sagebrush toward lower end. Hills to W have juniper, Douglas-fir, ponderosa, as well as sagebrush and associated desert species.

ACTIVITIES

Hiking: The canyon can be hiked, with difficulty; be sure to get current local advice and permission from private landowners. Elsewhere, no trails but 19 mi. of primitive ways, now reverting.

Swimming: Pool below Upper Falls.

ADJACENT: Ochoco National Forest (see entry).

HEADQUARTERS: Prineville District, Bureau of Land Management, 185 E. Fourth St., P.O. Box 550, Prineville, OR 97754; (503) 447-4115.

CROOKED RIVER, SOUTH FORK
U.S. Bureau of Land Management
19,660 acres.

19 mi. NE of US 20 at Hampton. Access is from Camp Creek Rd. on the S or off Crooked River Highway on the N end. E of Prineville. Inquire at the BLM's Prineville Office.

River has cut a steep-walled canyon up to 800 ft. deep in Twelvemile Table Mesa. Main canyon about 6 mi. long. E of canyon, mesa is relatively flat, open, offering miles of vistas. W of river are some low rolling hills, with steeper terrain in the NW portion. Area lies between the Ochoco Mountains to the N and high lava plains to S.

Canyon is open and relatively wide, with colorful pinnacles, caves, alluvial slopes and terraces. Several dirt tracks in or out. Several side canyons.

Plants: On N-facing slopes: juniper, big sage, Idaho fescue, bluebunch wheatgrass, Thurber's needlegrass. Dense juniper stands in W portion, small, isolated juniper on mesa. Many wildflowers along the river.

Fauna: No data, but wildlife is said to be abundant in this isolated, little-disturbed habitat.

Hiking, backpacking: Easier access and easier hiking through the canyon than in the canyon of the North Fork. Hikers often start at Pickett Canyon, travel 12 mi. downstream to Crooked River highway. Best hiking seasons are late spring, early fall. River flow dwindles in summer.

HEADQUARTERS: Prineville District, Bureau of Land Management, 185 E. Fourth St., P.O. Box 550, Prineville, OR 97754; (503) 447-4115.

DESCHUTES NATIONAL FOREST
U.S. Forest Service
1,602,809 acres/1,852,282 acres within boundaries.

On both sides of US 97 S of Bend, and NW of Bend. Also crossed by US 20, SR 242, SR 58, and SR 31.

Second largest National Forest in OR, part of a huge block of National Forest land extending from WA border to CA. On the E slope of the Cascade Mountains. Elevations from about 2,000 to 10,358 ft., most of the area between 4,000 and 5,000 ft. Snowcapped peaks, craters, cinder cones, and other volcanic formations, some formed as recently as 1,400 years ago. Over 200 lakes and reservoirs, many of them more than 1 mi. high. 730 mi. of streams, including the headwaters of the Deschutes and Metolius rivers. Forest slopes and valleys, high meadows.

The Forest is popular in all seasons, recording over 3 million visitor-days per year. However, it has extensive roadless areas, and those who travel on foot or horseback can easily find isolation.

Plants: Ponderosa pine predominates through most of the area and is the chief species harvested. Lodgepole pine is also common. Whitebark pine, usually found at altitudes over 5,000 ft., and sugar pine are widely distributed. Species occurring in more limited areas include Douglas-fir, incense cedar, Engelmann spruce, western larch, mountain hemlock, and six firs: grand, noble, Pacific silver, white, Shasta red, and subalpine. Western juniper in drier E sections. Although conifers predominate, deciduous species include willows, black cottonwood, quaking aspen. Understory species include serviceberry, elderberry, mountain mahogany. Wildflowers are most abundant in mountain meadows, along forest edges and roadsides, and in moist places. Species include asters, lupines, cinquefoil, false lily-of-the-valley, calypso, alpine pyrola, Indianpipe, lady's slipper, narrowleaf and roundleaf sundews, Indian paintbrush, penstemon, monkeyflower.

Birds: Checklist available. Large variety of species. Residents include great blue heron, Canada goose, mallard, ring-necked duck, Barrow's goldeneye, bufflehead, hooded and common mergansers, cormorant, goshawk; Cooper's, red-tailed, Swainson's, and ferruginous hawks; golden and bald eagles, prairie falcon, kestrel; blue, ruffed, and sage grouse; California and mountain quail, killdeer, 6 owl species, red-shafted flicker, 6 woodpecker species, horned lark; gray, Steller's, and pinyon jays; white-breasted, red-breasted, and pygmy nuthatches; water ouzel, winter and canyon wrens, mountain bluebird, evening grosbeak, pine siskin, red crossbill, Oregon junco, Many others in migration.

Mammals: Checklist available. Mule deer, spring until late fall. A few

Roosevelt elk. Pronghorn on desert fringe. Black bear, coyote, beaver, mink, otter, marten, skunk, badger. Also porcupine, pika, yellow-bellied marmot, cottontail, black-tailed jackrabbit, snowshoe hare, golden-mantled and Oregon ground squirrel, chipmunk, white-footed deer mouse, flying squirrel.

SCENIC DRIVES

Cascade Lakes Highway, also known as Century Drive, 76 mi. long, begins at Bend, extends W and S through the heart of the Forest, returning to US 97 at a point 25 mi. S of Bend. Fine views of the snowcapped Three Sisters, Bachelor Butte, Broken Top, and other peaks. The road passes near many high mountain lakes, beside the Deschutes River, through tall conifer forest. Spur roads, paved and unpaved, lead to other lakes, campgrounds, and viewpoints. Along the way are well-marked trailheads with parking areas. Highest section often closed by snow until June or July.

US 20, NW from Sisters, over Santiam Pass.

SR 242, W from Sisters, to McKenzie Pass. Closed in winter.

WILDERNESS AREAS

Three Sisters Wilderness. 245,302 acres (including acreage in Willamette National Forest). Addition proposed. Snowcapped Three Sisters are high peaks in Cascade Range. 14 glaciers. Area is usually accessible from July to Oct., snow remaining on some trails until Aug. Pacific Crest Trail crosses, about 40 mi. Volcanic landscape; many notable geological features. Forests, alpine meadows, many lakes, waterfalls. Evenings are cool; snow can occur in summer. Mosquitoes are a nuisance until mid-Aug. Good fishing, trout.

Diamond Peak Wilderness. 36,637 acres (including acreage in Willamette National Forest). Addition proposed. Diamond Peak, 8,744 ft., is a popular climb, as is 7,138-ft. Mt. Yoran. About 50 mi. of trails, including part of the Pacific Crest Trail system. Usually accessible July–Oct. Many small lakes. Fishing streams. Mosquitoes a nuisance until Sept.

Mount Washington Wilderness. 46,116 acres (including acreage in Willamette National Forest). Addition proposed. Adjoins Three Sisters Wilderness. Rugged volcanic landscape. Mt. Washington, 7,802 ft., is a challenging climb, for the experienced. 66 lakes and potholes; good fishing. Pacific Crest Trail passes through. Season: July–Oct.

Mount Jefferson Wilderness. 100,208 acres (including acreage in Mount Hood and Willamette National Forests). Many peaks, lakes. Extensive trail system. Popular hiking area, day and overnight. Mt. Jefferson, 10,497 ft., second highest peak in OR; perpetual glaciers. Nearly 100 lakes, many good for fishing. Season: July–Oct.

Windigo-Thielson Wilderness. (Proposed.) 55,000 acres (including acreage in Umpqua and Winema National Forests. On Cascade crest, elevations from 4,200 to 9,182 ft. Headwaters of the Deschutes and North Umpqua rivers, Cottonwood Creek. Vegetation representative of both E and W sides of the

Cascades. About 70% forested: Douglas-fir, mountain hemlock, lodgepole pine, some ponderosa. Pacific Crest Trail passes through.

VOLCANIC AND OTHER GEOLOGICAL FEATURES

Lava Butte Geological Area. Lava Butte is a 500-ft. cinder cone 6,000 years old. Extending W and N is a 6,117-acre lava field. Road access.

Newberry Crater. S of Lava Butte. Largest dormant volcano of the region, 8,000 ft. high, 25 mi. at base. The top has collapsed and enlarged repeatedly for hundreds of thousands of years. Cinder cones, lava, and pumice erupted as recently as 1,400 years ago. Two lakes within the crater at over 6,300 ft. elevation. Large obsidian flow also within the crater. Road access. Camping, trails, horse camp, boating, ski touring, snowmobiling.

Hole-in-the-Ground. Crater 450 ft. deep, 4,800 ft. wide, formed by volcanic steam explosion long ago.

Lava Cast Forest. N of Newberry Crater. An ancient forest invaded by lava.

Lava River Caves State Park, 12 mi. S of Bend off US 97. Main tunnel inside a lava flow extends almost 1 mi. Stairs down to chamber 58 ft. high. Visitors need sweaters and lights, can rent lanterns.

Arnold Ice Cave, Wind Cave, Skeleton Cave. SE of Bend, reached by Forest roads.

Lavacicle Cave has stalactites, stalagmites of frozen lava. Entrance is locked; trips arranged at Lava Lands Visitor Center.

LAKES

Cascade Lakes Highway provides access to over 100 lakes, some near the route and accessible by auto, others for backpacking. Lakes are stocked and known for excellent fishing, chiefly brook trout with rainbow, lake, cutthroat, and brown trout; whitefish, kokanee, coho, and Atlantic salmon in some lakes. Many of the higher lakes are blocked by snow until July.

Crane Prairie Reservoir, 3,850 acres, is shallow, with many stumps and snags. Elevation 4,445 ft. Protected nesting area for osprey and bald eagle. Many waterfowl in the fall. 5 campgrounds; boat launching; information center. Good place for wildlife observation. Road access.

Crescent Lake, 4,000 acres. Deep natural lake dammed to increase water storage. Elevation 4,580 ft. Surrounded by forest with stands of Douglas-fir, white fir, lodgepole, ponderosa. 12 mi. of shoreline. Campgrounds. Boat launching. Swimming. Fishing best in spring, early summer. Road access. Trails into nearby Diamond Peak Wilderness.

Odell Lake, 3,500 acres. Elevation 4,790 ft. Occupies an old glacial valley. About 6 mi. long, 1 1/2 mi. wide, deep. Surrounding forest of firs: Pacific silver, Shasta red, subalpine, white, with Engelmann spruce, western and mountain hemlock, Douglas-fir; ponderosa, lodgepole, and white pines. Annual precipitation of over 70 in. supports luxuriant understory. Abundant wildlife. Kokanee and lake trout. 4 campgrounds. Marina, boat launching. Road access.

Davis Lake, 3,000 acres. Elevation 4,390 ft. Formed behind a rugged lava dam. Moderate depth. Boat launching, but motors can be used only to and from fishing sites, speed limited to 10 mph. A good lake for canoeing. Shoreline marshes, grass and bulrush. Surrounded by pine forests. Good area for birding: waterfowl and songbirds. Fishing for rainbow, coho, kokanee, whitefish. Campgrounds. Road access.

Camping is prohibited within 100 ft. of the high-water line around these and many other lakes. Some setback zones are greater than 100 ft. Look for postings.

INTERPRETATION

Lava Lands Visitor Center, on US 97 SW of Bend. Exhibits, slide shows. Naturalist on duty. Near many of the area's geological features. *Nature trails:* 3 trails, 15–30 min. walking time each, near visitor center.

ACTIVITIES

Camping: 125 campgrounds, over 2,000 sites. Campgrounds differ in size, accessibility, and facilities. Many are on or near lakes or streams. Informal camping almost anywhere except restricted areas and special zones.

Hiking, backpacking: 550 mi. of trails. Also 10,000 mi. of roads, including dirt and primitive roads good for hiking. Many relatively short, undemanding trails to small lakes and other attractive camping locations. Also trails at lower elevations which can be used in winter. Although many hikers use the Forest, only a minority of trails are heavily traveled. Ask a ranger to suggest a lightly used trail if you seek solitude.

Hunting: Mule deer is principal game. Elk are summer residents, bear scarce. Waterfowl on the larger lakes. Upland game birds include blue and ruffed grouse, valley and mountain quail, chukar.

Fishing: 158 lakes and reservoirs, elevations 1,940–7,240 ft., have trout and salmon. Pools from less than 1 acre to over 5,000 acres. 247 mi. of fishable streams.

Swimming: Designated swimming areas on a number of lakes, usually at campgrounds. Elsewhere at your discretion.

Boating: Ramps on the larger lakes. Special restrictions on many of the lakes: no motors, 10 mph limit, etc.

Canoeing, kayaking, rafting: Deschutes River is popular. Several dangerous falls and cascades; get information before launching. Metolius River is for experts; here, too, current conditions should be ascertained. Good canoeing and canoe camping on several lakes.

Pack trips: Pack and saddle stock, guide services available; list of packers available. Some trails are closed to horses. In wilderness areas, horses are prohibited within 200 ft. of lakes and streams. Not allowed in campgrounds; but a few campgrounds have horse-holding facilities.

Skiing: Bachelor Butte Ski Area, elevation 6,200 ft. Usual season Nov.–May. Willamette Pass Ski Area, elevation 5,120 ft., usual season Dec.–Apr.

Ski touring, snowmobiling: Abundance of dry snow; many sunny days in winter. Snowmobile route at Bachelor Butte, Cascade, Newberry Crater, Paulina Lake. Many areas suitable for ski touring.

ADJACENT

Fremont, Winema, and Umpqua National Forests (see entries, zone 5). Willamette National Forest (see entry, zone 2).

PUBLICATIONS

Forest map. $1.00.
Summary description, leaflet.
Native Trees of the Deschutes, leaflet.
May I Dig Wild Plants?, leaflet.
The Crane Prairie Osprey Management Area, leaflet.
Bird checklist.
Wildlife on the Deschutes National Forest, description, checklists.
Lava Lands, folder.
Lava Cast Forest, nature trail guide.
Lava River Caves, pamphlet.
Cascade Lakes Highway, leaflet.
Mount Jefferson Wilderness map. $1.00.
Diamond Peak Wilderness map. $1.00.
Mount Washington Wilderness map. $1.00.
Three Sisters Wilderness map. $1.00.
Lakes of the Deschutes National Forest, folder.
The Newberry Crater, folder.
The Lava Butte Geological Area, pamphlet.
Information sheets (mimeo):
  Headwaters of the Metolius River.
  Bend Ranger District Trails.
  Sisters Ranger District Trails.
  Hiking Trails South of Crescent Lake.
  The Sisters Group of the High Cascades, ascent routes.
  Hunting on the Deschutes National Forest.
  Fishing on the Deschutes National Forest.
  Fishing Directory, pamphlet.
  Drifting on the Waters of the Deschutes National Forest.
  Floating the Deschutes River, leaflet.
  Map of Ranger District Boundaries.
  Guidelines and Regulations for Use of Undeveloped Areas, folder.
  Snow Guide.

HEADQUARTERS: 211 NE Revere, Bend, OR 97701; (503) 382-6922.

RANGER DISTRICTS: Bend R.D., 211 NE Revere, Bend, OR 97701; (503) 382-6922. Crescent R.D., P.O. Box 208, Crescent, OR 97733; (503) 433-

2234. Fort Rock R.D., 211 NE Revere, Bend, OR 97701; (503) 382-6922.
Sisters R.D., Sisters, OR 97759; (503) 539-2111.

DESCHUTES RIVER RECREATION LANDS
U.S. Bureau of Land Management

From US 197 at Tygh Valley, E about 8 mi. on SR 216.

We consider this site one of our most pleasant discoveries. Approaching the
river, SR 216 descends into a winding canyon to a modern bridge which
replaced Sherar's Bridge, built in 1860. This was a traditional Indian crossing,
and here pioneers floated their wagons across. Here the river drops over falls
and enters a narrow cut. Indians were fishing from high platforms with
long-handled nets. A state biologist was monitoring the fish ladder.

1/2 mi. E of the bridge, a BLM road enters the scenic canyon, following
the river downstream for 17 mi. The road is unpaved, rough in places but not
difficult. The canyon is 600–800 ft. deep, walls generally steep to vertical,
some talus. Occasional small side canyons. Basalt, shades of brown and tan
with hints of red. Sparse desert vegetation. The river is wide, moderately swift,
generally shallow but—at the time of our visit—deep enough for floating,
with sections used by fishermen with outboards.

The BLM land is a relatively narrow strip along the river. Some of the
private land along the rim is posted. The road dead-ends, with private land
beyond. Occasional trains use the tracks across the river from the road.

Local fishermen know about the canyon, but in a July visit only one
camping couple shared the canyon with us overnight.

No data on flora and fauna. Observed: chukar, kingfisher, Brewer's blackbird, seagulls, cottontail, golden-mantled squirrel.

ACTIVITIES

Camping: Primitive, informal campground at Sherar's Bridge, used by
fishermen. Camping in any suitable place along the 17-mi. road. Two primitive
campgrounds with latrines, managed by the BLM.

Hiking, backpacking: It may be possible to hike to the river's junction with
the Columbia, but this would require permission to cross several private
landholdings.

Fishing: Cutthroat, steelhead.

Boating: Rafting from US 26 to Sherar's Bridge, 53 mi., experts only. Don't
run falls at Sherar's Bridge. Put-in there for 45-mi. run to Columbia River.
Rapids to class IV; one portage around a class VI. Fishermen use powered
drift boats in river, launching near end of the canyon road.

HEADQUARTERS: Prineville District, Bureau of Land Management, 185 E. Fourth St., P.O. Box 550, Prineville, OR 97754; (503) 447–4115.

DRY RIVER CANYON; HORSE RIDGE
U.S. Bureau of Land Management
11,076 acres.

On both sides of US 20, from about 16 mi. SE of Bend to 1 mi. NW of Millican.

Dry River drained an Ice Age lake, spilled over Horse Ridge, cut a canyon through lava. Canyon is about 2 1/2 mi. long, N of the highway, roughly paralleling it. N of canyon are two low ridges. Scattered clusters of juniper, a few ponderosa, with Idaho fescue, bluebunch wheatgrass, mountain mahogany, gray rabbitbrush, yarrow. In the canyon, some trees used by nesting raptors.

S of the highway, Horse Ridge and Horse Ridge Summit are steep basalt hills. Vegetation is similar to the N side, except for a 600-acre Research Natural Area established to preserve a nearly pristine western juniper–big sage–threadleaf sedge plant community.

ADJACENT: On N, Badlands (see entry).

HEADQUARTERS: Prineville District, Bureau of Land Management, 185 E. Fourth St., P.O. Box 550, Prineville, OR 97754; (503) 447-4115.

JOHN DAY FOSSIL BEDS NATIONAL MONUMENT
U.S. National Park Service
14,402 acres.

Three widely separated units. (1) Sheep Rock: from Dayville on US 26, W 5 mi. (2) Painted Hills: from US 26 W of Mitchell, 6 mi. NW on marked county road. (3) Clarno: from Fossil on SR 19, 20 mi. W on SR 218.

One of the newest units in the National Park system; visitor facilities are developing gradually. Sedimentary strata of the John Day Basin contain one of the longest continuous records of plant and animal fossils, tracing evolution of life forms over 70 million years, from the subtropical climate of the Eocene Epoch through the Ice Age.

High desert region. The John Day River flows through the Sheep Rock Unit, borders part of S boundary of the Clarno Unit. The exposed strata are colorful, bands in shades of red, yellow, and green. Also around the valley are high buttes, escarpments, and pinnacles of basalt. Scattered juniper with sagebrush and bunchgrass. Cottonwood and willow beside streams. Many wildflowers in May. Surrounding mountains have forests of Douglas-fir, true firs, larch, pines.

Birds: Checklist in preparation. Species include Canada goose, ducks, great blue heron, California quail, chukar, pheasant, magpie, red-tailed hawk, golden eagle.

Mammals: Include coyote, bobcat, badger, mule deer, jackrabbit, cottontail, rodents.

Reptiles: Rattlesnake not uncommon.

FEATURES

Sheep Rock Unit, 9,614 acres. Strata sharply tilted, eroded into picturesque forms; cliffs, peaks, gorges, canyons. Colors from brick red and brown to bronze, bluish-green, buff, white. High viewpoint.

Painted Hills Unit, 3,129 acres. Dramatically eroded landscape, strikingly colorful layers: pale yellow to rich brick red, green, white. Sagebrush desert.

Clarno Unit, 1,659 acres. Hills, bluffs, towering palisades and pinnacles of brown to bronze rock.

INTERPRETATION

Information at HQ in John Day City. Fossil exhibits, publications.

Cant Ranch, in Painted Hills Unit, has restored ranch house and outbuildings. Visitor center: information, exhibits, publications. Good birding spot.

Painted Cove Trail, self-guiding, in Painted Hills Unit, passes colorful formations.

Wayside exhibits at overlooks along roads.

ACTIVITIES

Hiking: A few unimproved trails, gummy and slippery when wet.

Fishing: John Day River.

NEARBY: (Near to Clarno Unit) Spring Basin, BLM, 6,283 acres. About 3 mi. SE of Clarno. County road on W boundary. Elevations 1,340 to 2,827 ft. Three steep-sloped canyons almost join in S. Generally rugged topography. Scattered clusters of juniper with big sage, green rabbitbrush, snakeweed, buckwheat, hedgehog cactus, bluebunch wheatgrass. Camping, hiking, hunting.

PUBLICATIONS

Leaflet with map.
Painted Cove Trail guide.

The Geologic Setting of the John Day Country, U.S. Geological Survey. Superintendent of Documents, U.S. Government Printing Office, Washington, DC 20402. 30¢.

HEADQUARTERS: John Day, OR 97845; (503) 575-0721.

JOHN DAY RIVER

U.S. Bureau of Land Management, state, and private land.
147 river mi.

> From Service Creek on SR 19 (about 22 mi. S of Fossil) to 10 mi. upstream from the confluence with the Columbia River. Principal access points: bridge at Service Creek; SR 218 at Clarno; SR 206 crossing. Other access points are on private land, and landowner permission is needed.

The John Day River has been designated a Scenic Waterway from Service Creek to Tumwater Falls, 10 mi. above the mouth. It flows through National Forest and past private land for most of the distance from the headwaters on the North Fork of the John Day, nearly 140 mi. upstream from Service Creek, to about 6 mi. N of Clarno. The river canyon is within BLM land for most of the next 58 mi., but without rights-of-way to public roads. Further downstream, most of the land is private, but there are small blocks of BLM land, including several islands. Scenic Waterway designation limits further developments within 1/4 mi. of the river.

BLM recreation specialists estimate that the 100-mi. lower segment of the Deschutes River attracted 150,000 visitors in 1980, but only 5,000 visited the John Day. One reason is limited access. Also, river flow has extreme seasonal variations. August flow may be less than 1/30 of the Apr.–May flow. ("You can wade it without getting your shoes wet," said a BLM man.)

Even so, travel by shallow-draft boat is the preferred way to see the canyon. A few people can and do hike the canyon in the dry season, we were told, but the extremely rugged terrain, summer heat, and limited access discourage most hikers.

N of Clarno the river flows through a rugged canyon, generally 1,500 ft. deep. Elevations from 1,650 ft. at Clarno to 535 ft. at the end of the canyon. Reddish-brown basalt with a great variety of formations: cliffs, pillars, columns, isolated escarpments, blocks, small stepped plateaus. Many scenic side canyons. Vegetation is dominated by Idaho fescue and bluebunch wheatgrass, with some scattered juniper. Also big sage, hackberry, rabbitbrush, cacti, lupine, cheatgrass.

Upstream, from Service Creek to Clarno, the terrain is somewhat less rugged but still wild and scenic, with few sightings of ranch houses or other developments.

ACTIVITIES

Camping: Someone gave us a little map showing campsites used by boaters. The BLM says there are no designated sites. Certainly no facilities.

Boating: Powered boats can be used on some stretches when water is high. Inquire locally.

Canoeing, kayaking, rafting: Best in Apr.–May. 3 major rapids. Few people run the river N of Clarno, but those who do say it's outstanding; one class IV rapids. Most run from Service Creek to Clarno, 48 mi. Last takeout is above Tumwater Falls, 10 mi. above the Columbia. The falls drop into the slack water of the John Day Dam pool. Boaters usually take out at Cottonwood Canyon, SR 206. They must take out at McDonald Crossing, near Rock Creek, 20 mi. below SR 206.

Whether traveling by boat or on foot, check at the BLM office for maps, conditions, advice. The BLM emphasizes that one must obtain permission before crossing private land.

HEADQUARTERS: Prineville District, Bureau of Land Management, 185 E. Fourth St., P.O. Box 550, Prineville, OR 97754; (503) 447-4115.

OCHOCO NATIONAL FOREST
U.S. Forest Service
843,644 acres/978,470 acres within boundaries.

In 3 blocks. Largest block E and N of Prineville, crossed by US 26 and secondary roads. Second block NW of Burns, crossed by secondary roads only. Smallest block, about 22 mi. by 7 mi., SE of Prineville, S of Post on Crooked River Highway.

The *Central Oregon Rockhound Guide* (see Publications) shows digging locations scattered through the largest and the smallest units of the Forest. Many visitors come in search of thunder eggs, moss agate, petrified wood, vistaite, and other prizes.

Much of the Forest is over 5,000 ft. elevation, highest point over 7,000. Terrain varied, from flat and slightly rolling to broken topography with cliffs and river canyons to mountains. Numerous creeks. Small lakes, the largest 90 acres.

Plants: Mostly forested. Ponderosa pine with Douglas-fir, lodgepole pine, white and grand firs, western larch. Some old-growth stands. Some high desert scablands. Flowering species include mariposa lily, wyethia, balsamroot, Indian paintbrush. Best flowering season is Apr.–June.

Birds: No checklist available. Species reported include great blue heron, Canada goose, bittern, red-tailed hawk, owls, magpie, flycatchers, meadowlark, golden eagle, pheasant, chukar, ruffed grouse, valley quail.

Mammals: No checklist available. Species reported include pronghorn, mule deer, elk, porcupine, chipmunk, ground squirrel, coyote, badger, bobcat, skunk, raccoon.

FEATURES

Black Canyon wilderness, 13,400 acres. Elevations from 2,853 ft. at the mouth of Black Canyon Creek to 6,372 ft. at Wolf Mountain. Canyon rim about 5,700 ft. Steep slopes, rockslides, bluffs, timbered and open areas, relatively level benches and mesas. Mesas and benches generally forested with ponderosa, Douglas-fir, other conifers. Several perpetually flowing streams, tributaries of John Day River system. In Paulina Ranger District.

Mill Creek Recreation Management Area, in Prineville Ranger District. Variable terrain, some rugged, steep areas; some meadows, prairies. Ponderosa and lodgepole.

Lookout Mountain Recreation Management Area, in Big Summit Ranger District. Some of the most rugged terrain, elevations from 4,700 to over 6,900 ft. Parklike stands of ponderosa with Douglas-fir on steep N slopes. Open, grassy top; vistas.

Steins Pillar, near Mill Creek and Forest Route 33: stone monolith rising 350 ft. above base.

Wild Horse Range. Small bands of wild horses often seen in central and W half of Big Summit Ranger District.

Spanish Peak, 6,871 ft., in Paulina Ranger District, highest point in District, accessible by road. Vistas.

Snow Mountain, 7,163 ft., at NE edge of Snow Mountain Ranger District. Lookout station; viewpoint.

ACTIVITIES

Camping: 25 campgrounds, 196 sites. Most open all year. Informal camping elsewhere except as posted.

Hiking, backpacking: 61 mi. of trails, chiefly in N unit (largest block). Many miles of roads, most unpaved, some little used. Most trails open to ORV's, which discourages hikers. Bushwhacking feasible in many areas.

Hunting: Mule deer, elk, upland game birds.

Fishing: Streams and lakes. Trout, bass.

Horse riding: Considerable use of trails. Pack trips uncommon.

Snowmobiling: In large sections of the Forest, restricted to designated routes during hunting season. Otherwise few controls.

PUBLICATIONS
Forest map. $1.00. (Includes Crooked River National Grassland.)
Off-Road Vehicle Travel Map. (Includes National Grassland.)
Central Oregon Rockhound Guide.

HEADQUARTERS: P.O. Box 490, Prineville, OR 97754; (503) 447-6247.

RANGER DISTRICTS: Big Summit R.D., Prineville, OR 97754; (503) 447-3854.
Paulina R.D., Paulina, OR 97751; (503) 477-3373. Prineville R.D., Prineville, OR 97754; (503) 447-3825. Snow Mountain R.D., Hines, OR 97738;
(503) 573-7292.

PETER SKENE OGDEN SCENIC WAYSIDE
Oregon Parks and Recreation Division
98 acres.

9 mi. N of Redmond on US 97.

Another view of the Crooked River Gorge, also seen at Smith Rock State
Park and Crooked River National Grassland (see entries). Here the canyon
is 400 ft. wide, over 300 ft. deep. Not as spectacular as at Smith Rock, but
worth a brief stop.

PRINEVILLE RESERVOIR; PRINEVILLE RESERVOIR
STATE PARK
U.S. Bureau of Land Management/Oregon Parks and Recreation Division/
Oregon Department of Fish and Wildlife.
3,010 acres of water; about 5,500 acres of public land around the reservoir
administered by the Water and Power Resources Service; additional BLM
lands nearby.

For State Park: from Prineville 1 mi. E on US 26, then 16 mi. S on marked
county road. For dam: from Prineville, 19 mi. S on SR 27.

Reservoir formed by damming Crooked River. State Park is a popular resort
occupying a peninsula on the N shore. Chiefly water-based recreation. Lake
is surrounded by dry hills, sparse juniper and sagebrush. Interesting lava rock
formations: columns, pillars, blocks. Some private land on the lakeshore, but
development is limited chiefly to the N shore. Much of the remaining shoreline is undeveloped, without road access. Popular rockhounding area.
Much of the land outside the Park and near the lake is known as the
Prineville Reservoir Wildlife Area. The Department of Fish and Wildlife has

game management responsibility, not ownership. Deer are relatively abundant. Some waterfowl nest at the inlet in Apr.–May, which is also the best time for desert wildflowers, depending on rainfall.

ACTIVITIES

Camping: At State Park, 70 sites, mid-Apr. to Oct. Reservations. Informal BLM campsites along SR 27 (see entry, Crooked River Canyon).

Hiking: No trails, but bushwhacking is feasible. Few people hike, we were informed, but it's possible to hike around the lake, about 14 mi. of difficult hiking.

Hunting: Not within the State Park, but on BLM land.

Fishing: Rainbow trout, bass, catfish.

Swimming: Lake.

Boating: Ramp and other facilities at State Park. Informal ramp, poor access road, near dam; suitable for light boats only.

ADJACENT: Crooked River Canyon (see entry).

PUBLICATION: Park leaflet.

HEADQUARTERS: (Park) Prineville Lake Rt., Box 1050, Prineville, OR 97754; (503) 447-4363. Prineville District, Bureau of Land Management, 185 E. Fourth St., P.O. Box 550, Prineville, OR 97754; (503) 447-4115.

SAND HOLLOW; GERRY MOUNTAIN; LOGAN BUTTE; REDMAN RIM; SEARS CREEK; HAMPTON BUTTE; COUGAR WELL; HAMPTON; STOCKPILE
U.S. Bureau of Land Management
100,000 acres.

These are contiguous units of a block of BLM land about 30 mi. N–S, 8 mi. E–W. Just N of US 20. W boundary is about 1 mi. N of Hampton; E boundary meets US 20. Names read N to S.

High desert, above 4,200 ft., with buttes and mountains rising as much as 1,100 ft. above surrounding land. Juniper occurs throughout the area, sometimes in dense stands, more often well scattered. Principal plant species: low sage, big sage, green rabbitbrush, gray rabbitbrush, lupine, Idaho fescue, bluebunch wheatgrass, bitterbrush. Portions once seeded with crested wheatgrass.

Sand Hollow: Low, rolling hills; higher hills extending E–W forming part of Steens Ridge. In W and N, rugged dark brown basalt escarpments. Boundaries are county and BLM roads.

Gerry Mountain: Mountain is butte-shaped, elevation 5,200 ft., offering sweeping vistas. Two smaller mountains, rolling hills. NE portion relatively flat. N, E, and S boundaries are county roads.

Redman Rim: Rim rises about 1,000 ft. above surrounding land, about 1 1/2 mi. long, up to 1 1/4 mi. wide. Rimmed with dark brown basalt escarpments and outcroppings. Steep slopes. 650-ft. Ibex Butte is nearby. Also shallow basins, high rolling hills. County road on part of N boundary, BLM roads on S and E.

Logan Butte: A scenic outcropping of John Day clay formations covering nearly 2 sq. mi.

Sears Creek: Low rolling hills dissected by deep drainages. Canyon about 160 ft. deep extends E–W for 1 1/2 mi., rimmed with reddish-brown basalt. NE and SW portions have more varied terrain: hills and small ravines. Roads along parts of all boundaries.

Hampton Butte: Foothills rising to a rugged basalt rim, edge of a 600-acre plateau, part of the scenic Hampton Buttes. To the N, smaller plateaus, rolling hills, a shallow canyon. Roads on portions of N, S, and W boundaries.

Cougar Well: E half is relatively flat desert plain, sloping gradually up to W; a small N–S canyon bisects this portion. To the W, low rolling foothills join a large butte, offering sweeping vistas. W flank of butte drops sharply, forming a small secluded valley. Part of E boundary is county road; W boundary is BLM road.

Hampton: Divided by N–S ridge of reddish-brown basalt about 4 mi. long. To E, low rolling hills and desert plain. To W, low hills slope downward to shallow valley. Small escarpments in NW. County road on E, BLM maintenance roads on W and S.

Stockpile: Dry river bed in central portion with reddish-brown basalt outcroppings. Tributary dry river bed in E. In the W, low rolling hills sloping down to E. County roads on W and E. S boundary is US 20.

Much of the area has been used for grazing, signs of which are ways, fences, and small reservoirs, many now reverting to nature. Most of the area is now in a natural state. Utility power lines cross, but there are no residences or other developments.

ADJACENT: Crooked River, South Fork (see entry) on the N.

HEADQUARTERS: Prineville District, Bureau of Land Management, 185 E. Fourth St., P.O. Box 550, Prineville, OR 97754; (503) 447-4115.

SMITH ROCK STATE PARK
Oregon Parks and Recreation Division
623 acres.

From Redmond, 6 mi. N on US 97 to Terrebonne, then E 3 mi.

Scenic area on Crooked River. Winding canyon cut 300 ft. deep through colorful layers of sedimentary rock, contrast with flatlands surrounding. Cliffs on N side considerably higher than observation area on S. Spires, columns, vertical cliffs.

From observation area, one can hike down trail to canyon floor, cross river on footbridge. Trails on both sides of river. Day-use area.

HEADQUARTERS: c/o The Cove Palisades State Park, Route 1, Box 60 CP, Culver, OR 97734; (503) 546-3412.

THE COVE PALISADES STATE PARK
Oregon Parks and Recreation Division
4,130 acres.

From Culver on US 97, 5 mi. W.

Round Butte Dam formed Lake Billy Chinook, backing up water in canyons of Deschutes, Crooked, and Metolius rivers, forming lake with three long, narrow arms. State Park is chiefly on E side, a popular resort with marina, cafe, store, campgrounds, and other facilities. Activity at the Park is almost entirely water-based. Several scenic overlooks. Desert region. Juniper-sagebrush plant community.

Those interested in exploring surrounding land areas will find them scenic and uncrowded. Much adjacent area is within the Crooked River National Grassland (see entry).

ACTIVITIES
Camping: 2 campgrounds, 272 sites. Mid-Apr. through Oct. Reservations.
Fishing: Kokanee, rainbow, brown trout; bass.
Swimming: Usual season Apr.–Oct.
Boating: Ramps, marina, rentals.

Crowded most summer weekends, all holiday weekends.

PUBLICATIONS
Leaflet.
Peterson, N. V., and Groh, E. A. *Geologic Tour of Cove Palisades State*

Park Near Madras, Oregon. State of Oregon, Department of Geology and Mineral Industries, 1069 State Office Bldg., Portland, OR 97201. 1970.

HEADQUARTERS: Rt. 1, Box 60 CP, Culver, OR 97734; (503) 546-3412.

WHITE RIVER WILDLIFE AREA
Oregon Department of Fish and Wildlife
25,000 acres.

From The Dalles, S on US 197 about 33 mi. to Tygh Valley, then W past Wamic.

An irregularly shaped area along the White River between US 197 and the Hood River National Forest. Farming, timber, and rangeland area. Established to provide deer and elk an alternative to feeding on farmers' crops. Several thousand deer and several hundred elk are attracted here in winter, as they come down from the high country in the National Forest. Stop at site HQ to ask where viewing is best. In spring and fall this is a good birding area, between farms and forest. Elevation 1,500–2,000 ft.

HEADQUARTERS: Department of Fish and Wildlife, Region III, 61374 Parrell Rd., Bend, OR 97701; (503) 382-5113.

ZONE 4

1 Umatilla National Wildlife Refuge
2 McNary Wildlife Park
3 Cold Springs National Wildlife Refuge
4 Umatilla National Forest
5 Wenaha Wildlife Management Area
6 Wallowa-Whitman National Forest
7 McKay Creek National Wildlife Refuge
8 Hells Canyon National Recreation Area
9 Bridge Creek Wildlife Area
10 Ladd Marsh Wildlife Area
11 McGraw Creek; Homestead; Sheep Mountain
12 Malheur National Forest
13 Brownlee Reservoir
14 Farewell Bend State Park

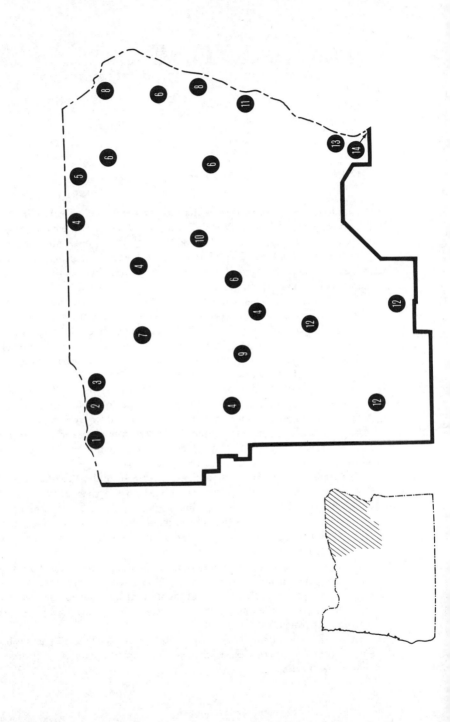

ZONE 4

Includes these counties:

Morrow	Wallowa	Grant
Umatilla	Union	Baker

Dominant feature of the area is the Blue Mountains range, extending from the NE corner to the John Day Valley in the SW. Part of the chain projects SE to the Snake River Valley, OR's border with ID in this zone. The mountains are generally from 5,000 to 6,000 ft. with numerous peaks over 7,000, the highest point 10,033 ft. Much of this high country is within the three National Forests of the region.

Even in the mountains, annual precipitation is only moderate, but much of it falls as snow, providing good skiing. The lower country is dry, including the broad plateau of the Columbia River and other river valleys. Snowmelt provides reliable water flow for many good trout and salmon streams. The zone has many lakes and reservoirs, most of them small. Reservoirs used for irrigation are often well down in summer.

Route I-84 cuts across the zone, NW to SE. US 395 is a N–S highway in the W portion of the zone, US 26 E–W along the John Day River in the S. A few good state and county roads also tend to follow river valleys. Large sections of the zone are either roadless or served by roads to be used with caution, especially in winter. The official highway map's designation of "all-weather roads" is, in some cases, optimistic.

The Hells Canyon National Recreation Area straddles the Middle Snake River in OR and ID. Publicity has focused on the river canyon and the popularity of rafting through the impressive rapids. However, the area is huge, 662,000 acres in the two states, much of it wilderness. Each of the National Forests has substantial wilderness acreage, offering almost unlimited opportunities for backpacking and pack trips.

Elk and deer take to the high country in summer, seek the valleys when snow falls, often invading farmers' fields. Several wildlife management areas provide limited alternatives. Most of the natural wetlands of the zone have been obliterated, so the refuges that provide good wintering grounds are well patronized by ducks and geese.

In the SE corner of the zone, below Hells Canyon, the Snake River has been dammed. The Brownlee Reservoir, in a scenic desert canyon, is easily accessible but lightly used.

BRIDGE CREEK WILDLIFE AREA

Oregon Department of Fish and Wildlife
13,086 acres.

From US 395 at junction with SR 244, E a short distance to Ukiah, then S on unpaved Forest Service Road 52 about 3 mi. Continue straight where road turns E toward Granite. Unimproved road runs S through the Wildlife Area to a point overlooking the North Fork, John Day River. Road best suited to pickups and 4-wheel-drive vehicles. Advisable to hike.

W boundary is canyon of Camas Creek. Forested valleys; open grassland. Bridge Creek crosses E–W at about midpoint. Elevation about 4,000 ft. Wintering ground for deer and elk which summer in Umatilla National Forest. The entire area is open to public entry by permit only Dec. 1–Apr. 30 to prevent harassment of game. Camping is permitted within 100 yds. of designated roads during the hunting season. Nonhunters would be well advised to limit their visits to the period May 1–Sept. 14.

ADJACENT

Ukiah-Dale Forest Wayside, 2,987 acres, along the Camas Creek Canyon, US 395, between Ukiah and Dale. Scenic. Campground, 25 sites. Season depends on winter weather.

Umatilla National Forest (see entry).

BROWNLEE RESERVOIR (OR side only)

Idaho Power Company/Oregon Parks and Recreation Division/U.S. Bureau of Land Management

Access from I-84 near Huntington. State Park is 4 mi SE. From Huntington, Snake River Road runs close to reservoir for about 30 mi., N to Richland on SR 86.

Idaho Power Company Dam on Snake River, 12 mi. S of Copperfield on SR 86, has backed up a 58-mi. pool, to a point 10 mi. W of Weiser, ID. Desert valley; brown, rounded, largely treeless mountains on both sides. Cliffs, slides, boulders; a few sand dunes on ID side. Snake River Road is gravel, reasonably well maintained, with sections of washboard. Land along the road is a patch-work of private holdings and BLM, but there has been little development. We saw a number of informal campsites and boat-launching places. The BLM's Spring Recreation Site is quiet, scenic.

River and upper portion of reservoir are quite shallow, but small outboards were operating from the State Park in Aug., with water level several feet below its high point.

The section N of Huntington has few visitors other than fishermen; the road is lightly traveled. For much of the distance, there is no road on the ID side. It offers an easy way to enjoy a scenic desert canyon in relative isolation.

Plants: Lower slopes along the reservoir: bluebunch wheatgrass, cheat-grass, bitterbrush, big sagebrush. In moist areas of draws: some Douglas-fir, white fir, huckleberry, snowberry. Higher and drier slopes have Idaho fescue, arrowleaf, balsamroot, serviceberry. Wildflowers include larkspur, buttercup, violet, penstemon, Indian paintbrush, mariposa lily, bluebells, clarkia, lupine, phlox, fireweed.

Birds: No checklist. Species noted include chukar, blue grouse, Steller's jay, Clark's nutcracker, red crossbill. Wintering area for bald eagle.

Mammals: Mule deer wintering range. Elk, black bear, coyote, chickaree, weasel. Mountain lion reported.

ACTIVITIES

Camping: At Farewell Bend, 53 sites, all year. The BLM's Spring Recrea-tion Site, 3 mi. N of Huntington, 14 sites, primitive, all year. Informal camping along the route.

Hiking: Snake River Road is lightly traveled, pleasant hiking. Numerous places to bushwhack into the hills.

Hunting: On BLM land. Deer, elk, grouse, chukar.

Fishing: Said to be good: bass, crappie, catfish.

Swimming: Local comment: "If you're hot enough."

Boating: Good launching facilities at Farewell Bend. Ramp at Spring is steep. Along the way, informal launching spots for light boats. More facilities on ID side near dam.

HEADQUARTERS: Farewell Bend State Park, Star Route, Huntington, OR 97907; (503) 869-2365. Baker District, Bureau of Land Management, Federal Building, P.O. Box 987, Baker, OR 97814; (503) 523-6391.

COLD SPRINGS NATIONAL WILDLIFE REFUGE
U.S. Fish and Wildlife Service
3,117 acres.

From I-84 N, exit on SR 207. 6 mi. N to Hermiston. E 8 mi. on Stanfield Loop Rd. Entrance on left.

About 1,550 acres of open water at full pool. Water is used for irrigation, and levels drop greatly in the summer dry season. Management has had difficulty controlling illegal and destructive use of ORV's on the dry lakebed but hoped this problem was being solved. Summer is the least desirable time to visit. Large numbers of waterfowl arrive in late fall. Peak winter populations vary but usually reach 30,000 ducks, 10,000 geese. Desert environment; about 7 in. of precipitation annually. A road with parking areas is on the S shore. Little upland, but one can hike around the lake, about 8 mi. Management advises that an information station stocked with brochures is at each entrance; this is new since our 1980 visit.

Plants: Cheatgrass steppe community: sagebrush, rabbitbrush, mustard, buckwheat, bitterbrush, Russian thistle. Cottonwood and Russian olive at the shoreline.

Birds: Chiefly mallard, pintail, green-winged teal, American wigeon, shoveler, Canada goose. Most waterfowl species common to the Pacific Flyway are seen here at times. Bald and golden eagle in winter. Marsh, red-tailed, and Swainson's hawks in summer, as well as American kestrel. White pelican, whistling swan, sandhill crane occasionally visit in migration. Many shorebirds.

Mammals: Often seen on and near the Refuge: mule deer, cottontail, black-tailed jackrabbit, muskrat, coyote, badger, beaver.

Reptiles and amphibians: Often seen: short-horned, side-blotched, and western fence lizards; Great Basin spadefoot toad, Pacific tree frog, bullfrog, western yellow-bellied racer, gopher snake.

PUBLICATIONS
Recreation activity sheet.
Hunting information.
Map.

HEADQUARTERS: P.O. Box 239, Umatilla, OR 97882; (503) 922-3232.

FAREWELL BEND STATE PARK
See Brownlee Reservoir.

HELLS CANYON NATIONAL RECREATION AREA
See Wallowa-Whitman National Forest.

LADD MARSH WILDLIFE AREA
Oregon Department of Fish and Wildlife
2,400 acres.

About 5 mi. SE of La Grande. Crossed by I-80 N; SR 203 is E boundary.

Of interest chiefly because few wetlands remain in NE Oregon. Marsh and cropland with small areas of open water. Canada goose, sandhill crane, several species of duck. Upland game birds are stocked. Except in hunting season, the area has been closed to the public, but self-guided nature trails were being constructed in early 1981. (Groups of naturalists and students can arrange guided visits.) Reasonably good viewpoints are just outside, worth checking if you pass this way in spring or fall.

HEADQUARTERS: Region IV, Department of Fish and Wildlife, Box 339, La Grande, OR 97850; (503) 963-2138.

MALHEUR NATIONAL FOREST
U.S. Forest Service
1,458,055 acres/1,540,423 acres within boundaries.

Few inholdings but very irregular shape. S of John Day, on both sides of US 395, but boundaries are 1–4 mi. away from the highway. Another large section generally N and E of John Day is connected with the S portion by a strip 6–8 mi. wide, on the E side.

In the SW sector of the Blue Mountains, extending S to the high desert. Elevations from 3,700 ft. to 9,038 ft. Highest country is in the Strawberry Mountain Wilderness. Elsewhere the forested mountains are rolling, with moderate slopes. Large, grassy mountain meadows, bright with wildflowers in season. The lower country, approaching the desert, is plateaulike, with open grassland and sagebrush. Precipitation is 14–30 in., increasing with altitude. Summers are dry. High country usually snow-covered Dec.–Mar.

Includes the headwaters of the Malheur and Silvies rivers, major part of the John Day headwaters. Numerous creeks and intermittent streams. 8 lakes, 3 to 50 acres.

4,600 mi. of roads within the Forest. Most are logging roads maintained only when needed, but there are ample opportunities for backcountry driving; one seldom encounters another vehicle.

Plants: Chief tree species: ponderosa pine. 77% of area is commercial forest land. Several forest types, depending on altitude: subalpine fir, mixed fir-pine, ponderosa, white fir, lodgepole, and sagebrush-juniper. Old-growth stands in scattered locations. Prominent understory species include huckleberry, bitterbrush. Flowering species include wild iris, Indian paintbrush, elephant heads, larkspur, lupine, fireweed, mariposa and snow lilies.

Birds: Common or distinctive species include golden eagle, red-tailed hawk, blue and ruffed grouse, raven, gray jay, great horned owl, Canada goose, mountain bluebird, killdeer. Also prairie falcon, mountain quail, mourning dove, kestrel, goshawk, mallard, cinnamon teal, Oregon junco, flicker, great blue heron, spotted sandpiper, sandhill crane, willet, long-billed curlew.

Mammals: Include mule deer, Rocky Mountain elk, pronghorn, bighorn sheep, black bear, beaver, muskrat, mountain lion, bobcat, Townsend ground squirrel, coyote, various rodents.

Reptiles and amphibians: Include gopher and garter snakes, western rattlesnake, short-horned and western fence lizards, Pacific tree frog.

FEATURES

Strawberry Mountain Wilderness, 33,000 acres plus 35,000 acres of proposed additions. Almost all of the area is above 6,000 ft., several peaks over 8,000 ft., Strawberry Mountain 9,038 ft. Five of the 7 major life zones of the United States are represented, roughly parallel bands, characteristic plant-animal communities changing with altitude. 5 high-altitude lakes. This is high country, but trails leading into the wilderness are, for the most part, not difficult.

Normal hiking season is July–Nov., but snow may occur until mid-July and in late Oct. Freezing night temperatures may occur in any month. Summer thunderstorms are common.

Hikers should have good maps and local information, such as availability of water. Horse travelers must carry all feed needed by their stock.

Baldy Mountain and Sheep Rock are within the proposed wilderness addition, lying immediately to the N of the present wilderness area. Accessible by trail only.

Scenic drive, about 70 mi., from John Day E on US 26 to Prairie City, SE and S on County Road 14, W on County Road 16 through Logan Valley, NW on County Road 15 to US 395, N to John Day. Grant County Chamber of Commerce at John Day has descriptive leaflet.

Vinegar Hill–Indian Rock Scenic Area, 29,077 acres, above timberline, high in Greenhorn Mountains at N end of Forest, nearly half of it in the Umatilla National Forest. Scenic views of mountain meadows, steep cliffs, timbered slopes, abundant wildflowers. Gold and silver mines dating back to late 1800s dot the countryside. Fire lookouts on Vinegar Hill, 8,131 ft., and Indian Rock, 7,353 ft.

Cedar Grove at W end of Forest, 60 acres of Alaska cedar, isolated hundreds of miles from other Alaska cedar stands.

Rosebud Fossil Area, N of Izee at W edge of Forest. Marine fossil shells are embedded in soft shale of exposed road banks. Forest Road 16020 approaches.

Magone Lake Slide. The landslide that formed Magone Lake in the early 1800s can be viewed from a good trail over rough, irregular ground. It supports grotesquely tilted trees carried down by the slide.

ACTIVITIES

Camping: 23 campgrounds, 249 sites. Open to camping whenever snow-free; piped water Jun.–Sept. Informal camping elsewhere, subject to regulations.

Hiking, backpacking: 250 mi. of trails, plus many more mi. of little-used Forest roads. Trails into Strawberry Mountain Wilderness are most popular. Attractive trails in other parts of the Forest have lighter use. Ask at Ranger Districts. New Forest map shows only maintained trails. Wilderness map is better, for that area, but shows little detail. There are also two National Recreation Trails, one along the Malheur River, the other into Cedar Grove.

Hunting: Mule deer, elk, some pronghorn and bighorn sheep, upland game birds, waterfowl.

Fishing: Streams, some lake, rainbow, cutthroat, steelhead, chinook, brook, Dolly Varden.

Swimming: Magone Lake. Season: July–Aug.

Canoeing: Magone and Yellowjacket lakes.

Rockhounding: Promising throughout the Forest: petrified wood, jasper, agate, thunder eggs.

Ski touring: About 120 mi. of marked snowmobile trails. High country usually has sufficient snow Dec.–Mar.

Snowmobiling: Prohibited in wilderness area.

ORV travel is permitted everywhere except in wilderness area, Vinegar Hill– Indian Rock Scenic Area, and on a few designated trails.

ADJACENT: Umatilla National Forest, Wallowa-Whitman National Forest, Ochoco National Forest (see entries).

PUBLICATIONS

Forest map. $1.00.
Strawberry Mountain Wilderness map. $1.00.
Malheur Activities, fact sheet.
Campground Information.

HEADQUARTERS: 139 N.E. Dayton St., John Day, OR 97845; (503) 575-1731.

RANGER DISTRICTS: Bear Valley R.D. and Long Creek R.D., same address as HQ. Prairie City R.D., P.O. Box 156, Prairie City, OR 97869; (503)

820-3311. Burns R.D., Box 12870, Burns-Bend Star Route, Burns, OR 97720; (503) 573-7292.

MCGRAW CREEK; HOMESTEAD; SHEEP MOUNTAIN
U.S. Bureau of Land Management
20,000 acres.

Three units, not quite adjacent; McGraw Creek and Homestead N and Sheep Mountain S of SR 86 at Copperfield. All have frontage on Snake River Rd.

Near but not on Hells Canyon and Oxbow Dam impoundments of Snake River. Steep sloping ridges, stream valleys, a canyon in McGraw and Sheep Mountain units. Some lava outcroppings. Elevations from 1,780 to 4,940 ft. All three units considered for wilderness designation. N unit adjoins proposed wilderness area in Wallowa-Whitman National Forest.

Plants: Ponderosa pine and Douglas-fir at higher elevations, with snowberry, bitter cherry, wild rose in understory. Pine, fir, aspen, and willow on lower NE-facing slopes and along riparian zones with understory of Oregon grape, snowberry, snowbrush. Also open grassy slopes. Botanists consider the Snake River Canyon area unique—many rare and unusual species occur.

Birds: No checklist for distribution. Noted: red-tailed hawk, great horned owl, chukar, magpie, Canada goose, killdeer.

Mammals: Deer and elk abundant. Black bear and mountain lion present.

ACTIVITIES
Hiking, backpacking: Generally steep, rather rugged terrain. Trail from end of Snake River Road, N along river through McGraw Creek unit to within 1-2 mi. of Hells Canyon Dam. Connecting trail leads NW at McGraw Creek to Hells Canyon National Recreation Area.

Hunting: Deer, elk, chukar, bear, mountain lion.

HEADQUARTERS: Baker District, Bureau of Land Management, Federal Building, P.O. Box 987, Baker, OR 97814; (503) 523-6391.

MCKAY CREEK NATIONAL WILDLIFE REFUGE
U.S. Fish and Wildlife Service
1,836 acres.

From Pendleton, US 395, S 6 mi. Entrance on left.

Open: Mar. 1–Sept. 30, 5 A.M.–10 P.M. After Sept. 30, hunting is permitted, in season, in designated areas, Wed., Sat., and Sun.; wildlife observation is permitted in these same areas, nonhunting days preferred.

An irrigation reservoir with a narrow strip of surrounding land. Desert region; about 7 in. of annual precipitation.

Plants: Cheatgrass steppe community: sagebrush, rabbitbrush, mustard, buckwheat, bitterbrush, Russian thistle.

Birds: Waterfowl concentrations can be observed late fall and winter. Peak populations vary, usually reach 30,000 ducks, 10,000 geese. Primary species: mallard, pintail, green-winged teal, American wigeon, shoveler, Canada goose. Bald and golden eagles common in winter. Marsh, red-tailed, and Swainson's hawks active all summer; also American kestrel. White pelican, whistling swan, sandhill crane seen occasionally in spring and fall migrations. Many shorebirds.

Mammals: Mule deer, cottontail, black-tailed jackrabbit, muskrat, coyote, badger, and beaver are often seen.

A gravel, 2-mi. wildlife observation drive with turnouts and parking areas is on the W shore.

PUBLICATION: Hunting leaflet.

HEADQUARTERS: P.O. Box 239, Umatilla, OR 97882; (503) 922-3232.

MCNARY WILDLIFE PARK
U.S. Army Corps of Engineers
500 acres.

1/2 mi. NE of Umatilla, immediately below McNary Lock and Dam.

Not a natural area but an interesting effort to create a viable wildlife habitat. Site was a gravel pit and disposal site during dam construction, 1947–57. Later, ponds were established and stocked with game fish. Further grading and plantings have created a variety of habitats: rabbitbrush-sage scabland, open marsh, closed marsh, open ponds and lakes, flowing streams, riparian woods, grassland, pine grove. The site is 1 1/4 mi. long by 1/4 mi. wide, bounded by the Columbia River, a paved road, the interstate bridge, and McNary Dam. However, a corridor of riparian habitat extends 9 mi. W into the Umatilla National Wildlife Refuge. The surrounding area is semiarid shrub steppe, so the richness and diversity of this site attract many species of wildlife.

On reading the site leaflet, we wondered if this were a kind of safari park. It is not; no animals are confined.

Plants: Checklist available. Many are native to the area, but exotic and cultivated species have also been used.

Birds: 129 species have been attracted and noted. Checklist available. Abundant or common, seasonally: pied-billed grebe, great blue heron, black-crowned night heron, mallard, pintail, gadwall, teals, American wigeon, wood duck, kestrel, California quail, pheasant, coot, killdeer, ring-billed gull, rock and mourning doves, nighthawk, kingbirds; bank, barn, and cliff swallows; magpie, raven, crow, robin, cedar waxwing, starling, house sparrow, western meadowlark, red-winged and Brewer's blackbirds, cowbird, evening grosbeak, house finch, goldfinch, rufous-sided towhee, lark sparrow, Oregon junco, song sparrow.

Mammals: Checklist available. Species reported include mule deer, jackrabbit, cottontail, Columbian and Washington ground squirrels, yellow-bellied marmot, northern pocket gopher, Great Basin pocket mouse, woodrat, voles, beaver, muskrat, coyote, raccoon, weasels, badger, skunks, river otter, shrews, mink, porcupine.

INTERPRETATION

Nature trail, 3/4 mi., self-guiding, pamphlet. *Naturalist* present all year. *Photo blinds,* chiefly for waterfowl.

Fishing: Rainbow trout, largemouth bass, bluegill, catfish.

PUBLICATIONS

Species checklists.
Nature trail guide.

HEADQUARTERS: U.S. Army Corps of Engineers, Building 602, City-County Airport, Walla Walla, WA 99362. Resource manager: (503) 922-3211.

UMATILLA NATIONAL FOREST

U.S. Forest Service
1,398,914 acres, including 311,209 acres in WA.

Three principal blocks. The largest lies across the WA border, NE of I-84, N of La Grande. It is crossed by SR 204. The two other pieces are E and W of US 395, between Pilot Rock and Long Creek. SR 244 from Ukiah crosses the E section.

In the Blue Mountains. Elevations from 1,900 ft. to 7,720 ft. Part of a large block of forest land, it adjoins the Malheur and Wallowa-Whitman National Forests. Diverse terrain. In the N, sharply dissected plateaus and steep slopes. The central portion is partly rolling, partly dissected, the S rolling to steeply rolling, the SW relatively flat or undulating. About 2/3 of the area is commercial forest. The balance is a mix of shrub and grassland.

Climate is generally temperate, semiarid, but with great variations depending on altitude and exposure. Annual precipitation is about 20 in. at lower elevations, up to 65 in. in high country, where snowfall averages 100 in. Summers are dry.

Headwaters of the Umatilla, North Fork John Day, and Walla Walla rivers are within the Forest. More than 1,100 mi. of fishing streams. Olive Lake, 145 acres, is the only natural lake larger than 3 acres. The largest reservoirs are under 100 acres.

Camping, hunting, and fishing are the principal visitor activities. Tens of thousands of hunters congregate in elk season. Although some campgrounds may be fully occupied at other times, few places in the Forest are heavily used, and hikers can easily find isolation. Unfortunately, almost all trails outside the wilderness area are open to use by ORV's, but it's not difficult to observe which trails they favor.

The Forest has 5,270 mi. of roads, of which only 96 mi. are paved. About 2,000 mi. are graveled, 1,000 graded and drained. About 2,000 are primitive, to be approached with caution.

Plants: Four major vegetation zones. At 2,800 to 3,600 ft., western juniper with big sagebrush, bluebunch wheatgrass, Idaho fescue. At 2,900 to 4,900 ft., more humid places, ponderosa pine forests with Douglas-fir, grand fir, lodgepole pine, western larch; understory includes sagebrush, bitterbrush, mahogany, snowberry, spirea, and grasses. From 4,900 to 6,600 ft., grand fir is dominant, with ponderosa and lodgepole pines, western larch, and Douglas-fir. Also in this zone are such flowering plants as twinflower, heartleaf arnica, bishop's cap, huckleberry, pipsissewa, pasque flower. From 4,500 ft. to timberline at 7,900, subalpine fir, Engelmann spruce, grand fir, western larch, and Douglas-fir, with huckleberry, heartleaf arnica, hawkweed, anemone, other subalpine flowers.

Birds: No checklist available. Species reported include goshawk, golden and bald eagles, osprey, prairie falcon, grouse; great horned, barred, and flammulated owls; pileated, hairy, downy, white-headed, and northern three-toed woodpeckers; flicker, Williamson's sapsucker, Steller's jay, Vaux's swift, water ouzel, winter wren, hermit thrush, kingfisher, Merriam's turkey, pine grosbeak, MacGillivray's and yellow warblers. Area said to be noted for numbers and variety of woodpeckers.

Mammals: No checklist. Species reported include black bear, river otter, marten, mink, beaver, badger, bobcat, mountain lion, pocket gopher, coyote, mule and white-tailed deer, elk, California bighorn. Exceptionally large elk population.

FEATURES

Wenaha-Tucannon Wilderness, 177,412 acres, of which 66,417 are in OR, remainder in WA. Elevations from 2,000 ft. at the Wenaha River to 6,401 ft. at Oregon Butte (WA). Rivers and streams have cut deep canyons into broad tablelands. High ridges have steep, gravelly slopes. Vegetation from bunchgrass at lower elevations to subalpine. Many streams. Wenaha River, Crooked Creek, Rock Creek, Butte Creek have good fishing. About 165 mi. of trails reached from a dozen trailheads. Saddle and pack horses used subject to special rules. Wilderness permit required.

Vinegar Hill–Indian Rock Scenic Area, 29,285 acres, about half in Malheur National Forest (see entry). Alpine topography, over 7,000 ft. elevation. Cirque basins, steep cliffs, rocky outcrops, with views of timbered slopes, mountain meadows with abundant wildflowers. Remains of old gold mines.

Thompson Flat and Potamus Creek, in the Heppner Ranger District. The Flat, about 1 1/2 mi. sq., is semiarid, sagebrush and bunchgrass with scattered juniper and ponderosa pine. At the edge, the land drops abruptly, providing scenic views of the North Fork John Day River and Potamus Creek. The creek canyon has steep, dissected side slopes, vertical rock outcrops, scattered trees.

Kendall-Skyline Road, on the crest of the Blue Mountains, extends 44 mi. from the N end of the Forest to SR 204. Fine views of the Wenaha-Tucannon Wilderness, Mill Creek, Walla Walla River. Segments vary from gravel surface to primitive. Check conditions.

Roadless areas: In the wilderness review process, 27 roadless areas totaling 413,332 acres were identified. Except for a 21,210-acre site on the North Fork John Day, it is unlikely that any of these areas will be added to the wilderness system. The existence of such large roadless areas is an indication of the hiking opportunities.

Scenic route: SR 204, Weston to Elgin, passes Umatilla Breaks Viewpoint, fine view of rugged canyon of the North Fork of the Umatilla River.

ACTIVITIES

Camping: 35 campgrounds, 351 sites. Earliest opening: Apr. 20. Most open June 1–July 1.

Hiking, backpacking: 633 mi. of mapped and maintained trails. Off-trail hiking is feasible in many areas.

Hunting: Outstanding elk hunting. Also deer, bear, turkey.

Fishing: 1,100 mi. of fish-bearing streams, of which over 700 mi. are capable of supporting salmon, steelhead. Fishing in lakes includes some ice fishing.

Swimming: At a few lakes.

Boating: Motors permitted only at Olive Lake. River floating between Rondowa and Troy in the gorge of the Grande Ronde River.

Horse riding: Outfitters in nearby communities provide pack and saddle stock, guides.

Skiing: Two commercial ski areas.

Ski touring: No special trails but many opportunities.

Snowmobiling: Several posted trails, but most snowmobilers use unplowed roads or travel cross-country. Banned only in wilderness area and certain winter game ranges.

PUBLICATIONS

Forest map. $1.00.

Information letter, sent on request.

Wenaha-Tucannon Wilderness map. $1.00.

ORV map, showing closures.

List of lakes with fishing information.

HEADQUARTERS: 2517 S.W. Hailey Ave., Pendleton, OR 97801; (503) 276-3811.

RANGER DISTRICTS: Dale, OR 97880; (503) 421-3311. Heppner, OR 97836; (503) 676-9187. Pendleton, OR 97801; (503) 276-3811. Ukiah, OR 97880; (503) 427-3231. Pomeroy, WA 99347; (509) 843-1891. Walla Walla, WA 99362; (509) 525-5500.

UMATILLA NATIONAL WILDLIFE REFUGE

U.S. Fish and Wildlife Service

8,879 acres in OR; 14,000 acres in WA zone 6; about 16,500 acres of water.

On the Columbia River. From I-84 N, exit at US 730 E of Boardman. NE on US 730 about 4 mi., then left on Paterson Ferry Rd.

Closing of John Day Dam in 1968 inundated much traditional waterfowl habitat. It also created McCormack Slough in OR and Paterson Slough in

WA. The Refuge was established to maintain this new waterfowl habitat. Peak winter populations are over 80,000 geese, 325,000 ducks.

Directions above are to McCormack Slough, largest land parcel on the OR side. When we visited in summer of 1980, no map or informative signs were posted. We have since been advised that signs are up and brochures are available. Road marked Parking A leads to a high point overlooking pond and cattail marsh. Next road to left marked Parking BCDE leads to junction of slough and Columbia River. From the parking areas, trails and gated service roads cross fields, sagebrush flats, and to shores of slough and river. We saw no AREA CLOSED signs. The Refuge is busy during hunting season but appears to have few visitors at other times.

Plants: Desert region, about 7 in. of rain yearly. Cheatgrass steppe community: sagebrush, rabbitbrush, mustard, buckwheat, bitterbrush, Russian thistle. Cottonwood and Russian olive along shores. Cattail, rushes, other marsh vegetation.

Birds: 189 species recorded; checklist available. Seasonally abundant and common species include pied-billed grebe, double-crested cormorant, great blue heron, whistling swan, Canada goose, mallard, gadwall, pintail, teals, wigeon, shoveler, goldeneye, bufflehead. Long-billed curlews are a special feature. Their return is celebrated locally as heralding spring weather. About 200 are produced on the Refuge each year. Other abundant or common species: marsh hawk, kestrel, California quail, pheasant, coot, killdeer, greater yellowlegs, Baird's and western sandpipers, avocet, ring-billed gull, terns, rock and mourning doves, flicker, kingbirds, horned lark, bank and barn swallows, magpie, raven, crow, long-billed marsh wren, robin, cedar waxwing, house sparrow, western meadowlark, yellow-headed and red-winged blackbirds, northern oriole, cowbird, house finch, goldfinch.

Mammals: Often seen: mule deer, cottontail, black-tailed jackrabbit, muskrat, coyote, badger, beaver, big brown bat, small-footed myotis. Less often seen: mink, river otter, porcupine, bobcat, skunks, raccoon, opossum, various rodents.

Reptiles and amphibians: Often seen: short-horned, side-blotched, and western fence lizards; Great Basin spadefoot toad, Pacific tree frog, bullfrog, western yellow-bellied racer, gopher snake. Present but seldom seen: long-toed salamander, Oregon alligator lizard, western skink, striped whipsnake, Oregon rattlesnake, wandering garter snake, western painted turtle.

FEATURE: 27 *blinds* on the marsh can be used for photography and observation as well as hunting.

PUBLICATIONS
Refuge leaflet with map.
Bird checklist.

Hunting information.
Hunting map.

HEADQUARTERS: P.O. Box 239, Umatilla, OR 97882; (503) 922-3232.

WALLOWA-WHITMAN NATIONAL FOREST
U.S. Forest Service
2,250,177 acres.

NE OR. Two major blocks. The larger, shaped like a backward C, lies against the ID border, close to the WA border. Access from points on SRs 86, 203, 237, 82, and 3, the last crossing a neck of the C. The other block, irregular in shape, is largely within the triangle formed by I-84, US 395, and US 26.

Mountainous region of great diversity, elevations ranging from 875 ft. at the Snake River to 9,839 ft. atop Sacajawea Peak. Matterhorn Peak is 9,833 ft. The Wallowa Mountains, a range about 80 mi. long, are high, rugged, snow-capped, granite slopes rising above the timberline, many high lakes. The Forest also includes part of the more extensive Blue Mountains, not quite so high, forested slopes generally more moderate. Along the E border, the Snake River flows through Hells Canyon. Here 662,000 acres, including parts of the Nez Perce and Payette National Forests in ID, became the Hells Canyon National Recreation Area by Act of Congress in 1975.

Climate is as varied as the terrain. Annual precipitation ranges from desert conditions, less than 10 in., to as much as 40 in., including much snow in the high country. Many streams feed the rivers flowing from the Forest, including the Burnt, Grande Ronde, Imnaha, John Day, Lostine, Minam, Powder, and Wallowa.

The Forest is well and favorably known by many backpackers, hunters, and fishermen, as well as skiers, but its distance from large cities limits crowding. The lakes are popular camping places in summer, but anyone who hikes can find as much solitude as he wants.

Plants: Only about half of the region is forested. The balance is a mixture of alpine zone vegetation, barren slopes, grassy meadows, desert plant communities, and riparian fringes. Principal tree species: ponderosa and lodgepole pine, Douglas-fir, white fir, western larch, Engelmann spruce. Great variations of altitude, soils, and moisture produce many different plant communities. More than 500 species have been identified on the lower slopes of Hells Canyon alone. Wildflower displays peak during Apr.–June at low elevations, July–Aug. on high slopes. Among many flowering species: buttercup, lupine, fleabane, western clematis, fawn lily, monkeyflower, penstemon, phacelia, aster, spring beauty, heather, bluebell, phlox, blazing star, arrowleaf balsam root, evening primrose.

Birds: No checklist available. Many habitats indicate wide assortment of species. Those reported include whistling swan, Canada goose, mallard, teals, wood duck, goldeneye, goshawk, golden and bald eagles, prairie falcon, blue grouse, Virginia rail, killdeer, long-billed curlew, spotted sandpiper, avocet, calliope hummingbird, white-headed woodpecker, mountain chickadee, water ouzel, varied and hermit thrushes, vireos, veery, marsh wren; yellow, yellow-rumped, and Townsend's warblers; yellow-breasted chat, Cassin's and gray-crowned rosy finches, pine siskin.

Mammals: No checklist available. Species reported include a few bighorn sheep, mountain goat, mountain lion, seldom seen. Also big brown, little brown, and silver-haired bats; long-tailed weasel, badger, spotted skunk, bobcat, coyote, black bear, beaver, deer mouse, porcupine, pika, snowshoe hare, elk, mule deer.

FEATURES

Hells Canyon National Recreation Area, 662,000 acres in OR and ID, includes the 190,000-acre Hells Canyon Wilderness and the Rapid River (ID) and Snake River segments of the National Wild and Scenic River System. Hells Canyon, cut by the Snake River, is the world's deepest river gorge, averaging 6,600 ft., 20 mi. long. The upper 5 mi. is flooded by Hells Canyon Dam, but the area is now protected against further alterations.

Numerous outfitters offer float and jet boat trips. The floating season is about May 20 to Sept. 10. Private parties who wish to float the river must make reservations and obtain a permit from Hells Canyon National Recreation Area, 2620 B Snake River Ave., Lewiston, ID 83501.

About 5,000 visitors travel the canyon each year by boat, horse, or on foot. This is wild country, and one should know what to expect before setting forth.

S entry into the canyon is from Oxbow, OR, on SR 86, crossing into ID, N to Hells Canyon Dam, across the dam back to OR, the road ending in 1/4 mi. From Enterprise on SR 82, roads lead to the Hat Point Viewpoint, overlooking the canyon. Ask about current road conditions from Imnaha to Hat Point. From Asotin, WA, a 23-mi. gravel road follows the Snake upstream to the Grande Ronde River.

The Wilderness Area, on the OR side, is a strip 4 to 6 mi. wide along the Snake River. This area is roadless. It is surrounded by the larger portion of the Recreation Area, which is penetrated by a few Forest roads. Check conditions before trying them. Many hiking trails in the entire area. Many streams, but purifying tablets are recommended for drinking water; many streams are dry July–Sept. Winter weather in the canyon is usually mild. The high country is usually snow-covered until late spring or early summer.

Eagle Cap Wilderness, 293,735 acres. Generally W and S of Enterprise. Includes the highest peaks of the Wallowa Mountains, more than 50 lakes, many in glacial cirques. The Minam, Lostine, Wallowa, and Imnaha rivers flow from the slopes of Eagle Cap. Fishing is good to excellent; special bag limits apply on some lakes.

The Wilderness map includes a planning chart with 58 destinations, most of them lakes, and information on trail conditions. A mileage chart is also included. Usual season is July 1–Oct. 30, shorter for some of the highest lakes and passes. Saddle and pack horses are used, subject to a few regulations. Wilderness entry points are Forest trails, though in several places a road is less than a mile away.

A 31,300-acre addition to the Wilderness has been proposed, 20 mi. NE of La Grande. The Minam River Gorge enters from the present Wilderness Area and extends NW. Prominent ridges, deep canyons. Heavily forested stream and river bottoms; bare and rocky ridges.

Anthony Lakes Recreation Area lies W of North Powder on I-84. Winter ski area. Summer camping, hiking, fishing, boating. Trail of the Alpine Glacier, 1/2 mi., self-guiding.

Phillips Lake, 2,450 acres, is a popular recreation area: camping, fishing, swimming, boating. *Nature trail,* 1/2 mi.

Wallowa Lake, about the same size, is just outside the Forest boundary, S of Joseph on SR 82. This is one of the gateways to the Forest and Eagle Cap Wilderness. *Wallowa State Park,* on the lake, 166 acres, opens when winter weather ends. 210 campsites. Reservations. Hiking, fishing, swimming, boating. Ramp; boat rentals.

Catherine Creek State Park, 168 acres, is just outside the Forest on SR 203 about 5 mi. SE of Union. 10 primitive campsites. Access to trails and Forest roads.

Elkhorn Drive is a 106-mi. loop road W of Baker, passing through a scenic part of the Forest, various plant communities. A brochure describes highlights of the trip, which includes the Anthony Lakes region and Phillips Lake.

Lostine Canyon Scenic Drive, 18.9 mi., follows the route of an ancient glacier. From Lostine on SR 82. Leaflet available.

ACTIVITIES

Camping: Approximately 60 campgrounds, 461 sites. Earliest opening Apr. 15, some as late as July 1.

Hiking, backpacking: No data, but Forest maps show hundreds of miles of trails, at all altitudes, plus hundreds of miles of little-used Forest roads. The Hells Canyon and Eagle Cap areas are favored by backpackers, but other parts of the Forest are also attractive, including areas accessible earlier in the year.

Hunting: Deer, elk, bear, pheasant, blue and ruffed grouse. Sheep subject to special permit.

Fishing: Brook, rainbow, cutthroat. In the Snake, smallmouth bass, sturgeon, channel catfish.

Swimming: Lakes.

Boating: Chiefly at Phillips, Wallowa, and Anthony lakes, and above Hells Canyon Dam. Rafting on the Snake River in Hells Canyon, with licensed outfitters or by permit. Also floating trips on the Grande Ronde and its upper tributary, the Wallowa, by raft or drift boat. Essential to obtain full information before beginning trip.

Horse riding: Pack trips in the Forest, especially the wilderness areas. Outfitters nearby; ask Forest HQ.

Skiing: Ski area at Anthony Lake. Wallowa Lake offers alpine and cross-country skiing. Gondola to 8,200-ft. Mt. Howard.

Ski touring: No special trails. Many unplowed Forest roads offer opportunities.

Snowmobiling: 850 mi. of signed trails. Users must register. Trail map with information.

PUBLICATIONS

Forest maps, N and S halves. $1.00 each. N half includes Hells Canyon National Recreation Area.

Eagle Cap Wilderness map.

Everything You've Always Wanted to Know About the Hells Canyon National Recreation Area.

Guide to the Common Plants of Hells Canyon.

The Elkhorn Drive, pamphlet.

The Lostine Canyon Scenic Drive, leaflet.

Campground directory.

Floating the Grande Ronde.

Snowmobile Trails, map.

HEADQUARTERS: P.O. Box 907, Baker, OR 97814; (503) 523-6391.

RANGER DISTRICTS: Baker R.D., Rt. 1, Box 1, Pocahontas Rd., Baker, OR 97814; (503) 523-6391, ext. 266. Wallowa Valley R.D., Rt. 1, Box 83, Joseph, OR 97846; (503) 432-2171. La Grande R.D., Rt. 2, Box 2108, La Grande, OR 97850; (503) 963-7186. Pine R.D., Halfway, OR 97834; (503) 742-2361. Union R.D., Star Route, Union, OR 97883; (503) 562-5191.

Unity R.D., P.O. Box 38, Unity, OR 97884; (503) 446-3351. Eagle Cap and Hells Canyon National Recreation Area, P.O. Box 490, Enterprise, OR 97828; (503) 426-3151.

WENAHA WILDLIFE MANAGEMENT AREA
Oregon Department of Fish and Wildlife
10,660 acres.

Difficult road access. SR 3 (Enterprise, Lewiston) to Grande Ronde River. Across river, county road SW to Troy, about 18 mi. Wildlife Area is around Troy, mostly SW.

Elk winter range. The elk move to higher ground about end of May. Present acreage is very irregular in shape; many inholdings. About 8 mi. of joint boundary with Umatilla National Forest; short section of joint boundary with Wenaha-Tucannon Wilderness. About 6 mi. of frontage on Grande Ronde and Wenaha rivers, E and W of Troy. Rivers flow through steep-sided canyons. Climate is semiarid.

Plants: Western juniper with big sagebrush, bluebunch wheatgrass, Idaho fescue. In more humid places, ponderosa pine with Douglas-fir, grand fir, western larch; understory includes sagebrush, bitterbrush, snowberry, spirea.

Birds: Species include great blue heron, Canada goose, mallard, green-winged teal, shoveler, wood duck, common and Barrow's goldeneyes, hooded and common mergansers, goshawk; sharp-shinned, Cooper's, red-tailed, and rough-legged hawks; golden and bald eagles, osprey, blue and ruffed grouse, California quail, chukar, coot, common snipe; screech, flammulated, great horned, pygmy, long-eared, short-eared, and saw-whet owls; black-chinned, rufous, and calliope hummingbirds; pileated, Lewis's, hairy, downy, and white-headed woodpeckers; gray jay, black-capped and mountain chickadees, canyon and rock wrens, bohemian and cedar waxwings, northern and logger-head shrikes; orange-crowned, yellow, yellow-rumped, MacGillivray's, and Wilson's warblers; evening, rose-breasted, black-headed, and pine grosbeaks.

Mammals: Elk, mule deer, white-tailed deer, black bear, mountain lion, bobcat, raccoon, striped skunk, mink, beaver, weasel, badger, Columbian ground squirrel, pine squirrel, marmot.

Reptiles and amphibians: Long-toed salamander, western toad, tree frog, spotted frog, western fence lizard, Pacific gopher snake, rubber snake, mountain and wandering garter snakes, Great Basin rattlesnake.

ACTIVITIES

Camping: Primitive sites. No water.

Fishing: Rainbow, Dolly Varden, whitefish, steelhead, Chinook salmon, largemouth bass.

PUBLICATION: Information sheet with map showing open roads.

HEADQUARTERS: Department of Fish and Wildlife, Rt. 2, Box 2283, La Grande, OR 97850; (503) 963-2138.

ZONE 5

1 Umpqua National Forest
2 Fort Rock State Monument
3 Christmas Valley Area
4 Glass Butte Recreational
   Rockhound Area
5 Winema National Forest
6 Fremont National Forest
7 Rogue River National Forest
8 Zane Grey
9 Rogue Wild and Scenic River
10 Oregon Caves National
   Monument
11 Soda Mountain
12 Klamath Wildlife Area
13 Klamath Forest National
   Wildlife Refuge

14 Sun Pass State Forest
15 Crater Lake National Park
16 Upper Klamath National
   Wildlife Refuge
17 Summer Lake Wildlife Area
18 Diablo Mountain; Wildcat
   Mountain; Coglan Buttes
19 Lake Abert
20 Abert Rim
21 Warner Lakes
22 Hart Mountain National
   Antelope Refuge
23 Spaulding Reservoir

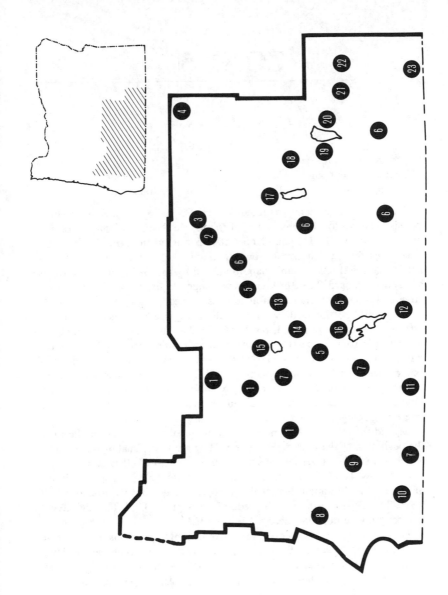

ZONE 5

Includes these counties:

Douglas (except portion on Coast)	Klamath	Josephine
	Lake	Jackson

The W portion of zone 5 is mountainous. On the SW and S are parts of the Siskiyou National Forest. Parts of the Rogue River National Forest are on the S and E. The Umpqua National Forest is on the NE.

I-5 runs through an area of low mountains, hills, and river valleys. On either side are tracts of public land managed by the BLM, but these tracts are a checkerboard. The BLM has a few campgrounds, but we found no sites large and interesting enough to include as entries.

The central portion of the zone straddles the Cascade Range. Most of this area is National Forest land, plus Crater Lake National Park. It includes many peaks from 5,000 to 9,500 ft. high, many rushing streams. Just E of the Park, extending N and S along US 97, is the Klamath Basin, a region of shallow lakes and wetlands, a stopover for some 4 million ducks and geese in migration, nesting grounds for many waterfowl and wading and shorebirds. Upper Klamath Lake is the largest in Oregon. The Basin includes several interesting refuges.

Beyond the mountains of the Fremont National Forest, E of the Basin, is the beginning of the high desert region. Here are many shallow alkali lakes and ephemeral lakes, vestiges of a huge, ancient lake, as well as some productive marshes. The NE portion of the zone has many volcanic features. In the SE is the Hart Mountain National Antelope Refuge, above a dramatic fault scarp. This E part of the zone is predominantly public land. The high desert is mostly public domain, managed by the BLM.

Thus the zone contains a great variety of habitats: elevations from 1,000 to almost 10,000 ft., climates from humid to dry. The zone has alpine meadows, extensive forests, wetlands, rivers, lakes, and sagebrush desert. Terrain includes jagged peaks, sheer fault scarps, rolling hills, canyons, green valleys, and desert flats.

ABERT RIM
U.S. Bureau of Land Management
22,800 acres.

Above US 395 about 25 mi. N of Lakeview.

One of the highest fault scarps in North America, rising some 2,500 ft. above the valley floor, overlooking Lake Abert (see entry). In the Miocene period, lava covered much of E Oregon. Later fractures occurred, and great blocks were tilted. The Rim is the W edge of one block; the lake is atop another.

Above the Rim, terrain is generally flat, sloping slightly to the E. Low basalt cliffs in the SE. An interesting feature is Colvin Timbers, a remnant stand of ponderosa pine. Sagebrush plant community over most of the area, some juniper in the SE. Pronghorn seen occasionally. Area used for grazing; fences, stock reservoirs, vehicle ways.

Most of the area adjoining to the NE is BLM land.

Hiking: Best access to top of Rim is from Fremont National Forest roads leading N from SR 140. Rim extends S into the Forest. Map and local information both needed. The view is exceptional, but the area is otherwise undistinguished.

HEADQUARTERS: Lakeview District, Bureau of Land Management, 1000 Ninth St., Lakeview, OR 97603; (503) 947-2177.

CHRISTMAS VALLEY AREA
U.S. Bureau of Land Management
210,000 acres.

From SR 31 (Lakeview to La Pine) about 18 mi. N of Silver Lake, E on county road to Fort Rock and Christmas Valley.

This entry describes the area generally N of the Valley. From the Valley, BLM roads lead to other parts of the area. Roads to Crack-in-the-Ground, Devils Garden, and Four Craters are usually in good condition. Others may be also, but inquire, especially in wet weather.

High lava plains. Elevations generally above 4,000 ft. Highest point is a 5,585-ft. lava cone. The area is of interest because of its volcanic features, fossil beds, and an unusual forest. Low, rolling terrain with shallow, dry lakebeds. Climate is dry. No permanent lakes or streams. Cool winters, hot summers. Spring and fall are the best hiking seasons.

Plants: Mostly big sagebrush, gray and green rabbitbrush, scattered juniper in the S, moderate to dense juniper with big sagebrush and bitterbrush to the N. Lava-associated plants include penstemon, threadleaf phacelia, woolly groundsel, biennial cinquefoil, western groundsel, Anderson's larkspur, showy townsendia, sulphurflower, sagebrush mariposa, hoary aster. Sand dunes and fossil lake plants include lance-leaved goldenweed, prostrate amaranth, silvery lupine, salt heliotrope, saltgrass; shrubs include greasewood, spiny hopsage, shadscale saltbush.

Birds: Species reported include bald and golden eagles, prairie falcon, rough-legged and red-tailed hawks, loggerhead shrike, pinyon jay, magpie, Brewer's blackbird, red-shafted flicker. Large wintering flocks of robin, mountain bluebird, Townsend's solitaire in juniper woods.

Mammals: Species reported include coast mole, black-tailed and white-tailed jackrabbits, cottontail, kangaroo rat, porcupine, yellow-pine chipmunk, wood rat, deer mouse, Townsend ground squirrel, coyote, mountain lion, bobcat, badger. Winter range for 25,000–40,000 deer.

FEATURES

Devils Garden Lava Bed, 8 mi. NE of Fort Rock. 45 sq. mi. lava flow. S half is rather smooth-surfaced, moderate irregularities. N portion very rugged, difficult walking, some cinder cones. Considerable variety of lava formations. The "garden" is the central area, not lava-covered, with sagebrush, grasses, some juniper. In NE of the area is *Derrick Cave,* a large lava tube, undeveloped.

Squaw Ridge Lava Bed, about 2 1/2 mi. E of the Devils Garden Bed, 12 mi. NE of Fort Rock. Feature is Lava Butte, large peak, surrounded by very rugged terrain.

Four Craters Lava Bed, 9 mi. N of Christmas Valley. Surrounding area has sagebrush flats and low, rolling hills. Craters area, about 5,000 acres, is recent lava flow, extremely rough surface features, with four large spatter cones. *Crack-in-the-Ground* is a unique geological feature, an extensive crack with depths up to 70 ft.

Fossil Beds, E of Christmas Valley. As an ancient lake dried, sand blew off exposing a bog where fossils had been preserved. Over 7,000 acres closed to all vehicles. Fossil collecting prohibited.

Lost Forest, NE of Christmas Valley. A Research Natural Area. Sand blowing into a ponderosa forest appears to have served as a mulch, maintaining an area of forest in a region with a dry climate, generally too dry for such growth. Sand dunes to the W.

ACTIVITIES

Camping: Any suitable place on BLM land. No facilities.

Hiking, backpacking: No trails. Bushwhacking is feasible; country is open with numerous landmarks. Some of the lava beds offer difficult footing. Essential to carry sufficient water.

Hiking in the lava beds is hazardous: rough footing, sharp rocks.
Sand dunes E of Fossil Lake are open to and much used by ORV's.
Advisable to consult BLM office for maps, current information on roads.

NEARBY: Fort Rock State Monument (see entry).

HEADQUARTERS: Lakeview District, Bureau of Land Management, 1000 Ninth St., Lakeview, OR 97603; (503) 947-2177.

CRATER LAKE NATIONAL PARK
U.S. National Park Service
183,180 acres.

From Klamath Falls, N on US 97 and SR 62, 57 mi.

About 6,700 years ago, vast quantities of lava were ejected from Mt. Mazama, leaving a cavity into which the mountaintop collapsed. Rain and snow collected in the cavity, forming a lake of 21 1/2 square miles, 4 1/2 to 6 mi. across, 1,932 ft. deep, one of the world's deepest lakes. A jagged rim surrounds the lake, rising almost vertically 500 to 2,000 ft. above its surface. Back of the rim, the outward slope is gradual.

The main visitor-access route enters from the S. Rim Drive, a 33-mi. auto route, circles the lake. The S and W entrance roads are open all year. Rim Drive and the N entrance road are closed by snow, usually from mid-Oct. to early July. Although the Park has over half a million visitors a year, most are day visitors who arrive at Rim Village, travel all or part of Rim Drive. Few enter the surrounding parklands.

The Park is surrounded by National Forests. Elevations from 4,400 ft. at the S entrance to 8,926 at Mount Scott, a parasitic cone on the E side of Mt. Mazama. Several treeless pumice-covered flats recall past volcanic activity. Most of the Park is heavily forested, open and parklike except in the SE.

The lake has no inflowing streams and no outlet. A number of streams originating on the mountainside drain to the Rogue or Klamath rivers. Most precipitation falls as snow, about 50 ft. per year at Park HQ. Only about 6% of precipitation falls June–Aug. Within the Park, precipitation varies with altitude and location. The E slopes, in rain shadow, are semiarid.

Plants: Four principal plant communities: ponderosa pine forest to about 5,500 ft. elevation; lodgepole pine forest from 5,500 to 6,500 ft.; and mountain hemlock forest to over 8,000 ft. The fourth is pumice desert, treeless except where lodgepole is invading. Each community is a complex of species. In all, about 570 species have been identified within the Park. Common trees are Douglas-fir; Shasta red, noble, white, and subalpine firs; western white, white-bark, and sugar pines; mountain and western hemlock. The many shrubs include willows, alders, California hazel, Sierra evergreen-chinquapin, currants, gooseberries, spireas, thimbleberry, raspberry, Sitka mountain-ash, serviceberry, ceanothus, dogwood, mountainheath, manzanita, snowberry, big sagebrush, rabbitbrush.

Wildflowers include phlox, western pasqueflower, painted-cup, sulphur eriogonum, violets, columbine, monkeyflower, gilia, monkshood, aster, lupine, fireweed, orchids. July and Aug. have best flower displays.

Birds: About 175 species recorded. Checklist available. Several species have declined: golden eagle, bald eagle (no recent sightings), aquatic species generally. Most often seen: Clark's nutcracker, gray jay, Steller's jay. Also common: blue and ruffed grouse, red-tailed hawk, hairy woodpecker, pygmy owl, black-backed three-toed woodpecker, mountain and chestnut-backed chickadees, red-breasted nuthatch, water ouzel, winter wren, kinglets, Cassin's finch, pine siskin, pine grosbeak, Oregon junco, western tanager. Warblers: orange-crowned, Nashville, Audubon's, hermit, MacGillivray's, Wilson's.

Mammals: Checklist available. Common species include vagrant shrew, shrew-mole, little brown myotis, big brown bat, black bear, marten, long-tailed weasel, badger, coyote, red fox, yellow-bellied marmot, golden-mantled squirrel, Townsend chipmunk, chickaree, deer mouse, long-tailed vole, porcupine, pika, snowshoe hare, elk, mule deer.

Reptiles and amphibians: Checklist available. Often seen: long-toed salamander, boreal toad, Pacific tree frog, Cascades frog. Valley garter snake is only snake reported.

FEATURES

Five *wilderness areas,* totaling about 70% of the Park's acreage, were proposed. This is most of the parkland away from the crater and rim, except for access corridors.

Rim Village is the center of visitor activity: overlooks, visitor center, shops, services. Gasoline is available in summer only.

Sand Creek–Pinnacles Area, in SE corner, extends into adjacent National Forest. Wide canyon with sloping walls of scoria and pumice. Branch road from Rim Drive.

Garfield Peak, 8,060 ft., reached by 1.7-mi. trail along the rim wall.

The Watchman, 8,025 ft., also offers sweeping vistas. On W side of rim, reached by 0.8-mi. trail.

Cloudcap, 8,070 ft., E side of rim, can be reached by auto, short spur road.

Castle Crest Wildflower Garden, near Park HQ, has species found in the Park.

Sphagnum Bog and *Boundary Springs* are among several unique ecological areas. Because they are fragile, they have been given special protection. Botanists and others with serious interest may inquire.

INTERPRETATION

Visitor center at Rim Village. At Sinnott Memorial Overlook, *frequent talks by rangers.*

Information counter at Park HQ.

33-mi. Rim Road has many wayside *exhibits and overlooks.*
Nature trails at Castle Crest Wildflower Garden and near Mazama Camp-
ground. Also Godfrey Glen Nature Trail.
Boat trips on Crater Lake include talks by rangers.
Evening programs at Rim Center Building and Mazama Campground,
summer months.

ACTIVITIES
Camping: Mazama Campground, 198 sites, mid-June to end of Sept., snow
permitting. Lost Creek: 12 primitive sites.
Hiking, backpacking: 65 mi. of trails, including 26 mi. of Pacific Crest
Trail, which crosses the Park. Many short hikes, easy to moderate. Backcoun-
try travel is very light, partly because of the short season. Estimate for a recent
year: 2,000 overnight visits.
Fishing is permitted but not popular. Stocking the lake has been discon-
tinued.
Ski touring: Ski touring in the area around Park HQ has been increasing.
Cafeteria and curio shop are open in winter.
Snowmobiling: Restricted to N entrance road, which is not plowed.

ADJACENT: Umpqua, Winema, and Rogue River National Forests (see entries, zone 5).

PUBLICATIONS
Leaflet with map.
The Origin of Crater Lake (2 pp., mimeo).
Checklists: trees, birds, mammals, amphibians and reptiles.
Snowshoeing, ski touring, and winter camping information.
Fishing information.

REFERENCES
Kirk, Ruth. *Exploring Crater Lake.* Seattle: University of Washington
Press.
The Crater Lake Natural History Association, c/o Crater Lake National
Park, offers a list of publications on Park history, geology, fauna and
flora.

HEADQUARTERS: P.O. Box 7, Crater Lake, OR 97604; (503) 594-2211.

DIABLO MOUNTAIN; WILDCAT MOUNTAIN; COGLAN BUTTES
U.S. Bureau of Land Management
333,360 acres.

NE of SR 31 between Lake Abert and Summer Lake. Access from local
roads NE from Paisley and E from town of Summer Lake.

High desert. The two lakes, now 25 mi. apart, were once part of a large lake. Both are shallow, too alkaline for fish, with extensive saltflats exposed in dry seasons. From Summer Lake, the land rises gradually to the E. Mt. Diablo, at 6,145 ft., is part of a N–S rim, the E edge dropping vertically 1,800 ft. Other high points in the area: Wildcat Mountain, 5,560 ft.; Tough Peak, 5,625 ft.; Euchre Butte, 5,315 ft.; Coglan Buttes, 6,207 ft. Most of the area is relatively flat; some low, rolling hills; many shallow, ephemeral lake basins. Several fault block ridges with steep escarpments, basalt rims. Sand dunes near Summer Lake.

Parts of the area are grazed, and ranchers have established a few small watering places. Hikers must bring all the water they need. Spring and fall are the best hiking times.

The area is crossed by a number of BLM roads. For information on road conditions and available maps, check the BLM office.

Mt. Diablo, E of Summer Lake, is surrounded by a 113,000-acre roadless area proposed for wilderness status. Few hikers or backpackers enter this harsh area. These few favor the Diablo Rim, chiefly for its sweeping vistas.

Plants: Near the two lakes, salt-tolerant species such as saltgrass, shadscale, greasewood, spiny hopsage, bud sage, Indian ricegrass, desert paintbrush, seablite, showy townsendia, hoary aster, common cryptantha, hairy evening-primrose. Between the lakes: sagebrush, rabbitbrush, squirreltail, needlegrass, death camas, Anderson's larkspur, specklepod milk-vetch.

Birds: Nesting golden eagle; prairie falcon, kestrel, red-tailed hawk. Around Coglan Buttes, sparse, scattered nests of burrowing and short-eared owls. For water and shorebirds of the lakes, see entries for Summer Lake Wildlife Area and Lake Abert.

Mammals: Sparse herds of deer and pronghorn. Deer mice, voles, wood-rats, rabbit. Wild horse sometimes seen in N of area.

HEADQUARTERS: Lakeview District, Bureau of Land Management, 1000 Ninth St., Lakeview, OR 97603; (503) 947-2177.

FORT ROCK STATE MONUMENT
Oregon Parks and Recreation Division
190 acres.

From US 97 near La Pine, about 26 mi. SE, then 7 mi. E on county road to Fort Rock.

One of OR's most spectacular geological features, an unusual crater known as a *tuff ring.* Almost 1/2 mi. in diameter, 325 ft. above base at highest point. Surrounded by sagebrush flats.

NEARBY: Christmas Valley Area (see entry).

FREMONT NATIONAL FOREST
U.S. Forest Service
1,196,351 acres; 1,710,750 acres within boundaries.

Two areas. (1) W of Lakeview, from the CA border to SR 31 near junction with US 97. (2) E of Lakeview, N and S of SR 140.

The Forest land includes over 100 fragments of less than 1 sq. mi., as well as several large blocks. Although the blocks include numerous inholdings, these do not obstruct visitor activities. On the Forest boundaries are the Deschutes and Winema National Forests, the Modoc National Forest in CA, and much BLM land.

Generally rolling terrain with numerous mountain peaks, on the E side of the Cascade Mountains. Elevations from 4,150 ft. to Crane Mountain, 8,454 ft. Precipitation averages 22 in. per year, with considerable variation depending on location and elevation. Dry summers. Substantial snowfall on the high slopes. Forest roads in the high country may be closed by snow Dec. 1–May 1.

Part of the W area is close to Summer Lake (see entry for Summer Lake Wildlife Area). Here forested slopes rise from the lakeshore to Winter Ridge, looking out over the lake and surrounding desert. This pattern is common to the region: timbered slopes rising from sagebrush flatland.

The E portion includes the S part of Abert Rim (see entry), highest fault scarp in the United States. A Forest road leads to a dramatic viewpoint overlooking Lake Abert.

Although most of the site is forested, it includes some meadows and high semidesert. Numerous small streams carry off snowmelt. Largest are the Sprague, Chewaucan, and Sycan rivers. Thompson Reservoir, 2,600 acres, is the largest body of water, a recreation area. Dog Lake, 491 acres, is the only other lake of more than 100 acres, but the Forest includes many smaller ones.

Plants: 85% forested. Three principal forest types: ponderosa pine, mixed conifer, lodgepole. Prominent tree species include ponderosa and lodgepole pines, white fir, incense cedar. Remaining old-growth stands are about 3%–5% of the total. Understory species include bitterbrush, sagebrush, currant. In sites not forested: juniper, low sage, fescues, bluegrasses. Flowering species include arrowhead balsamroot, aster, bleeding heart, fireweed, foxglove, clarkia, penstemon, phacelia, spreading phlox, twinflower, western yarrow. Plant checklists available.

Birds: 176 species recorded. Checklist available. 85 species are all-year residents. Species listed include grebes, white pelican; great blue, green, and black-crowned night herons; American bittern, whistling swan; Canada, white-fronted, snow, and Ross's geese; many ducks, goshawk; sharp-shinned, Cooper's, red-tailed, Swainson's, rough-legged, and ferruginous hawks;

golden and bald eagles; blue, ruffed, and sage grouse; 8 owl species, all woodpeckers found in the region; gray, Steller's, and scrub jays; varied and hermit thrushes, both kinglets; purple, Cassin's, house, and gray-crowned rosy finches. Warblers listed include orange-crowned, Nashville, yellow, yellow-rumped, black-throated gray, MacGillivray's, Wilson's.

Mammals: Checklist of 67 species available. Includes numerous shrews and bats, pika, white-tailed and black-tailed jackrabbits, marmot; California and Belding ground squirrels, golden-mantled squirrels; various mice and rats, porcupine, black bear, marten, fisher, long-tailed weasel, mink, badger, mountain lion, bobcat, elk, mule deer, pronghorn.

Reptiles and amphibians: 22 species said to be present, but no checklist.

FEATURES

Gearhart Mountain Wilderness, 18,709 acres. At 8,354 ft., Gearhart Mountain is the highest of many volcanic domes in western Lake County. Cirques and U-shaped valleys are the marks of vanished glaciers. Picturesque rock formations cap most of the ridgetops, which offer sweeping vistas. High mountain meadows. Lower, lodgepole pine forests and mixed ponderosa pine–white fir forests. Blue Lake is the only lake in the area.

A single 12-mi. trail with a 4-mi. spur crosses the wilderness, along the ridge, dropping down to Blue Lake. The terrain and open forests make bushwhacking feasible. (Snow drifts on the trail persist until mid-June or early July.) Terrain and snow cover favor ski touring and snowshoeing in winter, but access roads are likely to be blocked by snow. Saddle and pack horses are subject to special rules.

Crane Mountain roadless area, 23,396 acres, is near the CA border. Crane Mountain, 8,454 ft., is the highest point in the Forest. Other roadless areas, 4,114 acres to 13,615 acres, were identified in the RARE II process. Although none were recommended for wilderness status, they offer hiking opportunities. The Forest Service officer who reviewed this entry cautioned that these areas may not remain roadless after the Forest Plan is adopted in 1984. Consult Forest HQ or Ranger Districts.

North Warner Viewpoint, overlooking Crooked Creek Canyon, is on the same Forest road leading to the Abert Rim Viewpoint, mentioned earlier.

Scenic drive: Forest Road 290, along Winter Ridge, overlooking Summer Lake. Access from SR 31 N of Summer Lake (turning S) or from SR 31 via Forest Road 3313 near the S end of Summer Lake.

ACTIVITIES

Camping: 19 campgrounds. 181 sites. May 15–Oct. 15.

Hiking, backpacking: The Forest reports only 27 mi. of trails. However, it has 6,000 mi. of roads, most of them unpaved and little used. Also, most forest areas are open, inviting off-trail travel.

Hunting: Chiefly mule deer, blue grouse.

Fishing: 395 mi. of fishing streams. Brook and rainbow trout. Also lakes with bass, perch, catfish.

Boating: Power boats on Thompson Reservoir. 5 mph limit on Dog Lake. No motors on other lakes.

Canoeing: Lakes only. Canoe camping on Dead Horse Lake.

Horse riding: Some use of horses, but no nearby outfitters.

Skiing: Ski area on summit of Warner Mountain. Usual season Dec.–Mar.

Ski touring: On unplowed roads, suitable trails. Usual season Jan 1.–Apr. 15.

Snowmobiling: Forest reports about 90 mi. of suitable trails, not groomed.

PUBLICATIONS

Forest map. $1.00.

Gearhart Mountain Wilderness map.

List of recreation sites.

HEADQUARTERS: P.O. Box 551, Lakeview, OR 97630; (503) 947-2151.

RANGER DISTRICTS: Bly R.D., Bly, OR 97622; (503) 353-2427. Lakeview R.D., Lakeview, OR 97630; (503) 947-3334. Paisley R.D., Paisley, OR 97636; (503) 943-3114. Silver Lake R.D., Silver Lake, OR 97638; (503) 576-2503.

GLASS BUTTE RECREATIONAL ROCKHOUND AREA

U.S. Bureau of Land Management

10,911 acres.

10 mi. SE of Hampton on S side of US 20.

Dominant feature is pyramidal Glass Butte, elevation 6,385 ft., about 1,500 ft. above surrounding land. To NW and E are several canyons extending from Glass Butte, forming steep-sloped valleys and low, rolling hills with massive reddish-brown and gray basaltic outcroppings and boulders. Vegetation here: clusters of juniper, mountain mahogany, willow, big sage, rabbitbrush. Below the W and S slopes of the Butte, lower rolling hills with stands of juniper. Smaller N–S canyons to the S. Indians gathered obsidian here, and rockhounds still do. Site includes miles of fencing and ways, cattle troughs, reservoirs, a microwave station atop the Butte.

HEADQUARTERS: Prineville District, Bureau of Land Management, 185 E 4th St., Prineville, OR 97754; (503) 447-4115.

HART MOUNTAIN NATIONAL ANTELOPE REFUGE

U.S. Fish and Wildlife Service

275,000 acres.

From Lakeview, 5 mi. N on US 395. E about 16 mi. on SR 140, then NE 19 mi. on county road to Plush. Follow signs 25 mi. NE to HQ. (Also see note on alternate routes, cautions.)

One of the most unusual wildlife refuges. Remote, with relatively few visitors, but usually accessible by any auto in good condition. Massive fault block ridge. W side is a scenic, rugged escarpment rising 3,600 ft. above the Warner Lakes (see entry); cliffs, steep slopes, knife ridges. Several canyons extend from the valley floor to the ridgetop. Entrance road passes roadless canyons well worth exploring. Highest point is Warner Peak, 8,065 ft. E side descends gradually in series of hills and low ridges.

Somewhat surprisingly, the area has a number of reliable springs, cold and "hot." Rock Creek flows from the NE, emerging from a deep canyon onto open range near HQ. Other creeks rise on S end of mountain, flowing S and E.

Refuge was established to provide spring, summer, and fall range for pronghorn, most of which move S to the Charles Sheldon Antelope Range (NV) in winter. Mission has been expanded to include all high desert wildlife.

Entire Refuge is open to foot and horse travel. One of the few federal Refuges that has a campground and that permits trailside camping.

Plants: Mostly sagebrush community. An exhibit shows native plants important to wildlife: bluebunch wheatgrass, Thurber's needlegrass, squirreltail grass, Sandberg bluegrass, Indian ricegrass, Idaho fescue, wild buckwheat, low sagebrush, big sagebrush, bitterbrush. Isolated stands of juniper, aspen, some old-growth ponderosa. Colorful wildflower display in early summer.

Birds: Checklist of 213 species includes records from nearby Warner Lakes, a noted birding area. Seasonally common or abundant high desert species include turkey vulture; red-tailed, Swainson's, and rough-legged hawks; golden eagle, sage grouse (several strutting grounds), California quail, killdeer, mourning dove, great horned and short-eared owls, poor-will, nighthawk, red-shafted flicker, western kingbird, ash-throated flycatcher, Say's phoebe, Hammond's flycatcher, western wood pewee, horned lark, barn and cliff swallows, magpie, raven, common crow, black-capped and mountain chickadees, white-breasted nuthatch, canyon wren, robin, mountain bluebird, Townsend's solitaire, kinglets, northern shrike, yellow-breasted chat, meadowlark, western tanager, evening grosbeak, goldfinch, rufous-sided towhee, lark and sage sparrows.

Mammals: Include pronghorn, mule deer, bighorn sheep, coyote, wild horse, ground squirrel, kangaroo rat, yellow-bellied marmot, bobcat.

INTERPRETATION: *Information* is best obtained at the HQ in Lakeview. The field HQ is often unmanned.

ACTIVITIES

Camping: One campground open whenever the Refuge is accessible, 3 others during deer hunt. All primitive.

Hiking, backpacking: No trails, but cross-country hiking is said to be excellent, especially along Poker Jim Ridge to NE and on Warner Mountain to S. Permit required for overnighting.

Hunting: Pronghorn, mule deer, bighorn. Special regulations; inquire.

Fishing: Small streams, lake. Trout, crappie, bullhead, catfish.

Horse riding: Horse travel is permitted, but no special facilities or nearby stable.

Sometimes inaccessible in winter. Roads often closed because of muddy and hazardous conditions in spring. Nearest gasoline and telephone at Plush. Refuge may be unmanned.

NEARBY: Largely surrounded by BLM land. In dry weather, other routes shown on OR's official highway map are interesting. One leads NE from field HQ to Frenchglen, another S to SR 140 near Guano Lake. Don't try either without local advice.

PUBLICATIONS

Leaflet with map.
Bird checklist.
Native plant notes.
Public use regulations with map.

HEADQUARTERS: P.O. Box 111, Lakeview, OR 97630; (503) 947-3315.

KLAMATH FOREST NATIONAL WILDLIFE REFUGE
U.S. Fish and Wildlife Service
16,376 acres.

From US 97 about 45 mi. N of Klamath Falls, E 6 mi. on Silver Lake Rd.

Large natural marsh, an important nesting area for greater sandhill crane and waterfowl. The road crosses the marsh, and an unimproved side road goes S along the E side of the Refuge to Wocus Bay, where pelicans are sometimes seen. Birders say there's not much action here until June but much to see then and through August.

Birds: Most waterfowl species found at other Klamath Basin refuges are seen here, though not in such large numbers as at the Lower Klamath and Tule Lake units of the Klamath Basin complex (CA). Unlike these units, the Klamath Forest Refuge includes habitat for ruffed grouse, osprey; long-eared, spotted, great gray, pygmy, saw-whet, and screech owls; white-headed wood-pecker, Williamson's sapsucker. Red-necked grebe sometimes seen in road-side ditches.

Hunting: Designated area. Inquire.

NEARBY: Winema National Forest (see entry). Silver Lake Road continues into the Forest. The Klamath Marsh extends about 8 mi. NE of the Refuge. This is private land, but the Winema National Forest map shows several local roads that might reward exploration.

PUBLICATIONS
Refuge map.
Klamath Basin National Wildlife Refuges leaflet (CA map only).
Bird checklist.
Beginners Check List.

HEADQUARTERS: Klamath Basin National Wildlife Refuges, Route 1, Box 74, Tulelake, CA 96134; (916) 667-2231.

KLAMATH WILDLIFE AREA
Oregon Department of Fish and Wildlife
3,390 acres.

6 mi. S of Klamath Falls on Miller Island Rd.

On the Klamath River. Not a large refuge but, given its strategic point in the Klamath Basin, an important flyway. Midway between the Upper Klamath and Lower Klamath National Wildlife Refuges (see entries).

Five habitat types: farmland, marshland, potholes, saltgrass flats, and dry brushlands. Elevation 4,100 ft. 1,700 acres of wetland. Best time to visit is usually Apr.–May, when refuge serves as breeding, nesting, and rest area for migrants. Fall peak: late Oct.–early Nov.

Birds: Checklist available. Seasonally abundant and common species include eared and western grebes, white pelican, double-crested cormorant, great blue heron, great egret, black-crowned night heron, American bittern, whistling swan, Canada goose, lesser Canada goose, white-fronted and snow geese, mallard, gadwall, pintail, blue-winged and cinnamon teals, wigeon, shoveler, redhead, canvasback, lesser scaup, common goldeneye, bufflehead, ruddy duck, common merganser, red-tailed and marsh hawks, bald eagle, kestrel, pheasant, coot, killdeer, common snipe, spotted sandpiper, willet, greater yellowlegs, least sandpiper, dunlin, long-billed dowitcher, avocet, black-necked stilt, Wilson's phalarope; California, ring-billed, and Bona-parte's gulls; Forster's, Caspian, and black terns; mourning and rock doves, rufous hummingbird, barn owl, common flicker, western kingbird, horned lark; tree, barn, and cliff swallows; long-billed marsh wren, yellow-rumped warbler, meadowlark; red-winged, yellow-headed, and tricolored blackbirds; evening grosbeak, house finch, goldfinch; savannah, vesper, lark, and sage sparrows.

Mammals: Common species include mule deer, coyote, striped skunk, muskrat, black-tailed jackrabbit, cottontail, yellow-bellied marmot, Belding ground squirrel, harvest mouse, mountain vole, Pacific shrew, little brown bat.

Reptiles and amphibians: Include common and Klamath garter snakes, northwestern pond turtle, spotted frog.

PUBLICATIONS
Area Map.
Species checklist.

HEADQUARTERS: Region II, Department of Fish and Wildlife, 3140 NE Stephens St., Roseburg, OR 97470; (503) 440-3353.

LAKE ABERT
U.S. Bureau of Land Management

On US 395 about 25 mi. N of Lakeview.

A visitor unfamiliar with this region wonders why so large and scenic a lake is unused, no shoreline development, no boats in sight. The extensive flats are a clue. The lake, once part of a far larger body of water, is shallow and too alkaline for fish. Brine shrimp and other organisms attract shorebirds, and birding along the shore is rewarding in winter and spring: swans, waterfowl, occasional gang-feeding by pelicans from Warner Valley. Eared grebe, ruddy duck on the lake all year except midwinter. Marshes to the N, reached by a county road, are also lively. Further N on US 395, about 4 mi. S of Wagontire, a small lake at the roadside was well populated in Aug.: Canada goose, Wilson's phalarope, avocet, killdeer—and a golden eagle wading at the edge.

The highway beside Lake Abert is at the foot of the Abert Rim (see entry), one of the highest fault scarps in the United States. Roadside parking is scarce along the shore, especially to the N.

OREGON CAVES NATIONAL MONUMENT
U.S. National Park Service
480 acres.
Within Siskiyou National Forest (see entry, zone 1).

SW OR. From Cave Junction on US 199, 20 mi. SE on SR 46.

Feature is Marble Cave, a complex of chambers and passageways, dripstone and flowstone calcite formations. A 75-min. conducted tour climbs from the entrance at 4,020 ft. elevation to exit at 4,238 ft.

Above ground, mountainous forested terrain. Annual precipitation about 60 in.; wet winters, dry summers. Surrounding is a disjunct portion of the Siskiyou National Forest, E of US 199, which adjoins a disjunct portion of the Rogue River National Forest, both on the CA border, in the Siskiyou Mountains.

Plants: Checklist available. Site is entirely forested, a transition zone between forest types. Below 4,000 ft. is a mixed broadleaf-conifer forest: Douglas-fir and a few pines with tan oak, canyon live oak, Pacific madrone, bigleaf maple, golden chinquapin, rhododendron, manzanita. Higher is all conifers, Douglas-fir up to 6-ft. diameter, white fir, Port Orford cedar, incense cedar. Some virgin stands of Douglas-fir, largest specimen 12-ft. diameter, 182 ft. tall. Many flowering species including bleeding heart, inside-out flower, twinflower, bluebell, yarrow, pearly everlasting, St. Johnswort, fawn lily, Pacific trillium, rattlesnake plantain. Eight orchid species. Sword-, bracken, and lady ferns. Mosses, alumroot, many lichens.

Birds: Checklist available. Prominent are Steller's and gray jays, Clark's nutcracker. Also seen: turkey vulture; sharp-shinned, Cooper's, and red-tailed hawks; golden eagle, kestrel, blue and ruffed grouse, mountain quail, band-tailed pigeon, mourning dove; screech, great horned, long-eared, and saw-whet owls; pileated, hairy, Lewis's, and white-headed woodpeckers; mountain and chestnut-backed chickadees, white-breasted and red-breasted nuthatches, water ouzel, brown creeper; varied, hermit, and Swainson's thrushes; mountain bluebird, golden-crowned and ruby-crowned kinglets, Hutton's and warbling vireos. Warblers: orange-crowned, yellow-rumped, Nashville, black-throated gray, Townsend's, hermit, MacGillivray's, Wilson's. Also western tanager, black-headed and evening grosbeaks, lazuli bunting, pine siskin, green-tailed and rufous-sided towhees, Oregon junco; chipping, white-crowned, golden-crowned, fox, and song sparrows.

Mammals: Checklist available. Abundant or common species include chickaree, California and golden-mantled squirrels, Townsend chipmunk, western gray squirrel, white-footed mouse, bushy-tailed woodrat, California red-backed vole. Other species occurring in National Forest, such as black bear, occasionally enter the Monument.

INTERPRETATION

Information station near entrance. *Naturalist* on site Mar.–Sept. For programs, check at Ranger Station.

Guided tours every day except Christmas. *Note: Children under 6 not*

*permitted in cave. Cave tour not recommended for people with heart, breathing,
or walking difficulties: 550 steps; some long narrow passages.*
  Guided hikes by request.
  Cliff Nature Trail, self-guiding, about 45 min.

ACTIVITIES
  Hiking: 10 mi. of trails within the Monument. No Name Trail, 1.1 mi.,
passes mountain streams, mossy cliffs, dense forest. Big Tree Trail, 3 mi., to
virgin forest. Connecting trails into National Forest. *Snowshoes usually
needed winter and spring.*

  Pets are not permitted in cave or buildings or on trails.
  *Last 8 mi. of SR 46 narrow, winding. Trailers not recommended. Trailer
parking limited in summer.*

PUBLICATIONS
  Leaflet with map.
  Species checklists.
  Discovery Map.

HEADQUARTERS: 19000 Caves Highway, Cave Junction, OR 97523. Telephone: Toll Station 2 through Portland, OR operator.

ROGUE RIVER NATIONAL FOREST
U.S. Forest Service
638,259 acres, including 54,016 acres in CA.

  In two principal blocks, from the N and W boundaries of Crater Lake
National Park to and across the CA border. Crossed by SRs 230, 62, 140.
S block is just W of I-5.

The larger block, about 2/3 of the Forest, is in the Cascade Mountains, on
the N, W, and S boundaries of Crater Lake National Park, extending S along
the boundary of the Winema National Forest. On the NW it adjoins the
Umpqua National Forest. Highest point is 9,495-ft. Mt. McLoughlin, lowest
about 2,500 ft. The smaller block is in the Siskiyou Mountains and adjoins
the Siskiyou National Forest on the W. Highest peak is Mt. Ashland, 7,533
ft.; many peaks in the range are over 1 mi. high. The two blocks are about
25 mi. apart.

The N block is a high plateau with deep canyons, sloping W, many small streams gathering to form the Rogue River. Visitors who enter or leave the National Park by the W entrance can see spectacular sections of the Rogue River Gorge along SR 62.

Annual precipitation is moderate, ranging from 20 to 40 in., most of it Oct.–Mar., much as snow in the higher elevations. Snow usually limits access to the high country until mid-July. Summers are warm and dry, with occasional thunderstorms. The climate supports a dense forest of Douglas-fir and sugar pine. Alpine meadows occur on many high slopes.

The most accessible and popular lakes are Fish (350 acres), Willow (300 acres), Applegate (988 acres), and Squaw (45 acres). Many smaller lakes, chiefly in the Sky Lakes region, are reached only on foot or horseback.

Plants: About 90% forested: Douglas-fir, sugar pine, other conifers, including ponderosa and western white pine, white fir, incense cedar, western and mountain hemlocks, Shasta red fir. Associated in various habitats: bigleaf and vine maples, madrone, golden chinquapin, Oregon white oak. Understory species include western hazel, Oregon boxwood, baldhip rose, big huckleberry, western prince's pine, deerfoot vanillaleaf, Oregon grape, whitevein pyrola, slender-tubed iris, starflower, sedges. On rock outcrops and scree slopes: squawcarpet, pine-mat manzanita, western groundsel, collomia, great houndstongue, larkspur. Species in open meadows include false hellebore, fawn lily, spring beauty. The E–W-oriented Siskiyou Mountains are well known to botanists because they contain numerous rare and endangered species.

Birds: No checklist available. Some waterfowl and shorebirds occur at various lakes. Upland species reported include golden and bald eagles; sharp-shinned, Cooper's, red-tailed and rough-legged hawks; blue grouse, California and mountain quail, band-tailed pigeon, rock and mourning doves; screech, great horned, pygmy, short-eared, northern spotted, saw-whet, and snowy owls; Vaux's swift; rufous and Anna's hummingbirds; pileated, hairy, downy, and Lewis's woodpeckers; western kingbird; Traill's, Hammond's western, dusky, olive-sided, and ash-throated flycatchers; violet-green, tree, bank, rough-winged, barn, and cliff swallows; hermit, Swainson's, and varied thrushes; Bohemian and cedar waxwings. Warblers: orange-crowned, Nashville, yellow, yellow-rumped, Townsend's, MacGillivray's, common yellowthroat.

Mammals: No checklist available except for Abbot Creek Research Natural Area. Species reported for the Forest include black bear, mountain lion, bobcat, mule deer, elk, mink, long-tailed weasel, marten, fisher, raccoon, western spotted skunk, gray fox, coyote, mountain beaver, snowshoe hare, pika, porcupine, Townsend chipmunk, chickaree, northern flying squirrel.

FEATURES

The Forest map includes a new feature: a small map with sections in 5 colors, keyed to indicate degrees of isolation. The most isolated areas are on the boundaries shared with the Umpqua National Forest, Crater Lake National Park, Winema National Forest, and Siskiyou National Forest.

Sky Lakes Area, 107,900 acres, including 38,900 acres in the Winema National Forest. About 6 mi. wide, 27 mi. long, extending S from the National Park, straddling the Southern Cascades. Elevations from 3,800 to 9,495 ft. More than 200 lakes and ponds, the largest, Fourmile Lake, in the Winema. All motorized equipment is prohibited, and motorized vehicles are barred from trails leading into the area. Includes 35 mi. of the Pacific Crest Trail. Many side trails. Drinking water is scarce. Travelers should study the descriptive folder before entering the area.

Mazama Flats wilderness, 9,200 acres, including acreage in the Umpqua National Forest. On the N boundary of Crater Lake National Park, adjoining a wilderness area in the Park. Elevations from 5,000 to 6,200 ft. Includes a major part of the Rogue River headwaters, the deep canyon of Upper Mazama Creek, and Lake West.

Red Butte wilderness, 25,900 acres, including acreage in the Klamath and Siskiyou National Forests. Straddles the Siskiyou Mountains at the CA border. Terrain is highly dissected, steep slopes, scenic. Mosaic of meadows, brushfields, dense forest, rocky areas.

Red Blanket wilderness, 5,100 acres, on the W boundary of Crater Lake National Park, adjoining a wild area within the Park. On the SW flank of Mount Mazama. Elevations from 3,800 to 6,000 ft.; no prominent peak. N section includes Thousand Springs. S end terminates at walls of Red Blanket Canyon. Lower part of the canyon is prime winter range for elk, deer.

Sphagnum Bog wilderness, 6,800 acres, adjoins NW side of the National Park, wild area within the Park. It is separated from the Red Blanket wilderness only by SR 62. Also on the lower slopes of Mt. Mazama. Includes the 680-acre Sphagnum Bog Special Interest Scenic Area.

INTERPRETATION

Visitor center at Union Creek, on SR 62. *Nature trail* at Mammoth Pines, on SR 62.

Theater in the Woods at Union Creek campground has an exceptional schedule of summer weekend evening programs, featuring well-known speakers. Also weekend plant walks. Notices posted.

ACTIVITIES

Camping: 26 campgrounds, 408 sites. Most are open July–Sept.

Hiking, backpacking: 450 mi. of trails. In addition to Pacific Crest Trail, many lead into high country, to secluded lakes, into adjoining National Forests and the National Park. Trail guides available; see Publications.

Hunting: Deer, elk.

Fishing: The Rogue is a famous fishing stream. Other streams, lakes. Rainbow trout, steelhead.

Swimming: Mostly at Squaw Lakes and Applegate Lake. Others are cold.

Boating: Fish Lake, Applegate Lake. 10 mph limit. The sections of the Rogue suitable for rafting and kayaking are outside the Forest, downstream.

Horse riding: Most pack trips are in Sky Lakes Area and to Siskiyou Crest. For outfitters, ask Klamath Falls and Medford Chambers of Commerce.

Skiing: Commercial area at Mt. Ashland. Usual season: Dec.–Mar.

Ski touring: About 100 mi. of suitable trails.

Snowmobiling: About 150 mi. of suitable trails.

ADJACENT OR NEARBY

Crater Lake National Park.

Umpqua and Winema National Forests (zone 6).

Siskiyou National Forest (zone 1).

Klamath National Forest (in CA)

PUBLICATIONS

Forest map. $1.00.

Sky Lakes Users Guide, map.

Upper Rogue River Recreation Trails, booklet of maps and trail guides.

Mammoth Pines Nature Trail, guide.

Gin Lin Trail, historical trail guide.

HEADQUARTERS: P.O. Box 250, Medford, OR 97501; (503) 776-3579.

RANGER DISTRICTS: Ashland R.D., 2200 Highway 66, Ashland, OR 97520; (503) 482-3333. Applegate R.D., 6941 Upper Applegate Rd., Jacksonville, OR 97530; (503) 899-1812. Butte Falls R.D., P.O. Box 227; Butte Falls, OR 97522; (503) 865-3581. Prospect R.D., Prospect, OR 97536; (503) 560-3623.

ROGUE WILD AND SCENIC RIVER

See entry in zone 1.

SODA MOUNTAIN

U.S. Bureau of Land Management

5,640 acres.

18 mi. SE of Ashland, near CA border, E of I-5, S of SR 66. On Schohiem Rd., not shown on highway maps. Local information or consult BLM office.

Pacific Crest Trail borders NW portion. Very steep terrain, from 2,800 to 5,700 ft. Camp, Dutch Oven, and Salt creeks run through the site. Mixed conifers and hardwoods; extensive, dense brushfields; some open, grassy slopes. Surrounded largely by other BLM and private timberlands.

The BLM considers the area outstanding for backpacking, camping, horseback riding, wildlife observation, says that the site has great botanical diversity, abundant water, scenic vistas.

Birds: Species reported include Cooper's, sharp-shinned, and red-tailed hawks; golden eagle, kestrel, wild turkey, blue and ruffed grouse, California and mountain quail; screech, great horned, long-eared, and pygmy owls; pileated, acorn, Lewis's, hairy, and downy woodpeckers; ash-throated, dusky, and western flycatchers; horned lark; black-capped, mountain, and chestnut-backed chickadees; dipper; white-breasted, red-breasted, and pygmy nuthatches; Townsend's solitaire; orange-crowned, yellow, yellow-rumped, black-throated gray, MacGillivray's, and Wilson's warblers; purple, Cassin's, and house finches; green, rufous-sided, and brown towhees.

Mammals: Include vagrant and Trowbridge shrews, broad-handed and shrew moles, brush rabbit, black-tailed jackrabbit, California ground and golden-mantled squirrels, yellow pine and Siskiyou chipmunks, chickaree, beaver, porcupine, gray fox, coyote, black bear, raccoon, ringtail, long-tailed weasel, striped skunk, bobcat, mule deer.

HEADQUARTERS: Medford District, Bureau of Land Management, 3040 Biddle Rd., Medford, OR 97501; (503) 779-2351.

SPAULDING RESERVOIR
U.S. Bureau of Land Management
65,720 acres.

18 mi. E of Adel on SR 140. Also on BLM roads.

Variety of terrain. Site is narrow at S end, on SR 140 near NV border, broadens considerably to N. N–S distance about 18 mi. S portion a broad sage flat above Guano Rim, a 450-ft. fault scarp running N–S in W portion for about 12 mi. Rolling topography in central portion. Sage Hen Canyon begins as a small drainage in the S, deepens in 5 mi. to Spaulding Reservoir. N and NE portions contain broken rims, plateaus. Site contains 20 ephemeral lakebeds.

Much of area grazed. Three reservoirs for cattle; Spaulding, near center of site, is associated with Spaulding Ranch, a private inholding.

The BLM judges the area to be excellent for hiking and backpacking, especially the canyons and broken country in the central and E portions.

Except on the SW, the site is surrounded by other BLM land. To the W, below Guano Rim, is a large dry lakebed. To the NE is 6,510-ft. Lone Grave

Butte; this area is adjacent to Hart Mountain National Antelope Refuge and much used by hunters and trappers. To the E is Ryegrass Valley, a broad sage basin.

Plants: Mostly big and low sagebrush communities. Big sagebrush includes squirreltail, rabbitbrush. Wildflowers: desert paintbrush, Anderson's larkspur, clustered broomrape, Pursh's milk-vetch, big-fruited desert-parsley, sand lily, long-leaved phlox, cushion buckwheat. Low sagebrush includes Sandberg's bluegrass and squirreltail. Wildflowers: bitterroot, crag aster, mat buckwheat, scabland and line-leaf fleabane, prickly sandwort, Hood's phlox, stemless and narrowleaf goldenweed. Stands of willow and aspen below the rims on E and N.

Hiking, backpacking: Spring and fall best seasons. Bring all the water you need.

HEADQUARTERS: Lakeview District, Bureau of Land Management, 1000 Ninth St., Lakeview, OR 97603; (503) 947-2177.

SUMMER LAKE WILDLIFE AREA
Oregon Department of Fish and Wildlife
18,000 acres.

On SR 31 about 75 mi. NW of Lakeview.

Summer Lake was once part of a much larger lake. It is now shallow and alkaline; broad saltflats are exposed in dry seasons. Fresh water flows into the N portion, maintaining a large wetland with marshes, streams, potholes, and ponds. Surrounded on three sides by high desert, on the fourth by a wooded ridge, this wetland attracts many species of wildlife. The high desert to the E is mostly BLM land. (See entry, Diablo Mountain.)

Dikes provide a pleasant auto tour route and opportunities for hiking. Pick up a map at HQ and ask where the birding is best at the time.

Only the N tip of the lake is within the refuge. Pause at the pond on the W side of the highway just S of HQ. Concentrations of shorebirds are often seen on the lakeshore to the S, and it's possible to park beside the highway and walk across the flats.

Birds: Seasonally abundant and common species include grebes, white pelican, great blue heron, black-crowned night heron, bittern, whistling swan, Canada and snow geese, mallard, gadwall, pintail, teals, wigeon, shoveler, redhead, canvasback, lesser scaup, common goldeneye, bufflehead, ruddy duck, sandhill crane, Virginia rail, coot, gulls, terns. Hawks: red-tailed, Swainson's, marsh. California quail, pheasant. Abundant and common shorebirds: snowy plover, killdeer, common snipe, long-billed curlew, least sandpiper, long-billed dowitcher, western sandpiper, avocet, black-necked stilt, Wilson's phalarope. Also owls, nighthawk, flicker, many songbirds. Spring and fall are best seasons, but a visit is pleasant at any time.

About 170 species have been recorded, including a number of rarities.

Other fauna: No checklist. Deer, muskrat common.

ACTIVITIES

Camping: Primitive site near HQ. A Parks and Recreation Division wayside campground is nearby on SR 31.

Hunting: Designated areas; special rules; inquire.

Public access to dikes may be restricted during hatching season, beginning about July 1; some areas may be open to hunters only in hunting season.

NEARBY:

Fremont National Forest (see entry). A scenic Forest Road begins about 4 mi. N of Summer Lake.

BLM land. See Diablo Mountain entry.

PUBLICATIONS

Map with hunter information.

Bird checklist.

HEADQUARTERS: Box 8, Hines, OR 97738; (503) 573-6582.

SUN PASS STATE FOREST

Oregon Department of Forestry

20,250 acres.

SE of Crater Lake National Park. From SR 62 near Ft. Klamath, N about 2 mi. on SR 232, which crosses site.

SR 232 crosses Sun Pass at 5,405 ft. Mountainous, steep to moderate slopes with some relatively flat areas. Elevations 4,200 to 6,000 ft. Annual precipitation 14–30 in. Pumice from eruption of Mt. Mazama (the mountain forming Crater Lake) mantles the area.

Ponderosa pine forest managed for timber production. About 700 acres are logged off each year, another 1,000 acres thinned. Forest is open for public recreation, but primary use is wood fiber production.

Wood River originates near here in large springs. Sun and Annie creeks flow through.

Plants: All forest. Ponderosa with lodgepole pines, white fir, sugar pine, Douglas-fir, Shasta red fir, incense cedar, grand fir. Understory species: chinquapin, cottonwood, manzanita, snowbrush, aspen, sedge. Flowering species include aster, false Solomon's seal, penstemon, fireweed, wintergreen, dog-bane, hawkweed, pussytoes, lupine, phacelia.

Birds: 85 species recorded. Unpublished checklist. Those noted include bald eagle, raven, magpie, grouse, mountain bluebird, unspecified owls, hawks, woodpeckers, flycatchers, and warblers.

Mammals: Often seen: porcupine, squirrel, mule deer, badger, chipmunk. Present but seldom seen: elk, beaver, black bear, mink, weasel, mountain lion. Unpublished checklist.

ACTIVITIES

Camping: Permitted; no facilities. Preferred campsites are along Sun Creek.

Hiking: 2 3/4-mi. trail begins at Sun Creek Bridge, leads to S boundary of National Park. Beaver ponds along the trail. Also hiking on forest roads or bushwhacking.

Hunting: Elk, deer.

Fishing: Trout.

ADJACENT

Crater Lake National Park and Winema National Forest (see entries).

Jackson F. Kimball State Park, 19 acres, on SR 232, has 10 primitive campsites; opening depends on end of winter weather.

HEADQUARTERS: Klamath Lake District, Department of Forestry, P.O. Box 400, Klamath Falls, OR 97601; (503) 883-5681.

UMPQUA NATIONAL FOREST
U.S. Forest Service
988,149 acres.

SW OR. Between I-5 and US 97, S of SR 58. Crossed by SRs 138, 227, 230.

On the W side of the Cascade Range. Mountainous, deep valleys cut by streams carrying snowmelt toward the sea. Highest point is 9,182-ft. Mt. Thielsen, on the boundary with Winema National Forest. Here the E arm of the Forest extends S to the N boundary of Crater Lake National Park, with the Winema to the E, Rogue River National Forest to the W and S. Here, too, is Diamond Lake, over 3 mi. long, 3,000 acres, at an elevation of 5,183 ft. Downstream the North Umpqua flows beside SR 138 toward Roseburg, making this a scenic route used by many Forest visitors.

To the N, the Calapooya Mountains separate the Umpqua from the Willamette National Forest. An arm of the Forest extends N almost to SR 58, W of Oakridge.

Most of the W boundary is drawn sharply along section lines. To the W are forested hills in a checkerboard pattern of public and private ownership, the public lands managed for timber production.

A scenic area close to I-5 and population centers, the Forest attracts many visitors, summer and winter. However, the irregular terrain, cut by many large and small stream valleys, enables hikers to find secluded places even on holiday weekends. The popular centers, of course, are crowded at such times.

In addition to Diamond Lake, two reservoirs, Lemolo and Toketee, have more than 100 acres. The Forest includes 46 smaller lakes, many of less than 5 acres, all open to fishing.

In sharp contrast to the semiarid environment across the ridge, the W side is humid, annual precipitation averaging about 65 in. This promotes more rapid tree growth and a denser understory with many ferns and mosses as well as shrubs.

Plants: 90% forested, including extensive stands of old-growth Douglas-fir. Principal tree species: Douglas-fir, mountain hemlock, white fir, western hemlock, western white pine, sugar pine, lodgepole pine. Associated: Pacific yew, golden chinquapin, Pacific madrone, salal, swordfern, bracken fern. Rhododendron display in May. No wildflower checklist available, but species mentioned include yarrow, mountain arnica, Canadian thistle, Oregon grape, twinflower, snowberry, pipsissewa, lupine, California corn lily, beargrass, larkspur, monkeyflower, foxglove.

Birds: No published checklist. Species recorded include common loon; horned, western, and pied-billed grebes; double-crested cormorant, great blue and green herons, Canada and white-fronted geese, other waterfowl; sharp-shinned, Cooper's, red-tailed, and Swainson's hawks; golden and bald eagles, peregrine falcon, blue and ruffed grouse, California and mountain quail; barn, screech, great horned, pygmy, spotted, great gray, long-eared, and saw-whet owls; Anna's, rufous, Allen's, and calliope hummingbirds; common flicker, yellow-bellied sapsucker; pileated, acorn, Lewis's, hairy, downy, and black-backed woodpeckers; willow, Hammond's, dusky, western, and olive-sided flycatchers; gray, Steller's, and scrub jays; house, winter, Bewick's, long-billed marsh, and rock wrens; Hutton's, solitary, and red-eyed vireos; western tanager, black-headed and evening grosbeaks, lazuli bunting, pine siskin; chipping, white-crowned, golden-crowned, white-throated, fox, Lincoln's, and song sparrows.

Mammals: Species recorded include vagrant, dusky, Pacific, water, and Trowbridge shrews; pika, brush rabbit, snowshoe hare, mountain beaver, yellow-bellied marmot; Belding and California ground squirrels; northern and western pocket gophers, beaver, muskrat, porcupine, coyote, red and gray foxes, black bear, ringtail, raccoon, marten, fisher, long-tailed weasel, mink, wolverine, badger, river otter, mountain lion, bobcat, Roosevelt elk, mule deer, Columbian black-tailed deer.

Reptiles and amphibians: Include rough-skinned newt; Pacific giant, Olympic, northwestern, long-toed, clouded, Dunn's, Siskiyou Mountain, and western red-backed salamanders; tailed, western, Pacific tree, red-legged, and foothill yellow-legged frogs; rubber boa, common and California mountain kingsnakes; western, northwestern, and common garter snakes; western rattlesnake.

Windigo-Thielsen roadless area, 55,000 acres, including acreage in the Deschutes and Winema National Forests. On the crest of the Cascade Mountains. Douglas-fir forest on lower slopes, alpine vegetation above. Summer habitat for deer, elk, black bear, other mammals. Trails from Diamond Lake area. Pacific Crest Trail crosses N–S through the area.

Park Winema roadless area, 5,400 acres, including acreage in the Winema National Forest. On the N boundary of Crater Lake National Park, adjoining a wilderness area within the Park. On the lower N flanks of Timber Crater. On the Pacific Crest Trail.

Mazama Flats roadless area, 9,200 acres, including acreage in the Rogue River National Forest. On the N boundary of Crater Lake National Park, adjoining a wilderness area within the Park. (Separated from the Park Winema roadless area by the Park's N entrance road.) Includes the Boundary Springs Scenic Area, major part of the Rogue River headwaters, the deep canyon of Upper Mazama Creek, and Lake West.

(Portions of these areas may eventually be added to the Crater Lake National Park.)

Limpy Rock roadless area, 6,700 acres. Drainages on N side of North Umpqua River. Easy access. Elevations from 1,500 to 4,500 ft., moderate to steep slopes below, gentle above. Forest of Douglas-fir, incense cedar, western hemlock, chinquapin, madrone. Moderate use by hunters. No fishing streams.

Diamond Lake area, including *Lemolo Lake, Mt. Thielsen, Howlock Mountain,* attracts the largest number of visitors. Diamond Lake is developed with resorts, RV parks, campgrounds, summer residences, stores, marinas. Lemolo is somewhat less developed but has a resort, campgrounds, boat ramps. Trails connect with the nearby Pacific Crest Trail, also lead to the two principal mountains, and Mt. Thielsen. Mt. Bailey, Rodley Butte, and Lemolo Falls are other points of interest.

Fish Lake area, in the headwaters of the South Umpqua River, is reached only by trail. The nearest road is 3 mi. from the 90-acre lake. From the lake, formed by a landslide into Fish Creek Canyon, the creek cascades down the face of the natural dam. Nearby are Buckeye Lake (15 acres) and Cliff Lake (7 acres).

The numerous waterfalls include Steamboat, Fall Creek, Grotto, Toketee, Watson, Lemolo, Clearwater, Shadow, South Umpqua, Cow Creek. Watson,

272 ft., is highest in S OR. Most have viewpoints within 1 mi. of the nearest road.

INTERPRETATION: *Information center* at Diamond Lake. *Evening programs* Fri.–Sat. in summer. *Nature trail,* 1/2 mi.

ACTIVITIES

Camping: 57 campgrounds, 956 sites. Earliest opening date Apr. 15, latest closing Dec. 1.

Hiking, backpacking: 349 mi. of trails, 270 currently maintained. Forest map shows which are maintained. Also 3,780 mi. of Forest roads, most unpaved and lightly used. 28 mi. of the Pacific Crest Trail N of National Park. Each Ranger District has a leaflet describing popular trails: length, elevation, season, grades, points of interest.

Hunting: Deer, elk, grouse, quail.

Fishing: 49 lakes: brook, rainbow, and brown trout. Also streams. North Umpqua is famous for its summer steelhead run.

Swimming: Mostly the larger lakes.

Boating: Power boats restricted to 10 mph on Diamond Lake; 40 mph on Lemolo, with some no-wake zones.

Canoeing: Whitewater kayaking on North Umpqua River, spring months. Class III–IV rapids. Write to HQ for information.

Horse riding: Some use of horse, some pack trips.

Ski touring: About 26 mi. of marked cross-country ski trails, most originating in Diamond Lake and Lemolo Lake areas. Also use of unplowed Forest roads.

Snowmobiling: About 130 mi. of marked and groomed trails.

ADJACENT OR NEARBY

Crater Lake National Park (see entry).

Deschutes (zone 3), Rogue River and Winema, and Willamette (zone 2) National Forests (see entries).

Susan Creek State Park, 176 acres, 29 mi. NE of Roseburg on SR 138, just outside the Forest, on a whitewater section of the Umpqua River. Camping: 33 sites.

PUBLICATIONS

Forest map. $1.00.

Umpqua National Forest Facts.

Diamond Lake Area folder.

Pacific Crest National Scenic Trail (Umpqua section) folder.

Fish Lake Area folder.

Campground information.

Hiking trail information pages, by Ranger District.

Diamond and Lemolo Lake Nordic Trails.

Diamond Lake Snowmobile Trails.

HEADQUARTERS: P.O. Box 1008, Roseburg, OR 97470; (503) 672-6601.

RANGER DISTRICTS: Cottage Grove R.D., 78405 Cedar Park Rd., Cottage Grove, OR 97424; (503) 942-5591. Diamond Lake R.D., Toketee Route, Box 101, Idleyld Park, OR 97447; (503) 498-2531. Glide R.D., Glide, OR 97443; (503) 496-3532. Steamboat R.D., Toketee Star Route, Idleyld Park, OR 97447; (503) 498-2511. Tiller R.D., Rt. 2, Box 1, Tiller, OR 97484; (503) 825-3201.

UPPER KLAMATH NATIONAL WILDLIFE REFUGE
U.S. Fish and Wildlife Service
12,457 acres.

About 20 mi. NW of Klamath Falls on SR 140.

Marshy shallows of Upper Klamath Lake, bordering Agency Lake. Accessible only by boat; little of the waterfowl areas can be seen from shore.

The Klamath Basin is one of the great waterfowl areas. Most of the region's wetlands have been drained, but concentrations of 1 to 2 million birds still occur. Upper Klamath is one of a chain of five federal refuges in OR and CA maintained for these waterfowl. Upper Klamath is unique for its vast tule marsh, drowned stream channels with willow-lined banks.

Birds: Colonies of several hundred nests of double-crested cormorant, great blue heron, black-crowned night heron. Other nesting species include sandhill crane, white pelican, red-necked grebe, avocet, black-necked stilt, gadwall, mallard, redhead, cinnamon teal, ruddy duck, Canada goose, California and ring-billed gulls; Caspian, Forster's, and black terns; common merganser, shoveler, coot, Wilson's phalarope, willet. Most numerous species in migrations include pintail, mallard, wigeon; white-fronted, cackling, Canada, and snow geese; shoveler, ruddy duck.

Hunting: Designated areas. Special regulations. Inquire.

Fishing: Limited to designated areas. Inquire.

Boating: Launching ramps at Pelican Bay and Malone. For birding, canoe would be best craft. Inquire at HQ for current regulations and directions to marked canoe trail.

PUBLICATIONS
Klamath Basin National Wildlife Refuges, leaflet. Checklist.
Beginners Check List.
Public hunting area map.

HEADQUARTERS: Klamath Basin National Wildlife Refuges, Route 1, Box 74, Tulelake, CA 96134; (916) 667-2231.

WARNER LAKES
U.S. Bureau of Land Management
About 70,000 acres in several units.

From US 395 5 mi. N of Lakeview, E about 28 mi. on SR 140 to Adel. Then
N on county road to and beyond Plush.

The county road follows a chain of alkali lakes, some ephemeral, a few
watered, all vestiges of a large ancient lake. To the E a 3,600-ft. escarpment
rises abruptly to the high ground of Hart Mountain National Antelope Refuge (see entry).

Lakes at the S end of the chain—Hart, Crump, and Pelican—are largely
surrounded by private land. This section has wetlands attracting large numbers of waterfowl as well as white pelicans. Birding is good along the public
road.

The S BLM tract includes Lynch's Rim, a dramatic fault scarp rising 1,300
ft. above the valley. The S end of the tract drops sharply into Deep Creek
Canyon. Vegetation above the rim is generally dense: juniper and aspen
groves, mountain mahogany, big sagebrush, bitterbrush, Idaho fescue, low
sagebrush, Sandberg's bluegrass, Hood's phlox, bitterroot, big-fruited desert-
parsley.

Plants: In the Warner Valley, marsh and wet meadow communities include
baltic rush, hardstem bulrush, small-fruited bulrush, alkali bulrush, common
spike-rush, Missouri goldenrod, water hemlock, cut-leaved water-parsnip,
field mint, saltwort, alkali-marsh butterweed.

Dry saltgrass communities include alkali birdbeak, lance-leaved goldenweed, greasewood, Lemon's alkaligrass, borax weed, spiny hopsage, red
goosefoot.

In the N of the Valley, greasewood dunes with spiny hopsage, big sagebrush, rabbitbrush, gooseberry-leaved globemallow, basin wildrye, Indian
ricegrass.

Sand dunes in the S of the Valley have spiny hopsage, greasewood, big
sagebrush, rabbitbrush, shadscale, tansy mustard, smooth malocothrix, desert paintbrush, hairy evening-primrose, sea-purslane.

Birds: Hart Mountain Refuge publishes a checklist including species reported from the Warner Lakes. Seasonally abundant and common species:
loon; eared, western, and pied-billed grebes; white pelican; double-crested
cormorant, great blue heron, common and snowy egrets, black-crowned night
heron, American bittern, whistling swan, Canada goose, mallard, gadwall,
pintail, teals, wigeon, shoveler, redhead, canvasback, bufflehead, ruddy duck,
common merganser. For upland species, see Hart Mountain entry. In migration, large flocks of greater sandhill crane.

HEADQUARTERS: Lakeview District, Bureau of Land Management, 1000 Ninth St., Lakeview, OR 97603; (503) 947-2177.

WINEMA NATIONAL FOREST
U.S. Forest Service
1,045,003 acres.

In several large sections, on both sides of US 97 S of its intersection with SR 58. Access from SRs 140, 62, 138.

The several sections are arranged in a great, irregular oval. A section about 6 mi. wide, 38 mi. deep, extends S from Crater Lake National Park. Its W border adjoins the Rogue River National Forest. The Upper Klamath National Wildlife Refuge is on its E boundary. This section includes the Mountain Lakes Wilderness and parts of the Pacific Crest Trail.

The upper part of the oval surrounds the Klamath Marsh. On its W boundary are the National Park and Umpqua National Forest; Deschutes National Forest is on the N boundary, Fremont National Forest on the E. The S portion lies between Upper Klamath Lake and the Fremont National Forest.

Terrain is mountainous to flat and rolling. Elevations from about 4,100 ft. at the lakeshore to 9,182-ft. Mt. Thielson in the NW. W portion has typical glaciated landform features. The E portion is relatively flat, but has several peaks and buttes rising to about 7,000 ft.

Climate is semiarid, about 14 in. of annual precipitation at lower altitudes. Most of the precipitation at higher altitudes is winter snow, up to 10 ft. on the highest slopes.

Numerous lakes. Upper Klamath, largest natural lake in OR, lies between two sections of the Forest. Agency Lake, a large, shallow, marshy area providing good waterfowl habitat and fishing, is nearby. Launching ramps for both lakes are within easy reach of the Forest. Largest lakes within the Forest are Lake of the Woods (1,113 acres), Fourmile (over 900 acres), and Miller (565 acres). Of 36 other lakes, all are smaller than 100 acres, 25 less than 10 acres. Most are in the W portion of the Forest.

The Sycan River forms part of the boundary with the Fremont National Forest. Nearby it flows through the large, privately owned Sycan Marsh. The Sprague and Williamson rivers flow through portions of the Forest. Hundreds of small seasonal streams.

Plants: 95% of the area is forested. Three principal forest types, depending chiefly on elevation: ponderosa pine, mixed conifers, and lodgepole pine. Associated species include white fir, incense cedar, mountain hemlock, Douglas-fir. Understory species include bitterbrush, ceanothus, chinquapin, manzanita. Flowering species include arrowleaf balsamroot, aster, bleeding heart, clarkia, dandelion, penstemon, fireweed, foxglove, heartleaf arnica, phacelia, silvery lupine, twinflower, woolly wyethia.

Birds: 239 species recorded. Checklist available. While the Forest includes only modest wetlands, it borders on some of the principal wetlands of the Pacific Flyway. Winter concentration of bald eagle. List includes all the grebes, white pelican, double-crested cormorant; great blue, green, and black-crowned night herons; great and snowy egrets, American and least bitterns, white-faced ibis, whistling swan; Canada, white-fronted, snow, and Ross's geese; 23 duck species, many hawks, sandhill crane, many shorebirds, 11 owl species, all the woodpeckers that occur in OR, plus a great variety of songbirds.

Mammals: 80 species recorded. Checklist available. Prominent are mule deer, pronghorn, elk, black bear, coyote, bobcat, mountain lion. Also recorded: snowshoe hare, black-tailed jackrabbit, marmot, chickaree, beaver, porcupine, raccoon, marten, fisher, mink, wolverine, river otter.

Reptiles and amphibians: 26 species recorded. Checklist available includes frogs, toads, fence lizard, western skink, rubber boa, gopher snake. Western rattlesnake present, seldom seen.

FEATURES

Mountain Lakes Wilderness Area, 23,971 acres. A large glacial basin surrounded by high peaks and hanging valleys. Highest point is Aspen Butte, 8,208 ft. Many mountain lakes with forested shores. Area is square, 6 by 6 mi., easy access. Hiking season July–Oct., warm days, cool nights.

Sky Lakes Area, about 80,000 acres, partly within the Rogue River National Forest. Undeveloped except for trails and campsites. No motor vehicles except snowmobiles. High mountain plateau with many lakes and ponds. On the Pacific Crest Trail.

Park Winema roadless area, 5,400 acres, partly within the Umpqua National Forest. On N boundary of Crater Lake National Park, adjoining wilderness area within the Park. On the N flank of Timber Crater. Elevations 5,200 to 6,600 ft. Gentle slopes. On the Pacific Crest Trail.

Panhandle North roadless area, 2,700 acres, and *Panhandle South roadless area,* 1,330 acres. On the E border of Crater Lake National Park, adjoining wilderness area within. *North* area is flat to steep, 5,200 to 6,400 ft. elevation, deeply cut canyons. *South* includes lower E slopes of Mt. Scott, mostly gentle slopes, 6,000 to 7,280 ft. elevation. These areas and the Park Winema are being added to the National Park.

Spring Creek, on US 97, scenic area, noted for the large spring, 200 cu. ft. per second of water rising from lava formation. Many wildflowers.

Lake of the Woods is heavily used, with resorts, homes, campgrounds, etc., on the shoreline. Easy access to wilderness area and Pacific Crest Trail.

Miller Lake near crest of the Cascades is also a popular area for fishing, boating, camping. Trails into large undeveloped areas. Pacific Crest Trail is nearby.

Yamsay Mountain was the highest point in the Forest with road access. Now the upper 3 mi. has been closed to motor vehicles. Crater rim is at 8,196 ft. elevation. Sweeping views. Foot access into crater, then down Jackson Creek.

ACTIVITIES

Camping: 9 campgrounds, 295 sites. Mid-June to Oct.

Hiking, backpacking: Forest reports only 80 mi. of trails, including 50 mi. of Pacific Crest Trail. However, many mi. of unpaved, lightly used Forest roads. Also, open forest and moderate slopes make bushwhacking feasible in many areas.

Hunting: Chiefly deer, elk.

Fishing: Lakes and streams. Rainbow, cutthroat, German brown, eastern brook, kokanee. Spring runs of mullet in Williamson and Sprague rivers.

Swimming: Lakes.

Boating: Upper Klamath Lake, Miller Lake, Lake of the Woods.

Canoeing: Williamson and Sprague rivers; no white water. A fascinating 6-mi. canoe trail winds through a 15,000-acre marsh in the Forest and adjoining Upper Klamath National Wildlife Refuge. Excellent wildlife viewing. See leaflet listed under Publications.

Horse riding: Forest reports some use of horses, but no outfitter nearby.

Skiing: Tomahawk Ski Bowl.

Ski touring, snowmobiling: Some marked trails, but also on unplowed roads.

ADJACENT OR NEARBY

Deschutes National Forest (zone 3); Rogue River, Umpqua, and Fremont National Forests (zone 5); Klamath Forest and Upper Klamath National Wildlife Refuges (zone 5). (See entries.)

Collier Memorial State Park, 349 acres. 30 mi. N of Klamath Falls on both sides of US 97. At confluence of Spring Creek and Williamson River. Camping: 68 sites, season opening depending on end of winter weather.

Jackson F. Kimball State Park, 19 acres. 3 mi. N of Fort Klamath Junction on SR 232, at the edge of Sun Pass State Forest (see entry). Camping: 10 primitive sites, season opening depending on end of winter weather.

PUBLICATIONS

Forest map. $1.00.

Mountain Lakes Wilderness map. $1.00.

Forest fact sheet.

Jackson-Klamath Winter Trails, map.

Upper Klamath Canoe Trails.
Sky Lakes Users Guide, map.

HEADQUARTERS: 7th and Walnut, Box 1390, Klamath Falls, OR 97601; (503) 882-7761.

RANGER DISTRICTS: Chemult R.D., P.O. Box 150, Chemult, OR 97731; (503) 365-2229. Chiloquin R.D., P.O. Box 357, Chiloquin, OR 97624; (503) 783-2221. Klamath R.D., 1936 California Ave., Klamath Falls, OR 97601; (503) 882-7761, ext. 342.

ZANE GREY
U.S. Bureau of Land Management
18,460 acres.

From Grants Pass, about 16 mi. NW to Galice on county road, then 3 mi. N.

This irregularly shaped site includes 26 mi. of the Rogue Wild and Scenic River, upstream from the Medford County line. The W tip of the site adjoins the Wild Rogue Wilderness (see entries for Siskiyou National Forest and Rogue Wild and Scenic River, both in zone 1). Steep, mountainous terrain; elevations from 400 to 3,800 ft. Several smaller streams flow into the Rogue. Numerous small waterfalls, cascades, pools. Slopes of stream valleys commonly exceed 50%. Valley bottoms are narrow. Most of the surrounding land is forested and managed for timber production.

Plants: Dense vegetation. Mostly forested, mixed hardwoods and conifers. Some brushfields and open meadows.

Birds: Essentially the same species found in Siskiyou National Forest and along the Rogue Wild and Scenic River. (See entries, zone 1.)

Mammals: Species essentially same as in the National Forest. Winter range for deer. Reported: mountain lion, black bear, Roosevelt elk.

ACTIVITIES
Camping: One BLM Campground, Tucker Flat, near W end of site. Reached on local roads from Glendale. Local directions needed.

Hiking, backpacking: Rogue River Trail follows the river through the site.

Fishing: Chinook, coho, steelhead.

HEADQUARTERS: Medford District, Bureau of Land Management, 3040 Biddle Rd., Medford, OR 97501; (503) 779-2351.

ZONE 6

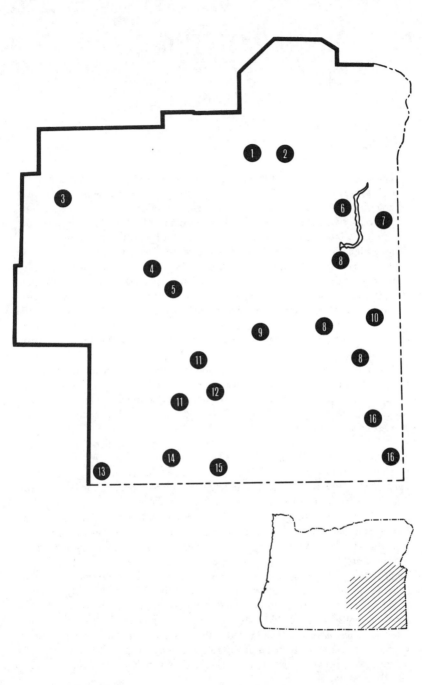

ZONE 6

Includes these counties:
Harney   Malheur

The high desert of SE Oregon is the least-known part of the state, one of the least-known regions of the nation. Only about 30,000 people live in an area of 20,000 sq. mi., most of them in five towns, the largest with a population of 8,000. Driving across it, one's impression is of an endless expanse of sagebrush, a few brown hills on the horizon. But highways follow the easiest routes; high ridges and deep canyons are off the main tracks.

It is a dry region, for the most part receiving 10 in. or less of moisture per year, most of that in winter. The relatively few springs, streams, and wetlands depend on the mountains high enough to catch heavy snow. Summers are hot, winters cold. Hikers and backpackers prefer spring and fall. River runners have no choice; only in late spring and early summer are a few streams high enough for rafting. Steens Mountain receives enough snow for ski touring and snowshoeing.

The highest point in the zone is just under 10,000 ft., but many mountains, ranges, and buttes rise several thousand feet above the flatlands. Most hikers prefer exploring the many canyons of the region, some as much as 1,500 ft. deep. Here they may find alder, willow, and cottonwood, perhaps a spring, as well as shade and isolation.

Well over 95% of the zone is federal land, most of it public domain administered by the Bureau of Land Management. The zone includes a portion of the Ochoco National Forest and the Malheur National Wildlife Refuge. The Refuge is famous, attracting birders from throughout the United States and from overseas.

The Steens Mountain Recreation Lands is the only major BLM site with formal boundaries. Its dramatic escarpment is one of the region's chief scenic features. The Steens high country attracts campers, backpackers, hunters, and cross-country skiers, though it is rarely crowded. Lake Owyhee, 52 miles long, is remarkably uncrowded, even in midsummer, both because it is far from any large city and because most of its shoreline is accessible only by boat.

We have necessarily been arbitrary in describing other portions of BLM lands. Usually we have selected a feature or cluster of features of special interest—such as a mountain, lake, or canyon—and as much of the surrounding country as seemed to be naturally related. The acreages need not be taken too seriously, because they do not measure sites with fixed boundaries. Usually the contiguous areas are also BLM lands.

An ordinary highway map is of little use in exploring the high desert. The roads described as "other all-weather" are usually good enough—at least in good weather. Those called "unimproved" are likely to be navigable by auto in dry weather. Thousands of miles of roads and ways are not shown on highway maps. Some have good surfaces; others are impassable. BLM offices have maps showing parts of their lands. It's advisable to talk with someone who knows the country before going far off the state and county roads. To explore this country, one needs a pickup truck or 4-wheel-drive vehicle.

No detailed descriptions of flora and fauna for these sites are available. However, the BLM District Offices do have much information about the features of their Districts, including lists of flora and fauna.

We asked these offices if we should recommend that strangers to the area visit them and ask for information and advice in trip planning. Could they respond to such requests? Both replies were unqualified: Yes, we can and will help. But both also said they don't have much printed information to send in response to letters of inquiry. Don't write; come.

Burns District Office, BLM
74 S. Alvord
Burns, OR 97720
(503) 573-2071

Vale District Office, BLM
100 Oregon St.
P.O. Box 700
Vale, OR 97018
(503) 473-3144

ALVORD BASIN
U.S. Bureau of Land Management
About 300,000 acres.

SW of Burns Junction. The official state highway map shows an unnumbered all-weather road running N from Denio, CA, through Fields and Andrews, meeting SR 78 about 26 mi. NW of Burns Junction. This marks the W boundary of the area. The map shows the area as roadless, but it has hundreds of miles of tracks and ways. Several routes begin at White-horse Ranch, 8 mi. S and 20 mi. E of Fields. All such routes should be used with caution, for the most part avoided in wet weather. Deep sand is a dry-weather hazard.

The Basin, though spectacularly scenic, has been described in such terms as "harsh," "barren," "inaccessible," "fearsome," and "hazardous." Yet BLM specialists say this area and neighboring Steens Mountain are the principal attractions of the Burns District.

The center of interest is the Alvord Desert, a flat playa—dry lakebed—of alkali, almost totally lacking in vegetation. The playa is light-colored, dazzling in bright sunlight, often windswept. Unfortunately, this expanse—like many other desert sites—is much used by ORV enthusiasts for competitions. We were told their tracks on the lakebed are erased by spring rains, but the surrounding area is more fragile.

The Basin is almost entirely ringed by mountains: Steens, Pueblo, Trout Creek, Sheepshead. Elevations begin at a bit over 4,000 ft., the highest butte rising to 6,170. Highest point on the periphery is Steens, 9,670 ft.

The Desert lies close to the W boundary road, just E of Andrews. E of the Desert are shifting and stabilized dunes, the latter vegetated with plants of interest to botanists. Beyond these to the E are cliffs rising 400–800 ft. above the desert floor, the W edge of a large, relatively flat plateau sloping gently E to the dry basin of Coyote Lake and its associated dunes.

Much of the Basin to the N and E is flat to gently rolling, Terrain is somewhat more rugged to the S and E, rising to Lookout Butte, 6,170 ft. Whitehorse Creek drains from Steens Mountain into Alvord Lake, just S of Andrews, but for most of the year the lake is dry. The S end is marshy, attracting many birds in season.

A variety of shrubs grow on the dunes. Otherwise, except for the barren lakebeds, this is a region of sagebrush and sparse grasses. Cottonwood and willow border some of the intermittent streams.

The region has been called an extension of the Sonoran Desert, some plant and animal species reaching here the N limit of their range.

This is wilderness. Large sections of the Basin are remote, far from any traveled road, seldom visited. They are fascinating to explore, by vehicle, horse, or on foot, but one should be aware of the special hazards of desert country and be able to cope with them.

Birds: In the desert, any temporary pond attracts waterfowl and shorebirds. Here, at times, are numbers of avocet, black-necked stilt, willet, plover, lesser yellowlegs, as well as Wilson's phalarope, cinnamon teal, other waterfowl. Songbirds favor the trees and shrubs beside streams. Chukar, California quail, sage grouse, red-tailed hawk, killdeer.

Mammals: Wild horse, pronghorn, coyote often seen. Mule deer and bighorn sheep in winter. Black-tailed jackrabbit, ground squirrel. Small mammals, especially, seldom seen in full daylight.

ACTIVITIES

Camping: No designated campground. Informal camping is generally unrestricted. Visitors are reminded that this is a fragile environment, asked to leave no scars or trash behind.

Hiking, backpacking: Desert hiking is increasing in popularity. Adequate preparation is essential.

For maps, information on current conditions, consult the BLM office at Burns.

HEADQUARTERS: Burns District, Bureau of Land Management, 74 S. Alvord St., Burns, OR 97720; (503) 573-2071.

ANTELOPE RESERVOIR
U.S. Bureau of Land Management
80 acres.

From Jordan Valley, about 12 mi. W on US 95, then 1 mi. S.

Campground on 4-mi.-long reservoir. Most of the surrounding land is BLM, leased for grazing and other purposes, of no special interest. However, this is a good base for visits to the Owyhee River above Rome, Lava Beds, Leslie Gulch, The Honeycombs, etc. See BLM map, Central Vale District. No bird data here, but similar reservoirs in the area attract many waterfowl.

Camping: Apr.–Nov. Primitive; no fixed sites.

HEADQUARTERS: Vale District, Bureau of Land Management, P.O. Box 700, Vale, OR 97018; (503) 473-3144.

CASTLE ROCK AREA
U.S. Bureau of Land Management
75,000 acres.

From Juntura on US 20, N on county road.

From Juntura, a good road follows the North Fork of the Malheur River, initially through farmland, then into a broad canyon, past a BLM riverside campground, and on to the Beulah Reservoir.

To the E is a 45,500-acre roadless area with great variety of terrain: mountains, buttes, ridges, canyons, foothills, flats. Numerous springs. Several creeks. Not a wilderness area, but excellent opportunities for primitive recreation. Vegetation is mostly juniper trees, sagebrush, native grasses.

4 mi. N of the reservoir is Castle Rock, 6,837 ft., an extinct volcano cone, a landmark visible for miles as one approaches Juntura from the W. A good area for day hikes. Horse Flat to the W, with Spring Creek flowing through. E section has steep slopes, rock outcrops, ponderosa pine stands.

5 mi. NE of Castle Rock is the Beaver Dam Creek area, under study for wilderness designation. Numerous canyons. Generally thick vegetative cover, sagebrush and mountain mahogany on slopes and ridges, aspen and riparian species in canyons. Heavy deer hunting pressure in season. Beaver in perennial streams.

Camping: The BLM's Chukar Park campground. 19 sites. Mar.–Dec. Primitive camping elsewhere. County primitive facilities on the reservoir.

HEADQUARTERS: Vale District, Bureau of Land Management, P.O. Box 700, Vale, OR 97018; (503) 473-3144.

CHICKAHOMINY RESERVOIR
U.S. Bureau of Land Management
200 acres.

From Riley, 2 mi. W on US 20.

Driving E from Bend, 106 mi. away, this was the first campground we saw. The reservoir is about 1 mi. long, shallow, surrounded—in summer—by hard-baked mudflats much used by cattle. Surrounding country is sagebrush flats, hills of the Ochoco National Forest visible to the N. A nearby road leads into the Forest, toward Buck Spring and Delintment Lake.

Birds: Desert lakes attract waterfowl and shorebirds; many were here even in midsummer. Observed: blue-winged teal with clutch, pied-billed and western grebes, mallard, Wilson's phalarope, great blue heron, willet, killdeer, sage sparrow.

ACTIVITIES
Camping: Primitive. No fixed sites. All year.
Hiking: Around the lake or toward the Forest.
Fishing: People we saw fishing said it's good. Ice fishing in winter.
Boating: Ramp.

HEADQUARTERS: Burns District, Bureau of Land Management, 74 S. Alvord St., Burns, OR 97720; (503) 573-2071.

COTTONWOOD CREEK
U.S. Bureau of Land Management
22,500 acres.

S and E of Jonesboro, 10 mi. E of Juntura, on US 20. Site extends about 15 mi. S, 7 mi. E. Access by local roads.

Cottonwood Creek flows NE, joining the Malheur River near Harper. In this area it flows through a steep, rugged canyon up to 1,200 ft. deep. Several steep, narrow side canyons entering from the N and W: Wildcat, Green, Long, Camp Creek. On E side, further S, West Fork and Little Cottonwood Creek are rugged tributaries. Scenic area. Numerous rims, rock outcrops. Numerous springs. Cottonwood Creek has both perennial and intermittent sections.

Sagebrush, cheatgrass, riparian plants, a few juniper. Above the canyon rim are sagebrush flats. The NW corner of the area, immediately SE of Jonesboro, has rough, broken terrain, rimrocked tables, three intermittent creeks in canyons 280 to 600 ft. deep. Wildlife said to be abundant: chukar, quail, raptors, jackrabbit, coyote, cottontail, mule deer, pronghorn, rattlesnake. General elevation about 4,000 ft. Accessibility of the area and availability of water make the area attractive for hiking or backpacking.

HEADQUARTERS: Vale District, Bureau of Land Management, P.O. Box 700, Vale, OR 97018; (503) 473-3144.

DIAMOND CRATERS
U.S. Bureau of Land Management
15,000 acres.

From Burns, 41 mi. S on SR 205, then E on Diamond Lane.

Recent lava flow, with an exceptional variety of relatively unweathered formations. The BLM has designated it an Outstanding Natural Area. Its features are comparable to those at Craters of the Moon National Monument (ID), but without visitor facilities and exhibits. Lava cones, ropy flows, cinder cones, spatter cones, and other products of volcanism cover several square miles. Vegetation includes a marsh community in the NW corner of the site; big sagebrush, greasewood, and juniper wherever they can sink roots; and low-growing pioneer plants adapted to the volcanic surface.

NEARBY: Malheur National Wildlife Refuge (see entry).

HEADQUARTERS: Burns District, Bureau of Land Management, 74 S. Alvord St., Burns, OR 97720; (503) 573-2071.

HAWKS VALLEY
U.S. Bureau of Land Management
340,000 acres.

On the NV border, W of Denio, NV. Area extends roughly 25 mi. W, 25 mi. N. Local and BLM roads from SR 140, at SW corner, and from SR 206 S of Frenchglen.

The area adjoins a large section of the Charles Sheldon Antelope Range in NV designated as wilderness. Just N of the border is a very large basin, ringed by hills on the W, N, and E, with an ephemeral lakebed known as "Hawksie Walksie." This S portion of the area includes Hawk Mountain, 7,000 ft., and Lone Juniper Mountain. To the E are rolling hills with minor rims.

A dominant feature on the NE is Catlow Rim, extending N–S about 15 mi., reaching elevations of nearly 6,000 ft. at Square Mountain in the N. Rugged rock cliffs face W. Several deep canyons cut the rim. Above the rim, plateau with some rolling hills. To the S, Lone Mountain, 6,520 ft., has interesting columns and pinnacles of volcanic rock. W of the rim is a flat, open valley. SE of Lone Mountain, about 1 mi. N of the border, is Oregon End Table, an irregularly shaped plateau about 3 by 5 mi., surrounded by rimrock.

Catlow Valley extends into the N portion of the area; flat, shallow, dry lakebeds; several rolling hills and buttes to the S. W of the Valley are flat plateaus edged by rimrock. The far NW is Beaty's Butte (7,916 ft.), high point of the steep, hilly terrain rising from Ryegrass Valley.

The area has many intermittent streams, generally dry in summer. Vegetation is mostly sagebrush community, sparse junipers at higher altitudes, areas of salt desert shrub. This is important range for pronghorn, including herds moving from the Hart Mountain National Antelope Refuge to the Sheldon for the winter.

Miles of ways penetrate and cross the area. Hiking and backpacking are most interesting in the hills and canyons.

HEADQUARTERS: W portion: Lakeview District, Bureau of Land Management, 1000 Ninth St., Lakeview, OR 97603; (503) 947-2177. E portion: Burns District, BLM, 74 S. Alvord St., Burns, OR 97720; (503) 573-2071.

LAKE OWYHEE
U.S. Bureau of Reclamation/U.S. Bureau of Land Management/Oregon Parks and Recreation Division
About 100,000 acres.

Principal access routes: (1) from Vale on US 20, S 41 mi. on well-marked county road to dam and State Park. (2) from Jordan Valley N 18 mi. on US 95, then N and W on local roads to Leslie Gulch.

An isolated lake, narrow, 52 mi. long, desert hills rising steeply from the shoreline. One paved road leads to the dam and State Park at the N end of the reservoir. The road to Leslie Gulch, near the S end, is said to be well maintained. The BLM map shows 3 other access routes by primitive roads. Otherwise the lakeshore is roadless.

The lake is not heavily used. On a fine July weekend, only half the campsites at the small State Park were occupied, but we were told it is crowded on many holidays. A modest commercial resort nearby is the only other development. The BOR reports about 70,000 visitor-days per year, 2/3 for fishing. On the busiest day, 150 boats were on the lake, but most were within a few miles of launching sites. A boat camper can easily find solitude.

Landscape is dramatically scenic. On the W, steep rocky slopes cut by deep ravines, rising to tall, rimrocked buttes and tables. Prominent high points: Red Butte, 4,584 ft.; Dry Creek Buttes, 4,226 and 4,303 ft.; North and South Table Mountains, Black Butte, Nanny's Nipple. (Lake elevation is 2,670 ft.) Colors are mostly shades of brown, tan, and gray, with areas of red.

Extremely rough, broken terrain to the E, many rugged breaks draining to the lake. Major canyons include Iron Mountain, Painted, Carlton, Three Fingers, Craig. Area is best known for striking formations called The Honeycombs. Here erosion has carved the rock into a great variety of columns, spires, cliffs, caves, ledges, ravines, and buttresses, with a variety of colors. Other prominent features: Steamboat Ridge, Shadscale Flat, Saddle Butte, Juniper Ridge, Sheepshead Basin.

Plants: Vegetation is sparse over most of the area, chiefly sagebrush community with scattered junipers. Willow, alder, cottonwood along watercourses. On foot one can see many wildflowers, depending on season, most of them not visible from passing automobiles.

Birds: No checklist available. Observed: magpie, chukar, California quail, house finch, goldfinch, rough-legged hawk, marsh hawk, tree swallow, crow, pied-billed grebe, mallard, Canada goose, meadowlark.

Mammals: No checklist. Species reported include pronghorn, mule deer, bighorn sheep, wild horse, black-tailed jackrabbit.

FEATURES

Scenic drives: Approach from the N through a 14-mi.-long canyon below the dam. Canyon walls are steep, heavily eroded, colorful. Grass and trees along the river. Numerous places to pull off the road to picnic, wade, fish, camp. The road in Leslie Gulch offers a sample of The Honeycombs.

The Honeycombs. The term is applied to a large area within which characteristic bizarre formations occur and to about 17 sq. mi. in which they are most concentrated. Easiest access is by boat, going ashore about 20 mi. above the dam. Primitive roads lead to the perimeter of the area, which is closed to vehicles. Consult the BLM Vale office for route and current conditions.

ACTIVITIES

Camping: State Park, 40 sites; opening depends on winter weather. The BLM has primitive campgrounds at Leslie Gulch and at Twin Springs, the latter about 4 mi. from the lake, on the W side, reached by an unpaved road beginning on US 20 4 mi. W of Vale. The Bureau of Reclamation has a primitive campground on the river below the dam.

Hiking, backpacking: Ample opportunities for those who enjoy desert hiking. Many seldom-traveled primitive roads, or go cross-country. Consult the BLM office for maps, best areas.

Hunting: Deer, pronghorn, chukar, quail, cottontail, duck.

Boating: Ramps at State Park and Leslie Gulch.

Fishing: Outstanding for black crappie. Largemouth bass in spring. Limited trout fishing.

HEADQUARTERS: Vale District, Bureau of Land Management, P.O. Box 700, Vale, OR 97018; (503) 473-3144.

MALHEUR NATIONAL WILDLIFE REFUGE
U.S. Fish and Wildlife Service
183,485 acres.

From Burns on US 20, 2 mi. E on SR 78; 24 mi. S on SR 205; 6 mi. E on county road to HQ.

One of the nation's principal wildlife refuges. An important nesting area for migratory birds and a major stop on the Pacific Flyway. The area also supports a diverse population of mammals. Established by President Theodore Roosevelt in 1908.

Roughly T-shaped, the stem extending S about 41 mi. along and generally E of SR 205. The crossbar includes Harney Lake and Double-O Ranch on the W, Malheur Lake on the E. Vast shallow marshes, small ponds, irrigated meadows, alkaline lakes, grass and sagebrush uplands with some greasewood-covered alkali flats.

Semiarid climate, dry and cloudless summers, temperatures seldom over 90° F or below zero. Droughts of 1–3 months not uncommon. Most of the year's precipitation is snow. All but spring-fed waters usually frozen Dec.–Feb.

The Refuge does not control its own water supply. The Silvies River, one of two major sources, is used for irrigation upstream, and in dry years no water reaches Malheur Lake. Flow of the Blitzen River, the other source, depends on the snow depth on Steens Mountain. It, too, enters Malheur Lake.

Overflow from Malheur, if any, enters Harney Lake, which has no outlet. Size of Malheur Lake has varied from 500 to 70,000 acres. Harney Lake is often dry. Refuge statistics show great year-to-year variations in waterfowl numbers, reflecting water supply.

Malheur Lake is a freshwater marsh with bulrush, bur-reed, and cattail as well as open water. It is both a feeding and breeding area for waterfowl. A current problem is controlling the population of carp, which interfere with the supply of sago pondweed, chief food supply for waterfowl.

Blitzen Valley, along SR 205, is flat and narrow, with many small ponds, willow-lined streams, irrigated meadows, bordered by sagebrush and juniper uplands. The valley is prime waterfowl nesting habitat.

Double-O Ranch was added to the Refuge in 1941. It has its own water supply, including a number of springs, developed in a series of ponds and meadows.

Birds: Checklist available listing 227 species observed. Notable nesting species include trumpeter swan, Canada goose, greater sandhill crane, gadwall, cinnamon teal, redhead, ruddy duck, great blue and black-crowned night herons, great and snowy egrets, western and eared grebes, bittern, black and Forster's terns, coot, killdeer, avocet, willet, long-billed curlew, Wilson's phalarope. Some migratory species are numerous in season: tens of thousands of avocets, snow geese. White pelican are regular visitors. Seasonally abundant upland species include nighthawk, tree and cliff swallows, magpie, robin, loggerhead shrike, yellow warbler, common yellowthroat, western tanager; savannah, Brewer's, white-crowned, and song sparrows.

The Refuge is also noted for its rarities: sightings of species seldom seen in OR. The HQ area is said to be an excellent birding spot for songbirds, especially in mid-May.

Mammals: Checklist available; 57 species observed. Includes 3 species of shrews, 13 bats, pygmy rabbit, cottontail, black-tailed jackrabbit, yellow-bellied marmot, 4 ground squirrels, Townsend and northern pocket gophers, Great Basin pocket mouse, dark kangaroo mouse, Ord's and chisel-toothed kangaroo rats, beaver, 3 field mice, 2 woodrats, 2 voles, muskrat, porcupine, coyote, raccoon, ermine, long-tailed weasel, mink, badger, 2 skunks, bobcat, mule deer, pronghorn.

INTERPRETATION: *Museum, information:* At HQ. Exhibits, publications,

FEATURE: *Blitzen Valley Auto Tour Route:* 42-mi. self-guided tour, assisted by printed guide. Begins at HQ, last station near Frenchglen. Alternate return route passes Diamond Craters (see entry).

When to go: Spring waterfowl migration usually peaks between mid-Mar. and early Apr. By early May, most migrants have left and breeding species are arriving. Songbird migration peaks in mid-May. Refuge Manager says he best likes the period including last 2 weeks of May, first 2 of June.

By end of June, marsh and meadow vegetation is high, making it difficult to see birds. Fall duck migration begins in Aug., peaks in Oct. Viewing isn't as easy as in spring. Ask about current best spots. Useful to call before visiting.

Fewer species are present in winter. They include mallard, Canada goose, trumpeter swan, upland game birds.

ACTIVITIES

Camping: Prohibited on the Refuge, but the BLM's Page Springs campground is near Frenchglen: 16 sites, Apr.–Nov.

Hiking: Restricted to public roads Mar. 1–Aug. 15. Unrestricted at other times except where posted.

Hunting: Designated areas. Special regulations. Inquire.

Fishing: Designated waters. Boats without motors permitted on Krumbo Reservoir in fishing season.

PUBLICATIONS

Leaflet with map.
Bird and mammal checklists.
Blitzen Valley auto tour route guide.
Regulations, with map.
Hunting Regulations.
Public Fishing Map.

HEADQUARTERS: P.O. Box 113, Burns, OR 97720; (503) 493-2323.

OWYHEE RIVER
U.S. Bureau of Land Management
About 100,000 acres.

Rome, on US 95, is midway in this section, which extends from Three Forks, SE of Rome, near ID border, to Lake Owyhee.

Tributaries forming the Owyhee River join at or near Three Forks. For 84 mi., to Lake Owyhee, the river flows in a deep canyon. Only at Rome, 32 mi. from the forks, does the terrain facilitate a road crossing. The section below Rome has been designated an Oregon Scenic Waterway, a legal bar to most streamside development. Although the section from Three Forks to Rome still lacks this protection, it is no less scenic and is unlikely to be much changed in the near future.

The river canyon is cut into a high plateau. From Three Forks to Rome, canyon depth is about 1,300 ft., walls of pinkish-brown rhyolite with tall pinnacles and chimneys. Walls are generally steep to sheer. Access is possible at only a few points. Canyon floor varies from wide, sandy bars to narrow rock-strewn rapids.

Rafting has become increasingly popular in recent years. Although the number of visitors is far less than in Hells Canyon, to the N, it is enough to arouse concern about damage to the fragile canyon vegetation, and the BLM is being urged to limit traffic.

It is not a river for the novice. At least 6 major rapids lie between Three Forks and Rome. Ratings differ according to water level and individual judgment, but we were told of one class VI rapid between Three Forks and Rome, two more between Rome and the lake. The season for river running is short, depending on snowmelt, about 6–8 weeks in late spring and early summer. Most rafters put in at Rome. Takeouts are possible at Black Rocks and Leslie Gulch. These are also access points for people visiting the canyon on foot.

Hiking or backpacking in the canyon is a memorable experience, but the BLM office should be consulted. Some sections are narrow, steep, rock-strewn, and virtually impassable. A section reported to be manageable extends from Rome N. Access roads should also be checked with the BLM. At the time of our visit, use of one was questionable for lack of an easement over some private land.

Several side canyons join the Owyhee above Rome. Antelope Creek is the largest. Others: Warm Springs, Long Canyon, Indian Canyon. Around Antelope Creek, land above the rim has rolling hills. Further N are sagebrush flats.

Downstream from Rome the canyon has greater variety, though it is never less than 500 ft. deep. In places the walls are vertical, in others a stairstep complex of cliffs, alluvial fans, ravines, and slopes. Several creeks and side canyons join the Owyhee. Terrain above the rim also has somewhat more variety: several lava beds, hills, buttes, and ridges as well as sagebrush flats.

ACTIVITIES

Camping: No established campgrounds. Informal camping is generally permitted on BLM land except where posted.

Hiking, backpacking: Many opportunities in the canyon, along the rim, and in surrounding country. Spring and fall preferred, though access roads may be muddy in spring. Consult BLM office at Vale for maps and advice.

Hunting: Mule deer, pronghorn, chukar, quail.

PUBLICATION: Map, Central Vale District. (Does not show area S of Rome.) No U.S. Geological Survey topographic maps are available for the S portion of the District. The BLM has a planimetric map.

HEADQUARTERS: Vale District, Bureau of Land Management, P.O. Box 700, Vale, OR 97018; (503) 473-3144.

OWYHEE RIVER, SOUTH FORK, AND LOUSE CANYON
U.S. Bureau of Land Management
About 200,000 acres.

SE corner of OR. Access by local and BLM roads from US 95. See BLM office for map and advice.

Some call this the best backpacking area in OR. It is certainly one of the wildest. A high plateau is cut by canyons up to 1,300 ft. deep, walls so steep or sheer as to allow only occasional access routes. From the ID border to Owyhee Reservoir, 150 mi. away, the Owyhee River canyon is crossed by only one way.

The 25 mi. of the South Fork from Idaho to Three Forks, where the main stem of the Owyhee is formed, has been designated an Oregon Scenic Waterway, an action that prohibits nearby commercial and other developments that would spoil the view. Most river running is further downstream, but the South Fork can be run when the water is high enough in spring, usually a period of 6–8 weeks. Some prefer it.

Upstream from Three Forks, several streams converge, including Louse Canyon and Toppin Creek, both impressive canyons. Somewhat smaller are Duke's Creek, Antelope, Twin Springs, Massie, Bald Mountain, Spring Creek, and Dry Canyons. In all, about 95 mi. of canyons. Canyon walls are mostly rhyolite in shades of red and yellow, with some sedimentary formations. Several caves are of interest to spelunkers.

Some sections of the canyon floors can be hiked. The going is uneven: ledges, boulders, sand, gravel, and streamside vegetation. At rapids it can be a difficult obstacle course, more rock climbing than hiking. Advice from the BLM could avoid a time-consuming descent into a forbidding section.

As recently as the 1940s, river runners reported that beaver, muskrat, deer, otter, and coyote had not yet learned fear of human beings. Wild animals are less wary of boats than of people on foot, so the change may not have been great. The cliffs are nesting sites for raptors. Ducks, geese, cormorants, and vultures are commonly seen.

Louse Canyon, shown on some maps as Larosa Canyon, is spectacular. The stream rises in high country near the NV border, flows N, and is joined by Toppin Creek. We found no evidence that rafting is ever feasible, but hiking the canyon, while certainly not easy, is said to offer fewer obstacles than the South Fork. Some experienced backpackers carry air mattresses for floating gear across deep pools. The BLM recreation guide map shows an unpaved road to the canyon, but advice from the Vale office should be obtained.

The plateau around the canyons is typical of OR high desert: sagebrush flats, playas, some gently sloping hills, a few buttes. Sacramento Hill, S of the confluence of Antelope Creek and the West Little Owyhee, is 5,395 ft. Horse Hill, about 20 mi. further S, is 6,440 ft., highest point in the area.

Annual precipitation is under 10 in. Winter is the "wet" season, often with snow rather than rain. Temperatures can be extreme, from −30°F to 100°F.

Two roads penetrate the area, and it has many miles of ways. All precautions advised for desert travel should be observed.

ADJACENT: Owyhee River (see entry).

HEADQUARTERS: Vale District, Bureau of Land Management, P.O. Box 700, Vale, OR 97018; (503) 473-3144.

PUEBLO MOUNTAINS
U.S. Bureau of Land Management
77,400 acres (additional acreage in NV).

4 mi. SW of Fields. Mountains roughly parallel road from Fields to Denio, NV. Local and BLM roads into the area from Field-Denio Road.

The Oregon High Desert Study Group (see OR bibliography) made this area their first recommendation for wilderness designation. Rugged topography, including the high peaks of the Pueblo Mountains, basins between peaks, steep slopes, large drainages, canyons, and foothills. Two N–S ridges. E ridge includes Pueblo Mountain, 8,725 ft. Western ridge, generally over 7,000 ft., continues into NV near the Charles Sheldon Antelope Range wilderness area.

Vegetation includes sagebrush and grasses in the lower foothills, aspen and mountain mahogany higher. Aspen, willow, cottonwood by springs and streams. Some mountain meadows, grassy slopes. Snowfall rather heavy at high elevations, limiting access until early summer. Snowmelt supports springs and perennial streams.

Area is said to be rich in wildlife, as habitat conditions would indicate, but few details are available. Similarly, hikers have mentioned splendid late spring wildflower displays, but no species list is available.

Hiking, backpacking: The Desert Trail Association, BLM, and State Department of Recreation have cooperated to mark a 22-mi. trail through the Pueblo Mountains from Denio Creek N to the Reoux Ranch. A trail guide has been prepared. In general, canyons are preferred travel routes, basins preferred campsites. June and Sept. are favored months for desert hikes. Consult the BLM Burns office for routes, current conditions.

HEADQUARTERS: Burns District, Bureau of Land Management, 74 S. Alvord St., Burns, OR 97720; (503) 573-2071.

SHEEPSHEAD MOUNTAINS
U.S. Bureau of Land Management
190,000 acres.

W and NW of Burns Junction. W of SR 78. E of Steens Mountain and the Fields-Crowley Road. Access by local and BLM roads from SR 78.

Nearby Steens Mountain attracts many more visitors. The roadless Sheepshead region is less dramatic but offers enough variety to interest hikers. E of the Steens Mountain escarpment are gently rolling hills and small ridges rising to a large N–S ridge. E of the ridge the land drops sharply to a valley with several dry lakebeds, small ridges and rimrocked buttes, scattered rock outcrops. Further E is a major N–S ridge with a steep, though not high, W-facing escarpment, while S of this area are many steep ridgelines, small flat-topped buttes, a large dry lakebed. Numerous small canyons offer hiking routes, but much of the terrain has gentle to moderate slopes.

The area is arid, in the Steens Mountain rain shadow, and treeless except for a few junipers. Vegetation is mostly sagebrush and grasses. Water is unavailable except in spring runoff. Wildlife is said to be abundant, including pronghorn, wild horse, chukar.

PUBLICATION: Steens Mountain Recreation Lands map, BLM, includes most of this area.

HEADQUARTERS: Burns District, Bureau of Land Management, 74 S. Alvord St., Burns, OR 97720; (503) 573-2071.

STEENS MOUNTAIN RECREATION LANDS
U.S. Bureau of Land Management
147,773 acres.

60 mi. S of Burns on SR 205. Loop road begins at Frenchglen. Hiking routes from the E, N of Fields, are demanding.

In the high desert. Steens Mountain is a huge fault block, 30 mi. long. E face is a rugged escarpment rising 1 mi. above the desert floor to a high point at 9,773 ft. From the top of the escarpment, the land slopes gradually to the W, rolling hills cut by canyons. From the escarpment, one looks out over the Alvord Basin (see entry). Seen to the W is the high plateau of Hart Mountain (see entry).

Climate is semiarid. Most precipitation falls as winter snow. Winters are cold, summers moderate. Because of snow, access to the high elevations is usually mid-July through late October. Summer thunderstorms are common, sometimes severe, sometimes with hail or snow.

An unusual feature is the presence of several U-shaped gorges, products of glaciation. Canyon of the Donner und Blitzen River runs generally N about

10 mi., up to 700 ft. deep, 1/4–1/2 mi. wide, cut into the desert plateau. Kiger Gorge, also running N, is in the NE corner of the site. Most other drainages are canyons or gorges cut into the escarpment by E-flowing streams.

Chronic overgrazing altered the mountain's vegetation. Cattle are still grazed under permit, but domestic sheep have been removed.

Numerous streams, a few perennial, most intermittent. In the high country, a few small lakes formed by glacial action.

Plants: Below 5,500 ft., mostly sagebrush community. The juniper belt lies between 5,500 and 6,500 ft., aspen belt from there up to 8,000 ft., the alpine bunchgrass belt beyond. Variations depend on terrain, soils, and microclimate. Thickets of aspen, willow, alder along drainages. Mountain mahogany on some high slopes. An oddity is Fir Canyon, with several groves of white fir, remote from the general range of that species. We could find no wildflower list but were told that the displays are spectacular, moving up the slopes with the receding snow, reaching a climax in the upper alpine meadows where they appear as seas of yellow, sometimes purple.

Birds: No checklist. Game species include chukar, sage grouse, California quail, mourning dove. Others noted: golden eagle, red-tailed hawk, kestrel, prairie falcon, great horned owl, common flicker, western kingbird, barn and cliff swallows, mountain bluebird, magpie, raven, rock wren, loggerhead shrike, yellow warbler, western meadowlark, sage sparrow, Cassin's finch.

Mammals: No checklist. Bighorn sheep reintroduced. Mule deer; pronghorn on lower slopes. Coyote, bobcat, mountain lion, yellow-bellied marmot, beaver, black-tailed jackrabbit, ground squirrels, chipmunk, wild horse.

FEATURE: *Steens Mountain Road* begins at Frenchglen, ascends the slope to the ridge, turns S, and returns to SR 205 about 10 mi. S of the starting point. The highest section is usually closed Nov. 1–July 1, others Dec. 1–May 15, depending on weather. The road can be hazardous in summer storms.

ACTIVITIES

Camping: In designated sites only. Four campgrounds, 44 sites. Limited facilities. Season linked to road opening.

Hiking, backpacking: Moderately popular backpacking area. BLM maps show primitive roads, not trails. Canyons and gorges are the natural routes, and most have visible trails, but conditions vary. Approaches from the E are steep, some with difficult sections, those from the W more gradual. Hiking along the ridge is impractical. Consult BLM Burns office for current conditions. In the high country, be prepared for sudden changes in weather.

Hunting: State regulations.

Fishing: Fish and Wildhorse lakes stocked; also lower Donner und Blitzen River. Rainbow, redband, brook, and Lahontan trout. Special regulations established by OR Fish and Wildlife Commission.

Ski touring: Above 6,500 ft. elevation.

Snowmobiling: Prohibited below 6,500 ft. and above 8,000 ft.

Alpine vegetation is fragile. Vehicles must stay on roads, and visitors are urged to walk only on well-defined paths.

PUBLICATION: BLM area map.

HEADQUARTERS: Burns District, Bureau of Land Management, 74 S. Alvord St., Burns, OR 97720; (503) 573-2071.

SUCCOR CREEK STATE RECREATION AREA
Oregon Parks and Recreation Division
1,910 acres.

From Nyssa on US 20/26, 30 mi. S on SR 201. Left turn into park is well marked.

Directly E of The Honeycombs (see entry, Lake Owyhee) and also an area of exceptionally colorful and scenic rock formations: pinnacles, towers, spires, buttresses, slides, balanced rocks. Good rockhounding, including thunder egg beds, and the usual State Park rules have been modified to permit amateur collecting. Elevation about 2,650 ft., mountains over 5,000 ft. nearby. Succor Creek flows all year, very heavily in spring.

Plants: Sagebrush and scrub brush. On hillsides, dark-leaved antelope bitterbrush, choke cherry, broom snakeweed. Streamside: bluebunch wheatgrass, alder, willow.

Birds: No checklist. Reported: California quail, chukar, rock dove, red-tailed hawk, kestrel, golden eagle, swallows.

Mammals: No checklist. Reported: mule deer, raccoon, black-tailed jackrabbit, cottontail, ground squirrels, coyote. Bighorn sheep reintroduced just W of site.

Reptiles and amphibians: No checklist. Reported: rattlesnake, gopher snake, yellow-bellied racer, garter snake, tree frog, side-blotched lizard, sagebrush lizard, collared lizard.

ACTIVITIES
Camping: 19 primitive sites. Late spring (May) through Sept. and early Oct., depending on weather.
Hiking: A good base for exploring adjoining BLM lands. No marked trails.
Hunting: Usual State Park rules modified to permit seasonal hunting of upland game birds in portions of site. Inquire.

Access road is impassable during and immediately after heavy rain.

PUBLICATION: Special regulations.

HEADQUARTERS: c/o Farewell Bend State Park, Star Route, Huntington, OR 97907; (503) 869-2365.

TROUT CREEK MOUNTAINS
U.S. Bureau of Land Management
140,000 acres.

Just N of the NV border, E of Denio, NV. Within an area bounded by the border, a county road 13 mi. N from Denio, a road from there NE through Whitehorse Ranch to US 95, then along US 95 to the NV border at McDermitt. Access can be a problem because roads into the area cross private land and can be closed by landowners. Also, these roads require pickup trucks or 4-wheel-drive vehicles. Consult BLM office for current conditions.

A fault block range rising gradually from the N and W, much more sharply on the E side. Elevations to more than 7,000 ft. The high country receives heavy snow. Creeks have cut canyons, some over 1,000 ft. deep. Flowing generally NW and N: Trout, Willow, Whitehorse, Antelope, and Twelvemile creeks.

Mountains have steep slopes, rugged terrain. On the W, rounded hillsides with intermittent streams. To the NW, flat-topped ridges deeply cut by streams. The N foothills have steep, rimrocked canyons, rounded ridges, plateaus. From the high places, tremendous views of distant mountains, Alvord Desert, Paradise Valley.

By contrast with the surrounding desert, the hills and ravines are refreshingly green. In addition to the usual sagebrush and bunchgrass, one sees scattered groves of aspen and mountain mahogany, clumps of snowberry and serviceberry, occasional junipers, alder and willow beside streams and springs. Wildflower displays are colorful as snow melts in late spring.

Wildlife is said to be abundant, as the habitat would indicate, but no details are available. Species mentioned include beaver, mule deer, pronghorn, coyote, black-tailed jackrabbit, ground squirrel, bobcat.

The area is well known to hunters, not yet discovered by many hikers and backpackers.

Hiking, backpacking: Late spring and early fall offer the best hiking weather. Spring is preferred, since by fall some streams are dry. Miles of ways, but hikers generally prefer the canyons.

HEADQUARTERS: W portion of area: Burns District, Bureau of Land Management, 74 S. Alvord St., Burns, OR 97720; (503) 573-2071. E portion: Vale District, BLM, P.O. Box 700, Vale, OR 97018; (503) 473-3144.

WASHINGTON

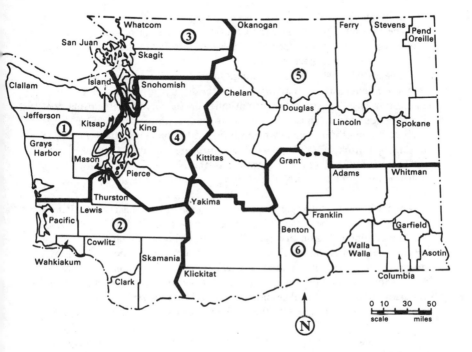

Whatcom		Okanogan	Ferry	Stevens	Pend Oreille

San Juan

③

Skagit

Clallam

Island

Snohomish

Chelan

⑤

Jefferson

Kitsap

King

Douglas

Lincoln

Spokane

Grays Harbor

Mason

④

Kittitas

Grant

Adams

Whitman

Pierce

Thurston

Yakima

Franklin

Lewis

②

Benton

Walla Walla

Garfield

Pacific

Cowlitz

Skamania

⑥

Asotin

Wahkiakum

Clark

Klickitat

Columbia

0 10   30   50
scale   miles

N

WASHINGTON

Washington's best-known features are the Olympic Peninsula, Puget Sound and the associated Straits, and the Cascade Range, a splendid array of high mountains extending from Canada to Oregon. For those interested in natural areas, there is much more.

Travelers who have driven N along Oregon's scenic coastal highway will find no counterpart in Washington. In the S, US 101 briefly skirts some interesting bays, but for only a dozen miles on the Olympic Peninsula does it run beside the sea. Those who take spur roads to the seacoast will find that little of it remains in public ownership. Several points and jetties offer good birding opportunities. Of the remaining natural areas on the S Coast, Leadbetter Point is by far the most interesting. In the N, a long strip of seacoast is a disjunct part of Olympic National Park, a wilderness beach with few access points.

The Park and the Olympic National Forest occupy the heart of the Peninsula. Several roads penetrate the Park, but none cross it. On the W side of this mountainous region are rain forests receiving as much as 130 in. of precipitation yearly; on the E, in the rain shadow, precipitation is as little as 20–30 in. In the warmth of an area where snow rarely falls, one can look up to see snowfields in midsummer. Auto routes are wonderfully scenic, but this is chiefly country for the hiker and backpacker. One can stroll on an easy trail among giant trees or pack into the roadless high country where an ice axe is needed even in summer.

For sailors, NW Washington is heaven. Under sail or power one could spend several lifetimes exploring the sounds, bays, straits, coves, and harbors of the region, as well as the hundreds of islands. Unfortunately for our purposes, little of the shoreline remains in public ownership. Of the fragments still owned by the state, most are state-owned only up to the high-water mark, with no access from any public road. Those we saw offered little of interest except to clam diggers. We found a few sites to include as entries, chiefly on the San Juan Islands.

The Cascade Range is a formidable barrier both to the E flow of moist air and to human traffic. Until a few years ago, US 2 over Stevens Pass was the most N transstate route, and only one other E–W crossing was kept open in winter. Now the heaviest traffic moves on I-90 from Seattle to Spokane. Completion of SR 20 across the North Cascades provides a N route into the previously isolated NE quarter of the state. One result has been a marked increase in visitors to the Pasayten Wilderness.

National Parks and Forests form an almost solid block of public land along the Cascade Range, more than 7.6 million acres. Most of this region is heavily forested and wildlife is abundant. The region has many lakes, more on the E side than the W, and many streams flow down from the high snowfields. Although few roads cross the range, many Forest roads enter it, usually following streams. Many Forest Service campgrounds and trailheads are along these roads, a number of which end near the boundaries of wilderness areas.

Much of the central part of the state is within the Columbia River basin. The once free-flowing river is now a series of impoundments, and dams have also been built on a number of its tributaries. The climate of the basin is semiarid, annual precipitation averaging only 8–10 in. While the dams caused inundation of much wildlife habitat, they created some; the basin has many seep lakes, potholes, marshes, and other wetlands which support large numbers of nesting and migrating waterfowl, wading birds, and shorebirds.

The NE corner of the state is mountainous, but these mountains are neither as high nor as rugged as the Cascades. Hiking trails in the Colville National Forest are open earlier in the season than those in the high Cascades. Even though SR 20 has made the Colville more accessible, most visitors from the W stop at the Cascades.

The E central portion of the state is agricultural land, mostly planted in wheat. The far SE corner includes a bit of the Blue Mountains, extending N from Oregon, and there is interesting country here and along the canyons of the Grande Ronde and Snake rivers.

Unlike Nevada, California, and Oregon, Washington includes very little public domain land. These lands, managed by the federal Bureau of Land Management, make up 25% of the acreage of Oregon, less than 1% of Washington. Washington has more Indian reservations; more public domain land went into railroad grants; more was suitable for homesteading; and the terms of statehood differed. Until 20 years ago, the policy was to sell off the public domain.

The first and most devastating eruption of Mt. St. Helens occurred while we were gathering data for this volume and just before a planned two-month field trip in Oregon and Washington. We soon learned that the most destructive effects were within the Gifford Pinchot National Forest. A much larger area had received heavy ash-fall. Most of the Pinchot had been closed to visitors and a number of State Parks were closed. Substantial ash-fall extended all the way to Idaho.

By the time we arrived in mid-July, almost all sites except the Pinchot had reopened. Life had not returned to normal, for the ash was both pervasive and abrasive. Farmers wore dust masks during the wheat harvest, and the dust ruined many cutting blades. Two eruptions occurred during our visit, adding slightly to the dust blanket.

By early 1981, most of the Pinchot had been reopened, although visitors were warned to take special precautions. Unless more major eruptions occur, visitors to other sites need expect no problems.

FEDERAL AND STATE AGENCIES

FEDERAL AGENCIES
U.S. Forest Service
Pacific Northwest Region
P.O. Box 3623
Portland, OR 97208
(503) 221-2971.

The Mt. Baker–Snoqualmie National Forest maintains an information office in downtown Seattle that can supply many Forest Service publications:

1018 First Ave.
Seattle, WA 98104
(206) 442-0170.

Among the publications below, *Wilderness Solitude Catalog* is of special interest. For each wilderness area in a Washington National Forest, it lists the crowded areas and trailheads to avoid and suggests how to find quiet places.

PUBLICATIONS
Pacific Crest National Scenic Trail—Washington.
Resorts and Packers in the National Forests.
Campground Directory (booklet, maps).
Wilderness Solitude Catalog.
List of Recreation, Wilderness, and Special Area maps for sale.
Northwest Ski (list of commercial ski areas).

National Park Service
Pacific Northwest Regional Office
1424 Fourth Ave.
Seattle, WA 98101
(206) 442-5565

Washington has three National Parks: Mt. Rainier, North Cascades, and Olympic. The Ross Lake and Lake Chelan National Recreation Areas are not, technically, within the North Cascades National Park. The NRA classification permits developments and activities excluded from National Parks. However, both are administered by the North Cascades National Park, and they adjoin it. We have written a combined entry.

Coulee Dam National Recreation Area is a strip of land along Franklin D. Roosevelt Lake, formed by Grand Coulee Dam.

U.S. Fish and Wildlife Service
Pacific Region
500 NE Multnomah St.
Portland, OR 97232
(503) 231-6121

National Wildlife Refuges are scattered throughout the state. We have
written 12 entries. The largest, Columbia, 28,952 acres, is in the Columbia
basin. The smallest is a string of almost 900 tiny islands along the seacoast,
none large enough to permit visitors ashore, many close enough that their
seabird colonies can be observed from the mainland with binoculars. The
islands are administered by the Willapa NWR and are described in that entry.

U.S. Bureau of Land Management
Spokane District Office
Room 551, U.S. Court House
Spokane, WA 99201
(509) 456-2570

The BLM administers about 311,000 acres in Washington. Their Spokane
office recommended four areas for entries, and we found no others. Two of
the four are in the San Juan Islands, for which there is a collective entry.

STATE AGENCIES
Washington Parks and Recreation Commission
7150 Cleanwater Lane
Olympia, WA 98504
(206) 753-5755

Washington has about 135 State Parks. We have entries for 33. A number
of these are not, in themselves, natural areas. We included them because they
adjoin natural areas.

In the early stages, we had difficulty gathering information about the parks.
No one seemed able to tell us about their fauna, flora, and other natural
characteristics. Later discussions with park officials explained why. It is not
the function of Washington State Parks to preserve natural areas. Their
primary mission is public recreation. Interpretive programs emphasize historical and cultural themes; only one park emphasizes natural history. No great
effort has been made to gather information about the parks' fauna and flora.

We had to see for ourselves. If a park's size, location, or other factor
suggested that it might be a suitable entry, we put it on our itinerary.

Most parks we saw are attractive and obviously serve a public purpose. No
doubt the presence of such large National Parks and National Forests has
made it seem less necessary for the state to take initiatives in preserving
natural sites.

Of the State Parks, 95 have campgrounds. Most are open all year. An experimental campsite reservation system started in 1980 at 16 of the most popular parks. Park managers we talked with expected this list would change from year to year, at least for the next few years. Reservations in the listed parks could be made, by telephone only, at the Olympia reservation center. (Toll free within Washington: 1-800-562-0990. Outside Washington: [206] 753-2002.) Since the system, too, may change, write for the circular listed below.

PUBLICATIONS

Washington State Outdoor Recreation Guide. (Issued annually, listing parks and facilities.)
Park rules and regulations.
Campground reservation information.

Washington Department of Natural Resources
Public Lands Building
Olympia, WA 98504
(206) 753-5327

The DNR manages about 3 million acres of land. Most of this was given to the state by the federal government in 1889 to support public schools. Some was acquired by foreclosures on tax delinquent properties. The DNR is under legal mandate to manage these lands for maximum long-term net revenue.

Critics of the DNR, including some professionals on the DNR staff, argue that the mandate is bad public policy. Acknowledging that DNR management has brought about recovery of some devastated areas, they contend that achieving high income, chiefly from timber sales, improperly subordinates good water and wildlife management, public recreation, and survival of plant species other than those which produce revenue.

Management of these lands would seem next to impossible because of their distribution. The area of the state is more than 68,000 square mi. At the time of statehood, the state was divided into townships, each a square 6 by 6 mi.: 36 1-mi.-square sections. The federal land grant deeded every Section 16 and Section 36 to the state. Although some of these 1-mi. blocks have been sold or traded, most have not. They appear as red freckles on the public lands map. Foreclosures, purchases, and exchanges have established state ownership of a few larger blocks of land. The five largest, ranging from 33,000 acres to 177,000 acres, are now managed as Multiple Use Areas, much the same as State Forests in other states. Each has one or more campgrounds, fairly good roads, and hiking opportunities. All five are entries. The MUA's are not well known even in Washington. We talked with local campers who had never heard of them. They are likely to be busy places in hunting season. In our midsummer visits, we saw visitors in each of them but no campground was full.

The DNR maintains about 75 camp and picnic sites on its other lands. (The leaflet lists 116 camp and picnic sites, including those in MUA's. A DNR publication says there are 160.) These sites are generally on 25- to 40-acre plots within a DNR landholding that may total 640 acres or less. Most sites are fenced to exclude cattle. Some have pit toilets, tables, perhaps hand water pumps. Neither they nor the MUA campgrounds are listed in popular national campground directories. We were told the leaflet noted hereafter is distributed at state and county fairs in Washington.

The sites are used mostly by hunters and fishermen. We could not visit all of them. Those we did were unoccupied in midsummer. The sites were wooded and attractive. Most were near paved roads. The short access roads were from good to poor but not impassable. We did not consider these sites as entries, with a few exceptions, because we could not assess surrounding areas. One can't tell where state land ends and private land begins. The traveler who prefers simple, quiet campsites will find the leaflet useful.

PUBLICATIONS
Five Million Acres. (Describes DNR operations.)
Guide to camp and picnic sites.

Department of Game
600 N. Capitol Way
Olympia, WA 98504
(206) 753-5700

This department manages about 800,000 acres of land for wildlife-oriented recreation. The largest Habitat Management Area* is about 150,000 acres; several have less than 1,000. All are busy in hunting season. At other times, especially in spring and early summer, they are delightful places for camping, hiking, birding, and—in some cases—canoeing.

Like wildlife departments in many states, Washington's Game Department is giving increasing attention to nonhunted wildlife species and to "nonconsumptive users," visitors who don't hunt or fish. The shift in emphasis is never easy. Usually it is vigorously opposed by the potent hunter lobby and by old-timers in the wildlife service.

The hunters have an argument. Game departments are generally supported by hunting and fishing license fees, which the nonconsumptive user doesn't pay. One Washington Habitat Management Area manager told us that more than half of his visitors today are nonconsumptive users. He welcomes this, he said, but his budget is pinched by the influx of visitors in spring and summer. He still has maps for free distribution to hunters, but he can't afford to hand them out after the hunting season.

---

*After our entries had been written, the department renamed all of its Wildlife Recreation Areas, now calls them Habitat Management Areas. We hope we've made the substitution everywhere. The WRA title still appears in many publications.

Camping is permitted in most Habitat Management Areas. HMA camp-sites are simple. Most have latrines. Few have water. Few have waste bins; you're expected to carry away your trash. We saw a number of campgrounds beside small lakes. Overnight RV parking is generally permitted at the depart-ment's many boat-access points. Game Department campgrounds are not listed in popular national directories. In midsummer, we were the only camp-ers at several of them; we saw none crowded.

Many of the Habitat Management Areas, chiefly the larger ones, have on-site headquarters. We were advised to list the regional offices rather than local headquarters in our entries. Local managers are more likely to be out in the field than in their offices, and they aren't equipped to handle mail inquiries.

PUBLICATIONS
Wildlife Recreation Areas. (Map and descriptions.)
Columbia Basin Recreation Areas.

REFERENCES
The following publications do not constitute a comprehensive bibliography, more a sampling of what is available. Many of the publishers listed specialize in regional items, including but not limited to natural history. Most will send their current lists on request.
Books pertaining to more than one state are listed in the main Preface, not here.

GENERAL
Evans, Brock, and Cooper, Ed. *The Alpine Lakes.* Seattle: Mountaineers.
Hansen, Mel. *Indian Heaven Back Country.* Beaverton, OR: Touchstone Press.
Kirk, Ruth. *Exploring the Olympic Peninsula.* Seattle: University of Wash-ington Press, 1979.
Yakima Scenic and Recreational Highway. Washington State Parks and Recreation Commission, Olympia, Washington.

WILDLIFE
Schwartz, Susan, and Spring, Bob and Ira. *Wildlife Areas of Washington.* Seattle, WA: Superior Publishing. $9.95.
Larrison, Earl J. *Washington Wildflowers.* Seattle, WA: Seattle Audubon Society. $7.95.
Larrison, Earl J. *Mammals of the Northwest.* Seattle, WA: Seattle Audubon Society. $8.50.
Pyle, Robert M. *Watching Washington Butterflies.* Seattle, WA: Seattle Audubon Society. $4.50.
Washington State Game Department. *Washington Wildlife.* Quarterly.
Lyons. *Trees, Shrubs, and Flowers to Know in Washington.* Available from

Pacific Northwest National Parks Association, North Cascades Branch, at Park HQ, North Cascades National Park. $2.00.

HIKING

Dean, John. *Hiking the Inland Empire.* Lynnwood, WA: Signpost Publications. $3.95.

Manning, Harvey, and Spring, Bob and Ira. *Footsore 1, 2, 3,* and *4.* Seattle, WA: Mountaineers. $5.95 each.

Spring, Ira. *101 Hikes in the North Cascades.* Seattle, WA: Mountaineers. $6.95.

Manning, Harvey, and Spring, Bob and Ira. *102 Hikes in the Alpine Lakes, South Cascades and Olympics.* Seattle, WA: Mountaineers. $6.95.

Sterling, E. M. *Trips and Trails 1* and *2.* Seattle, WA: Mountaineers. $5.95 each.

BOATING

Bultmann, Phyllis and Bill. *12 Cruises Through the San Juans and Gulf Islands.* Seattle, WA: Pacific Search Press.

Mueller, Marge. *San Juans Afoot and Afloat.* Seattle, WA: Mountaineers. $6.95.

Furrer, Werner. *Water Trails of Washington.* Lynnwood, WA: Signpost Publications.

SKI TOURING

McDougall, Randy. *Snow Tours in Western Washington.* Lynnwood, WA: Signpost Publications.

ZONE 1

1 Olympic National Forest
2 Olympic National Park
3 Dungeness National Wildlife
   Refuge
4 Bogachiel State Park
5 Dosewallips State Park
6 Lake Cushman State Park
7 Hood Canal Beaches
8 Tahuya Multiple Use Area

9 Olympic Beaches
10 Oyhut Habitat Management
   Area/Ocean Shores
11 Twin Harbors Beaches
12 Olympic Habitat Management
   Area
13 Schafer State Park
14 Johns River Habitat
   Management Area

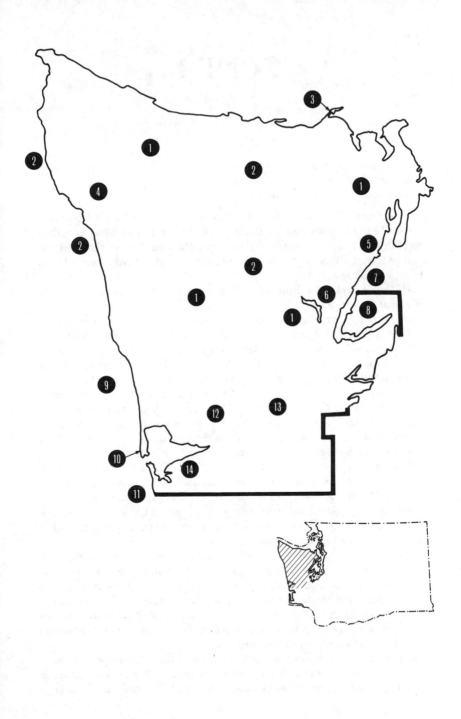

ZONE 1

Includes these counties:
Clallam   Grays Harbor
Jefferson   Mason

The Olympic Peninsula is bounded on three sides by the Pacific Ocean, the Strait of Juan de Fuca, and the Hood Canal. The central portion, more than half the total area, is within the Olympic National Forest and Olympic National Park. This central portion is mountainous, heavily forested, and largely wilderness.

US 101 encircles the Peninsula. N of Aberdeen, the traveler enters the National Forest. Even a short detour to Quinault Lake offers a look at splendid old-growth rain forest. US 101 then turns seaward. A side road follows the Queets River into the S part of the National Park, another through state-owned forests to the Hoh River. US 101 enters the Pacific Coast Area of the National Park, then turns inland, following the Hoh. In about 10 miles it turns NW, while a side road continues E into the Hoh Rain Forest.

Just beyond Forks is the road to La Push, a seaside fishing community within the Pacific Coast Area of the Park. Beyond here, the only access to the Park beach is on foot. Soon 101 turns E, passes through a part of the Forest, and—for the only time—passes through a bit of the main Park, following the S shore of Lake Crescent.

Now 101 becomes a somewhat busier road for a while, entering the city of Port Angeles, gateway to the principal Park entrance. One can turn back to the W on SR 112, following the Strait of Juan de Fuca, coming eventually to Cape Flattery, westernmost point of the conterminous United States. A path leads to a viewpoint on a rocky cliff, looking down at caves and arches worn into the rock by breaking waves.

US 101 stays on private land, passing through or near several communities, until it turns S, passes Quilcene, and enters the National Forest again. At Dosewallips a road leads W through the Forest and into the Park. Then, for some miles, 101 is beside or near the Hood Canal. Here and on the shore of the canal after it turns NE are a number of small State Parks. We have not included them as entries, because they are recreation sites rather than natural areas, but most have boat-launching ramps.

Along this route are various sites described in the following entries, such as the Dungeness National Wildlife Refuge to the E of Port Angeles. One can also find many opportunities to wander and explore. For example, a large block of state-owned forest lies N of the Hoh River, between the main body of the Park and its Pacific Coast Area. This is managed by the Washington Department of Natural Resources for timber production, but it's open to visitors. Ten small primitive campgrounds are within this area, none mentioned in any of the campground directories we have at hand.

But by far the greatest opportunities for exploration are within the more than 1.5 million acres of National Park and Forest. Most of the Park is roadless. The surrounding Forest is not. You need the Forest map, which shows hundreds of miles of Forest roads, few carrying any traffic.

REFERENCES
Kirk, Ruth. *Exploring the Olympic Peninsula.* Seattle: University of Washington Press, 1980. $4.95.
Spring, Bob and Ira, and Manning, Harvey. *102 Hikes in the Alpine Lakes, South Cascades, and Olympics.* Seattle: Mountaineers. $5.95.
*Stewart, Charles. *Wildflowers of the Olympics.* $4.25.
Namkung, Johsel, and Kirk, Ruth. *The Olympic Rain Forest.* Seattle: University of Washington Press, 1973.

BOGACHIEL STATE PARK
Washington Parks and Recreation Commission
119 acres.

On US 101, 6 mi. S of Forks.

Small park with 2,800-ft. frontage on the Bogachiel River. Sample of rain forest. Nearby trail along the Bogachiel River into the National Park.

ACTIVITIES
Camping: 41 sites. All year.
Fishing: Salmon, steelhead, rainbow, Dolly Varden, cutthroat.

HEADQUARTERS: Box 369, Forks, WA 98331; (206) 374-6356.

DOSEWALLIPS STATE PARK
Washington Parks and Recreation Commission
425 acres.

---

*This and other publications about the region are offered for sale by Pacific Northwest National Parks Association, 2800 Hurricane Ridge Rd., Port Angeles, WA 98362. A list is available.

On US 101 and Hood Canal, 1 mi. S of Brinnon.

On the Hood Canal and Dosewallips River. From here a road goes W along the river, through a section of the National Forest, and in the W entrance of the National Park, about 14 miles from the State Park.

The flat meadows were old homesteads before acquisition as a park. Some wooded upland. The Park is a wintering ground for a herd of about 150 elk.

Camping: 153 sites. All year. Reservations.

HEADQUARTERS: P.O. Drawer K, Brinnon, WA 98320; (206) 796-4415.

DUNGENESS NATIONAL WILDLIFE REFUGE
U.S. Fish and Wildlife Service
756 acres.

From 4 mi. W of Sequim on US 101, N 3 mi. on local roads to Refuge, following signs.

When most of the Olympic Peninsula is wet and chilly, this site is likely to be dry and sunny; Sequim is in the mountains' rain shadow and receives less than 18 in. of rain per year. A favorite spot for birders, partly because of large numbers of bird species, with many shorebirds, ducks, geese.

The Refuge is a natural sand spit projecting 5 1/2 mi. into the Strait of Juan de Fuca. Parking is at the entrance. Only foot travel beyond that point. The sand spit curves to the NE. About 2 miles before the tip, Graveyard Spit projects due S into New Dungeness Bay.

Sand beaches, tidelands, protected bay waters, open saltwater beds of eelgrass, a small forested area near the base of the spit.

Most of the mainland bordering the harbor is outside the Refuge; several developments have been proposed here that would disturb or gravely damage the bay as a wildlife habitat.

Birds: Checklist available. The Fish and Wildlife Service lists as the site's primary species "black brant, ducks, shorebirds." The checklist includes 28 "accidentals," among them yellow-billed loon, New Zealand shearwater, mute swan, gyrfalcon, skua, parakeet auklet, and skylark.

Not including these, 246 species have been recorded. Winter populations include up to 1,500 black brant as well as arctic and red-throated loons, grebes, double-crested and Brandt's cormorants, Canada goose, mallard, pintail, green-winged teal, canvasback, greater scaup, common and Barrow's goldeneye, bufflehead, oldsquaw, harlequin duck; common, white-winged, and surf scoters; common and red-breasted mergansers. Also killdeer, surfbird, dunlin, black turnstone, sanderling. Many more species are seen in spring and fall migrations, while species such as rhinoceros auklet and tufted puffin are most often seen in summer.

ADJACENT: Dungeness Recreation Area, 216 acres. On the Strait of Juan de Fuca, at the National Wildlife Refuge entrance. Camping, hunting.

PUBLICATIONS Bird checklist. Leaflet with map.

HEADQUARTERS: c/o Nisqually National Wildlife Refuge, 100 Brown Farm Rd., Building A, Olympia, WA 98506; (206) 753-9467.

HOOD CANAL BEACHES
Washington Department of Natural Resources

The publication listed for this entry describes 16 state-owned beaches in the Hood Canal area. As explained in the preface, the DNR has responsibility for the remaining fragments of Washington's public beaches. In the great majority of cases, state ownership goes only to the mean high-water line. The adjoining beaches and area above high water are privately owned, and the state has no right-of-way.

Of the 16 beaches described, 15 are thus inaccessible except by boat. Frontages range from 514 ft. to 12,050 ft. One beach just N of Hoodsport is accessible by land; the state owns the strip from the water's edge to the highway. This beach, of cobbles, is 2,951 ft. long.

PUBLICATION: *Your Public Beaches; Hood Canal.* 1978.

HEADQUARTERS: DNR, Division of Marine Land Management, Olympia, WA 98504; (206) 753-5324.

JOHNS RIVER HABITAT MANAGEMENT AREA
Washington Department of Game
1,450 acres.

From Aberdeen, 12 mi. SW on SR 105. Just beyond bridge, turn SE, then N to access.

From near SR 105 and the river's mouth on Grays Harbor, the site extends upstream about 4 mi. on both sides of the Johns River. A dike extends upstream for about 1 mi. on the S side, with a footpath on the dike. The opposite shore is also diked. Tidewater, with tides fluctuating as much as 14 ft. The floodplain is grassy, often wet, cut by channels. Higher ground is woodland, young alder and fir.

Fishermen use the ramp at the HQ area, as do hunters in season. Hunters also hike along the S dike to reach upstream hunting grounds. Otherwise public use is light. We met no one in a visit of several hours.

Birds: Partial checklist in leaflet. Upland game species include blue and ruffed grouse, band-tailed pigeon, Chinese pheasant. Waterfowl in migration: dusky Canada goose, mallard, wigeon, green-winged teal, pintail, scaup. Also noted: red-tailed, marsh, and Cooper's hawks; merlin, kestrel, osprey, buffle-head, wood duck, goldeneye, killdeer, great blue heron, rufous hummingbird, red-winged and Brewer's blackbirds, downy woodpecker, Oregon junco, evening and black-headed grosbeaks; violet-green, cliff, barn, and tree swallows; varied thrush, marsh wren, golden-crowned kinglet. Warblers: orange-crowned, yellow-rumped, black-throated gray, yellow, Wilson's.

Mammals: Big game species include mule deer, Roosevelt elk, black bear. Other mammals include muskrat, mink, coyote, weasel, raccoon, river otter.

ACTIVITIES

Camping: Not prohibited, but no campground and few suitable sites.

Hiking: Easy hiking on dikes, both sides. Leaflet mentions a new access road on the N side of the river.

Hunting: Designated areas, including an island N of the river's mouth.

Fishing: Cutthroat, steelhead, silver salmon.

Boating: Ramp at HQ.

Horse riding: On dikes and established roads only.

PUBLICATION: *Wildlife Recreation Areas 4 & 24.* Leaflet with map.

HEADQUARTERS: Department of Game, Aberdeen Regional Office, 905 E. Heron, Aberdeen, WA 98520; (206) 533-9335.

LAKE CUSHMAN STATE PARK
Washington Parks and Recreation Commission
603 acres.

From Hoodsport on US 101, 7 mi. W on Staircase Rd.

Lake Cushman was formed by damming the Skokomish River, North Fork, which flows from Olympic National Park. The NW tip of the 10-mi.-long lake is about 1/2 mi. from the SE corner of the Park. The lakeshore road ends inside the Park's Staircase entrance, a major trailhead. National Forest land is on both sides of the lake's upper third, but with little actual waterfront. Most of the lakeshore is privately owned.

Plants: Most of the State Park is forested: Douglas-fir with hemlock, western redcedar, white pine. Deciduous trees include alder, bigleaf maple, wild cherry. Understory includes Oregon grape, huckleberry, salal, vine maple, swordfern. Much beargrass, usually seen only at higher elevations. Lake elevation is 750 ft.

Birds: Essentially the species noted in the Olympic National Park and Forest entries.

Mammals: Seen at or near the lake, include Olympic elk, mule deer, raccoon, rabbit, coyote, squirrel, chipmunk, river otter.

ACTIVITIES
Camping: 80 sites. All year.
Fishing: Rainbow, cutthroat, Dolly Varden, kokanee.
Swimming: Lake, unsupervised.
Boating: Ramp.

HEADQUARTERS: P.O. Box 128, Hoodsport, WA 98548; (205) 877-5491.

OLYMPIC BEACHES

Coast of lower Olympic Peninsula, along SR 109.

This section of the Coast is more scenic than most of the coastline further S. In the N section, land rises rather steeply from the beach. Hills are mostly forested, and some sections of forest are quite handsome. Viewpoints are limited, however, and the land is almost all privately owned. Especially in the N section, development outside the resort communities is, as yet, relatively light.

Ocean City State Park, 112 acres, is the largest public site and heavily used. Pacific Beach State Park is a 9-acre in-town campground, congested and unattractive. The state has also provided a number of beach-access points. Motor vehicles are allowed on the beach. Perhaps for this reason beach hiking is not popular.

The most interesting area is the S tip. See entry for Oyhut Habitat Management Area.

Camping: Ocean City State Park, 177 sites. Pacific Beach, 138 sites. Ocean City requires reservations. Ocean City HQ: Rt. 4, Box 283, Hoquiam, WA 98550; (206) 289-3553.

OLYMPIC HABITAT MANAGEMENT AREA
Washington Department of Game
962 acres.

15 mi. N of Aberdeen on Wishkah Rd.

Mostly open fields and brushlands surrounded by tree farms. Managed to promote winter use by elk, deer, and bear. Crossed by the Wishkah River and its West Fork. The area is well away from traveled routes and likely to be people-free outside hunting season. The road passes field HQ just beyond Greenwood, and a stop is worthwhile when it's open.

HEADQUARTERS: Department of Game, Regional Office, 905 E. Heron St., Aberdeen, WA 98520; (206) 532-9680.

OLYMPIC NATIONAL FOREST
U.S. Forest Service
651,487 acres.

Olympic Peninsula. All access roads from US 101, which circles the Peninsula.

The Forest surrounds the Olympic National Park (see entry). Together they occupy the mountainous heart of the Olympic Peninsula. Although parks and forests are governed by different policies (e.g., no logging or hunting in National Parks), for the hiker these two are an entity, many trails from the Forest leading into and crossing the Park.

Highest point in the complex is 7,965-ft. Mt. Olympus at the center of the Park. The range of high, craggy peaks extends into the Forest. Mt. Fricaba, 7,134 ft., is the highest of many high peaks in the E part of the Forest. Terrain is rugged, mountains and ridges radiating in all directions, a pattern carved by ice and water. On the W, some of the land is somewhat less steep, more rolling. The backcountry has alpine meadows, high lakes, rushing streams with falls and cataracts.

The Peninsula is known for sharp contrasts of climate: Mt. Olympus has 200 in. of precipitation per year, while an area 40 mi. away has only 17. Contrasts in the National Forest are not quite so great: about 140 in. a year on the W side, 60 in. on the E. Winters are wet, midsummers dry. The climate is generally mild. At lower elevations winter temperatures are seldom below freezing, and summer days are seldom as hot as 80°F. Heavy snow falls on the high elevations, but most trails are open by June, almost all snow-free in July. Snow rarely accumulates below 1,500 ft.

US 101 is the only state highway within the Forest boundaries. It cuts across the SW corner near Quinault Lake, across the NW corner, and for a mile or two on the E side. Otherwise wheeled travel is on Forest roads, built for logging, their pattern on a map resembling a mass of worms. The wilderness inventory identified 10 roadless areas of 5,000 or more acres.

A moderate climate and 12 ft. of rainfall per year produce a lush rain forest, one of the major timber production areas of the nation. Countless streams carry the runoff, combining in a number of rivers: the Dungeness, Big Quilcene, Dosewallips, Duckabush, Hamma Hamma, South Fork Skokomish, Wynoochee, Humptulips, Quinault, Sitkum, and Soleduck. The Forest borders on 3,730-acre Lake Quinault (controlled by the Quinault Tribal Council) and 1,600-acre Lake Cushman. Wynoochee Lake, 1,120 acres, is within the Forest, although a few inholdings are on its shores. The Forest has about 1/2 mi. of tideland on the Hood Canal.

A few resorts have been developed in the Forest, notably on the S shore of Quinault Lake, and the popular campgrounds are often full in July and August. However, only limited areas of the Forest are accessible by road. The backcountry is open to hikers, hunters, fishermen, and others who travel on foot.

Plants: Heavily forested below 4,000 ft. except for areas recently logged. Principal tree species: Douglas-fir, western hemlock, western redcedar, Sitka spruce. Groves of bigleaf maple. Vegetation is lush and dense in the rain forest, the ground thickly carpeted with mosses, ferns, wood sorrel, oxalis, and decaying vegetation, tree branches draped with moss, giant trees forming a dark canopy overhead. More than 1,000 plant species have been identified on the peninsula, the variety attributable to the wide range of elevations and climate conditions.

Common understory species include coastal rhododendron, salal, swordfern, red and blue huckleberry. Other rain forest species include western coolwort, Dewey sedge, nodding trisetum, false lily-of-the-valley, western springbeauty, ladyfern, oakfern. Alpine wildflower meadows with avalanche lily, phlox, glacier lily, yellow cinquefoil, red paintbrush, white valerian.

Birds: 136 species recorded. Partial checklist available. Includes great blue heron, whistling and trumpeter swans, Canada goose, black brant, white-fronted and snow geese, green-winged teal, many duck species, goshawk; Cooper's, Swainson's, and red-tailed hawks; bald eagle, blue and ruffed grouse, California and mountain quail; pileated, Lewis's, hairy, downy, black-backed three-toed, and northern three-toed woodpeckers; violet-green, tree, rough-winged, barn, and cliff swallows; black-capped, mountain, and chestnut-backed chickadees; red-breasted nuthatch, water ouzel; house, winter,

Bewick's, and long-billed marsh wrens; water pipit, Bohemian and cedar waxwings, Hutton's and warbling vireos. Warblers include orange-crowned, yellow, black-throated gray, Townsend's, MacGillivray's, common yellow-throat, Wilson's. Sparrows include savannah, vesper, chipping, white-crowned, golden-crowned, Lincoln's, song.

Mammals: The Olympics have the nation's largest herd of Roosevelt elk. Mountain goat, introduced to the area, have multiplied. The mountain lion (cougar) population is exceptionally large, although seldom seen. Mule deer are abundant. A curiosity of the area is that, for reasons going back to the Ice Age, a number of mammals common to the Cascades are not found here, among them red fox, lynx, golden-mantled ground squirrel, pika, and wolverine.

A partial checklist of the species found here includes coyote, black bear, raccoon, marten, fisher, short-tailed and long-tailed weasels, mink, spotted and striped skunks, river otter, mountain beaver, yellow pine and Townsend chipmunks, chickaree, beaver, porcupine, snowshoe hare, mountain cottontail, brush rabbit, opossum.

Reptiles and amphibians: Partial checklist includes seven species of salamanders, tailed frog, northwestern toad, Pacific tree frog, Washington frog, bullfrog, Pacific green turtle, Pacific blue-bellied lizard, northwestern rubber snake, dusky garter snake, northwestern garter snake.

FEATURES

Twelve areas totaling 155,000 acres were considered in the 1978 Roadless Area Review and Evaluation (RARE II). Although less than half were recommended for wilderness status, others also have attractive backcountry qualities. As in other cases, we use "wilderness" without a capital "W" descriptively, for areas that had not, at the time of writing, been accorded Wilderness status.

The Brothers wilderness, 15,700 acres. Mountainous, rugged terrain including Mt. Jupiter, 5,701 ft., and The Brothers, 6,866 ft. Adjoins the E boundary of the National Park. Trail along the Duckabush River links with backcountry Park trails. Forest of western hemlock and Douglas-fir up to timberline. Includes Jupiter Lake and several small ponds.

Mt. Skokomish wilderness, 15,900 acres. At the SE corner of the National Forest, a large roadless area, bounded by the Park on the N and W. High mountains, notably Skokomish, 6,434 ft., Stone, 6,612 ft., Pershing, 6,154 ft., Cruiser, 6,104 ft., Washington, 6,255 ft. Headwaters of the Hamma Hamma River. Includes the three Mildred Lakes totaling 55 acres, several smaller ponds. S boundary is close to Lake Cushman. Valley bottoms have dense stands of western hemlock, Douglas-fir, western redcedar. At higher elevations: subalpine fir, western white pine; dwarf juniper near timberline. Upper slopes are rocky, barren, except many wildflowers in the few mountain meadows.

Buckhorn wilderness, 43,300 acres. On the E boundary of the Park, N of The Brothers wilderness, separated from it by the Forest road leading to the Park's Dosewallips entrance. Heavily forested lowland valleys lead into this high-peak mountain meadow country from the N and E. Includes Mt. Fricaba, 7,134 ft., highest in the Forest, several others over 5,000 ft. Several lakes and ponds. Many streams.

Colonel Bob wilderness, 12,200 acres. Just E of Quinault Lake. Rain forest. Colonel Bob Mountain, 4,492 ft., is one of a cluster of peaks between the Quinault and Humptulips rivers. Features include the Fletcher Canyon fault escarpment, Gibson slide. Small, open, marshy area E of Colonel Bob Mountain. Dense coniferous forest.

Quinault Lake area. Just off US 101. Forest borders the S shore, Park the N, Quinault Indian Reservation on the W; the Tribal Council controls the lake. On the S shore, resorts, campground, marina. Nearby: Big Tree Grove, prime example of old-growth rain forest, with 1/4-mi. nature trail, other trails. Also nearby: Quinault Research Natural Area, 1,468 acres. Old-growth western hemlock, Sitka spruce, western redcedar, Douglas-fir with luxuriant understory. Quinault area is wintering ground for Roosevelt elk. Forest road continues beyond the lake, along the river, ending a few miles inside the Park at Graves Creek campground.

Mt. Walker viewpoint. From US 101 near Quilcene, a 5-mi. drive to the 2,800-ft. summit. Views of the Olympic Mountains, Puget Sound, Cascades. Rhododendron display June–July. 2-mi. moderately steep trail to summit begins at start of Forest Road 2730.

Wynoochee Lake. Popular area for camping, boating, fishing, swimming. Nature trail. Trails into the Park. A National Recreation Trail makes a 10-mi. circuit of the lake.

ACTIVITIES

Camping: 19 campgrounds, 356 sites. 6 campgrounds open all year, others closed mid-Sept. to May.

Hiking, backpacking: 212 mi. of trails, many links to trails in the National Park. Backcountry permits not required in the Forest, required in the Park; access to some backcountry Park areas is limited by reservations.

Hunting: Elk, deer, mountain goat.

Fishing: Good fishing in many streams and lakes. Rainbow, cutthroat, brook trout.

Swimming: Wynoochee and Quinault lakes, Hood Canal, a few other lakes.

Boating: Some power boating on Wynoochee Lake. Ramps at Lake Quinault; rules fixed by Tribal Council.

Canoeing: Lakes. Humptulips River, from Fish Trap Rd., about 21 mi. upstream from Humptulips. Some class II rapids.

Horse riding: Forest HQ reports some trail riding; no livery within the site.

Ski touring: Some, on unplowed roads.

PUBLICATIONS
Forest map (includes Olympic National Park). $1.00.
Campground information.
Trail information.
Quinault Rain Forest nature trail guide.
Seal Rock Beach leaflet.
Recreation Opportunity Reports are issued weekly, describing trail conditions.

REFERENCE: Namkung, Johsel, and Kirk, Ruth. *The Olympic Rain Forest.* Seattle: University of Washington Press, 1973.

HEADQUARTERS: P.O. Box 2288, Olympia, WA 98507; (206) 753-9534.

RANGER DISTRICTS: Hoodsport R.D., P.O. Box 68, Hoodsport, WA 98548; (206) 877-5254. Quilcene R.D., Quilcene, WA 98376; (206) 765-3368. Quinault R.D., Quinault, WA 98575; (206) 288-2525. Shelton R.D., P.O. Box 520, Shelton, WA 98584; (206) 426-8265. Soleduck R.D., Star Route 1, Box 185, Forks, WA 98331; (206) 374-6522.

OLYMPIC NATIONAL PARK
U.S. National Park Service
892,578 acres.

Center of the Olympic Peninsula; circled by US 101. Several entrances on the perimeter.

Established by Theodore Roosevelt as an elk refuge in 1909, National Park status was achieved in 1938 after a planning period. The natural terrain and planning combined to make the Park less vulnerable to overuse than many others. Several roads penetrate the Park, but none cross it. Most of the area, including the central portion, is roadless. No overnight accommodations except campgrounds have been permitted on interior Park roads. Those who travel by car enjoy splendid vistas and close-up looks at many Park features, but most of the area can be visited only on foot or horseback.

Near the Park's center is 7,965-ft. Mt. Olympus, the highest point, snow-capped for much of the year, six major glaciers visible in midsummer. Several other peaks exceed 7,000 ft., with many ridges and crests between 5,000 and 6,000 ft. The Park has a total of 60 glaciers, their area totaling 25 sq. mi. Peaks are jagged, sign of geological youthfulness, while below are glacier-carved U-shaped valleys.

Below the glaciers are alpine meadows, bright with wildflowers when the snowfields melt. Lower elevations are forested. Many streams flow from the mountains, join in a number of rivers, notably the Soleduck, Elwha, Dosewallips, Duckabush, Quinault, Queets, Hoh, and Bogachiel. Lake Crescent is the largest body of water, about 10 mi. long, at the N edge of the Park. US 101 passes along its S shore; resorts are at each end of the lake. Numerous small lakes are found in the high country, in basins formed by glaciers.

The Park is surrounded by the Olympic National Forest (see entry) and is linked to it by numerous trails.

Most visitors enter the Park by driving S from Port Angeles and up a good mountain road to Hurricane Ridge, one of the Park's most scenic points. In summer cars can drive several miles more on a steep gravel road to Obstruction Point, 6,450 ft. elevation, with a fine view of Mt. Olympus. Another paved road enters the Park along the Elwha River, a few miles to the W.

Another popular entrance, on the W side, leads to the Hoh Rain Forest, which receives about 140 in. of rainfall yearly. On the SW, roads penetrate the Park at the Queets River and near the N shore of Lake Quinault. On the E and SE, several roads lead to campgrounds a short distance inside Park boundaries.

The separate Pacific Coast Area of the Park is described in the Features section of this entry.

Plants: The life zones and plant species of the Park are much the same as those in the adjoining National Forest and described in that entry. A principal difference is that the Forest is logged, and old-growth stands will be preserved only in wilderness areas and research natural areas. Another is that Park roads reach higher elevations, giving motorists views of the Hudsonian and Arctic-Alpine life zones.

Timberline is at about 5,000 ft. In the upper part of the Hudsonian zone, as at Hurricane Ridge, are prairielike meadows. In early summer some slopes are carpeted with white avalanche lilies; some have great patches of yellow glacier lilies. Other wildflowers of the zone are lupine, larkspur, buttercup, cinquefoil, paintbrush, arnica, tiger lily, and mountain buckwheat. The Arctic-Alpine zone has only perennials adapted to its harsh conditions: rocks, shallow soil, long winters, high winds. Plant life includes mosses, lichens, and a variety of tough, ground-hugging flowering species. The Olympic Mountains have a number of species of mountain plants found nowhere else.

Rain forests are characteristic of the west side of the Park, especially in the Hoh, Queets, and Quinault valleys. The Hoh is most accessible, by road to a visitor center and by an easy, well-maintained trail beyond. Some trees in the rain forest are gigantic: a western redcedar over 21 ft. in diameter, a Sitka spruce over 13 ft., a Douglas-fir over 14 ft. The ground, including the trunks of fallen trees, is thickly carpeted with mosses, clubmosses, oxalis, beadruby, and other plants. Many trees have sprouted from the downed trunks and by now attained considerable size. Bigleaf maples are covered with fantasy draperies of clubmoss.

Birds: Checklist available. About 140 species identified, generally the same species as reported in the National Forest, cited in that entry. Principal difference is for the Pacific Coast Area; species noted there include common, arctic, and red-throated loons; sooty and pink-footed shearwaters, Leach's petrel; double-crested, Brandt's, and pelagic cormorants; white-winged and surf scoters, black oystercatcher, surfbird, black turnstone, knot, dunlin, short-billed and long-billed dowitchers; glaucous-winged, western, herring, ring-billed, mew, and Bonaparte's gulls; pigeon guillemot, common murre, marbled and ancient murrelets, Cassin's and rhinoceros auklets, tufted puffin.

Mammals: Checklist available. Essentially the same species as those in Olympic National Forest entry. Because hunting is not permitted in the Park, some species are seen more often and show little fear of humans. Roosevelt elk, mule deer, and black bear are often seen. The Olympic marmot, similar to the hoary and yellow-bellied marmots, occurs only in the Olympic Mountains.

FEATURES

Pacific Coast Area. A narrow strip of Pacific coastline, 57 mi. long. US 101 runs near the S 12 mi. of the strip. A road leads to the Coast at La Push. Otherwise the area is roadless, reached and traveled only on foot. The coastline is a succession of sandy beaches separated by rocky points and headlands. Numerous needle rocks and small islands are offshore. (About 870 islands off the Washington Coast, from Cape Flattery to Copalis Beach, are included in the Washington Islands National Wildlife Refuge. All are small, some only a few yards across. Together they support vast numbers of nesting and resting seabirds, as well as seals and sea lions. All are closed to visitors, but many can be observed from the Coast with binoculars or spotting scope.) In many places, rockfields and tidepools are exposed at low tide, showing a rich assortment of marine flora and fauna. Coastal forest is just above the beach. Raccoon, skunk, deer, bear, and elk are sometimes seen on beaches.

One of the most popular trails to the beach begins at the N end of Lake Ozette. Indeed, so many people hiked the trail that a single-plank boardwalk was installed to minimize damage to the environment. One of the attractions on the beach but within the Ozette Indian Reservation is an archeological dig of Washington State University, on the beach, open to visitors.

Beach hiking and backpacking are popular, especially in winter when the high country is snowbound. Most campers don't travel far from the access trails. Walk a few miles more and you'll have little company.

Before hiking far, study the leaflet *A Strip of Wilderness.* Some points can't be rounded except at low tide, some not at all; trails lead over them. Fatalities have occurred when hikers were trapped by incoming tides.

Backcountry permits are required.

INTERPRETATION

Three *visitor centers:* at the Hoh Rain Forest, at Lake Crescent, and the Pioneer Memorial Museum near Port Angeles. Audio-visual programs, talks, exhibits, literature, information.

Nature trails are at numerous places, among them Lake Crescent, Hurricane Ridge, Heart O' the Hills, Staircase, Hoh, and Lake Ozette.

Campfire programs and *guided walks* in summer. Schedules posted.

ACTIVITIES

Camping: 17 campgrounds. 946 sites. Some campgrounds at lower elevations open all year. Those at high elevations usually closed by snow from early Nov. to late June or early July.

Hiking, backpacking: About 600 mi. of trails. Many short day trips. Longer, more difficult routes may take a week or more. Backcountry permits required for all overnight trips. Daily entry quotas limit access to Lake Constance and Flapjack Lakes. Check trail conditions and necessary equipment before backpacking into the high country.

Fishing: Cutthroat, rainbow, brook, Dolly Varden, and steelhead in streams. Rainbow and brook trout in some mountain lakes. Special regulations.

Swimming: Crescent Lake, Lake Ozette.

Boating: Ramps on Crescent Lake, Lake Ozette. Boat-in campsite on Lake Ozette.

Canoeing, kayaking: Hoh River, from the road's end at the rain forest visitor center to the sea. Upstream portion is in the Park. Class II and III rapids. Quinault River from bridge on road to Graves Creek Campground to Lake Quinault, about 10 mi. Some class II rapids. Best in summer. River below lake is controlled by Quinault Tribal Council.

Horse riding: HQ will provide current list of packers. Several backcountry trail routes are suitable for pack trips. Hitchracks and loading ramps at several locations. Special regulations.

Snowshoeing, ski touring: Late fall to spring. Trails suitable for short day trips or overnight.

PUBLICATIONS

Park map (includes National Forest).

Park leaflet with map.

A Strip of Wilderness. Leaflet with map for Pacific Coast Area.

Mammals, amphibians and reptiles, checklists.

Bird checklist.

Trees checklist.

Mimeographed information sheets:

    Park history.

    Significant Values of Olympic National Park.

    Rain forests.

    Glaciers.

    Hazards.

    Climbing Mount Olympus.

    Snowshoeing and ski touring.

Backcountry restrictions and regulations.
Summer fishing regulations.
Pack and saddle stock use.
Climate and seasons.

REFERENCES

Hanify, Mary Lou, and Craig W. Blencowe. *Guide to the Hoh Rain Forest.*
Seattle: Superior Publishing.
The following are among the publications offered for sale by the Pacific
Northwest National Parks Association, 2800 Hurricane Ridge Rd., Port
Angeles, WA 98362. Names of publishers and full authors' names are not
shown. Prices are exclusive of handling, postage, and WA sales tax.
Kirk, Ruth. *The Olympic Seashore.* $3.95.
Radlauer. *Olympic National Park.* $2.95.
Leissler. *Roads and Trails of Olympic National Park.* $3.95.
Stewart, Charles. *Guide to Hurricane Ridge.* 25¢.

HEADQUARTERS: 600 East Park Ave., Port Angeles, WA 98362; (206) 452-
4501.

OYHUT HABITAT MANAGEMENT AREA; OCEAN SHORES
Washington Department of Game
682 acres.

From Hoquiam, W 16 mi. on SR 109, then S on SR 115 2 mi. to end. Left
through Ocean Shores gates and 4.6 mi. on South Point Brown Ave. Right
on South Tonquin, over bridge, to end.

Ocean Shores, a burgeoning resort, is on a peninsula, the northernmost of two
enclosing Grays Harbor. At the S end are several areas of interest: the ocean
beaches ending at Point Brown, North Jetty, the Oyhut Habitat Management
Area, and Damon Point.

The Habitat Management Area is marked by a parking area, latrines, and
a small building housing some sort of electronics operation beyond a locked
gate. When we visited, no identifying signs were posted and the bulletin board
was bare. The operator at the electronics station said the area has visitors in
hunting season; otherwise he sees few. No trails, but easy walking over brushy
salt meadow. Walk SW. On the left is salt marsh and Armstrong Bay.

An alternative approach is to turn seaward at Ocean Shores and take Ocean
Shores Boulevard S to the North Jetty, turn left, drive along the seawall and
park near the sewage treatment plant. The Habitat Management Area bound-

ary is behind the plant. Keep to the right and out along the sand spit enclosing Armstrong Bay.

To reach Damon Point, drive N from the sewage plant, turn right on Marine View Drive, pass the first entrance just mentioned and turn right over a jetty onto Protection Island. Park and explore the beach.

We don't know the ownership of the dunes and ocean beach near Pt. Brown. Admonitory signs were refreshingly absent. We saw people swimming, sunbathing, beachcombing, surf fishing; several had apparently camped or parked RV's overnight in the dunes. Fishing and picnicking seemed to be popular at North Jetty. We saw no one within the Habitat Management Area.

Birds: The area is well known to local birders. Geese, mallard, pintail, wigeon, and green-winged teal are the chief game species. Species noted along the shores, dunes, marsh, and meadow include black turnstone, surfbird, rock sandpiper, wandering tattler, snowy plover, semipalmated plover, golden plover, whimbrel, willet, knot, dunlin, short-billed dowitcher, marbled godwit, Virginia rail, sanderling, marsh hawk, horned lark. The jetty is said to be excellent for seabirds, including species such as shearwaters, kittiwake, murre. Rafts of ducks are often seen near the jetty. Like many coastal peninsulas, this one is a funnel for migratory species.

NEARBY: Ocean City State Park, 112 acres. 1 mi. N of Ocean Shores. Also said to be a good birding area. Camping, 177 sites, all year. Seacoast.

HEADQUARTERS: Department of Game, 600 N. Capitol Way, GJ-11, Olympia, WA 98504; (206) 753-5700.

SCHAFER STATE PARK
Washington Parks and Recreation Commission
119 acres.

From Elma on US 12, 12 mi. N on East Satsop Rd.

Heavily wooded site, including large old-growth fir. On the East Fork of the Satsop River. Canoeing and kayaking on the Middle and West forks, nearby. Some class II and III rapids.

Camping: 53 sites. All year.

HEADQUARTERS: Rt. 1, Box 87, Elma, WA 98541; (206) 482-3852.

TAHUYA MULTIPLE USE AREA
Washington Department of Natural Resources
33,000 acres.

On the Tahuya Peninsula, SW corner of Kitsap Peninsula, SW of Bremerton, within the Big Bend of the Hood Canal. By local roads from Belfair.

The area was logged off and abandoned. County governments deeded it to the State Forest Board in return for 75% of future income. As noted in the preface, much of the land managed by the DNR consists of widely scattered small tracts. Here and in a few other cases, blocks are large enough to be managed for broader purposes. The DNR emphasizes, however, that these are trust lands managed primarily for timber production, with annual timber sales on tracts of 20–100 acres.

About 2/3 of the acreage is in one large, irregularly shaped block. Two smaller blocks lie to the NE and SW. A number of much smaller tracts are nearby. Although close to the Hood Canal, the Multiple Use Area has little actual frontage on it. Most of the peninsula is between 200 and 500 ft. elevation. The Green and Gold mountains in the NE reach about 1,700 ft.

Tidelands, brushy swamps, bogs. About 95% of the site is forested. 68 small lakes on the peninsula. Annual precipitation is about 55 in.; summer is the dry season.

Like other Multiple Use Areas, this site is not shown on the state's official highway map and its campgrounds are not listed in popular campground directories. Thus it is most used by residents of the nearby area for hunting, fishing, camping, hiking, horse riding, and motorcycle riding.

Plants: 95% forested: Douglas-fir with western redcedar and hemlock, red alder, cottonwood, quaking aspen along streams and beside swamps. Thousands of acres planted in Christmas trees. Understory of Oregon grape, salal, manzanita, evergreen huckleberry, swordfern, rhododendron. Many wildflowers, including tiger lily, daisy, twinflower, prince's pine, avalanche lily.

Birds: More than 180 species recorded; checklist not available. Game species include waterfowl, ring-necked pheasant, mountain and California quail, ruffed and blue grouse, band-tailed pigeon. Also common flicker, goldfinch, osprey, great blue heron, Steller's jay, kingfisher, marsh wren.

Mammals: Species reported include black bear, coyote, bobcat, mule deer, river otter, beaver, red fox, rabbit.

FEATURES

Viewpoint on Green Mountain. *Bald Point Vista* near tip of the peninsula. *Interpretive signs* at Camp Spillman, Tahuya Horse Camp, Howell Lake.

ACTIVITIES

Camping: 11 campgrounds; 61 sites. All year.

Hiking: 13-mi. trail system used by hikers, horses, and ORV's. Other trails under construction.

Hunting: Deer, bear, game birds.

Fishing: Many of the lakes are stocked. Game Department has provided 14 public accesses.

Swimming: Lake, unsupervised.

Boating: Ramps at Aldrich, Howell, Robbins, and Twin Lakes. Nearby access to Hood Canal.

NEARBY: Belfair State Park, 81 acres. 3 mi. W of Belfair on SR 300. On the Hood Canal. 194 campsites. Popular swimming site.

PUBLICATION: Leaflet with map.

HEADQUARTERS: Department of Natural Resources, South Puget Sound Area, 28239 SE 448th St., Enumclaw, WA 98022; (206) 825-1631.

TWIN HARBORS BEACHES
Washington Parks and Recreation Commission

Coast, between Grays Harbor and Willapa Bay, along SR 105.

Generally a wide sand beach sloping gently to shallow water. Backed by low dunes. Behind the dunes, in undisturbed locations, are shrubs and wildflowers; few trees. Most of the coastal land is privately owned. Largest public sites are Grayland Beach State Park, 210 acres, and Twin Harbors State Park, 168 acres, both heavily used. The state has also provided a number of beach-access points. Motor vehicles use the beach.

Camping: Grayland Beach, 60 sites. Twin Harbors, 332 sites. Both require reservations. Headquarters for both: Westport, WA 98595; (206) 268-6502.

ZONE 2

1 Capitol Forest Multiple Use Area
2 Nisqually National Wildlife Refuge/Nisqually Delta Habitat Management Area
3 Scatter Creek Habitat Management Area
4 Leadbetter Point
5 Long Beach
6 Willapa National Wildlife Refuge
7 Fort Canby State Park
8 Rainbow Falls State Park
9 Lewis and Clark State Park
10 Mount Baker–Snoqualmie National Forest
11 Gifford Pinchot National Forest
12 Columbian White-tailed Deer National Wildlife Refuge
13 Ridgefield National Wildlife Refuge
14 Battle Ground Lake State Park
15 Yacolt Multiple Use Area
16 Beacon Rock State Park

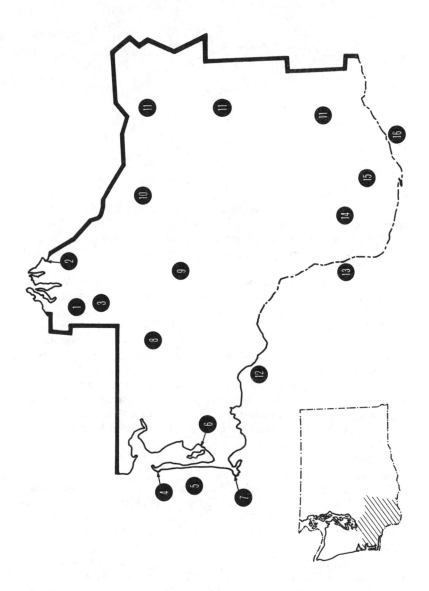

ZONE 2

Includes these counties:

Thurston	Wahkiakum	Clark
Pacific	Cowlitz	
Lewis	Skamania	

This zone extends from the Olympic Peninsula to the Columbia River, from the ocean to the Cascades. By far the largest block of public land is in the Gifford Pinchot National Forest, most of which was closed to public use following the Mt. St. Helens eruption in May 1980. A major part of the closed area has been reopened; see entry.

Tourists who have followed the Oregon Coast N are likely to find Washington's S Coast a disappointment. Grays Harbor and Willapa Bay divide it into three sections. Except for a few miles of SR 109 in the N section, there is no scenic drive. The coastal roads are behind low dunes. Most of the land is privately owned. A few small State Parks and state rights-of-way provide access to the beach. Most of the beach is wide and sandy, sloping gently to shallow water. Motor vehicles are allowed to drive on the beach.

Coastal peninsulas tend to concentrate the flow of migrating birds, and this coastline has a number of birding hot spots. S of Ocean Shores, on Grays Harbor, are the Oyhut Habitat Management Area and North Jetty. At the extreme S, Fort Canby State Park on Cape Disappointment attracts many birders in season. The most outstanding natural area on this section of Coast is Leadbetter Point, its tip a federal wildlife refuge, the adjacent land an undeveloped State Park.

Near the Coast and along the Columbia River are a number of fine state and federal wildlife refuges. Some offer good wildlife viewing from your automobile, others pleasant hiking, while several can be visited only by private boat. The state areas are likely to be almost deserted except in hunting season.

The two largest state-owned sites are the Capitol Forest Multiple Use Area a few miles SW of Olympia and the Yacolt Multiple Use Area a few miles NW of Vancouver. Washington's Multiple Use Areas have some unusual aspects, mentioned in the state preface.

Other public recreation sites are small, scattered, and with limited natural features. We have included a few as entries despite their smallness because no larger natural areas are nearby.

BATTLE GROUND LAKE STATE PARK
Washington Parks and Recreation Commission
280 acres.

From Vancouver, 8 mi. N on I-5. 8 mi. E on SR 502, then 3 mi. on local road to Park.

Rolling terrain, elevations 500 to 690 ft. 28-acre lake. Site is about 65% forested, balance brush and grassy meadows. Douglas-fir dominant, with some old growth. Precipitation about 80 in. annually. Most development is on the SE side of the lake. Heavily used in season.

No data on flora and fauna available. Park Manager says about 150 flowering plant species are present, good dogwood display in spring. Many Steller's jay, crow, sapsucker, flicker, robin, wrens, snow bunting. Some ducks come to the lake. Mammals include deer, cottontail, raccoon, opossum, coyote, fox.

INTERPRETATION: *Nature trail*, 1/3 mi., self-guiding.

ACTIVITIES
Camping: 50 sites. All year, weather permitting. Reservations May 23–Sept. 1.
Hiking: About 9 mi. of trails and fire roads.
Fishing: Rainbow, cutthroat trout.
Swimming: Lake, supervised.
Boating, canoeing: Electric motors only.
Horse riding: 5 mi. of trails. Horse camp. No rentals.

HEADQUARTERS: 17612 NE Palmer Rd., Battleground, WA 98604; (206) 687-4621.

BEACON ROCK STATE PARK
Washington Parks and Recreation Commission
4,250 acres.

On the Columbia River Highway, SR 14, 4 mi. W of Bonneville Dam.

Hilly to steep terrain. Highest point about 2,800 ft. elevation. 2,700 ft. of shoreline. Beacon Rock, a huge monolith, is between the highway and the river, rising 848 ft. Nearly 1 mi. of trail, 15% grade, to top; spectacular views of Columbia Gorge. Most of the Park is across the highway, including all of Hamilton Mountain, most of Little Hamilton, part of Table Mountain. Two high, rocky ridgelines. A popular Park, close to Vancouver and Portland, campground often full on summer weekends. However, most of the site is undeveloped except for trails, and it's usually possible to enjoy a hike without too much company.

Plants: About 60% forested, most of the remainder in tall, heavy brush. Douglas-fir predominates, including some old-growth specimens, over 300 years old, mixed with hardwoods. Other tree species include western hemlock, bigleaf maple, red alder. Heavy understory of vine maple, Pacific dogwood, willow, serviceberry, snowberry, Oregon grape, poison oak, mock orange, ocean spray, salmonberry, hazelnut, blackberry. The high ridges resemble subalpine areas, open with many wildflowers. Over 100 flowering species occur in the park, among them trillium, vanillaleaf, miner's lettuce, bleeding heart, violets, penstemon, monkeyflower, phlox, buttercup, cinquefoil, wallflower, Indian paintbrush.

Birds: No checklist available. Park ranger reports many hawks, ducks, woodpeckers, thrushes, sparrows, jays, finches, and swallows, naming: turkey vulture, red-shafted flicker, pileated woodpecker, varied thrush, Oregon junco, violet-green swallow, ruffed grouse, Canada goose, mallard, red-tailed hawk, great blue heron, rufous hummingbird, Steller's jay, western tanager.

Mammals: No checklist. Park ranger reports mule deer, chickaree, skunk, opossum, porcupine, ground squirrel, cottontail, muskrat, raccoon, coyote, with occasional sightings of elk, otter, beaver, black bear, mountain lion. We saw pika, usually found only at much higher elevations.

INTERPRETATION: *Nature trail,* 1 1/2 mi.; partial list of species posted at trailhead.

ACTIVITIES
Camping: 35 sites. All year.
Hiking: About 10 mi. of trails to such destinations as Rodney Falls, Hardy Falls, crest of Hamilton Mountain. Also 15 mi. of fire road in the back area of the Park, open to ORV's and hiking. To date, ORV use has been light.
Fishing: River, stream. Salmon, sturgeon, shad, trout, smelt.
Boating: Ramp on river. Dock with limited moorage.

PUBLICATION: Site map.

HEADQUARTERS: M. P. 34.83 L. State Road 14, Skamania, WA 98648; (509) 427-8265.

CAPITOL FOREST MULTIPLE USE AREA
Washington Department of Natural Resources
70,000 acres.

SW of Olympia. Coming from the S on I-5, take Maytown exit. US 101 through interchange at Capitol Lake and Tumwater, taking South Tumwater–Black Lake exit to Littlerock and signs to Capitol Forest.

Logging and fires had devastated this area by the early 1900s. State land acquisition began in the 1930s, much bought for 50¢ an acre. Intensive tree planting and forest management began, some 7 million seedlings being planted by 1942. The area was opened to public use in 1955.

In the Black Hills, the area bounded roughly by SR 8 on the N, US 12 on the W, the Black River on the E. Highest point is Capitol Peak, 2,658 ft., lowest 120 ft. Several cold, fast-flowing creeks flow to the Chehalis River, just outside the W boundary. No lakes, but beaver dams have formed some large, shallow ponds.

Annual precipitation is 50 to 65 in. Summers are dry, pleasantly warm days, cool nights.

This is a working forest, managed for timber production. Facilities for recreation are simple. The 75 mi. of roads suitable for pleasure driving are mostly single-lane and gravel. The DNR's Multiple Use Areas are not shown on the official state highway map, and the DNR's campgrounds aren't listed in major campground directories. Thus the site is seldom crowded.

The N half of the trail system has been designated for ORV use. The DNR reports that trail biking is the most popular recreation in the Forest. Hollywood Camp is the focal point for ORV activity.

Plants: Lower ridges and midslopes have a mix of Douglas-fir, western hemlock, western redcedar, red alder, bigleaf maple, with scattered grand fir and Sitka spruce. Subordinate species include cascara, dogwood, vine maple, Pacific yew; willow, alder, and maple along creeks. Abundant groundcover of salal and swordfern. Some higher peaks have silver fir/Douglas-fir forest with grand and noble firs, vine maple, pine-mat manzanita, Oregon boxwood, Pacific rhododendron, big huckleberry. Meadow flowers include camas, violets, wild daisy, buttercup.

Birds: No checklist available. Species noted or reported include goshawk, red-tailed and marsh hawks, kestrel, blue and ruffed grouse, rock dove; screech, great horned, pygmy, and spotted owls; Vaux's swift, common flicker; pileated, hairy, and downy woodpeckers; western flycatcher, wood pewee, violet-green swallow, Steller's jay, raven, crow, Clark's nutcracker, chestnut-backed chickadee, red-breasted nuthatch, brown creeper; house, winter, and Bewick's wrens; varied, hermit, and Swainson's thrushes; Hutton's and solitary vireos. Warblers: yellow, yellow-rumped, Townsend's, hermit. Also western tanager, Cassin's finch, American goldfinch; chipping, white-crowned, fox, and song sparrows.

Mammals: No checklist available. Better forest management has yielded larger, more diverse mammal population. The numbers of deer and black bear have increased; beaver have returned, especially in Upper Sherman Valley. Other species noted or reported include brush rabbit, cottontail, mountain beaver, Townsend chipmunk, chickaree, coyote, long-tailed weasel, bobcat.

FEATURES

Mima Mounds, grass-covered hummocks 5–10 ft. high, 15–25 ft. in diameter, scattered over a natural meadow. Several theories have been advanced to explain their origin.

Old Fuzzy Top is a hill with young forest on its slopes, a patch of 200-year-old Douglas-fir and hemlock near the crest.

Chehalis Valley Vista, overlook at the end of Wood Road.

INTERPRETATION

McLane Creek Nature Trail, 1.1 mi., self-guiding.

Interpretive signs at many campgrounds and along main visitor routes.

ACTIVITIES

Camping: 9 campgrounds. 88 primitive sites.

Hiking: Trail mileage figures seem confused. However, site map shows a number of trails in the S half, where use is limited to hikers and horses. Some forest roads offer good hiking, and bushwhacking is feasible in some areas.

Hunting: Deer, grouse, pigeon.

Fishing: Beaver ponds stocked.

Horse riding: Designated trails. Horse tie rails.

PUBLICATIONS

Leaflet with map.

McLane Creek nature trail guide.

HEADQUARTERS: Department of Natural Resources, Central Area Office, Chehalis, WA 98532; (206) 748-8616.

COLUMBIAN WHITE-TAILED DEER NATIONAL WILDLIFE REFUGE

U.S. Fish and Wildlife Service
4,757 acres, including 1,980 acres in OR.

SW WA, on Columbia River. From Skamokawa on SR 4, SE on Steamboat Slough Rd.

A small Refuge established to maintain this endangered deer subspecies. River bottomland: moist floodplain, pastures separated by blocks of trees.

Numerous sloughs and channels. Several islands are included within the Refuge. Wintering area for waterfowl. Many shorebirds.

The mainland portion of the Refuge is not open to visitors, but it is readily observed from a county road on the perimeter. One can hike along the road, but automobiles are effective blinds. Tenasillahe Island, accessible only by boat, about 2 1/2 mi. by 1 1/2 mi., offers good hiking and birding.

Birds: No checklist. Large wintering populations most years of wigeon, whistling swan, dusky Canada goose, mallard, pintail, loon. Other resident or migratory species often seen include bald eagle, great blue heron, common snipe, western grebe, red-tailed hawk, varied thrush, goldfinch, Steller's jay, Bewick's wren, many gulls.

Mammals: Deer often seen from county road, morning and evening. Also present: mink, beaver, river otter, raccoon.

ACTIVITIES

Hunting: Waterfowl. Designated area. Special regulations.

Fishing: Prohibited within Refuge boundaries but permitted in sloughs on the perimeter.

Boating: Launching sites on SR 4, 4 mi. W of Cathlamet and at Cathlamet Moorage Basin. Boats prohibited on the interior waters of the Refuge.

NOTE: *This HQ also manages the Lewis and Clark National Wildlife Refuge, a large area of islands, bars, and mudflats on the OR side of the Columbia River main channel.*

PUBLICATIONS

Leaflet.

Hunting regulations.

HEADQUARTERS: P.O. Box 566, Cathlamet, WA 98612; (206) 795-3915.

FORT CANBY STATE PARK

Washington Parks and Recreation Commission
1,770 acres.

From US 101 at Ilwaco, 2 1/2 mi. SW.

A developed, heavily used Park on Cape Disappointment, on the Columbia River and Pacific Ocean. More than 11 mi. of ocean shoreline (Benson Beach) as well as frontage on the river and Baker Bay. Includes 40-acre lake. Historical site.

Natural features of interest include the beach, a patch of virgin Sitka spruce–western hemlock forest with trees up to 500 years old, and North Jetty, well known to local birders as a hot spot for sea- and shorebirds.

ACTIVITIES:
Camping: 250 sites. All year. Reservations.
Boating: Two ramps.
Swimming: Ocean, unsupervised.

PUBLICATIONS
Leaflet.
Forest trail guide.

HEADQUARTERS: Ilwaco, WA 98624; (206) 642-3078.

GIFFORD PINCHOT NATIONAL FOREST
U.S. Forest Service
1,251,160 acres of Forest land; 1,356,232 acres within boundaries.

From Mount Rainier National Park to the Columbia River. Crossed by US 12. Access from S via SR 141 through Trout Lake.

In February 1980, Forest HQ returned our data sheets with a fine stack of maps, trail guides, and other information. We knew this Forest fairly well from previous visits and planned no extensive field work there. In the file was this note on geological history: "Although Mt. St. Helens has been dormant since 1857, its active and violent history leads many geologists to predict that the mountain will erupt again, perhaps before the end of the century."

The mountain erupted violently on May 18. In the National Forest, 20,000 acres were devastated, another 200,000 heavily damaged. The destruction included 1.6 billion board ft. of timber, 100 mi. of streams, 27 recreation sites, 63 mi. of roads, 12 bridges, 97 mi. of trails, 15 Forest Service buildings.

For all practical purposes, the Forest was closed to the public. The Pacific Crest Trail segment through the Forest was closed; hikers had to find some kind of transportation around the gap. Outside the area of destruction, much of the Forest had a layer of volcanic ash. No one knew what the mountain would do next.

When we visited in August, coming in from Trout Lake, we could get as far as the Mt. Adams Ranger Station. We studied maps and photographs of the devastation, talked to some of the Forest Service workers. Firefighters told us they must now carry whiskbrooms along with their chainsaws; unless ash is brushed carefully from a tree trunk, it ruins the saw teeth in seconds.

One reason for keeping people out was concern about what would happen in another eruption. We heard stories of hikers who had been on Mt. Adams at the time of the March eruption. The dense cloud of ash had caused a blackout, blinding them, and they had to grope their way down on hands and knees. While we were in Washington two more eruptions occurred, both minor, but enough to dust ash on our campground 100 mi. from the mountain.

On January 23, 1981, two-thirds of the Forest was reopened to public use. Still closed was a zone extending about 20 mi. from Mt. St. Helens. This action opened most of the campgrounds outside the St. Helens Ranger District, the Mt. Adams Wilderness, Indian Heaven Backcountry, and the Pacific Crest Trail. The Goat Rocks Wilderness had been opened earlier. Mt. St. Helens is near the W boundary of the Forest. The open areas outside the blue zone are in the N, E, and S.

The announcement warned that "the public must realize that a certain amount of risk still exists if they enter the newly opened area." Most of those who died in March 1980 were suffocated by ash inhalation. The announcement explained precautions to take that would increase chances of survival.

In March 1981 we asked Forest HQ for a status report, and we owe them thanks for a careful, detailed review of the situation, area by area. A new volcano map showing devastated areas and a number of other publications were being revised for reissue later in the year.

The red zone, roughly a 12-mi. radius around the mountain, will remain closed indefinitely. The blue zone, extending 5 to 10 mi. beyond the red zone, is less restrictive but still closed to recreation use. Visitors are asked to camp outside the blue zone. The zone boundaries are posted. Gates have been placed where roads enter the zone. Forest personnel patrol inside.

Except for a general description, this entry deals with places outside the blue zone. Considerable ash is still lying about, but the quantity differs greatly from place to place. Roads have been cleared, but ash may blow back. Wet ash is slippery. Dry ash kicks up to become a dust cloud. Airborne ash is rough on engines. The ash is gradually being incorporated into the soil, and in parts of the Forest it is inconspicuous.

The Gifford Pinchot is one of the oldest National Forests, parts of it set aside in 1897. It lies along the W slope of the Cascade Mountains. Average elevation of the mountain ridges is between 3,000 and 4,000 ft. Mt. St. Helens *was* 9,677 ft. Mt. Adams is 12,326 ft. Several peaks in the Goat Rocks area approach 8,000 ft.

Average annual precipitation is 60 in. on the W side of the range, up to 100 in. at the summit. It is far less on the E side, about 25 in. per year in the lower valleys. June, July, and August are dry on both sides of the range.

Temperatures seldom reach as low as 0°F on the W side, often drop to

—10°F on the E. Snowfall is between 250 and 500 in. on the summit at 4,000 ft., between 30 and 60 in. in the lower valleys. Summers are hot.

Many streams flow from the peaks. The Forest has nearly a hundred alpine lakes.

Within the Forest are many signs of past volcanic activity: vast lava beds, numerous lava tube caves.

Plants: Difference in precipitation between W and E is reflected in forest vegetation. The moist W slopes have heavy stands of timber, impressive Douglas-fir, western hemlock, western redcedar. At higher elevations: Pacific silver fir, Alaska yellow cedar, noble fir, western white pine. On the E fringe of the Forest: grand fir; white, ponderosa, and lodgepole pines.

The wide range of elevations, exposures, precipitation, and soils produces many different plant communities, from ferns and thick mosses in the moist and shaded ravines of the W side to the short-lived, summer-blooming heathers on the high slopes of the Goat Rocks. Shrubs of the W slopes include vine maple, Pacific rhododendron, small golden chinquapin, western hazel, western yew, Pacific dogwood, red huckleberry, Oregon grape, salal, trailing blackberry. Wildflowers include deerfoot vanillaleaf, evergreen violet, trillium, twinflower, white inside-out flower, starflower, beargrass, prince's pine.

On the high slopes: avalanche fawnlily, elkslip marsh-marigold, subalpine lupine, Indian paintbrush, red mountain heath, spreading phlox, mountain daisy, alpine cat's-ear, penstemon.

Birds: No checklist available. Species differ markedly from habitat to habitat. White-tailed ptarmigan, for example, occur on Mt. Adams, not on the W slopes. Hermit warbler have been observed near US 12 W of White Pass, not on the E side. Species noted in various parts of the Forest include western and pied-billed grebes, great blue heron, American bittern, mallard, gadwall, pintail, all three teals, wood duck, turkey vulture; sharp-shinned, Cooper's, red-tailed, Swainson's, and rough-legged hawks; common and bald eagles; blue, spruce, and ruffed grouse; ring-necked pheasant, spotted sandpiper, band-tailed pigeon, rock and mourning doves; screech, great horned, snowy, pygmy, and long-eared owls; common nighthawk, Vaux's swift, rufous hummingbird, belted kingfisher, common flicker; hairy, downy, and white-headed woodpeckers; Say's phoebe, Hammond's flycatcher, western wood pewee, horned lark; violet-green, tree, rough-winged, barn, and cliff swallows; gray and Steller's jays, common raven, common crow, Clark's nutcracker.

Also black-capped, mountain, boreal, and chestnut-backed chickadees; red-breasted and pygmy nuthatches; dipper, house, and Bewick's wrens; American robin; varied, hermit, and Swainson's thrushes; mountain bluebird, golden-crowned and ruby-crowned kinglets, water pipit, cedar waxwing, solitary and warbling vireos. Warblers include orange-crowned, Nashville, yellow, yellow-rumped, black-throated gray, Townsend's, hermit, MacGillivray's, yellowthroat, Wilson's. Also yellow-headed and red-winged blackbirds, northern oriole, western tanager, black-headed and evening grosbeaks, Cassin's and house finches, pine siskin, red crossbill, rufous-sided towhee; savannah, vesper, lark, chipping, Brewer's, white-crowned, fox, Lincoln's, and song sparrows.

Mammals: Species reported include opossum; masked, vagrant, dusky, water, Trowbridge, and Merriam shrews; many species of bats; pika, snowshoe hare, white-tailed jackrabbit, mountain beaver; least, yellow pine, and Townsend chipmunks; yellow-bellied and hoary marmots, California and Cascade golden-mantled squirrels, western gray and Douglas squirrels, northern and western pocket gophers, beaver, deer mouse, various voles, coyote, red fox, black bear, raccoon, marten, long-tailed weasel, badger, western spotted and striped skunks, river otter, mountain lion, bobcat, Roosevelt elk, mule deer, Columbian black-tailed deer, mountain goat.

FEATURES

Goat Rocks Wilderness, 82,680 acres. (22,940 acres of this is within the Mount Baker–Snoqualmie National Forest, but in an area administered by the Wenatchee National Forest.) Between Mt. Rainier and Mt. Adams. US 12 passes near the N boundary. Several Forest roads lead to trailheads near the W and E boundaries. Mountainous terrain; elevations from 3,000 ft. to 8,201-ft. Gilbert Peak. Much of the central portion of the Wilderness is above timberline. Pinnacles rise from snowfields. Glaciers are surrounded by colorful mountain meadows. Streams meander through meadows, cascade down rocky slopes. Many small alpine lakes. Most of the area is under heavy snow in winter and spring. Some visitors take the White Pass chairlift, ski cross-country to Hogback Mountain. Snowshoes are also used.

Trails are usually open to foot travel by about July 15, but some snow persists into August. The 95-mi. trail system permits both day hikes and long loop trips.

Permits are required. Sudden, violent storms can occur in any season. 85 mi. of trail are open to horse travel; feed must be carried in. The Wilderness map has trail information.

Mount Adams Wilderness, 32,356 acres. (10,000 additional acres on the E side of the mountain are managed by the Yakima Indian Tribal Council; travel in this area requires Council permission.) Mt. Adams, 12,276 ft., is second only to Mt. Rainier among WA mountains. Average elevation in the Wilderness is 5,500 ft.; absolute timberline is about 6,000 ft. The summit is a mile-long ridge. Heavy snow here feeds a number of glaciers. Adams Glacier, 3 mi. long, fan-shaped, dominates the NW face.

The lower slopes have an exceptionally diverse flora, species native to the moist W slopes and the drier E side sometimes intermixed. Many alpine meadows, flowers usually at their peak in late July, early Aug.

The Wilderness has had heavy use in the hiking season, and it shows, in groundcover damage and erosion. Permits are required. Hikers are asked to camp at forest edges, not in fragile meadows, practice meticulous sanitation, camp at least 100 ft. from water, leave no traces behind. The Wilderness map shows access routes.

The usual hiking season is July–Nov., but early and late snowstorms occur.

Indian Heaven, 15,400 acres, a roadless area about 13 mi. directly W of Trout Lake. Gently rolling, benchy area, elevations from 3,900 ft. to 5,927 ft. Large and small meadows, sparse forest of true firs and hemlock at higher elevations, denser stands of true firs, hemlock, lodgepole pine, and white pine at lower elevations. The area includes 175 lakes and ponds, the largest about 20 acres, most less than 5 acres. Marshy areas. Snow melts about mid-July, patches remaining on N slopes. Best season is Sept., when mosquitoes are gone. Pacific Crest Trail crosses the area.

Big Lava Bed, 12,500 acres, SW of Trout Lake. Elevations from 2,000 ft. to 3,360 ft. at the base of the crater, which rises 800 ft. Numerous cracks, crevasses, tall rock piles, short caves, oddly shaped lava formations. An interesting site; hiking into it is difficult going.

Cougar Lakes roadless area, 129,000 acres, including portion within the Wenatchee National Forest. Adjoins Mount Rainier National Park. Straddles the Cascade Crest. Terrain varies from gently rolling plateau in the S to steep ridges, crags, in the N. Elevations from 3,500 ft. to 7,766 ft. Many small lakes on the plateau. Vegetation varies from dense fir thickets in valley bottoms to open stands of mountain hemlock, subalpine fir; also mountain meadows. On the Pacific Crest Trail. US 12 is near the S boundary.

Tatoosh roadless area, 13,900 acres. On the S boundary of Mount Rainier National Park. Elevations from 1,400 ft. to 5,900 ft., from riverbottoms to subalpine ridgetops. Upper elevations almost entirely open or semiopen meadows; rocky outcrops on steeper slopes. Several lakes, waterfalls.

Mount Beljica area, about 4,000 acres. On the W boundary of Mount Rainier National Park, technically within the Mount Baker–Snoqualmie National Forest but administered by Gifford Pinchot. Said to be one of the most scenic areas of the Forest. Advocates urge that it be added to the National Park or accorded wilderness status. Good trails. Glacier View Point, 5,500 ft., looks out toward Mt. Rainier. Several lakes, streams, marshes.

Wind River Valley. From SR 14 on the Columbia River, turn NW at Carson to Ranger Station at Wind River. Self-guiding auto tour.

These are by no means all of the areas of interest in the Forest. Indeed, some of the less well known areas, also accessible by trail, are no less attractive and have fewer visitors. Consult the various hiking guides and inquire at Ranger Stations.

ACTIVITIES

Camping: As of spring 1981, 46 campgrounds, 904 sites. (Campgrounds in the St. Helens Ranger District were destroyed.) Seasons vary, most opening May or June, closing Sept.–Oct.

Hiking, backpacking: See trail guides.

Hunting: Elk, mountain goat, deer, game birds.

Fishing: Many lakes, streams. Rainbow trout, steelhead, salmon, cutthroat, eastern brook trout.

Swimming: Lakes, ponds, unsupervised.

Boating: Walupt, Takhlakh, and Goose lakes. Only Walupt is as much as 1 mi. long. Packwood Lake, near the W boundary of Goat Rocks Wilderness, is larger but a 3-mi. hike from trailhead.

Canoeing, kayaking: Cispus and Upper Lewis rivers.

Horse riding: Many good trails. One outfitter had applied for a permit by the end of Mar. 1981.

Skiing: Ski area at White Pass.

Ski touring: Many possibilities. Prepared trails at Upper Wind River area.

Snowmobiling: Special areas and regulations; inquire.

Mosquitoes are a problem in spring, early summer. Fire hazard closures are possible in Aug.

PUBLICATIONS

Forest map. $1.00.

Goat Rocks Wilderness map.

Mount Adams Wilderness map.

Mt. St. Helens. (Description of the eruption.)

Wilderness Solitude Catalog (leaflet).

Mimeographed sheets:

  Notes on Geologic History.

  Indian Heaven.

  The Big Lava Bed.

  List of campsites.

  Mt. Adams, Mountain Climbing Information.

  List of waterfalls.

  Resume of Forest history.

Horse camps information.

Trail Guides, issued by each Ranger District

Off-Road Vehicles Policy.

Upper Wind River Winter Sports Area.

REFERENCE

Hiking the Gifford Pinchot Back Country. 1976. Columbia Group, Sierra Club, 2637 S.W. Water Ave., Portland, OR 97201.

HEADQUARTERS: 500 W. 12th St., Vancouver, WA 98660; (206) 696-7500.

RANGER DISTRICTS: Packwood R.D., Packwood, WA 98361; (206) 494-5515. Wind River R.D., Carson, WA 98610; (509) 427-5645. Mt. Adams R.D., Trout Lake, WA 98650; (509) 395-2501. Randle R.D., Randle, WA 98377; (206) 497-7565.

LEADBETTER POINT

U.S. Fish and Wildlife Service/Washington Parks and Recreation Commission
Refuge: 1,433 acres/Park: 808 acres.

From US 101 at Seaview, N on SR 103 to its end at Oysterville, then N on Stackpole Road to end.

Called "one of the most outstanding natural areas of the Pacific Northwest." The Refuge occupies the tip of the Long Beach peninsula, between the ocean and Willapa Bay. Only foot travel is permitted within the Refuge. The adjacent State Park, which also extends from sea to bay, is as yet undeveloped except for the single road. Conservationists urge that it be kept that way, as part of a unique seacoast wilderness. We saw numerous tracks of ORV's within the Park, damaging to the vegetation, but little other disturbance. Although such a dune ecosystem is fragile, often greatly altered by storms, recovery is rapid. This area was logged and grazed until the 1940s, but few signs of this remain.

The ocean beach is sandy, flat, about 300 ft. wide. Back of the beach and at the tip of the peninsula are young, unstable dunes. Older dunes stabilized by vegetation occupy the central portion. Between the two sets of dunes are troughs that become ponds in winter, the wet season. Between the sand and Willapa Bay are an extensive salt marsh and mudflats. In the bay just E of the point is a small island, surrounded by marsh and mudflats.

The sea-to-bay width is greater in the State Park. Here there is a back dune forest with a dense understory. At the forest margin, trees are beginning to invade the Refuge dunes.

Dunes are up to 45 ft. high, and one can easily become lost wandering among them if the sun is obscured. One can hear the sound of surf, but it seems to come from all directions.

The bay and salt marsh are an important feeding and resting area for waterfowl, the mudflats for shorebirds. One source calls Willapa Bay "the last major undeveloped estuary on the West Coast of the United States."

A snowy plover nesting area, from mean high-tide mark up to the dunes, is closed to all entry Apr. through Aug.

Plants: Species establishing vegetative cover on dunes include beachgrass, American dunegrass, sea rocket, coastal strawberry, beach pea, pearly everlasting, seashore lupine, smooth and hairy cat's-ear, dune goldenrod, western tansy, sand verbena, pussytoes, kinnikinick. In the winter pond zone, sedge, mints, rushes, owl clover, buttercup, yellow-eyed grass. Tree species include lodgepole pine, spruce, western hemlock, red alder, dense understory including California wax myrtle, thimbleberry, salal, evergreen huckleberry, rattle-snake plantain, salmonberry, swordfern, bracken fern, nootka rose. In salt marsh, chiefly salicornia and arrowgrass.

Birds: Checklist available for Willapa National Wildlife Refuge (see entry), which includes Leadbetter Point. 180 species identified at the Point. Offshore: fulmar, parasitic jaeger, Brandt's cormorant, common murre, tufted puffin, rhinoceros auklet, Cassin's auklet; large numbers of sooty shearwater pass each August. Waterfowl include many black brant, as well as common and arctic loons; horned, eared, western, and pied-billed grebes; Canada and white-fronted geese, mallard, gadwall, pintail, wigeon, greater scaup, goldeneye, bufflehead, white-winged and surf scoters, common merganser. Shorebirds include dunlin, black turnstone, black-bellied plover, long-billed dowitcher, western sandpiper, sanderling. Gulls: black-legged kittiwake, Bonaparte's, Heermann's, glaucous-winged, western, herring, California, mew. Upland species include sharp-shinned, red-tailed, Swainson's, rough-legged, and marsh hawks; merlin, bald eagle, ruffed grouse, ring-necked pheasant, killdeer, kingfisher, flicker, Traill's and western flycatchers, cedar waxwing, red crossbill; white-crowned, golden-crowned, fox, and song sparrows.

Birding is generally most productive along the bayshore, fall and spring.

Mammals: Include red-backed vole, vagrant shrew, Trowbridge shrew, raccoon, muskrat, beaver, deer mouse, snowshoe hare, chickaree, mule deer.

Reptiles and amphibians: Include five salamander species, rough-skinned newt, red-legged and tailed frogs, western toad, painted turtle, northern alligator lizard, garter snake.

Hunting: In National Wildlife Refuge only, subject to special regulations.

PUBLICATIONS
Leaflet.
Bird checklist (Willapa National Wildlife Refuge).
Hunting regulations (Willapa National Wildlife Refuge).

HEADQUARTERS: Willapa National Wildlife Refuge, Ilwaco, WA 98624; (206) 484-3482. Parks and Recreation Commission, 7150 Cleanwater Lane, Olympia, WA 98504; (206) 753-5755.

LEWIS AND CLARK STATE PARK
Washington Parks and Recreation Commission
534 acres.

From Chehalis, S about 12 mi. on I-5; E about 2 mi. on US 12; S at Marys Corner on old US 99.

Washington's second State Park included the largest easily reached stand of virgin timber in this part of the state. A storm in 1962 downed two-thirds of it, but many impressive specimens remain. Douglas-fir was planted in the blowdown area. A nature trail passes through old-growth and recovering areas.

Rolling terrain. The Park is about 30 mi. from Mt. St. Helens. An interpretive center includes a seismograph, video program, telecopier link with U.S. Geological Survey HQ, and exhibits pertaining to the eruptions.

Plants: 99% forested: Douglas-fir, western redcedar, hemlock; understory including vine maple, swordfern, salal. Flowering species include bleeding heart, lady's slipper, trillium, dogwood, gooseberry, rhododendron.

ACTIVITIES
Camping: 32 sites. All year.
Hiking: 7 mi. of trails.

PUBLICATION: Leaflet.

HEADQUARTERS: 4583 Jackson Highway, Winlock, WA 98596; (206) 864-2643.

LONG BEACH
Public and private lands.

SW WA, along SR 103.

28 mi. of sand beach, from Cape Disappointment on the S to Leadbetter Point on the N end of the peninsula. Most of the land area is privately owned, and there are several small resort communities. The beach is wide, backed by small dunes. The sea is shallow close to shore; distance between high- and low-tide marks is exceptionally great.

The largest developed public site is Fort Canby State Park at the S end (see entry). The state maintains 6 beach-access points at intervals along the ocean shore. At the N end is Leadbetter Point, a fine natural area (see entry).

Motor vehicles are allowed on the beach.

MOUNT BAKER–SNOQUALMIE NATIONAL FOREST
About 70,000 acres of this Forest are in zone 2. The entry appears in zone 4, which has over a million acres of the Forest. The zone 2 portion is isolated from the main body of the Forest and is administered by the Gifford Pinchot National Forest. On the state highway map, this portion appears as a solid

block N of Morton and W of SR 7. It is actually a checkerboard of 1-mi. squares, alternating with private land. The highest point is about 4,300 ft. No Forest campgrounds are within the area. Principal visitor activities are hunting and fishing.

NISQUALLY NATIONAL WILDLIFE REFUGE/ NISQUALLY DELTA HABITAT MANAGEMENT AREA
U.S. Fish and Wildlife Service/Washington Department of Game
2,824 acres/665 acres.

> From Tacoma, SW on I-5 to exit 114. Turn N (right, under the freeway), then right again on Brown Farm Road to National Wildlife Refuge entrance.

The National Wildlife Refuge leaflet makes no mention of the Habitat Management Area, and its map includes within the "proposed boundaries" all the land in the HMA. The HMA leaflet's map shows the NWR area, without identification, and makes no mention of the NWR in text. The Fish and Wildlife Service Division of Realty in Washington, D.C., provided an authoritative map, the legally vested federal acreage (2,824), and clarification.

The area lies between I-5 and Puget Sound. It includes the delta of the Nisqually River, McAllister Creek, and tidal flats. A large part of the federal land, between the two streams, is diked, creating freshwater ponds and marshes. The federal land extends from I-5 out to the extreme low-tide line. Within the boundaries are several large blocks of state and private land.

"Land" is not a precise term. Two of the three blocks of state land are tidal flats: mud, sand, and muck at low tide. The federal boundary seaward of these blocks encloses no dry land. This area is reached only by boat. The third block of state land lies along McAllister Creek, which is canoeable.

Access to the National Wildlife Refuge area is by foot trail only, beyond the HQ area. There are two short walks, one of them a nature trail and the other a loop to an education center and observation deck at "Twin Barns." A 5-mi. circuit of the dike offers a longer walk past most of the major habitat types.

In addition to the freshwater impoundment, the tidal flats, and salt marsh, the area includes open grassland, mixed coniferous woods along McAllister Creek, and a patch of deciduous forest near I-5. The entrance road crosses a meadow edged with second-growth red alder, maple, and willow.

Birds: Some 10,000 waterfowl winter here, and up to 20,000 pass through in migration. Birds commonly observed include wigeon, mallard, pintail, green-winged teal, goldeneye, bufflehead, Canada goose, scaup, scoters, western grebe, red-tailed and marsh hawks, kestrel, great blue heron, greater yellowlegs, western sandpiper. A few eagle, white-fronted goose, and brant. Also many gulls, shorebirds, and passerines.

Mammals: Include Trowbridge shrew, Townsend vole, cottontail, squirrel, mountain beaver, river otter, coyote, raccoon, muskrat, mink, mule deer, seals.

ACTIVITIES
Hunting: In all of the Habitat Management Area and in designated areas of the National Wildlife Refuge. Obtain map at Refuge HQ.
Boating, canoeing: Ramp at Luhr Beach.

NOTE: Gates of the National Wildlife Refuge close at 4 P.M.

PUBLICATIONS
National Wildlife Refuge leaflet.
Habitat Management Area leaflet.

HEADQUARTERS: Nisqually National Wildlife Refuge: 100 Brown Farm Rd., Olympia, WA 98506; (206) 753-9467. Nisqually Delta Habitat Management Area, Department of Game, Regional Office, 905 E. Heron, Aberdeen, WA 98520; (206) 532-9680.

RAINBOW FALLS STATE PARK
Washington Parks and Recreation Commission
125 acres.

From Chehalis, W 18 mi. on SR 6.

A small park with some old-growth timber and 3,400 ft. of frontage on the Chehalis River, including Rainbow Falls and a basalt gorge. Level to rolling terrain. 45 acres N of the river are developed; 80 acres S of the river, reached by bridge, are hilly, forested, undeveloped except for trails. Self-guiding nature trail.

ACTIVITIES
Camping: 50 sites. All year.
Fishing: Trout.
Swimming: Pool at foot of falls.
Canoeing: River.

HEADQUARTERS: 4008 State Highway 6, Chehalis, WA 98532; (206) 291-3767.

RIDGEFIELD NATIONAL WILDLIFE REFUGE
U.S. Fish and Wildlife Service
3,017 acres.

From Vancouver, 15 mi. N on I-5 to Ridgefield exit; W 3 mi. to Ridgefield. HQ is in town at 210 N. Main St. Refuge adjoins the town.

Low-lying land along the Columbia River: pastures, marshes, woodlands. Mild, rainy winter climate produces an ideal environment for migrating waterfowl. Many sloughs, ponds, and shallow lakes within the Refuge and in nearby areas along the river. Most of the area is flooded each year by the spring runoff. An alternate route from Vancouver begins on Fruit Valley Road. Slower, it keeps closer to the river, passes near Vancouver and Shillapoo lakes, both good birding areas; each has a small State Habitat Management Area.

The Refuge has three units, although only a small gap divides N and S portions. Just north of Ridgefield, the Carty Unit has outcroppings of basalt forming knolls above the high-water mark, wooded with ash, oak, and Douglas-fir. In spring the knolls are bright with wildflowers; in summer they become dry, in contrast to surrounding marsh. The Roth Unit, at the far S of the Refuge, includes the N end of Campbell Lake. This is typical river floodplain, flat, forested with cottonwood, ash, and willow. These two units are relatively undeveloped. Management plans to maintain them as natural areas.

The central portion is the River "S" Unit, protected from flooding by 6 mi. of dike on the perimeter. Here feed crops are grown for waterfowl, pumps control water levels in each pond and lake, and grasslands are cut for hay and silage. The objective is to maximize waterfowl-carrying capacity.

Winter is the big season here, with up to 15,000 geese and 50,000 ducks in residence, but birders will find much of interest in any season. A parking area at the edge of the Carty Unit gives access to the 3/4-mi. Oak Grove Trail and to a longer management road, closed to unofficial vehicles but open to foot travel. Just south of Ridgefield, another entrance gives access to the dike around the River "S" Unit, a 6-mi. hike and a road beside Bower Slough. Here an observation blind overlooks Rest Lake.

Birds: 182 species reported. Checklist available. Species mentioned prominently include dusky and lesser Canada geese, whistling swan, wigeon, mallard, pintail, cinnamon and green-winged teal, shoveler, gadwall, snipe, sandhill crane, great blue heron, red-tailed hawk, great horned owl, band-tailed pigeon, Steller's jay, red-winged blackbird, goldfinch, red-breasted nuthatch, Bewick's wren, golden-crowned kinglet, many shorebirds.

Mammals: Include mule deer, coyote, fox, raccoon, skunk, beaver, otter, brush rabbit, nutria.

ACTIVITIES

Hunting: Waterfowl, in designated area, by reservation. Special rules. Inquire.

Fishing: State and Refuge regulations.

PUBLICATIONS

Leaflet with map.
Hunting information.
Bird checklist.
Wildlife leaflet.

HEADQUARTERS: P.O. Box 471, 210 N. Main St., Ridgefield, WA 98642; (206) 887-4071.

SCATTER CREEK HABITAT MANAGEMENT AREA
Washington Department of Game
1,161 acres.

18 mi. S of Olympia, just W of I-5. Turn W at Maytown exit, then immediately S on Case Rd. to Case Segment of Habitat Management Area. For Township Segment, continue to Lincoln Rd., then W.

The two segments are about 1/2 mi. apart, but they adjoin other state land and a large timber company holding. Flat prairie: heavy grassfields, Scotch broom, oak and evergreen woodlands. The state's most heavily hunted pheasant release site. Case Segment is used year around for dog training and field trials. Township Segment is closed to this activity Apr.–July. For those with interests other than hunting and dogs, Township Segment in spring and summer is the choice. Vehicles are banned; foot travel only.

Scatter Creek, crossing the Township Segment, is dammed to attract waterfowl but is usually dry in summer. Both segments, but especially Case, have a number of Mima Mounds, gravel hummocks of uncertain origin.

Birds: Checklist of 64 species. A few waterfowl in season, plus hawks, great blue heron, California quail, band-tailed pigeon, many songbirds.

PUBLICATION: *Wildlife Recreation Areas* [now Habitat Management Areas], *26, Scatter Creek WRA* [Habitat Management Area], leaflet with map and bird checklist.

HEADQUARTERS: Department of Game, 600 N. Capitol Way, Olympia, WA 98504; (206) 753-5700.

WILLAPA NATIONAL WILDLIFE REFUGE

U.S. Fish and Wildlife Service
9,608 acres.*

HQ on US 101, 8 mi. NE of Seaview. Long Island, largest section of Refuge, is directly across a narrow channel. A second section is at the S end of the bay. For the third section, see entry for Leadbetter Point.

Willapa Bay has been called the largest undisturbed estuary in the western United States. About 20 mi. long, the bay is shallow, almost empty at extreme low tides, with vast areas of mudflats exposed. The waters, flats, salt marshes, and higher ground are richly productive, providing excellent wildlife habitat.

Long Island is reached by boat from a ramp in the HQ area. Much of the 5,000 acres is forested, including a virgin stand of western redcedar. The island is surrounded by salt marshes and mudflats. Camping is permitted on the island, and there are miles of trails and roads.

About 5 1/2 mi. SW on US 101, just beyond a small bridge, Jeldness Road, to the right, leads 1.2 mi. to a parking area and locked gate, entrance to the Lewis Unit. The Riekkola Unit can be reached by Yeaton Road from Long Beach. This area has pastures and freshwater marshes protected by dikes and tidegates. Roads open to foot travel provide excellent opportunities to see waterfowl.

Some areas are closed to nonhunters in hunting season.

Birds: Over 256 species recorded, 118 of these common in one or more seasons, 86 known to nest on the Refuge. Common species include common and arctic loons; red-necked, horned, eared, western, and pied-billed grebes; double-crested, Brandt's, and pelagic cormorants; great blue heron, whistling and trumpeter swans, Canada goose, black brant, mallard, gadwall, pintail, green-winged teal, American wigeon, shoveler, wood duck, ring-necked duck, canvasback, greater scaup, common goldeneye, bufflehead, oldsquaw, white-winged and surf scoters; hooded, common, and red-breasted mergansers. Also blue and ruffed grouse, ring-necked pheasant, snipe, spotted sandpiper, greater and lesser yellowlegs, least sandpiper, dunlin; stilt, semipalmated, and western sandpipers; sanderling. Also many birds of prey, gulls, owls, songbirds.

Mammals: Notably on Long Island. Good populations of black bear, Roosevelt elk, coyote, mule deer, beaver, otter, muskrat.

---

*Plus 21,000 acres, mostly water, closed to waterfowl hunting.

ACTIVITIES

Camping: Designated sites at 7 locations on Long Island. Primitive.
Hiking: Miles of roads, trails, dikes.
Hunting: Designated areas. Special rules. Inquire.
Boating: Although the crossing to Long Island seems easy, those unfamiliar with the bay should inquire. Low tide can leave a beached boat far from the water, and wind can kick up rough water quickly.

PUBLICATIONS

Leaflet.
Long Island leaflet.
Bird checklist.
Hunting regulations.

HEADQUARTERS: Ilwaco, WA 98624; (206) 484-3482.

YACOLT MULTIPLE USE AREA
Washington Department of Natural Resources
168,000 acres.

From Vancouver, NE about 20 mi. to Hockinson, then E on NE 139th St. into the Multiple Use Area. This is one of several access routes. Signing is good, but MUA map is desirable.

Much of this area was swept by repeated forest fires, nine major burns in the first half of this century. Since then forest rehabilitation has made great progress: felling snags, planting, fertilizing, thinning, and improving fire protection. With recovery well along and wildlife populations restored, the area has been opened for recreation. Production and harvesting of timber continue to have priority, but visitors find much to enjoy.

Elevations from about 500 ft. to 3,500 ft. Terrain above 1,500 ft. is steep and rugged, considered part of the Cascade Range. Below 600 ft. are bottomlands and alluvial terraces. Climate is affected by proximity to the Columbia Gorge and highly variable. Summer temperatures are generally in the upper 70's by day, 50's at night, but readings of over 100°F are not unknown. Winter temperatures tend to be moderate. Ice storms occur. East winds up to 70 mph may occur in Jan.–Feb. and late July to early Nov.

Numerous small creeks, several of them tributaries to the Washougal River. Three reservoirs are formed by dams on the North Fork of the Lewis River.

Good blacktop roads lead into the Multiple Use Area. Unpaved roads differ in design and maintenance. Some are unsuitable for ordinary automobiles. All should be approached with caution in bad weather.

Like other Multiple Use Areas, the Yacolt is not well known even to Washingtonians. It isn't shown on the official highway map, nor are its campgrounds listed in popular directories.

Plants: Douglas-fir is the dominant tree species, with western hemlock and firs. A variety of soil types occur, influencing vegetation. Western redcedar, western hemlock, vine maple, red alder, willow, hazel, cherry, bigleaf maple, black cottonwood, dogwood, and cascara are found on poorly drained soils and along streams. Brush and groundcover species include salal, beargrass, salmonberry, huckleberry, blackberry, snowberry, thimbleberry, with mosses and ferns.

Birds: No checklist available. Species mentioned include grouse, ring-necked pheasant, bald eagle, nighthawk. One would expect to find most of the species common to the Douglas-fir/western hemlock forests of the Western Cascades.

Mammals: Include black bear, mule deer, coyote, chipmunk, squirrel, badger, marmot. One small elk herd.

FEATURES: *Viewpoint* on top of Larch Mountain, accessible by car. Vistas of Mt. Hood, Mt. Adams, Mt. St. Helens, Mt. Rainier. *Grouse Creek Vista* is reached by DNR Road No. L-1200.

INTERPRETATION: *Interpretive signs* at Tarbell Trail Camp, Larch Mountain Picnic Area, Rock Creek, and Grouse Creek camp and picnic areas.

ACTIVITIES

Camping: Three campgrounds; 21 sites. Jones Creek is used largely by trailbikers.

Hiking: Trails and unimproved roads. No mileage available. Trails designated for both hikers and horses. 12 1/2-mi. system of trailbike trails keeps most of this traffic off hiking trails. Proposed relocation of Pacific Crest Trail would route it through here, but plans are uncertain since Mt. St. Helens' eruptions. Status of trails into Gifford Pinchot National Forest also uncertain.

Hunting: Deer, bear, game birds. State regulations.

Fishing: Rainbow and cutthroat trout. Runs of silver, chinook, and jack salmon.

Horse riding: Stanchions, manure boxes, loading ramp.

ADJACENT OR NEARBY: Gifford Pinchot National Forest (see entry). Beacon Rock State Park (see entry). Battle Ground Lake State Park (see entry).

PUBLICATIONS: Leaflet.

HEADQUARTERS: Department of Natural Resources, Southwest Area, Box 798, Castle Rock, WA 98611; (206) 577-2025; in WA, 1-800-562-6010.

ZONE 3

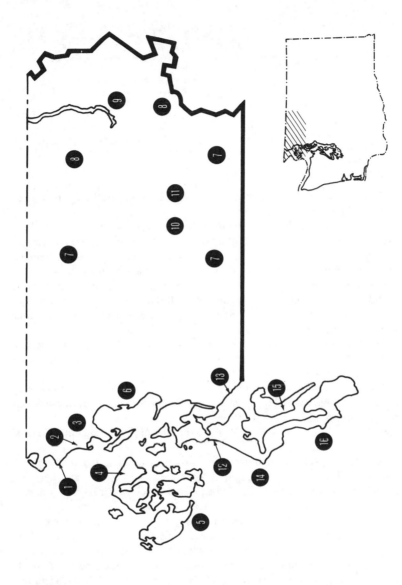

ZONE 3

Includes these counties:

San Juan	Skagit
Whatcom	Island

This is the smallest of the six zones we delineated, but it offers a great variety of fine natural areas.

The San Juan Islands and surrounding waters are a special case. The land area of all the islands combined is not large, and the four ferry-served islands, largest of the group, are, for the most part, privately owned and developed as resorts. Federal and state sites, including parks and refuges, are scattered through many of the islands. Most of these holdings are small. Most of the islands in the federal refuge system are off limits; one can look but not go ashore. Getting to any of these publicly owned sites, except those on the four main islands, requires a private boat.

If one has a suitable craft, however, this is a fascinating area to explore. Even the ferry trip is scenic, and one is likely to spot seabirds not often seen from the mainland.

Without a boat, and without boarding the ferry, one can join those who consider Fidalgo and Whidbey islands part of the San Juans. Both are linked to the mainland. SR 20 is a well-traveled highway. But they are islands, with complex and interesting coastlines and a number of interesting natural areas, as well as splendid scenery.

No road clings to the mainland coast. I-5 is generally a few miles inland. Spur roads lead to such coastal points of interest as Birch Bay and Larrabee State Parks. Largest of the coastal natural areas is the Skagit Habitat Management Area, a major station on the Pacific Flyway.

Well over half of the land area in zone 3 is to the E, a large block made up of portions of the Mount Baker–Snoqualmie National Forest, North Cascades National Park, and Okanogan National Forest. This is a region of mountains, glaciers, high lakes, dense forests, and rushing streams. A single road, SR 20, crosses it. Large portions of it are roadless wilderness, accessible only on foot or horseback.

REFERENCE: Tivel, Tracy M., and Adkins, Jack. *A Field Guide to Bird Watching in Skagit County.* Department of Game. (Map, text, checklist.)

BIRCH BAY STATE PARK
Washington Parks and Recreation Commission
193 acres.

From I-5, exit 266. W on Grandview Rd.; N on Jackson Rd.; W on Helwig Rd. About 8 mi. from I-5.

About 1 mi. of frontage on Birch Bay, off the Strait of Georgia, N of the San Juan Islands, near the Canadian border. Slightly rolling terrain sloping gently from the bayshore. Birch Bay Drive is between the bay and the major Park area. Terrell Creek flows through a freshwater marsh at the S of the Park, then turns and flows N beside the Drive. Most of the upland area is forested: fir, cedar, birch, alder, maple. Highest point is about 150 ft. Winter and spring are "wet" seasons, but annual rainfall is only about 20 in.

Birds: The shallow bay is a good feeding, resting, and wintering area for waterfowl, and the Park is one of the best observation sites. No checklist. Species mentioned include brant, green-winged teal, mallard, coot, harlequin duck, common loon; black, surf, and white-winged scoters. Many shorebirds. Also noted: kingfisher, cormorant, wood duck, robin, starling, red-winged blackbird.

Mammals: Mule deer, raccoon, skunk, opossum, muskrat, beaver.

ACTIVITIES
Camping: 156 sites. All year. Reservations required.
Swimming: Bay. Unsupervised. Scuba and snorkeling popular.
Boating: Ramp nearby.

PUBLICATION: Leaflet.

HEADQUARTERS: 5105 Helwig Rd., Blaine, WA 98230; (206) 366-5944, 5970.

CAMANO ISLAND STATE PARK
Washington Parks and Recreation Commission
134 acres.

From I-5, 10 mi. N of Marysville, NW 9 mi. on SR 530 to Stanwood; W on SR 532 to Camano Island; follow signs to Park.

On Saratoga Strait between Whidbey Island and the mainland. 6,700 ft. of beach. Rolling hills. Highest point 312 ft. Cliffs along the shore. About 85%

forested, chiefly Douglas-fir and white fir. Some old growth; specimens 300–500 years old along the nature trail. Cliff Trail has scenic overlooks. Climate is moderate and relatively dry, 15–20 in. of rain annually, most of this in winter and spring. Park is popular, likely to be at capacity on major holidays and—according to the manager—at low clam tides.

Birds: Good birding area. No checklist. Bald eagle winter here. Many waterfowl, shorebirds, as well as upland species.

Mammals: Manager reports mule deer, raccoon, opossum, rabbit, squirrel, weasel, fox, muskrat.

ACTIVITIES
Camping: 87 sites. All year.
Boating: Ramps.

PUBLICATIONS
Leaflet.
Nature trail guide.

HEADQUARTERS: 2269 S. Park Rd., Stanwood, WA 98292; (206) 387-3031, 2575.

DECEPTION PASS STATE PARK
Washington Parks and Recreation Commission
3,000+ acres.

On SR 20, 8 mi. N of Oak Harbor.

At Deception Pass, SR 20 crosses a high bridge linking Whidbey and Fidalgo islands. Many motorists stop at the parking area next to the bridge to enjoy the view. The channel between the islands looks like a deep gorge with rocky cliffs, forested slopes. Tidewater flows swiftly, forming whirlpools and boils, dangerous for a small craft.

The Park is on both islands, with 15 mi. of saltwater shoreline on Rosario Strait, Deception Pass, Cornet Bay, Bowman Bay, and Canoe Island. It includes Cranberry Lake, on Whidbey Island, and Pass Lake, on Fidalgo, with a combined shoreline of over 4 mi.

Hilly. Moderate to steep slopes. The Park has great variety: sandy and stony beaches, tidepools, rocky headlands, coves, bays, cliffs, wetlands, coastal brush, forested hills.

Plants: Forest of Douglas-fir, western hemlock, western redcedar, shore pine, grand fir. Some old growth. Understory and forest openings have salal, Oregon grape, ocean spray, red huckleberry, rhododendron, ferns. Also wetland plant communities.

Birds: No checklist or site record. Species mentioned include great blue heron, cormorants, puffin, bald eagle, glaucous-winged gull, terns, great horned owl, winter wren, Oregon junco. Local birders recommend the site because of its diverse habitats.

Mammals: Species mentioned include raccoon, bats, cottontail, chipmunk, sea lion, seal, red fox, beaver, muskrat, river otter, weasel, mule deer. Orca (killer whale) and other whales sometimes seen.

INCLUDES

Hope Island, 166 acres, in Skagit Bay. Boat access. Undeveloped except for small picnic area. Bluffs, beach, forest.

Canoe Island lies between Whidbey and Fidalgo, serving—in effect—as the bridge's center span. Parking area. Trails along the cliffs to the E tip. Stunted trees, brush, grasses, wildflowers. Exercise caution on trails.

Cranberry Lake, about 0.8 mi. long, on NW tip of Whidbey. Campground; fishing; swimming; boating (no motors). Nature trail in forest. Hilly, forested area. Nearby: West Beach, West Point, North Beach. Rocky headlands, stony and sandy beaches, dunes, bog.

Bowman Bay, on Fidalgo, W of SR 20. On the S is Reservation Head, almost an island, rocky shore, hilly, forested, trails. Rosario Head, on the N, is smaller. Seabirds on offshore rocks. Campground; hiking; boat launching.

Rosario Bay, NW of Bowman, is noted for marine life, tidepools. A marine research site. Seabirds on offshore rocks.

Cornet Bay, on Whidbey E of the highway, is more sheltered, Launching and other marine facilities. Nearby salt- and freshwater marshes. Side road continues to Hoypus Point. Trail circles Hoypus Hill.

Pass Lake, 100 acres, on Fidalgo, can be seen from the highway. Only boats without motors are allowed. A quiet area; wildlife often seen at dawn and dusk.

Goose Rock, 450 ft., is the highest point. On Whidbey Island. Trail. Vista.

Deception Pass Nature Trail.

ACTIVITIES

Camping: 2 campgrounds. 254 sites. All year.
Hiking: 8 mi. of trails.
Fishing: Fresh and salt water. Lakes stocked with trout.
Swimming: Lakes. Supervised in summer.
Boating: Launch and other facilities on salt water.
Canoeing: Lakes. Rentals, summer, on Cranberry Lake.

PUBLICATIONS

Hiking trail maps.
Nature trail guide.
Cornet Bay Environments (leaflet).

HEADQUARTERS: Oak Harbor, WA 98277; (206) 675-2417.

LAKE TERRELL HABITAT MANAGEMENT AREA
Washington Department of Game
1,041 acres.

From Ferndale on I-5 (N of Bellingham), W about 5 mi. on Mountain View Rd.; N on Lake Terrell Rd.

Managed for waterfowl and pheasant. All duck species found in western WA are seen here as winter residents or migrants. Used by duck and pheasant hunters in the fall season. Few visitors at other times.

HEADQUARTERS: 5975 Lake Terrell Rd., Ferndale, WA 98248; (206) 384-4723.

LARRABEE STATE PARK
Washington Parks and Recreation Commission
1,886 acres.

From Bellingham, 7 mi. S on SR 11, Chuckanut Dr.

WA's first State Park attracts almost half a million visitors per year. However, the manager says that while summer weekends are "quite busy," the Park is never uncomfortably crowded. About 1,800 acres are undeveloped forest, with two lakes that can be reached only on foot.

3,600 ft. of frontage on Samish Bay. Steep, rolling terrain back of the bayfront. Sandstone headlands worn into bizarre shapes by wind and sea. Highest point is 1,940 ft. The bay is cold and shallow close to shore; people wade rather than swim.

Plants: About 96% forested. Typical NW coastal forest, logged 40–60 years ago. Douglas-fir, western redcedar, grand fir, western hemlock, red alder, bigleaf maple. Scattered old-growth specimens. Lush understory of willow, elderberry, salmonberry, swordfern, salal, so dense that off-trail hiking is difficult. The many wildflowers include bleeding heart, trillium, Indian paintbrush, pink currant, dogwood, columbine, wild rose, calypso orchid, skunk cabbage. Peak season: Mar.–June.

Birds: No checklist. Said to be a reasonably good birding site: seabirds offshore, shorebirds at low tide, upland species.

FEATURES

Fragrance Lake (7 acres) and *Lost Lake* (12 acres), are reached by 2-mi. forest trail from developed area.

Cyrus Gates overlook, reached by Cleator Rd., 1900 ft., looks out toward San Juan Islands. Short trail to E-facing overlook, with views of Mt. Baker, North Cascades.

ACTIVITIES

Camping: 100 sites. All year.
Fishing: Lakes stocked.
Boating: Ramp on bay.

PUBLICATION: Site map. (Brochure in production.)

HEADQUARTERS: 245 Chuckanut Dr., Bellingham, WA 98225; (206) 676-2093.

MORAN STATE PARK
See San Juan Islands.

MOUNT BAKER–SNOQUALMIE NATIONAL FOREST

819,082 acres of this Forest are in zone 3. The entry appears in zone 4, which includes a larger acreage. Most of the portion in zone 3 is along the W boundary of the North Cascades National Park. It includes Mt. Baker, highest point in the Forest, the approach road to the Mt. Baker ski area and Heather Meadows, along the Nooksack River. This part of the Forest is crossed by SR 20, the highway leading to the National Park. A part of the Glacier Peaks Wilderness is in the SE corner of the zone.

The Forest land on the E side of the National Park, including part of the Pasayten Wilderness, is technically part of Mount Baker–Snoqualmie National Forest but is administered by the Okanogan National Forest and described in that entry (zone 5).

NORTH CASCADES NATIONAL PARK SERVICE COMPLEX, including ROSS LAKE and LAKE CHELAN NATIONAL RECREATION AREAS
U.S. National Park Service
674,000 acres.

Both sides of SR 20, between Burlington and Twisp. Access to the Lake Chelan National Recreation Area is by boat, float plane, or trail from Chelan on US 97.

One of the newest National Parks and unusual in many ways. Until 1968, almost all of the area was National Forest land. Some developments were in place: Ross Dam, forming Ross Lake; Gorge and Diablo dams, the power-houses and associated structures, including residences; tourist facilities at Newhalem, Diablo, and Stehekin. SR 20, which had ended at the lake, was pushed E to link with the road from Twisp shortly after the Park was inaugurated. A broad band of land on both sides of SR 20 and on both sides of Ross Lake was designated as the Ross Lake National Recreation Area. The Stehekin Valley area became the Lake Chelan National Recreation Area. Limited recreation development is permitted within these National Recreation Areas. Hunting, forbidden in National Parks, is also allowed. The National Park itself is in two huge blocks, N and S of SR 20, roadless, accessible only by foot or on horseback. The Park and National Recreation Areas are under common management. In this entry, "the Park" includes the entire complex. In the rugged Cascade Range, the Park extends from the Canadian border to the upper tip of Lake Chelan. It is surrounded by National Forests: Mount Baker–Snoqualmie, Okanogan, and Wenatchee. The Pasayten Wilderness is to the E, the Glacier Peak Wilderness to the S.

The region has so many peaks it would be misleading to mention one or two. Numerous peaks are between 7,000 and 9,000 ft., still more over 6,000, steep, jagged, carved into spires, horns, and ridges. On the slopes are 318 glaciers, countless snowfields. Slopes on the W side receive as much as 516 in. of snow per year. More than 127 alpine lakes are in cirque basins. Valleys are U-shaped, narrow, deep, the valley floors up to 2,000 ft. elevation. One description compares the North Cascades with the European Alps—"but with better weather, more diverse forests, and richer wildlife."

Annual precipitation on the upper W slopes is as much as 110 in., on the E slopes 34 in. Snowfall on the E side, which includes the Stehekin Valley, is thus much less than on the W. Snow is off all but the higher trails by July, but summer storms are common, so hikers should be prepared for rain and wind. Lower elevations and the big lakes are generally snow-free from early Apr. to mid-Oct.

SR 20 is a fine scenic route, and development is limited to a few short stretches. Trailheads along the way offer opportunities for short and easy day hikes or strenuous wilderness treks. Campgrounds on Ross Lake can be reached by boat or trail. From Chelan, a privately operated boat makes the 55-mi. trip to Stehekin daily in summer, several days weekly in winter.

Ross Lake, formed by a power company dam, is 24 mi. long, 2 mi. wide. Conservationists have long resisted a proposal to build the dam higher, widening the lake and extending it further into Canada. Diablo and Gorge lakes, also formed by dams, are smaller, both near SR 20.

Only the upper end of Lake Chelan is within the Park. About 35 mi., the center portion, is within the Wenatchee National Forest. The lower end is in private ownerships; Chelan is a busy resort.

Principal rivers are the Chilliwack and Baker in the North Unit, the Skagit in the Ross Lake National Recreation Area and the Stehekin in the South Unit and Lake Chelan National Recreation Area. Many creeks.

An unpaved road leads from Marblemount, on SR 20 W of the Park, through the National Forest, and into the South Unit, ending below Cascade Pass. A trail leads over the pass and down to the Stehekin Valley road.

SR 20 is normally kept open in winter from the W entrance to Diablo Lake.

The only other road penetrating the Park crosses the Canadian border to Hozomeen at the upper end of Ross Lake.

Plants: Great differences in moisture between E and W slopes, as well as variation in altitude, have produced a wide variety of plant communities: rain forest, subalpine coniferous forest, high meadows, alpine tundra, pine forest, dry shrublands.

At low elevations, W side, western hemlock with Pacific silver fir, grand fir, Sitka spruce, lodgepole and western white pines, Douglas-fir, western yew, quaking aspen, black cottonwood, Pacific willow, red alder, black birch, California hazel, vine maple, bigleaf maple, Pacific dogwood, bitter cherry, cascara. This is the plant community most visitors see. Trails pass through lush vegetation under the high canopy: ferns, mosses, herbs, shrubs. Moving upward, there is a shift toward species such as subalpine fir, alpine larch, whitebark pine, ponderosa pine, mountain hemlock, Alaska cedar, with red mountainheath, huckleberry, Cascades azalea, showy sedge, pine-mat manzanita.

Birds: Checklist indicates species reported and the habitats where they occur, including mountain streams, lake and ponds, and marsh areas as well as vegetation types. Areas said to offer good birding: Skagit River, the head of Lake Chelan, Big Beaver Valley. The wetland areas attract a great variety of swans, geese, ducks, herons, shorebirds. Relatively few species occur in the alpine tundra zone, these including horned lark, magpie, mountain bluebird, water pipit, northern shrike, gray-crowned and Hepburn's rosy finches, lapland longspur. Lowland areas are generally more populated. Species here include blue and ruffed grouse, California and mountain quail, chukar, bald and golden eagles, numerous hawks and owls, woodpeckers, flycatchers, swallows. Species found in a number of the habitats include black-capped chickadee, Swainson's thrush, northern shrike, orange-crowned and MacGillivray's warblers, western tanager; chipping, fox, and song sparrows.

Mammals: Checklist available is preliminary, because the Park is relatively new. Some species marked "doubtful," others probable but not yet confirmed. Known to be present: various shrews, moles, bats; snowshoe hare, pika, mountain beaver, yellow-bellied and hoary marmots, golden-mantled squirrel, yellow pine and Townsend chipmunks, chickaree, red squirrel, northern flying squirrel, beaver, several voles, muskrat, porcupine, red fox, coyote, black bear, raccoon, marten, long-tailed and short-tailed weasels, mink, striped and spotted skunks, otter, wolverine, mountain lion, lynx, bobcat, mule deer, mountain goat.

FEATURES

Ross Lake National Recreation Area, 107,000 acres. Skagit River drainage, ringed by mountains, separating the Park's North and South Units. Roughly L-shaped, the bottom is the route of SR 20. Resorts and other developments are along SR 20, chiefly at Newhalem, Diablo, and Ross Dam. Also on the route are two drive-in campgrounds: Goodell Creek and Colonial Creek. A third campground is scheduled for the 1982 season. The vertical stroke of the L is a broad N–S corridor on either side of Ross Lake, extending to the Canadian border. The only road access is from Canada by a 40-mi. unpaved road branching S from Canadian Route 1 to Hozomeen on the upper end of the lake. Hozomeen has a campground, launching ramp, nature trail.

Diablo Lake, on SR 20, is a center of visitor activity, site of the Colonial Creek campground, launching ramp, and the head of Thunder Creek Trail. Many people make short day hikes, enjoying an impressive forest and the deep stream canyon, with falls and rapids. The trail can be followed all the way to Stehekin, and several loop routes are possible. Evening programs are offered in an amphitheater just beyond the parking area; check bulletin boards for schedule. Just upstream from the amphitheater is the 0.8-mi. Thunder Wood Nature Trail.

Except at Hozomeen, Ross Lake is accessible only by trail and boat, the latter over Diablo Lake. Small craft are launched at Colonial Creek; at the upper end they must be portaged over a 1-mi. jeep road. Ross Lake Resort portages small boats and canoes by truck, rents boats, and operates a water taxi service. A boat makes twice-daily runs from Diablo Dam to Ross Dam carrying only people and personal gear.

17 boat-in camping areas are on the lakeshore. Most of them can also be reached by trail. Seven major trails lead from the lake into the backcountry.

Lake Chelan National Recreation Area, 62,000 acres. On both sides of the upper 5 mi. of Lake Chelan, extending along the Stehekin Valley and N toward Twisp Pass. No road access. Most visitors take the cruise boat from Chelan, which makes the 55-mi. run to Stehekin daily in summer, several times weekly in winter. This small community has lodge, shops, and marina. A shuttle bus operates on a road along the valley to within a few miles of Cascade Pass in the South Unit. (Autos can reach Stehekin only by weekly barge.) A boat-in campground is on the lakeshore. Several campgrounds are spaced along the Stehekin Valley. Trails lead into the adjacent National Forests and the South Unit.

Stehekin has information and visitor centers. A nature trail is at Rainbow Falls, 3 1/2 mi. upstream.

Park HQ (information, maps, publications) is at 800 State St., Sedro Woolley, near SR 20, about 45 mi. W of the Park entrance. Weekdays, 8 A.M.–4:30 P.M.

Visitor information center at Concrete, on SR 20 about 22 mi. W of the Park entrance. Exhibits, slide programs, publications, maps. (Summer only.)

Ranger Stations at Marblemount, on SR 20 about 4 mi. W of the Park entrance, and at Stehekin. Information and backcountry permits. 8 A.M.–4:30 P.M., all year.

ACTIVITIES

Camping: 24 sites at Goodell Creek, 165 sites at Colonial Creek; 122 at Hozomeen. Goodell is open all year, others Apr. 15 through Nov. Newhalem, scheduled to open in 1982, will have 130 sites. All other campgrounds are boat-in or hike-in.

Hiking, backpacking: A Park leaflet warns: "There are no other mountains like the North Cascades in the U.S., and for this reason people who are familiar with mountains in other parts of the country sometimes encounter difficulties traveling here." Hazards include steep, rugged terrain, treacherous glaciers and snowfields, swift and cold streams. The region has no monopoly on insects, but bring repellent.

Over 300 mi. of trails in alpine wilderness. The Pacific Crest Trail crosses the South Unit. Most trails follow streams, leaving dense timber at 4,000–5,000 ft. Backcountry permits are required for overnight use. Overuse has damaged some sites, and access to these may be limited.

Hunting: Prohibited in North and South Units. Permitted in designated portions of National Recreation Areas, subject to special regulations.

Fishing: A major activity. Lakes, streams. Rainbow, brook, cutthroat, Dolly Varden trout. State license required; state rules apply.

Boating: Ross, Diablo, and Chelan lakes. Commercial rentals.

Horse riding: One outfitter, at Stehekin, offers pack trips. Not all trails are suitable for horses, and horse parties are restricted to use of designated campgrounds. Inquire.

Ski touring: No developed ski areas. Rangers report increased winter use by skiers and snowshoers.

Dogs and other pets are prohibited in the North and South Units except on the Pacific Crest Trail, where they must be leashed. Pets must be leashed in the National Recreation Areas.

PUBLICATIONS (Items marked * are mimeograph sheets.)
Park leaflet with map.
Visitor Activities.
*Geologic history.
*Weather and climate.
*Questions and answers; general information.
Ross Lake National Recreation Area.
Mountains in the Stehekin District.

Lakes in the Stehekin District.
Tree checklist.
Bird checklist.
*Mammal checklist.
Natural Fire in the North Cascades.
Foods and Wilderness Survival.
Thunder Woods nature trail guide.
Obelisk nature trail guide.
*Campground information.
Hiking in the North Cascades.
Selected Long Hikes.
Main Trails and Backcountry Camp Areas (map, information).
*Boating regulations.
*General regulations.
(Trail reports are issued at frequent intervals.)

REFERENCE: Manning, Harvey, and Spring, Bob and Ira. *101 Hikes in the North Cascades.* Seattle: Mountaineers. $6.95.

HEADQUARTERS: 800 State St., Sedro Woolley, WA 98284; (206) 855-1331.

NORTH PUGET SOUND BEACHES
Washington Department of Natural Resources

See discussion of DNR beaches in preface. The publication listed in this entry provides maps and information for 10 beaches, 9 of them on Whidbey Island. Frontages range from 800 ft. to 9,000 ft., average about 3,500 ft.

8 of the 10 beaches can be reached only by boat. State ownership extends to the mean high-water line. Adjacent beaches and the upland are privately owned.

Beach No. 144, S of Dugulla Bay, can be reached by car or on foot across state-owned land. It has 4,800 ft. of frontage. The DNR description indicates it is of interest chiefly to clam diggers.

Point Partridge Recreation Site, Beach No. 140, can be reached by car and has been developed with parking, campsites, and beach trail. It is on the W side of Whidbey Island, W of Coupeville on SR 20, reached by taking Libby Rd. W from SR 20 toward West Beach, turning S on the marked access road.

PUBLICATION: *Your Public Beaches, North Puget Sound, 1978.*

HEADQUARTERS: Department of Natural Resources, Division of Marine Land Management, Olympia, WA 98504; (206) 753-5324.

ROCKPORT STATE PARK
Washington Parks and Recreation Commission
457 acres.

1 mi. W of Rockport on SR 20.

On the lower slope of Sauk Mountain, close to (though not on) the Skagit River. Includes a fine stand of old-growth Douglas-fir. Close to the Mount Baker–Snoqualmie National Forest. Sauk Mountain Road, beginning on the Park's W boundary, leads 7 1/2 mi. to a parking area and trailhead for a 1 1/2-mi. trail to an observation tower at the summit. Several short trails in and around the Park.

The Skagit River Bald Eagle Natural Area (see entry) is across the river. Eagles can often be seen from the Park and nearby in winter.

Rockport is about 12 mi. W of the entrance to North Cascades National Park.

Camping: 50 sites plus 12 walk-in sites. All year.

PUBLICATION: Leaflet.

HEADQUARTERS: 5051 Highway 20, Concrete, WA 98237; (206) 853-4705.

ROSS LAKE NATIONAL RECREATION AREA
See North Cascades National Park, zone 3.

SAN JUAN ISLANDS*
Multiple private, federal, state, and local ownerships.
About 170,000 acres.

By ferry from Anacortes or private boat.

The islands are the tips of submerged mountains, projecting above the water in the Straits of Georgia and Rosario, where they meet the Strait of Juan de Fuca and Puget Sound. Three large islands—Orcas, Lopez, and San Juan—comprise 4/5 of the total area. 169 other islands are large enough to have names. The total depends on how small a rock is counted and the height of the tide, but the accepted number is about 700.

Ferries from Anacortes serve the four largest islands (those just men-

---

*Entry does not include sites on Fidalgo and Whidbey islands, which are linked to the mainland by highways and bridges.

tioned, plus Shaw). These are popular resorts, and motorists are warned of long delays at times. Indeed, the State Ferries leaflet urges motorists to leave their cars behind and walk aboard without delay. The ferry-served islands are, of course, the most developed. The largest single public site, Moran State Park, is on Orcas Island. The smaller islands can be reached only by private boat.

Cruising the islands is, for the naturalist, the way to enjoy them. Developments and the many No Trespassing signs are less visible from afloat. Some public areas can be approached only by boat, because they are hemmed in by private holdings. About 80 of the islands in the San Juan National Wildlife Refuge can be seen only from a boat; going ashore is forbidden, to protect colonies of nesting seabirds. This hardly matters; these islands are so small one can see quite well from offshore. All of these federal islands together have only 458 acres.

Three islands—Martin, Turn, and Jones—within the federal Refuge are open to visitors. Each has a small State Park with a campground. However, increasing public use and disturbance of wildlife and habitat required change. Martin has been brought into the federal wilderness system, and its use as a State Park is restricted.

Moran, 4,064 acres, is by far the largest of 14 State Parks on the islands. (See following information.) The others total only 1,555 acres; 7 have less than 100. The state also lists 7 Natural Area Parks, ranging in size from 1/2 to 5 acres. All but one of the parks have campgrounds.

Here as elsewhere the Department of Natural Resources has the difficult task of managing what's left of Washington's beaches. Scattered among the islands are beaches the state owns—up to the mean high-water line, with private beaches on either side. Most such beaches can't be reached by land without trespassing. The DNR's attempts to install markers visible from the water have been at least partially frustrated by vandalism. The DNR plans to publish a directory of these beaches, but it had not appeared when we last inquired.

The DNR has 7 small, primitive campgrounds, two on Orcas Island, two on Cypress, one on Lummi, one on San Juan, one on Strawberry. Five are boat access only. These campgrounds aren't listed in popular campground directories; see *DNR's Camp and Picnic Sites* leaflet, or ask State Park Rangers.

The San Juan Island National Historical Park, 1,752 acres, is the largest single federal site. It is not managed as a natural area.

A few bits of the public domain still remain, managed by the Bureau of Land Management. A 60-acre tract on Pt. Colville, Lopez Island, is a little-disturbed coastal natural area with a quarter mile of shoreline, two small bogs, some old-growth Sitka spruce and Douglas-fir, brush, meadow, and bluffs. Iceberg Point, also 60 acres and on Lopez Island, is a long, narrow point, 2 mi. of irregular shoreline, half forested, half open grassland with rock outcrops. Informal camping is permitted at both sites. So is hunting, although the only likely game is rabbit. Public access is by water only.

Highest point on the islands is Mt. Constitution, 2,408 ft., on the edge of Moran State Park, reached by road or trail. Climate is moderate, with less than 30 in. of rain per year. Temperatures rarely exceed 80°F or drop below 32°.

The reference listed for this entry *(The San Juan Islands Afoot and Afloat)* is excellent. In 223 pages, it summarizes what can be found in this fascinating and complex area. It estimates that all publicly owned lands combined total only about 12,000 acres, 7% of the total. Not all of these come within our broad definition of "natural area." Cruising, however, adds the spaciousness of open water and interisland passages, the countless birds afloat as well as ashore, and the enjoyment of setting foot on a deserted island or isolated beach.

INCLUDES

Moran State Park (Washington Parks and Recreation Commission), 4,064 acres. On Orcas Island near Rosario. Occupies the interior portion of the E lobe of Orcas Island. Rolling to mountainous terrain. Includes Mt. Constitution, Mt. Pickett, and Little Summit. Mountain Lake is about 1 1/2 mi. long, Cascade Lake a bit under 1 mi., Twin Lakes much smaller. 26 mi. of trails, including trails to mountain peaks, around the lakes, and beside the falls of Cascade Creek. Considerable forest, with some virgin cedar and hemlock, salal and Oregon grape in understory. A plant list is in preparation. Bird and mammal lists available at office. *Camping:* 4 campgrounds, one open in winter. 136 sites. Reservations. *Fishing:* Brook, rainbow, cutthroat, silver trout. *Swimming:* Lake; supervised July–Aug. *Boating:* Two large lakes. No motors. Rowboat rentals. Leaflet available. Headquarters at Star Route, Box 22, Eastsound, WA 98245; (206) 376-2326.

Stuart Island Marine State Park (Washington Parks and Recreation Commission), 84 acres. 10 mi. NW of Friday Harbor. Boat access. Irregular coastline; long narrow bays; forested. *Camping:* 19 sites. *Boating:* Mooring, floats and buoys in sheltered harbor.

Jones Island Marine State Park (Washington Parks and Recreation Commission), 188 acres. SW of Orcas Island. Boat access. Valley between two hills links North Cove and South Cove. Rocky ground, heavily wooded. Open bluffs above the sea. One large meadow. Woodland is cool, damp, with mosses, ferns, mushrooms, wildflowers. *Camping:* 2 campgrounds, 21 sites. *Boating:* Dock, mooring float and buoys.

Clark Island Marine State Park (Washington Parks and Recreation Commission), 55 acres. 1 3/4 mi. NE of Orcas Island. Boat access. Narrow island about 1 mi. long. Largest of a cluster of rocky islands, it has a bit of forest, brush. Low tide exposes sandflats, tidepools. *Camping:* 8 sites. *Boating:* Mooring buoys but no sheltered harbor.

Spencer Spit State Park (Washington Parks and Recreation Commission), 130 acres. E side of Lopez Island. Heavily used because of location on a ferry-served island. Sand spit with shallow lagoon, sandy slopes, forested hillside. *Camping:* 28 sites plus primitive hiker-biker camp. *Boating:* Mooring buoys. No ramp. (A 50-unit campground is being prepared.)

Sucia Island Marine State Park (Washington Parks and Recreation Commission), 562 acres. 2 1/2 mi. N of Orcas Island. Boat access. One of the most popular marine parks and often crowded. A cluster of islands arranged in a horseshoe, with numerous bays and coves. The state has made several land purchases but some private holdings remain. Rocky and sandy beaches; eroded cliffs; upland forest. One of the few boat-access islands with opportunities for hiking. Some trails are steep, slippery when wet. Many seabirds. *Camping:* 51 sites at several locations. *Boating:* Docks and buoys, often fully utilized. Check weather and tides.

Turn Island Marine State Park (Washington Parks and Recreation Commission), 35 acres. E of San Juan Island. So close to ferry-served San Juan Island that a canoe or rowboat crossing is feasible in good weather. Thus the campsites are often crowded in summer. The island is part of the National Wildlife Refuge. Partially wooded; tideflats on the W; steep banks back of the beach on the N and E. *Camping:* 12 sites. *Boating:* Mooring buoys.

Matia Island Marine State Park (Washington Parks and Recreation Commission), 145 acres. NE of Orcas Island. Boat access. Part of the federal wildlife refuge and wilderness system. The former campground is closed. About 3/4 mi. long. Most of the shoreline is rocky, some steep banks sculptured by wave action. Forested, trees coming close to shoreline. Trails. A sandy cove at the E end looks out on Puffin Island, one of those off limits to visitors. Public use is presently restricted to 5 acres at the NW end of the island. *Boating:* Pier, hinged dock, float, buoys.

ACTIVITIES

Camping: Moran is the only State Park that accepts reservations. Several county parks have campsites, and there are a few commercial facilities. The total is small by comparison with demand in busy periods.

Hiking: Moran State Park offers the only substantial trail mileage.

Hunting: Land-based hunting is almost nonexistent.

Fishing: Fresh and salt water.

Swimming: Many beaches and a few interior lakes and ponds.

Boating: These are popular boating waters, but one needs a sound craft, navigation charts, and ability to handle both.

REFERENCES

Ferry information: Washington State Ferries, Pier 52, Seattle, WA 98104; (206) 464-6400.

Mueller, Marge. *The San Juan Islands Afoot and Afloat.* 1979. The Mountaineers, 719 Pike St., Seattle, WA 98101.

SKAGIT HABITAT MANAGEMENT AREA
Washington Department of Game
10,160 acres.

From I-5, Conway/LaConner exit. W through Conway on Fir Island Rd.
Left on Mann Rd. and S 1 mi. to HQ.

Said to be the most important waterfowl area in western WA. About 5 mi.
of frontage on Skagit Bay between the mouths of the N and S forks of the
Skagit River. Extensive tideflats, sloughs, cattail salt marsh, sedge-bulrush
areas, wooded stream banks, cultivated fields, lowland brush, and upland
forest.

The Area has two large pieces and a number of smaller ones, with different
access points, so it's advisable to stop at HQ for a map and advice. Fall and
spring are the peak seasons, but thousands of waterfowl winter here, and
broods of nesting species are seen in spring and early summer.

Near HQ is a 2-mi. walk on the dike. Fir Island Rd. leads into Maupin Rd.
and the Jensen Access, strategic point for overlooking tideflats. Turning N,
then left on Rawlins Rd., leads to a parking area near the Skagit's N fork.
Other access points to areas of interest are reached by turning S from Conway
on Old Highway 99.

Birds: No checklist. Nearly 200 species said to have been recorded, including all waterfowl species common to the region. 20,000 to 35,000 snow geese
winter here. Also many whistling swan, brant. Mallard, wood duck, cinnamon and blue-winged teal, Virginia and sora rails, and long-billed marsh wren
are among the nesting species. Many gulls, terns, shorebirds. Eagles and
hawks most numerous in winter.

Mammals: Mule deer, coyote, fox, raccoon, opossum, weasel, mink, beaver,
otter, muskrat.

ACTIVITIES
Hunting: Designated areas. Special regulations. Inquire.
Fishing: Spring through fall best seasons. Dolly Varden, cutthroat trout,
steelhead, salmon.
Canoeing, boating: Ramp near HQ. Boaters are advised to check tide
tables, watch out for tidal and river currents—and not to become lost in the
twisting tidal channels.

PUBLICATION: Leaflet.

HEADQUARTERS: Department of Game, 600 N. Capitol Way, Olympia, WA
98504; (206) 753-5700.

SKAGIT RIVER BALD EAGLE NATURAL AREA
Washington Department of Game/The Nature Conservancy
1,500 acres.

Along the Skagit River, beside SR 20, between Rockport and Marblemount.

Each winter up to 300 bald eagles gather at the Skagit River to feed on spawned-out salmon. The first of them arrive in late Oct. By mid-Feb. the eagles begin migrating to their northern nesting grounds.

For survival, the eagles require an undisturbed habitat with large hardwood trees for perching near the sand and gravel bars where they feed. To provide this protected habitat, The Nature Conservancy purchased over 870 acres of land along the river. Most of this was sold to the Department of Game, added to lands already in state ownership. TNC organized a national fund-raising drive to complete the project.

Eagles can be seen from various points along SR 20.

PUBLICATION: Leaflet.

HEADQUARTERS: Department of Game, 600 N. Capitol Way, Olympia, WA 98504; (206) 753-5700. The Nature Conservancy, 618 Smith Tower, Seattle, WA 98104; (206) 624-9623.

SOUTH WHIDBEY STATE PARK
Washington Parks and Recreation Commission
87 acres.

On Whidbey Island, 4 1/2 mi. SW of Greenbank by county road.

A small park with 4,500 ft. of shoreline on Admiralty Inlet. Wooded site on a bluff.

Camping: 54 sites.

HEADQUARTERS: 4128 S. Smugglers Cove Rd., Freeland, WA 98249; (206) 321-4559.

TENNANT LAKE NATURAL HISTORY INTERPRETIVE CENTER
Washington Department of Game/Whatcom County Parks
700 acres.

From Ferndale on I-5 (N of Bellingham), S 1/4 mi. on Hovander Rd., then SW 1 1/2 mi. on Nielson Rd.
Open: 10 A.M. to dusk.

The site borders the Nooksack River, includes Tennant Lake and surrounding wetlands. An observation tower overlooks the lake. Boardwalk, 1/2 mi. long, through the swamp. Upland nature trail.

Birds: Checklist available. Great blue heron seen regularly. Green heron, uncommon in the NW, is seen almost daily in summer. Summer ducks include blue-winged and cinnamon teals, mallard, wood duck. Common winter species include wigeon, shoveler, ring-necked duck, scaup, bufflehead, pintail, Barrow's and common goldeneyes, ruddy duck. Red-tailed and marsh hawks seen all year. Barn, screech, and great horned owls nest. Marsh birds include long-billed marsh wren, common yellowthroat, red-winged blackbird. Many others.

INTERPRETATION: *Interpretive Center* is open Wed.–Sun. Exhibits. Special programs, tours.

PUBLICATIONS
Leaflet.
Bird checklist.

HEADQUARTERS: 5236 Nielson Rd., Ferndale, WA 98248; (206) 384-5545.

ZONE 4

1 Mount Pilchuck State
    Recreation Area
2 Wallace Falls State Park
3 Mount Baker–Snoqualmie
    National Forest
4 Blake Island State Park
5 South Puget Sound Beaches

6 Flaming Geyser Recreation
    Area/Nolte State Park/
    Green River Gorge
    Conservation Area
7 Federation Forest State Park
8 Mount Rainier National Park

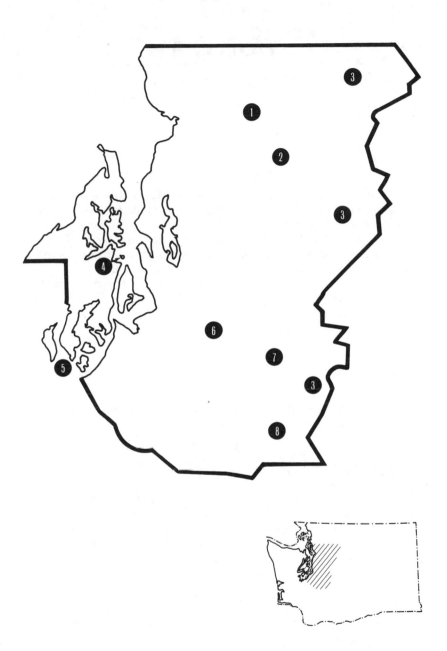

ZONE 4

Includes these counties:
  Snohomish   King
  Kitsap   Pierce

The E portion of this zone is occupied by the Mount Baker–Snoqualmie National Forest and Mount Rainier National Park, on the slopes of the Cascade Range. Puget Sound is on the W.

We reviewed all of the State Parks in the zone and visited most of them, finally omitting all but a few. Those we visited are attractive but small, generally surrounded by developed areas, and heavily used.

The entry on "Puget Sound Beaches" does not signify that these beaches are more significant natural areas than the omitted parks. We thought it useful to report the status of public beaches.

BLAKE ISLAND STATE PARK
Washington Parks and Recreation Commission
476 acres.

In Puget Sound near Seattle. Boat access only. Twice-daily ferry service from Pier 56, Seattle, June 3–Oct. 15.

Once an elaborate private estate with fine gardens, abandoned after 1929, structures later burned. Now densely wooded. Mostly native plants, but some exotics remain. The developed area includes Tillicum Village, offering Indian dancing and barbecued salmon. Four miles of beaches. Wildlife includes a few deer, plus small mammals; no data on birds.

ACTIVITIES
  Camping: 36 sites. All year.
  Hiking: Trail circles island.
  Boating: Many visitors come by private boat. Dock and mooring buoys.

PUBLICATION: Leaflet.

HEADQUARTERS: Box 287, Manchester, WA 98353; (206) 447-1313.

FEDERATION FOREST STATE PARK
Washington Parks and Recreation Commission
609 acres.

From Enumclaw, 18 mi. SE on SR 410.

Traveling to or from Mount Rainier National Park on SR 410, this is a mandatory stop. The site, with much virgin timber, was acquired through efforts of the Washington State Federation of Women's Clubs. Funds willed to the Federation were used to build the Catherine Montgomery Interpretive Center, one of the best anywhere, unique in the Washington State Parks system.

Exhibits inside the structure describe the flora and fauna of Washington's principal life zones. Through large windows, one looks out on small gardens with living specimens of many of the plants mentioned in the exhibits. Two nature trails.

PUBLICATION: Leaflet.

HEADQUARTERS: Star Route, Enumclaw, WA 98022; (206) 663-2207.

FLAMING GEYSER RECREATION AREA/NOLTE STATE PARK
Washington Parks and Recreation Commission
1,332 acres. See Green River Gorge entry below.

GREEN RIVER GORGE CONSERVATION AREA
Washington Department of Natural Resources
117 acres.

About 6 mi. N of Enumclaw on SR 169.

The Green River attracts whitewater enthusiasts in winter and early spring. The Gorge is scenic. One viewpoint is the highway bridge near the Park entrance. Others are nearby; inquire locally.

The Flaming Geyser Recreation Area has well-manicured day-use facilities beside the river: extensive lawns, playground, picnic tables. About 60% of the site is forested: second-growth Douglas-fir, western hemlock, western redcedar, bigleaf and vine maples, black cottonwood, red alder, willow, Sitka spruce, cascara, with salmonberry, thimbleberry, Oregon grape, swordfern, red elderberry, devil's club, twinflower. A small swamp has cattails, reeds, bamboo. A 1-mi. River Trail follows the river upstream into the Gorge, where there are Indian petroglyphs. A 1 1/2-mi. Hill Trail ascends the wooded hillside above the day-use area.

The "flaming geyser" is an old drill hole that spouts methane, but these days spouts only about 18 in. high.

Nearby Nolte has a small lake, self-guiding nature trail. Neither of these sites has a campground.

Also nearby is the DNR's recreation site. An unimproved, poorly maintained road leads around a loop on which are some primitive campsites in the woods. The bulletin board was blank, and we could not ascertain the size of the site. We saw trails, unmarked, but did not find one leading to the Gorge.

ACTIVITIES

Camping: DNR area. 12 sites.

Hiking: The two short trails at Flaming Geyser are pleasant. Those leading from the DNR campground may be worth exploring.

Hunting: DNR area only.

Fishing: River and Deep Lake at Nolte.

Swimming: Unsupervised. The area at Flaming Geyser seemed better for wading than swimming. Beach at Nolte State Park.

Canoeing: Above the Park, from Palmer, 5 to 6 mi. of class III and IV rapids, then class II and III into the Park. The 2.7 mi. from within the Park to the second bridge take-out has class II rapids. Water level is controlled at Howard Hansen Dam and can change from day to day.

PUBLICATIONS

Flaming Geyser leaflet.

Nolte nature trail guide.

HEADQUARTERS: Flaming Geyser Recreation Area, 23700 SE Flaming Geyser Rd., Auburn, WA 98002; (206) 931-3930.

MOUNT BAKER–SNOQUALMIE NATIONAL FOREST
U.S. Forest Service
2,100,000 acres within boundaries; 1,700,000 acres of Forest land.

On the W slopes of the Cascade Range, from the Canadian border to Mt. Rainier. Crossed by SR 20, US 2, I-90, SR 410.

Mount Baker and Snoqualmie were combined as one National Forest in 1974. They are elements of a huge block of National Forest and National Park land extending along the Cascades from Canada to Oregon. The Forest is on the W side of the Range, from Canada to Mt. Rainier. Rugged, mountainous terrain; peaks, ridges, deep glacier-carved valleys. More than 100 of the glaciers are still here. Several hundred alpine lakes, many in cirque basins below glaciers. Elevations range from 400 ft. to 10,778 ft. Annual precipitation ranges from 40 in. to 180 in., depending on elevation and location. Most of this falls as snow at high elevations.

The Forest is not a solid block of federal land. S of the Canadian border it adjoins the North Cascades National Park. This entry is concerned only with the area W of the Park; that to the E, including part of the Pasayten Wilderness, is administered by the Okanogan National Forest and is described in that entry.

On the W, the continuity of Forest land is broken by a wide band of private holdings along SR 20. Another wide band extends from the W boundary along SR 530 to Darrington. These are linked by a N–S band of private land along the Sauk River.

Next to the S is a large block of Forest land adjoining the South Unit of the North Cascades National Park and the Wenatchee National Forest. Irregular in shape, this block includes some inholdings, especially in the S portion. It ends just N of I-90. For the next 22 mi. S, the Forest land is a checkerboard of 1-mi. squares, alternating with private holdings. Then comes another solid block on the N boundary of Mount Rainier National Park.

To the S and SE of the Park is a large block of Forest land technically within Mount Baker–Snoqualmie but administered by Wenatchee, and is described in that entry.

Although the Forest is one of the largest in the national system, the available information describing it is surprisingly scanty. The Seattle office sent us all the publications they had and filled in our data sheets. All together, this was far less than we received from many much smaller sites. No fauna and flora checklists. Only a few brief notes on areas of special interest. We visited the Forest during our field work, but gathering all the needed information firsthand would have required months or years, not days.

The Forest includes some of the wildest country in the Northwest. Half of it is still covered by virgin timber, preserved thus far by the difficult terrain. Large areas are roadless wilderness.

Several roads are the principal corridors for Forest visitors. Generally these are scenic routes with campgrounds and trailheads along the way.

- SR 542, E from Bellingham, along the Nooksack River, dead-ending at the Mt. Baker ski area, within the Heather Meadows area.
- SR 20, E from Sedro Woolley, access to Baker Lake, continuing into the North Cascades National Park.
- SR 530, from I-5 to Darrington, beyond which are several Forest roads.

- SR 92 to Granite Falls, continuing E beyond Verlot to Forest roads along the Stillaguamish River.
- US 2 along the Skykomish River. About 8 mi. beyond Gold Bar, a Forest road follows the North Fork to the NE. US 2 continues along the South Fork and over Stevens Pass.
- SR 410, E from Enumclaw and SE to Mount Rainier National Park.

These are the primary routes for the motorist-sightseer and RV camper. The Forest has hundreds of miles of Forest roads, shown only on the National Forest map. People familiar with the Forest know the routes to the more secluded campgrounds and to trailheads for trails into the wilderness areas.

Weather and snow cover depend on altitude and location. Trails over the high passes may be closed by snow until late July or even early Aug., then remain open through Oct. Main highways are usually kept open. Many Forest roads are left unplowed unless in use for logging. At lower altitudes the camping season is Apr.–Oct., a few campgrounds remaining open all year.

Plants: 85% forest. Most of the remainder is above timberline. About half the forest is virgin; some old growth. Dense stands of Douglas-fir and western hemlock on W slopes up to about 3,000 ft. elevation. Associated species include western redcedar, bigleaf maple, red alder. Understory is luxuriant, including raspberry, rhododendron, salal, vanillaleaf, wild ginger, dogwood, cascara, evergreen huckleberry, devil's club, western yew. The many ferns include swordfern, bracken, ladyfern, spiny wood fern, maidenhair fern. Between 3,000 and 5,000 ft., Douglas-fir with western white pine, grand fir, lodgepole pine. In the subalpine zone, open stands of mountain hemlock and subalpine fir.

Still higher are open heather-covered meadows with stunted subalpine fir and mountain hemlock, many brightly colored flowers in season.

More than 200 flowering species recorded, including Indian paintbrush, glacier lily, mountain valerian, shooting star, queen's cup, orange honeysuckle, bleeding heart, columbine, mountain spirea, blue Jacob's ladder.

Birds: No checklist available. Forest reports over 200 species recorded. Species include grebes, great blue heron, whistling and trumpeter swans; Canada, white-fronted and snow geese; various ducks, goshawk; sharp-shinned, Cooper's, red-tailed, and Swainson's hawks; golden and bald eagles, osprey, merlin, kestrel; blue, spruce, ruffed, and sharp-tailed grouse; California and mountain quails; screech, flammulated, great horned, pygmy, snowy, spotted, great horned, long-eared, and short-eared owls; black and Vaux's swifts, common flicker; pileated, Lewis's, hairy, and downy woodpeckers; yellow-bellied and Williamson's sapsuckers; willow, Hammond's, dusky, western, and olive-sided flycatchers. Also violet-green, tree, rough-winged, barn, and cliff swallows; gray and Steller's jays, magpie, raven, crow, Clark's nutcracker; black-capped, mountain, boreal, and chestnut-backed chickadees; white-breasted, red-breasted, and pygmy nuthatches; varied, hermit, and Swainson's thrushes; golden-crowned and ruby-crowned kinglets; solitary, red-eyed, and warbling vireos. Warblers include orange-crowned, yellow,

yellow-rumped, black-throated gray, Townsend's, hermit, MacGillivray's, and Wilson's.

Mammals: No checklist available. Species reported include opossum; various shrews, moles, and bats; pika, cottontail, snowshoe hare, mountain beaver; least, yellow pine, and Townsend chipmunks; yellow-bellied and hoary marmots, golden-mantled squirrel, red squirrel, chickaree, northern flying squirrel, beaver, deer mouse, various voles, porcupine, coyote, red fox, black bear, raccoon, marten, fisher, mink, wolverine, otter, mountain lion, lynx, bobcat, Roosevelt elk, mule deer, mountain goat.

FEATURES

Glacier Peak Wilderness, 464,237 acres, slightly more than half of this in the Wenatchee National Forest. Glacier Peak elevation is 10,528 ft. This huge wilderness area, roadless and undeveloped, has more than 30 other peaks, 3 of them over 9,000 ft., and over 90 glaciers. Glaciers and snowfields are the sources of hundreds of streams with many cascades, falls, and pools, as well as many high lakes. Vegetation ranges from lush rain forests along several of the lower valleys, notably the Suiattle, to high meadows and rocky peaks supporting little more than lichens.

Fish and game are plentiful, and the wilderness attracts many hunters and fishermen, on foot and horseback. Climbers are challenged by several of the peaks. The principal visitor activity is backpacking. The Pacific Crest Trail crosses the area. Connecting trails enter from the E and W, generally follow the drainages. Several large areas, shown in pink on the wilderness map, have no maintained trails, and the terrain is unsuitable for horses; these are areas for experienced hikers.

Commercial outfitters are located on the principal approaches, experienced in providing stock, gear, and guidance. Ask Forest HQ for addresses. Trails that have much horse traffic during the hunting season are likely to be in bad condition for hikers, at least temporarily: muddy, chewed up. Inquire at a Ranger District.

Wilderness permits are required, but backcountry travel is not yet rationed.

Goat Rocks Wilderness. Although a portion of this Wilderness is in the Mount Baker–Snoqualmie National Forest, that portion is administered by the Wenatchee National Forest. See entry in zone 5. (The other portion is in the Gifford Pinchot National Forest, entry in zone 2.)

Skagit Wild and Scenic River. In 1978 Congress so designated the Skagit and its tributaries. This includes the river and a strip of land 1/4 to 1/2 mi. wide along the main stem of the Skagit and along these tributaries: Cascade River, Suiattle River, Sauk River, N and S Forks of the Sauk. Included are large portions of these streams outside the National Forest. A management plan is being prepared. No special restrictions are yet in effect, but the designation is based on the generally wild and undisturbed condition of the river system.

Alpine Lakes Wilderness, 305,318 acres, 61% in the Wenatchee National

Forest. The Mount Baker–Snoqualmie portion is generally to the N of I-90 at Snoqualmie Pass. This is also rugged country, but less so than the Glacier Peaks area. Here the highest peak in the Mount Baker–Snoqualmie portion is 6,800 ft. More than a dozen others are over 1 mi. high. The most striking feature of the area is the lakes, more than 700 of them if you include those as small as an acre. The map is dotted with them, the largest about 1 1/2 miles long, three others close to a mile, perhaps a dozen in the 1/4-mile range. Lake elevations from 2,100 to 6,000 ft. Trails generally follow the drainages, and a number of them are easy going, the destination lakes being only a couple of miles from the trailhead.

Permits are not yet required, nor is access rationed. But the popularity of several lakes has been such that camping is not permitted within 100 ft. of the shoreline.

Glacier Ranger District

- *Picture Lake.* An easy 1/2-mi. scenic walk on Path No. 735 from Mt. Baker Highway 20 mi. E of the Ranger Station. Circles Picture Lake in the Heather Meadows area.
- *Mt. Baker Viewpoint.* Because of intervening ridges, Mt. Baker can't be seen from most areas. An exception is at the end of Glacier Creek Rd. (No. 3904). Parking area overlooks Coleman Glacier.
- *Nooksack Falls.* Turn at sign on Mt. Baker Highway 7 mi. E of the Ranger Station. Follow Wells Creek Rd. 1/2 mi. to parking. Falls, 170 ft. high.

Monte Cristo Ranger District

- *Mountain Loop Highway.* From Granite Falls E through Verlot. From Barlow Pass NW to Darrington, a usually good gravel road follows the Sauk River. This section was closed by flood damage in 1981.
- *Lake Twenty-two.* Lake is in a large cirque on the side of Mt. Pilchuck (see entry). Trail No. 702 begins in the Lake 22 Research Natural Area. Trail is 2 1/2 mi. one way.
- *Ice Caves.* Trail No. 723, a National Recreation Trail, begins at the site of an old inn, crosses the river on a footbridge, then through timber to a snowfield at the base of Big 4. Caves form as snow melts in early summer. Dangerous to enter.

Baker River Ranger District

- *Shadow of the Sentinels National Recreation Trail,* a primitive area adjacent to Baker Lake Highway 1/2 mi. N of Koma Kulshan Guard Station. Exhibit near trailhead, signs along the trail.
- *Rainbow Falls.* Turn off Baker Lake Rd. just beyond Boulder Creek bridge; follow Road No. 385, 4 1/2 mi. High falls.
- *Baker Lake,* 5,000 acres, is largest in the Forest. About 9 mi. long. Numerous campgrounds and launch points. Fishing, boating, swimming. Speed limits on motorboats.

Skykomish Ranger District
- *Deception Falls Nature Trail* is 8 mi. E of the Skykomish on US 2. 1/2-mi. loop.
- *Alpine Falls,* on US 2, 5 mi. E of the Skykomish Ranger Station. Wide double falls on the Tye River.
- *Bridal Veil Falls,* on Mt. Index River Rd. just below Lake Serene near Mt. Index.
- *Eagle Falls,* 2 1/2 mi. E of the Index turnoff on the S side of US 2.

North Bend Ranger District
- *Franklin Falls,* about 150 ft., on the South Fork, Snoqualmie River, W of Snoqualmie Pass. Exit 52 from I-90 E, then Forest Road 2219 about 1 mi. W. Short trail.
- *Asahel Curtis Nature Trail* through old-growth Douglas-fir and western hemlock. 600-year-old trees, 250 ft. tall, 5 ft. diameter. Off I-90 W of Snoqualmie Pass.

White River Ranger District
- *Suntop Lookout.* Spectacular view of Mt. Rainier. Forest Roads 186 and 188, 8 mi. from SR 410.
- *Crystal Mountain Area.* Alpine ski area in winter. Chairlifts operate on weekends in summer. SR 410 and Forest Road 1802.

INTERPRETATION

Information is available at Ranger Stations or at the visitor information center in downtown Seattle: Room 110, 915 Second Ave.

Campfire programs in summer at Horseshoe Cove and Gold Basin campgrounds.

ACTIVITIES

Camping: 73 campgrounds; 1,150 sites. Some all year, others Apr.–Oct. and June–Sept.

Hiking, backpacking: 1,200 mi. of trails. Numbered trails are shown on the Forest map, but the scale does not permit sufficient detail. Each Ranger District has good information on trails and can suggest routes. Four Ranger Districts have published Visitor Guides with detailed trail information; however, budget cuts make it unlikely that these will be available for distribution. They can be seen at Ranger Stations. Glacier Peak Wilderness map, at 3/4 in. per mi., shows contours and detail. Topo maps advisable for backcountry travel.

Hunting: Deer, elk, bear, mountain goat.

Fishing: Many lakes, streams. Trout, salmon.

Boating: Baker Lake.

Canoeing, kayaking: Whitewater streams include sections of the South Fork, Stillaguamish River; Upper Skykomish River; Upper Sauk River. Other whitewater streams are just outside the Forest. Water levels are generally best late spring to fall.

Horse riding: About half the trail system is usable by horses. About 80% of that use occurs in the two-week early deer hunt in Sept. Forest HQ can provide a list of outfitters. Riding is more popular in the Wenatchee, Okanogan, Colville, and Umatilla National Forests.

Skiing: Downhill: 7 ski areas, commercially operated. Usual season: Thanksgiving to end of Apr. Ski touring: when and where snow conditions permit. Weather is often rainy, snow wet. Better ski conditions are usually found E of the Cascades crest.

Snowmobiling: Prohibited in wilderness areas. Elsewhere as conditions permit, generally on unplowed Forest roads.

Note: Many areas have high avalanche hazard in winter. Visitors should inquire about current snow conditions in areas they plan to enter.

PUBLICATIONS

Forest map. $1.00.
Glacier Peak Wilderness map.

HEADQUARTERS: 1022 First Ave., Seattle, WA 98104; (206) 442-5400. USFS-NPS Outdoor Recreation Information Office, 1018 First Avenue, Seattle, WA 98104.

RANGER DISTRICTS: Baker River R.D., Concrete, WA 98237; (206) 853-2851. Darrington R.D., Darrington, WA 98241; (206) 436-1155. Glacier R.D., Glacier, WA 98244; (206) 599-2714. Monte Cristo R.D., Granite Falls, WA 98252; (206) 691-7791. North Bend R.D., North Bend, WA 98045; (206) 888-1421. Skykomish R.D., Skykomish, WA 98288; (206) 677-2414. White River R.D., Enumclaw, WA 98022; (206) 825-2571.

MOUNT PILCHUCK RECREATION AREA

Washington Parks and Recreation Commission/U.S. Forest Service
1,975 acres.

From Granite Falls on SR 22 (NE of Everett), E 19 mi., following signs to Mt. Pilchuck.

Beyond Verlot, turn right on a steep, narrow paved road that ascends 5,324-ft. Mt. Pilchuck. The mountainside is wooded, with some impressive stands. At the top is a large parking area. This was a state-managed ski area, but state management ended in 1981 and the ski lifts and buildings are being removed. The site is now administered by the Mt. Baker–Snoqualmie National Forest, which adjoins.

The view from the top is impressive, marred only by the patchy appearance of the forest hills. The principal visitor activity is hiking. Several trailheads are marked along the mountain road. A trail near the parking area is marked for Lookout No. 2.

The National Forest has a roadside campground at Verlot. If you proceed beyond the Mt. Pilchuck Road, the route enters the Forest along the Stillaguamish River, a popular area with many campgrounds. Portions of the river offer whitewater canoeing.

HEADQUARTERS: Verlot Ranger Station, Mount Baker–Snoqualmie National Forest, Verlot, WA 98252; (206) 691-7791.

MOUNT RAINIER NATIONAL PARK
U.S. National Park Service
235,404 acres.

70 mi. SE of Tacoma on SR 410. Other approaches via US 12 and SR 123, SR 706, SR 165.

Part of the huge block of National Forest and National Park land extending from Canada to Oregon along the Cascades. Mt. Rainier, 14,410 ft., is the most prominent peak of the Cascades, a composite volcano surrounded by 34 sq. mi. of glaciers on its upper slopes.

Many visitors come to climb the mountain, many more to hike on its extensive trails, most simply to look. This is one of the National Parks threatened by overuse. On our most recent visit, backpacking above timberline, we were shocked to see how much damage had occurred since our visit a few years before. A section of the Wonderland Trail had become a muddy ditch beaten into the tundra by cleated boots. A high park we remembered as exquisite had been ruined, its grasses and wildflowers trampled by the many parties camping here. To limit damage, backcountry travel is rationed now. Management is encouraging additional public transportation, has moved some support facilities outside the Park, and is adopting other changes designed to protect the environment without curtailing public enjoyment.

It is one of the snowiest places on earth. At Paradise in the winter of 1971–1972 snowfall totaled 94 ft., a world record; the average here is 48 ft. Snowfall is heaviest from Paradise, at 5,500 ft. elevation, up to 9,500 ft. Annual precipitation ranges from 60 to 110 in. per year in different locations.

Moisture, soil conditions, and topography—from 1,560 to 14,410 ft.—combine to produce rich plant growth. Four major life zones are represented: Humid Transition, Canadian, Hudsonian, and Arctic Alpine. Deep forests, including extensive virgin stands, are on the lower slopes. Between 5,000 and 6,500 ft. are spectacular subalpine meadows and fields of bright flowers.

Heaviest visitor traffic is from the Nisqually entrance at the SW corner to Paradise, site of the Paradise Inn and other facilities. Along the way are trailheads and such features as Longmire Meadow, Christine Falls, and Narada Falls. Beyond Paradise are several lakes, Martha Falls, Box Canyon, Grove of the Patriarchs, and Silver Falls. Near the SE corner of the Park, one can turn N to Cayuse Pass and the White River entrance, then W to Sunrise, said by some to offer the most splendid view of the mountain. The entire route is scenic, and all along are places to stop to enjoy a vista, waterfall, cascade, lake, canyon, or meadow. Turning S on SR 123 leads to Silver Falls and the tall trees and hot springs of Ohanapecosh.

Much less traveled are two other Park routes. One turns N about 1 mi. beyond the Nisqually entrance. The other enters the Park at its NW corner, following the Carbon River to Ipsut Creek.

The Park is open in winter. The road from Nisqually entrance to Paradise is plowed; snow may close it temporarily, and chains may be required. The Paradise Visitor Center is closed Mon.–Fri., Jan.–Mar. Other Park roads are usually closed from late Nov. to June or July. About 70% of the 2 million visitors per year come in June–Sept., less than 10% in Dec.–Mar. More than half of them come on weekends. 90% come only for the day.

Plants: Over 700 plant species have been identified. In the Humid Transition zone, dense stands of Douglas-fir and western hemlock with western redcedar, bigleaf maple, red alder. Dense understory includes lichens, mosses, swordfern, bracken fern, ladyfern, rhododendron, salal, vanillaleaf. From 3,000 to 5,000 ft., Douglas-fir and Pacific silver fir with western white pine, grand fir, Sitka spruce. In the understory and forest openings: vine maple, bleeding heart, fireweed, queen's cup, coltsfoot. The subalpine meadows are dominated by herbaceous flowering species. A long list of wildflowers recorded at Paradise includes beargrass, bog orchid, white heather, avalanche lily, pearly everlasting, spring beauty, pasqueflower, cinquefoil, broadleaf arnica, pedicularis, glacier lily, columbine, rosy spirea, scarlet paintbrush, moss campion, alpine aster, mountain daisy.

Birds: Preliminary checklist of 157 species, 24 considered accidental or very rare. Abundant or common species include rough-legged and red-tailed hawks, kestrel, blue grouse, band-tailed pigeon, Vaux's swift, rufous hummingbird, common flicker, yellow-bellied sapsucker, western flycatcher, western wood pewee, barn and violet-green swallows, Steller's and gray jays, Clark's nutcracker, raven, mountain chickadee, brown creeper, hermit thrush, golden-crowned kinglet, water pipit, Oregon junco.

Mammals: Common species include elk, mountain goat, mule deer, black bear, coyote, raccoon, pine marten, mountain lion, porcupine, beaver, snowshoe hare, hoary marmot, pika, golden-mantled squirrel, yellow pine chipmunk. Checklist available.

INTERPRETATION

Visitor centers at Longmire and Paradise are open all year, except Paradise closes weekdays Jan.–Mar. Those at Sunrise and Ohanapecosh are summer only.

Nature walks and *evening slide programs,* late June through Labor Day. Notices posted.

Nature trails at Kautz Creek Mudflow, Longmire Meadows, Sourdough Ridge, Nisqually Vista, Emmons Vista, Ohanapecosh, Hot Springs, Grove of the Patriarchs, Carbon River, and Ipsut.

ACTIVITIES

Camping: 5 campgrounds, over 500 sites. Only Sunshine Point, near the Nisqually entrance, is open all year. No reservations.

Hiking, backpacking: Rainier is a hiker's park. Many trails offer day hikes to points of interest. Hiking season in the high country is usually mid-July to mid-Oct.

The Wonderland Trail, 95 mi. long, encircles the mountain crossing alpine meadows, glacial streams, mountain passes, valley forests, reaching a maximum elevation of 6,500 ft. 10 days is the minimum recommended time for a complete circuit. Many trails from below meet the Wonderland Trail, so there are many opportunities for loop hikes of less than 10 days. Backcountry permits are required from June 1 to Oct. 15, and camping in some areas is limited. Reservations can be made up to 90 days in advance for high camps Muir and Schurman. Permits specify the campsites to be used. Off-trail camping is available but specific rules apply.

The Pacific Crest Trail skirts the Park's E boundary.

The climbing zone begins at the glacier line, about 7,000 ft. About 2,500 people climb the mountain each year. Climbers generally spend the first night at Camp Muir or Camp Schurman. Climbers must register on climbing cards.

ACTIVITIES

Fishing: Stocking of lakes has been or will be discontinued. Fishing is not a major activity.

Horse riding: Terrain is not favorable for horse travel. Horses are limited to 90 mi. of designated trails. No livery or grazing is available in the Park.

Ski touring: No downhill slopes with tows. Ski touring has become increasingly popular. Usual season: Dec.–May.

Pets permitted only in developed areas, on leash. No pets in backcountry.

ADJACENT: Gifford Pinchot, Wenatchee, and Mount Baker–Snoqualmie National Forests. (See entries.)

PUBLICATIONS

Leaflet with map.
Evolution of Mount Rainier's Landscape.
Checklist of trees.

Wildflowers of Paradise.
Bird checklist.
Mammal checklist.
Amphibian and reptile checklist.
Fish checklist.
Hiking in Mount Rainier National Park.
Backcountry trail mileages.
Trail mileage chart.
Backcountry reservation system information.
Climbing Mount Rainier (leaflet).
Backcountry trip planning information.
Fishing regulations.

REFERENCES

Kirk, Ruth. *Exploring Mt. Rainier.* Seattle: University of Washington Press. $4.95.

Spring, Ira; Manning, Harvey; and Mueller, Marge. *50 Hikes in Mt. Rainier.* Seattle: Mountaineers. $5.95.

Hiking Map, Southwest Corner of Park. 75¢. (Southeast and North sections in production, due 1981.)

HEADQUARTERS: Ashford, WA 98304; (206) 569-2211.

SOUTH PUGET SOUND BEACHES
Washington Department of Natural Resources

The publication listed for this entry describes 23 state-owned beaches in the South Puget Sound area. As explained in the preface, DNR has responsibility for the remaining fragments of Washington's public beaches. In the great majority of cases, state ownership goes only to the mean high-water line. The adjoining beaches and area above mean high water are privately owned, and the state has no right-of-way.

Of the 23 beaches in this area, 21 are thus inaccessible except by boat. Frontages range from 627 ft. to 5,872 ft. As described, these beaches seem to be of interest chiefly to clam diggers.

The Robert F. Kennedy Education and Recreation Area is 2 mi. W of Longbranch, N of Whiteman Cove, at Joemma Beach. It has 8 tent sites and a launching ramp on a partially wooded site. Road access.

Maple Hollow Beach, 1,420 ft., also with road access, is a day-use area. About 5 1/2 mi. N of Longbranch by Longbranch–Gig Harbor Road, turning E on Van Beek county road. Mooring buoys.

PUBLICATION: *Your Public Beaches, South Puget Sound, 1978.*

HEADQUARTERS: DNR, Division of Marine Land Management, Olympia, WA 98504; (206) 753-5324.

WALLACE FALLS STATE PARK
Washington Parks and Recreation Commission
518 acres.

From I-5 at Everett, E about 30 mi. on US 2 to Gold Bar, then N on marked
county road.

A park for hikers, featuring the 2 1/2-mi. trail to the falls. In the Cascade
foothills near the boundary of the Mt. Baker–Snoqualmie National Forest
(see entry). The trail enters a mixed second-growth forest, winds along the
Wallace River, then moves higher on a bench above the river. Viewpoints of
smaller falls at the 2-mi. rest stop. Viewpoints further up the switchbacking
trail look out at 250-ft. Wallace Falls and the Skykomish River valley.

Plants: Forest of Douglas-fir, western redcedar, western hemlock, red
alder, bigleaf maple, black cottonwood. In the understory: vine maple, red
elderberry, swordfern, salal, Oregon grape, salmonberry, red huckleberry,
wild blackberry, strawberry.

Return from the falls can take the Old Railroad Grade Trail—1 mi. longer,
gentle grade.

Camping: 6 sites. Tents only.

PUBLICATION: Leaflet with map.

HEADQUARTERS: P.O. Box 106, Gold Bar, WA 98251; (206) 793-0420.

ZONE 5

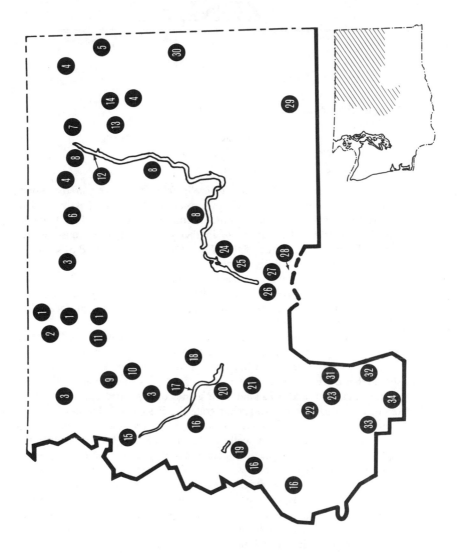

ZONE 5

Includes these counties:

Okanogan	Chelan	Spokane
Ferry	Douglas	Kittitas
Stevens	Grant (N tip only)	
Pend Oreille	Lincoln	

The W boundary of this zone generally follows the crest of the North Cascade Mountains. The W and N portions of the zone are mountainous. The Selkirk Mountains are in the NE corner, on the Canada and Idaho boundaries. Most of the public lands are in these mountainous regions: several National Forests and a part of the North Cascades National Park.

The SE part of the zone, roughly half of its total acreage, lies in the Columbia Basin. Most of this area is agricultural, chiefly great fields of wheat. Here there are many State Parks, Habitat Management Areas, and Department of Natural Resources sites, much smaller than the National Forests but offering much of interest.

For those seeking escape from crowds, this is a good place to look. Spokane is the only large city in the zone. Most of Washington's residents live on the other side of the Cascades. With so many delightful places closer to them, why should they drive the additional hours to—say—the Colville National Forest?

Hunters are attracted by a kind of big game hunting more typical of Canada than the United States. Backpackers rate the Pasayten Wilderness high on their lists, but the zone also offers much backcountry at lower elevations, to be enjoyed in April and May while waiting for the deep snow to melt in the high country. Canoeists have a choice of many lakes, several quiet streams, and a few whitewater courses.

Climate of the zone is much affected by the Cascade Range. At high elevations, annual precipitation is high and winter snow is deep. Lower elevations are in the rain shadow. Parts of the Columbia Basin are semiarid.

Exploring the zone in midsummer, we found the heaviest clusterings of people around the larger and most accessible lakes, including the Columbia River impoundments. We had no difficulty finding natural areas with few if any visitors. When we stopped for the night at Department of Game or DNR campsites, we were usually alone; in National Forests we had only to avoid the few large campgrounds.

ALTA LAKE STATE PARK
Washington Parks and Recreation Commission
177 acres.

From Pateros on US 97, NW a short distance on SR 153, then SW on marked road.

A small park at the edge of Okanogan National Forest, on a route to Twisp and SR 20 across the North Cascades. More than half a mile of shoreline on an attractive lake. In pine forest.

Camping: 200 sites.

NEARBY: A recent PRC bulletin mentions Ice Caves State Park-Natural Area as an Alta Lake satellite. We could obtain no further information. If visiting Alta Lake, inquire.

HEADQUARTERS: 40 Star Route, Pateros, WA 98846; (509) 923-2473.

BANKS LAKE HABITAT MANAGEMENT AREA
Washington Department of Game
44,662 acres, including 27,000 acres of water.

Between Grand Coulee Dam and Coulee City, on SR 155.

The lake is a narrow irrigation reservoir, 27 mi. long, between high cliffs of basalt. SR 155, on the E shore, is an exceptionally scenic drive. The Habitat Management Area land extends from the water's edge to the cliffs, width averaging about 1/4 mile. A similar strip on the W shore is also within the HMA; this seems accessible only by boat. Sections of the shore are tule marshes. Sagebrush and grasses are on the slightly higher ground near the cliffs. The valley is 2–4 mi. wide, between clifftops.

Public access is limited. Along the lower two-thirds of the lake we saw no parking areas, and few places on the road shoulders offered adequate parking. About 13 mi. from Coulee City is a public-access point with parking and an unpaved boat ramp. Further to the N is a larger access area with enough level parking for RV camping. Most campers use one of the campgrounds noted later in the entry.

Birds: No checklist. The Department of Game says the lake is "noted for its waterfowl," without giving details. We visited in summer, when populations were small. Geese are attracted by the lake and nearby wheatfields. Upland species include raven, chukar, pheasant, golden eagle.

Mammals: A few mule deer. Also coyote, marmot, porcupine, raccoon, bobcat.

Apr.–June is said to be the best time for a visit. To fully enjoy the scenery, drive N in the morning, when sunlight is on the W cliffs; return in the afternoon, with the sunlight on your side.

ACTIVITIES

Camping: Informal, in access area.

Fishing: Said to be good. Rainbow, kokanee, largemouth bass, perch, pike.

ADJACENT

Steamboat Rock State Park (see entry).

Municipal parks at Coulee City and Electric City have boat ramps, swimming; Coulee City includes a campground.

NEARBY: Sun Lakes State Park (see entry).

HEADQUARTERS: Regional Office, Department of Game, P.O. Box 1237, Ephrata, WA 98823; (509) 754-4624.

CHOPAKA MOUNTAIN
U.S. Bureau of Land Management
5,520 acres.

From US 97 N of Tonasket, W on local road to Loomis. N about 2 mi. on local road, left on Toats Coulee Rd. about 2 mi., right on gravel road about 6 mi. to Chopaka Lake.

Wilderness study area. Elevations 1,200 to 5,600 ft. Most of the unit lies on the steep, rugged E slopes of the Chopaka Mountain Range. The S third of the unit contains Bowers Lake, the N half of Chopaka Lake, and steep grassland. Unit adjoins the Okanogan Multiple Use Area (see entry). Pasayten Wilderness is 6 mi. W.

Slopes are partially forested, with pockets of subalpine fir, whitebark pine, lodgepole pine, Engelmann spruce, Douglas-fir, ponderosa pine, with associated shrubs and grasses. Mountain goats sometimes seen.

Steep terrain limits recreation opportunities, generally to the two lakes. A site at the N end of Chopaka Lake is often used for informal camping. A DNR campground is just S of the BLM land, on Chopaka Lake.

Fishing: Fly fishing, barbless hooks only.

HEADQUARTERS: BLM, Spokane District Office, Room 551, U.S. Court House, Spokane, WA 99201; (509) 456-2570.

COLOCKUM HABITAT MANAGEMENT AREA
Washington Department of Game
119,167 acres.

From Kittitas, on I-90 E of Ellensburg, the highway map shows a local road running N and NE over Colockum Pass to Malaga. Colockum Pass is within the Habitat Management Area. Unimproved roads lead from it. The Pass road may require 4-wheel drive.

Largest single holding by the Department of Game. E boundary is the Columbia River. Rolling, open sagebrush hills drop off to steep cliffs along the river. At higher elevations, timbered draws merge with stands of ponderosa pine. Cottonwood and brush along streams.

Roads within the Habitat Management Area may require 4-wheel drive, but hiking is a fine way to see the area, outside of hunting season. The diversity of habitats is reflected in the many species of wildlife.

A smaller, separate portion of the Habitat Management Area, also on the Columbia River, lies N and W of Vantage. The S boundary is the Old Vantage Highway, paralleling I-90 between Ellensburg and Vantage.

Birds: No checklist. Grainfields, flats, and protected bays along the Columbia River attract waterfowl. Other game species include chukar, valley quail, Merriam turkey, ruffed grouse, sage hen, pheasant, mourning dove. Upland species include western tanager, Bullock's oriole, lazuli bunting, western meadowlark, lark sparrow, red-winged blackbird, rock wren, Lewis's woodpecker, yellow-bellied sapsucker, western kingbird, violet-green and cliff swallows, magpie, mountain bluebird.

Mammals: Species reported include Rocky Mountain elk, mule deer, pronghorn, bighorn sheep, coyote, bobcat, yellow-pine chipmunk, marmot, ground squirrel.

INTERPRETATION: Information published by the Department of Game is not adequate for pathfinding in the Habitat Management Area, nor is signing. For anything more than an exploratory visit, prepare by a visit to HQ.

HEADQUARTERS: Regional Office, Department of Game, 2802 Fruitvale Blvd., Yakima, WA 98902; (509) 575-2740.

COLOCKUM HABITAT MANAGEMENT AREA: CHELAN BUTTE, ENTIAT, AND SWAKANE UNITS
Washington Department of Game
28,488 acres.

W of Columbia River and US 97, between Wenatchee and Chelan.

These three units border the Wenatchee National Forest. Department of Game publications describe them briefly but don't say how to find them. Even with maps we could not find the Entiat and Swakane Units, and the road that apparently leads into the Chelan Butte Unit was unsuitable for our vehicle. We suggest inquiring at HQ, on US 97 about 2 mi. beyond where it turns N along the Columbia River. Chances are you'll need a 4-wheel-drive vehicle.

The *Chelan Butte Unit,* 8,614 acres, is reached by a road leading off US 97 just E of Chelan marked "Chelan Butte Lookout." For a mile or two the road is paved, steep, narrow, passing private homes, offering fine views of Lake Chelan. Then it becomes a gravel road. This unit is characterized by flat ridges, deep canyons, steep grassy slopes. It has frontage on the Columbia River. High chukar and valley quail populations.

The *Entiat Unit,* 9,675 acres, is just W of US 97, N and W of Entiat. Ponderosa pine forests on steep hillsides; grasslands; basalt benches. Abundant quail and chukar.

The *Swakane Unit,* 11,199 acres, is also just W of US 97, along Swakane Creek, N of Wenatchee. Ponderosa forest on steep slopes, grassy areas, basalt cliffs near the Columbia River. Bear, mountain lion, blue grouse, mule deer, chukar, quail. California bighorn sheep were introduced in Swakane Canyon in 1969. The herd increased, but we have no current status report.

In hunting season, these three units are best left to hunters. At other times they offer opportunities for hiking, birding, and primitive camping in solitude, near a main highway.

HEADQUARTERS: Local HQ is on US 97 near the S boundary of the Swakane Unit. Regional Office: Department of Game, 2802 Fruitvale Blvd., Yakima, WA 98902; (509) 575-2740.

COLVILLE NATIONAL FOREST
U.S. Forest Service
1,095,368 acres.

NE WA. In several blocks, crossed by or reached from SR 20, SR 21, US 395, SR 25, SR 31.

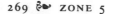

The mountains of NE Washington are neither as high nor as rugged as those to the W. The highest peak is Gypsy Peak, 7,309 ft., near the NE corner. About a dozen peaks are above 6,000 ft., many more between 4,000 and 6,000.

The Colville Forest is a collection of many parts, large and small. The largest solid block extends from the Canadian border S across SR 20 to the Colville Indian Reservation, a block about 20 mi. wide, between Republic and the Columbia River. To the W is a somewhat narrower block with the same N and S boundaries, broken into several parts by inholdings. Across the Columbia River, the E half is even more fragmented. The largest solid block, in the NE corner, adjoins the Kaniksu National Forest, which extends into Idaho. Just W of the Pend Oreille River the Forest land is irregular in shape, broken by many inholdings, with areas of checkerboard further S. Some of the inholdings are state land. The Forest has no frontage on the Columbia River, only a few miles on the Pend Oreille.

Because of the more gentle terrain and the drier climate, the hiking season is longer here than in the Cascades. The Forest has one ski area, and ski touring is growing in popularity, but the snow season generally ends by the beginning of March. The main hiking season begins at the end of May, but many trails are open earlier.

This is a region of mixed forest types and winding valleys, offering good hiking, fishing, hunting, and camping. The Forest has 59 lakes, from 1 acre to 1,291 acres in size. Despite these attractions, visitation is relatively light. The only large city nearby is Spokane. Residents of the more populous W counties are likely to stop at the Cascade Mountains rather than drive another hundred miles or so.

Plants: Largely Douglas-fir and western hemlock forest, local plant communities varying according to elevation, history of fire and logging, and other factors. In general, medium dense to open forest, fairly open groundcover of grasses and scattered shrubs. Associated tree species may include western larch, western white pine, lodgepole pine, ponderosa pine, grand fir. At higher elevations: subalpine fir with Engelmann spruce and whitebark pine.

Understory of the ponderosa forest may include snowberry, snowbush, ceanothus, lupine, hawkweed, western yarrow, bluebunch wheatgrass, hawkweed, kinnikinick, fawn lily, cinquefoil, pussytoes. Understory associated with Douglas-fir forests includes ninebark, redstem ceanothus, pinegrass, lupine, prince's pine.

Plants of high open ridges may include beargrass, huckleberry, white rhododendron, green fescue, woodrush.

Western hemlock forests support an understory that includes huckleberry, queenscup bead lily, wintergreen, rattlesnake plantain.

Birds: Checklist available. Lakes, streams, and marshes attract some waterfowl, gulls, shorebirds: western and pied-billed grebes, whistling swan, Canada goose, mallard, pintail; green-winged, blue-winged, and cinnamon teals; wigeon, shoveler, redhead, ring-necked duck, lesser scaup, common and Barrow's goldeneyes, common merganser, ruddy duck, great blue heron, Virginia rail, common snipe, lesser yellowlegs, ring-billed gull. Birds of prey include sharp-shinned, Cooper's, goshawk, red-tailed, and marsh hawks; osprey, kestrel; screech, great horned, pygmy, and barred owls. Also Franklin's blue and ruffed grouse; mourning dove, common nighthawk, Vaux's swift; black-chinned, rufous, and calliope hummingbirds; common flicker, pileated woodpecker, yellow-bellied sapsucker, hairy and downy woodpeckers, northern and black-backed three-toed woodpeckers. Also eastern and western kingbirds, six species of swallows, gray and Steller's jays, black-capped and mountain chickadees, brown creeper, dipper; varied, hermit, and Swainson's thrushes; mountain bluebird, water pipit, solitary and red-eyed vireos. Warblers include orange-crowned, Nashville, yellow, yellow-rumped, MacGillivray's, yellowthroat, Wilson's, American redstart. Also western tanager, evening grosbeak, lazuli bunting, Cassin's and house finches, pine siskin, red crossbill, rufous-sided towhee, savannah and vesper sparrows.

Mammals: Checklist available. Include masked, vagrant and dusky shrews; big brown, California brown, and little brown bats; pika, snowshoe hare, red squirrel, yellow-bellied marmot, Columbian ground squirrel, yellow pine and red-tailed chipmunks, northern flying squirrel, beaver, deer mouse, boreal red-backed vole, porcupine, coyote, black bear, raccoon, short-tailed and long-tailed weasels, mink, marten, striped skunk, mountain lion, bobcat, elk, white-tailed and mule deer. Caribou frequently cross the Canadian border into the Salmo Priest roadless area.

Reptiles and amphibians: Checklist available. Include northern long-toed and northwestern tiger salamanders, northwestern boreal toad, Pacific tree frog, western spotted frog, western painted turtle, northern alligator lizard, western skink, Rocky Mountain rubber boa, valley garter snake, western yellow-bellied racer, Great Basin gopher snake, northern Pacific rattlesnake.

FEATURES
Salmo Priest roadless area, 41,000 acres, including acres in the Kaniksu National Forest. In the far NE corner. Includes Gypsy Peak, highest in eastern WA, 7,309 ft. Lowest elevation: 2,720 ft. Mountainous, slopes averaging 50% or greater. Except for high peaks and ridges, heavily forested. Includes the Salmo Research Natural Area, 1,390 acres, established in part because of its exceptional wildlife. Caribou, grizzly bear, lynx, and gray wolf have been seen here, although not regularly. Several species are here at their range limits; these include boreal chickadee, pine grosbeak, crossbills.

Kettle Range Limited Access Area, 80,000 acres in the W half of the Forest, N and S of Sherman Peak. This area was proposed for wilderness status by conservationists; the Forest Service was opposed.* Four roadless areas: rolling peaks, ridges, meadows, grassy open forest. Most of the area is over a mile high.

Sullivan Lake, SE of Metaline Falls, largest lake in the Forest, about 3 1/2 mi. long. Elevation 2,583 ft. Road along the W shore, trail along the E. Campgrounds at N and S ends. From the N end of the lake, Forest Road 654 leads NE to Salmo Mountain, near the Canadian border, skirting the wilderness area. Good area for birding; pine forests, large stands of cottonwood and aspen, open meadows, streams. SW of the lake is the 630-acre Maitlen Creek Research Natural Area, where bighorn sheep are sometimes seen. Sheep are also seen on 6,222-ft. Hall Mountain, E of the lake, reached by trail from the S end.

Crawford Cave State Park, 41 acres, is within the Forest, N of Metaline Falls, within 1/4 mi. of the Canadian border, off SR 31. Feature is Gardner Cave, largest limestone cavern in WA. 1,500-ft. underground trail, half of it illuminated. Bring flashlight and sweater. Nearby: Boundary Dam on the Pend Oreille River; Crescent Lake. About 1 mi. S of the dam, on the W side, misnamed Peewee Falls drops into the reservoir.

East Portal Interpretive Area on SR 20, 6 mi. W of Kettle Falls. On Sherman Creek. Steep slopes forested with Douglas-fir, western redcedar, larch, ponderosa pine. *Bangs Mountain Auto Tour,* 5 mi., self-guiding, passes Donaldson Draw, old-growth ponderosa, other points of interest; viewpoint at end of route. *Log Flume Nature Trail,* 1/2 mi., explains old logging methods. Nearby is Sherman Creek Habitat Management Area (see entry).

Crystal Falls, just off SR 20 about 16 mi. E of Colville. Water drops 30 ft. over large boulders.

Little Pend Oreille Information Site is on SR 20 about 28 mi. E of Colville. Sign shows facilities in the Gillette Lake area.

Old Dominion Mountain Vista, about 20 mi. NE of Colville, is a picnic area and viewpoint. The road to the top is very rough, best suited to pickup trucks and 4-wheel-drive vehicles.

Lake Thomas is among the Little Pend Oreille Lakes. Campground.

ACTIVITIES

Camping: 25 campgrounds, 346 sites. Campgrounds are at elevations from 2,000 to 5,400 ft. Most are on lakes or streams. Camping season: May 31–Sept. 15. These dates vary according to weather conditions.

Hiking, backpacking: 305 mi. of trails, most maintained yearly. The Forest has available simple but valuable trail guides. Each has a trail map and text giving mileage, trail conditions, other features. Obtain from HQ.

---

*Active advocates: Kettle Range Conservation Group, P.O. Box 150, Republic, WA 99166.

Hunting: Selkirk Mountains are known for outstanding mule deer hunting. Also white-tailed deer, bear, quail, chukar, dove, pheasant, Canada goose, brant.

Fishing: Lakes, streams. Cutthroat, rainbow, brown, brook trout.

Swimming: Several lakes, including Sullivan, Leo, Trout.

Boating: Power boats on Sullivan.

Horse riding: Mostly in the Salmo Priest area, the Abercrombie-Hooknose area NW of Metaline Falls, and the Kettle Crest. No outfitters were operating when we inquired.

Skiing: One downhill ski area, 10 mi. E of Chewelah. Ski touring wherever conditions are suitable. For information on groomed trails: (509) 327-3791 (Spokane).

NEARBY: Little Pend Oreille Habitat Management Area (see entry). Coulee Dam National Recreation Area (see entry). Sherman Creek Habitat Management Area (see entry). Curlew Lake State Park, 130 acres, 10 mi. NE of Republic on SR 21; 4,600 ft. of freshwater shoreline; camping (70 sites), hiking, fishing, boating, ice skating.

ADJACENT: Kaniksu National Forest, mostly in Idaho, not described in this volume.

PUBLICATIONS

Forest map. $1.00.

Campground list.

Bangs Mountain Auto Tour guide.

Log Flume nature trail guide.

Checklists of birds, mammals, reptiles and amphibians.

Trail guides available at Ranger Districts.

HEADQUARTERS: Federal Building, Colville, WA 99114; (509) 684-5114.

SPOKANE INFORMATION OFFICE: Federal Courthouse, W. 920 Riverside, Spokane, WA 99202; (509) 456-2574.

RANGER DISTRICTS: Colville R.D., Colville, WA 99114; (509) 684-4557. Kettle Falls R.D., Kettle Falls, WA 99141; (509) 738-6111. Newport, R.D., Newport, WA 99156; (509) 447-3129. Republic R.D., Republic, WA 99166; (509) 775-3305. Sullivan Lake R.D., Metaline Falls, WA 99153; (509) 446-2681.

CONCONULLY STATE PARK

Washington Parks and Recreation Commission

81 acres.

From Omak on US 97, 22 mi. NW on marked road.

The Park is on a small irrigation reservoir. The site is developed, not a natural area, but it's a pleasant base for exploring areas nearby. A bit over a mile beyond the Park, the road enters the Colville National Forest (see entry), a part of the Forest with numerous trails and campgrounds. A road to the NE —which first looks likely to become impassable but then greatly improves— passes several small lakes and enters the Sinlahekin Habitat Management Area, a delightful, broad valley.

ACTIVITIES
Camping: 81 sites.
Swimming: Artificial pond.

NEARBY: Okanogan Multiple Use Area (see entry).

HEADQUARTERS: Box 95, Conconully, WA 98819; (509) 826-2108.

COULEE DAM NATIONAL RECREATION AREA
U.S. National Park Service
80,000 acres of water, 20,000 acres of land.

From Coulee Dam on SR 174 almost to the Canadian border. SR 25 parallels for some miles. SR 20 crosses at Kettle Falls.

Franklin D. Roosevelt Lake, formed by damming the Columbia River, is 130 mi. long, has 660 mi. of shoreline within the National Recreation Area. Although 20,000 acres of land seems large, extended along so much shoreline it makes a narrow band, too narrow to be shown on the site map.

The basin is generally drier to the S of Fort Spokane than to the N. About a fourth of the surrounding land is rolling dry land, grass and sagebrush; another fourth is rolling hills and bluffs with scattered ponderosa pine; about half, mostly in the N, is mixed conifer forest.

Winter is the drawdown period for the reservoir. The lake is raised to its maximum level in late June or early July and remains full during the warm season. Summer daytime temperatures range from 75°F to 100°, nights from 50° to 60°.

S of Kettle Falls, the developed areas are on the S and E sides of the lake, except for several areas administered by Indian tribes on the W side. In all there are 22 campgrounds, several large and developed, others primitive, a few accessible only by boat. All can be reached by boat, and most have launching facilities.

The lake is on a secondary flyway, attracting considerable numbers of migratory waterfowl. Bald eagle in fall and winter. Bird and mammal species are essentially the same as those of the nearby Colville National Forest (see entry).

Roads parallel the lakeshore from Fort Spokane N, with many scenic sections. SR 21 crosses the lake by a free ferry. On the N side of the lake, SR 21 follows the Sanpoil River through the Colville Indian Reservation. The lake is a water route into Canada; boaters should ask about border inspection procedures before crossing.

INTERPRETATION

Largest campgrounds are those near Coulee Dam, Fort Spokane, and Kettle Falls.

Campfire programs in summer. Occasional guided hikes. Schedules posted.

Nature trails at each of the three major campgrounds.

ACTIVITIES

Camping: 22 campgrounds, 542 sites. Some open all year.

Hiking: Few opportunities when Lake Roosevelt is full, in summer. In winter and spring, when the water level is down, one can hike for miles on sandy shores.

Hunting: Chiefly deer, game birds.

Fishing: Trout, walleye, sunfish, bass.

Swimming: Gravel and sand beaches. Most are unsupervised.

Boating: Many launching points. Several marinas with services. No horse-power limit, but HQ says a noise limit will soon be enforced.

Campgrounds often at capacity on holidays and summer weekends.

PUBLICATIONS

Leaflet with map.

Walleye Fishing on Lake Roosevelt. 26¢.

Fishing, Coulee Dam National Recreation Area. (Out of print in 1981.)

Checklists: trees, birds, mammals, reptiles, and amphibians.

HEADQUARTERS: P.O. Box 37, Coulee Dam, WA 99116; (509) 633-1360.

RANGER DISTRICTS: Coulee Dam, P.O. Box 37, Coulee Dam, WA 99116; (509) 633-1360. Fort Spokane, Star Route, Box 30, Davenport, WA 99122; (509) 725-2715. Kettle Falls, Route 1, Box 537, Kettle Falls, WA 99141; (509) 738-6266.

CURLEW LAKE STATE PARK
Washington Parks and Recreation Commission
128 acres.

From Republic, 10 mi. N on SR 21.

A pleasant out-of-the-way campground in a valley between two sections of the Colville National Forest. The lake is narrow, about 5 mi. long. The first state fly-in park; airplane tiedowns.

Camping: 94 sites, including walk-in sites.

HEADQUARTERS: Rt. 1, Box 219, Republic, WA 99166; (509) 775-3592.

GINKGO PETRIFIED FOREST STATE PARK; includes WANAPUM STATE PARK
Washington Parks and Recreation Commission
7,684 acres.

E of Ellensburg, where I-90 crosses the Columbia River. On W side of bridge, look for marked right turn.

A visit should begin at the Interpretive Center, about 1 mi. N of the bridge, high above the impounded river with a splendid view. Open 9 A.M.–6 P.M. Some millions of years ago, climate, terrain, and soil were quite different, and a great variety of trees grew here: redwood, magnolia, cypress, mahogany, hickory, elm, Douglas-fir, sassafras, banded gordonia, maple, myrtle, coffee tree, box elder, Spanish cedar, and many more. Mature trees fell, were carried by streams into a swamp, eventually were engulfed by lava. Six other sites in the United States are noted for petrified wood, but none has so many tree species.

Petrified ginkgo is found nowhere else. The ginkgo is known today only as a tree grown in cultivation; no wild specimens remain.

A map inside the center shows the site. 2 1/2 mi. up the road are trails: a 3/4-mi. interpretive trail with a number of petrified logs shown as found, and a 3-mi. hiking trail. Other hiking routes are also possible, between the highway and the river. Temporary permits are needed for backcountry travel. Hiking is most pleasant in the early morning, because this is desert country.

Petrified wood specimens cannot be collected within the Park. No such prohibition applies within the Quilomene Habitat Management Area 9 mi. to the N, at milepost 19. According to the map, 2 mi. of passable gravel road lead to a public dig; beyond is another dig on a road requiring 4-wheel drive. Needless to say, these digs have been well picked over. The quantity you may take is limited.

The Columbia River is impounded by Wanapum Dam, below the I-90 bridge. The Park has 5 mi. of shoreline. The Wanapum area, sometimes listed separately as Wanapum State Park, has campground, beach, and boating facilities.

Birds reported in the area include bald eagle, white-throated swift, prairie falcon, raven, sage thrasher, sage sparrow, meadowlark. Deer, elk, and coyote are common. Reptiles are common, including the Pacific rattlesnake.

ACTIVITIES

Camping: 50 sites. All year.

Fishing: Trout, steelhead, salmon.

Swimming: 3,500 ft. of beach, unsupervised.

Boating: Launching ramps. 13 mi. between dams. High winds are common.

NEARBY: Quilomene Habitat Management Area (see entry).

PUBLICATION: Leaflet.

HEADQUARTERS: Vantage, WA 98950; (509) 856-2700.

IDAHO PANHANDLE NATIONAL FOREST, also known as KANIKSU NATIONAL FOREST

U.S. Forest Service

283,353 acres in WA.

Along the Idaho border, from Canada to just N of Newport. No paved road access in Washington. Access by Forest roads from Colville National Forest or from a paved secondary road W of Priest Lake, Idaho.

Most of this National Forest is in Idaho, beyond the geographic limits of this volume. The acreage in Washington adjoins the Colville National Forest (see entry) and, from the visitor's viewpoint, can be considered an extension of the Colville. Highest peaks in this WA section, over 6,000 ft., are on the ridge that is the boundary between the two Forests. Several Forest roads and trails lead in from the Colville. This portion of the Kaniksu has only one small campground.

HEADQUARTERS: 1201 Ironwood Dr., Coeur d'Alene, ID 83814; (208) 667-2561.

LAKE CHELAN NATIONAL RECREATION AREA

See North Cascades National Park, zone 3.

LAKE CHELAN STATE PARK
Washington Parks and Recreation Commission
127 acres.

9 mi. W of Chelan, off US 97, on the lakeshore.

Most of the shoreline at the lower end of this long, narrow lake is privately owned, much of it developed. At the Park, the boundary of Wenatchee National Forest is about 2 mi. W of the lake. Beyond the Park, the strip of privately owned land is narrower; it ends near Twenty-Five-Mile Creek State Park (see entry), as does the road.

The upper end of the lake, reached only by boat, float plane, or on foot, is within the Lake Chelan National Recreation Area of the North Cascades National Park (see entry, zone 3).

The Park has 6,454 ft. of waterfront. A forested, hillside site. Nearby an unpaved road leads into the Forest a short distance.

ACTIVITIES
Camping: 144 sites.
Swimming: Lake. Supervised in season.
Boating: Ramp, dock.

HEADQUARTERS: Rt. 1, Box 90, Chelan, WA 98816; (509) 687-3710.

LAKE WENATCHEE STATE PARK
Washington Parks and Recreation Commission
474 acres.

From US 2 at Coles Corner, 3 mi. N on SR 207.

The Park is deep within the Wenatchee National Forest, though in an area with many inholdings, including about half of the lakeshore. Three National Forest campgrounds are also on the lake. Beyond the lake the road divides, branches going W and N, both leading to Forest campgrounds and trails into the Glacier Peak Wilderness (see entry, Wenatchee National Forest).

The Park has 12,623 ft. of frontage on Lake Wenatchee, 7,000 ft. on both sides of the Wenatchee River. The lake is about 6 mi. long, a bit less than 1 mi. wide, surrounded by ponderosa pine forest. Elevation is about 1,870 ft. The Park is popular, often near capacity in season. Most visitor activity is water-based.

INTERPRETATION: *Evening programs, nature hikes,* summer weekends.

ACTIVITIES

Camping: 197 sites. Some kept open in winter.

Hiking: Trails into the National Forest. 7-mi. hike to Alpine Lookout, 6,237 ft.

Swimming: Supervised beach.

Boating, canoeing: Ramps. Local canoe outfitters offer day and overnight trips, May–Oct.

Ski touring: Chiefly on trails and unplowed Forest roads.

Horse riding: Rentals.

Snowmobiling: Dec.–Mar. State Parks and Forest Service cooperate in trail grooming.

PUBLICATION: Leaflet.

HEADQUARTERS: Star Route, Leavenworth, WA 98826; (509) 763-3101.

LENORE LAKE HABITAT MANAGEMENT AREA
Washington Department of Game

See Sun Lakes State Park.

LITTLE PEND OREILLE HABITAT MANAGEMENT AREA
Washington Department of Game
40,861 acres.

From Colville, 7 mi. E on SR 20. S on Rocky Lake Rd. and look for marked left turn. Then follow signs. Entrance is 13 mi. from Colville. HQ is on this road.

One of the largest and most popular State wildlife habitat areas. The area was homesteaded, logged, and grazed. Most of it was acquired by the Resettlement Administration in the 1930s. It became a federal wildlife refuge. When the Fish and Wildlife Service suffered severe budget cuts, the site was placed under state management. The site now has a managed forest and supports a vigorous population of wildlife.

Near the entrance one enjoys a splendid view across a valley to the N-facing slopes. Elevations range from 1,800 ft. in the SW to 5,610 ft. on the E drainage divide. Terrain is gently rolling in the SW, steep in the E. The Little Pend

Oreille River forms part of the N boundary. The Kaniksu National Forest adjoins on the E, the Colville National Forest on the S.

Temperatures are moderate in summer, usually cold Dec.–Feb. Annual precipitation is 18–24 in. Snowfall is fairly heavy, and accumulations of several feet persist through late spring on N-facing slopes. However, the area is popular with backpackers in spring, because it is snow-free weeks earlier than the higher country in the National Forests.

Bear Creek, tributary of the Little Pend Oreille, and Bear Canyon Creek are the principal streams. Bayley Lake (70 acres) and McDowell Lake (about 60 acres) are within the site, Long Lake, on the E boundary, partially so.

More than 100 mi. of roads cross the area. The principal roads are all-weather and well maintained. A new road-numbering system helps pathfinding, once you know how it works, but visitors should stop at headquarters and study the wall map there.

Hunters and fishermen make up more than half of the visitors, but nonconsumptive use is increasing. Don't be surprised if you encounter bands of military men; the Air Force uses the site for survival training.

Plants: Three principal forest types: pine, pine-fir, and mixed woodlands. Pine woodland, at lower elevations, is important winter range for white-tailed deer. Here ponderosa pine predominates with understory of bluebunch wheatgrass, Idaho fescue, bearberry, bitterbrush. Somewhat higher are stands of ponderosa and Douglas-fir, denser on N-facing slopes, understory species including red-stemmed ceanothus, serviceberry, huckleberry, snowberry, bearberry, spirea. Other tree species occurring include tamarack, lodgepole, western hemlock, western white pine, western redcedar, Engelmann spruce, alpine fir, cottonwood, quaking aspen, western yew. Many even-aged stands reflect past history of logging and fires. Forest openings occur throughout the site, but they are larger and more numerous on the W side and along major drainages.

Birds: No checklist for distribution. Site is a transition zone between eastern and western species. Some waterfowl. Nesting mallard, green-winged teal, ring-necked duck, hooded merganser. Whistling swan, great blue heron, grebes, and shorebirds make some use of water areas. Golden and bald eagles, osprey; great horned, barred, and flammulated owls; peregrine falcon. Ruffed, spruce, and blue grouse; a few pheasant. American redstart, common yellowthroat, catbird, Vaux's swift, common snipe, northern waterthrush. Pileated and northern three-toed woodpeckers.

Mammals: Refuge was established for a western race of white-tailed deer; latest population estimate, 2,000. Mule deer present in limited numbers. Elk have been seen but are not considered resident. Black bear common. Also resident: mountain lion, lynx, bobcat, coyote, beaver, mink, muskrat, badger, weasel, skunk, raccoon, red squirrel, Columbian ground squirrel, northern flying squirrel.

ACTIVITIES

Camping: Several informal campgrounds in attractive places. Latrines. Not listed in popular campground directories. Information at HQ. Some are crowded on fine weekends, but you can find a spot.

Hiking, backpacking: No trail map available. A 10-mi. trail is under development. Many good places to hike, and in much of the site bushwhacking is pleasant. Some old logging roads are now closed to vehicles.

Hunting: Deer, bear, upland birds.

PUBLICATION: Site map.

HEADQUARTERS: Rt. 1, Box 171, Colville, WA 99114; (509) 684-5343.

L. T. MURRAY HABITAT MANAGEMENT AREA
Washington Department of Game
103,000 acres.

On foot, from Yakima Canyon Scenic Highway (see entry), into S unit. By road, W from Ellensburg on I-90 to exit 106. S over bridge; left on Brown Rd. to end; right on Damman Rd., which becomes Umtanum Rd. 4 mi. from end of Brown Rd. go S on Durr; Habitat Management Area boundary is then about 2 mi. ahead. N unit is W of I-90, NW of Ellensburg. Several roads lead in: Robinson Canyon, Watt Canyon, Taneum Creek. Local advice on road conditions is desirable.

Typical E slope timberland, grassy rangeland. Pine forests, bald hilltops, canyons cut through lava, attractive streams. Roads range from fairly good to difficult, not for cars or RV's; muddy spring conditions may last until May. Considerable traffic in hunting season, otherwise very little. Spring and early fall are the best times to visit.

The backpacker can park at the Umtanum Creek Recreation Site on SR 821, in the Yakima River Canyon S of Ellensburg, walk over a footbridge, and be in a roadless part of the Habitat Management Area, with a choice of trails.

Elevations range from about 1,500 ft. to 2,500 ft., with a high point of about 4,900 ft. in the S unit. Climate is semiarid. Vegetation is fairly sparse: some open stands of ponderosa on N-facing slopes, scattered trees on other hillsides. Grassy slopes, some with sagebrush. Willow, cottonwood, and aspen along streams.

Flora and fauna lists can be seen at the Regional Office. Species are much the same as in the E portion of the Tieton and Naches Ranger Districts, Wenatchee National Forest. Good chukar population. Birds reported include

Swainson's hawk, prairie falcon, sage grouse, white-headed woodpecker, pine grosbeak, flammulated and spotted owls, sage and Brewer's sparrows, pine siskin, Williamson's sapsucker. Game mammals include elk, bighorn sheep.

Game Department maps show no local headquarters, no designated campgrounds, no facilities other than roads. Camp where you wish.

For such a large area, the information we could gather was scanty. Our motor home could not negotiate several of the roads, including a narrow track that dropped steeply into a canyon with several tight switchbacks. Hiking, we found the area delightful even in midsummer. It offers solitude; we met only one party, a botanist couple studying the area.

NEARBY: Oak Creek Habitat Management Area (see entry, zone 6).

PUBLICATIONS: North and South Unit maps.

HEADQUARTERS: Department of Game, Regional Office, 2802 Fruitvale Blvd., Yakima, WA 98902; (509) 575-2740.

METHOW HABITAT MANAGEMENT AREA
Washington Department of Game
23,364 acres.

About 2 to 4 mi. E of SR 20 between Winthrop and Twisp. Take local road on E side of Methow River; turn E on road to Davis Lake; follow signs to HQ.

A 17-mi. strip, 1–3 mi. wide. Area lies between lowland river valley and high mountains. Rolling to rugged terrain. Open sage and bitterbrush at lower elevations, semiopen ponderosa pine forest above. Several small lakes.

Key winter range for mule deer. Other mammal species include mountain lion, black bear, red squirrel, bobcat, snowshoe hare, porcupine. Bird checklist available; species noted include ruffed, blue, and spruce grouse; valley quail, mallard, Clark's nutcracker, Lewis's woodpecker.

Late Mar. into Apr. is best time to see deer. May and June offer good birding and wildflower displays.

Camping: Informal.

ADJACENT: Pearrygin Lake State Park (see entry), Okanogan National Forest (see entry).

HEADQUARTERS: Department of Game, Regional Office, P.O. Box 1237, Ephrata, WA 98823; (509) 754-4624.

MOUNT SPOKANE STATE PARK
Washington Parks and Recreation Commission
16,040 acres.

From Spokane, N 6 mi. on US 2, then NE 15 mi. on SR 206.

Mt. Spokane, 5,881 ft., dominates the landscape. A paved road goes 7 1/2 mi. to the top with fine views along the way. From the top one can see the Selkirks and the Rockies, look into three states and Canada. The park includes most of the mountain and adjoining ridges. Most of the slopes are forested.

This was the first Washington State Park E of the Cascades, and it is one of the largest in the state. We were surprised to find it lightly used. The small campground, we were told, is almost never full. In two hours at the top, we saw one other party.

On the way up, the road passes a ski area: tows, runs, ski lodge. Nearby, on the mountain but just outside the park, are 7 condominium buildings with restaurant, pool, tennis court, and other facilities. Judging from the size of the parking area, the ski slopes are popular.

At the time of our visit, we saw no sign marking an office or information point; we had no map or leaflet; the bulletin board was bare. Looking for hiking opportunities, we saw what might be trailheads, unmarked. We're told a new park office has been built and signed at the entrance, though it cannot be manned continuously. Trailheads are marked No Motor Vehicles. A trail development system has been approved that, when completed, will include a hike-in primitive campground. Many local hikers, we learned, know the area and enjoy the mountain trails.

Plants: Almost entirely forested except for tundralike vegetation near the crest and a few high mountain meadows with shrubs and beargrass. Marked contrast between vegetation of N-facing and S-facing slopes. Trees are mostly conifers: alpine fir, grand fir, lodgepole pine, western larch, Douglas-fir, western hemlock, western redcedar, western white pine. Also cottonwood, quaking aspen, alder, Rocky Mountain maple. Understory includes willow, huckleberry, ocean spray, serviceberry. Many ferns in lower, moister areas. Many wildflowers, including paintbrush, purple aster, lupine, golden aster.

Birds: No checklist. Species noted by ranger include black-capped chickadee, red-breasted nuthatch, dipper, raven, Steller's jay, hairy woodpecker, Oregon junco, fox sparrow, varied thrush, red-tailed hawk, cedar waxwing, pine grosbeak.

Mammals: Noted by ranger: coyote, bobcat, porcupine, ground squirrel, black bear, badger, skunk, mule and white-tailed deer. Ranger says moose have been sighted.

ACTIVITIES
Camping: 12 sites. June 1–Oct. 15.
Hiking: 20 mi. of trails. Inadequately shown on map in Park leaflet. Several trails are described in *Hiking the Inland Empire* (see references in preface).
Horse riding: All trails open to horses. Tie-up racks.
Skiing: 5 chairlifts, 2 rope tows, 31 runs, 2 day lodges. Usual season Dec.– Apr.
Ski touring: On trails.
Snowmobiling: Groomed trails.

PUBLICATIONS
Park leaflet.
Ski information.

HEADQUARTERS: Route 1, Box 336, Mead, WA 99021; (509) 456-4169.

OKANOGAN MULTIPLE USE AREA; SINLAHEKIN HABITAT MANAGEMENT AREA
Washington Department of Natural Resources/Washington Department of Game
177,000 acres/14,035 acres.

W of US 97, N of Okanogan. For the Habitat Management Area, W from US 97 at Tonasket to Loomis, then S. The larger portion of the Multiple Use Area adjoins the HMA on the W and extends N to the Canadian border. A smaller portion lies S of Conconully, adjoining the Okanogan National Forest; it is crossed by SR 20.

Much of the land in this region is publicly owned and boundaries are not always conspicuous. Within a 5-mi. drive one can be within a State Park, a National Forest, the Multiple Use Area, and the Habitat Management Area.

We turned N at Conconully, along Lake Conconully (not to be confused with the reservoir). The lake is long, narrow, with steep slopes on either side, forested with talus and rock outcrops. The narrow road, surfaced but rough, is on a ledge. Part way along the lake the road deteriorates, passing through a narrow canyon with impressive talus slopes. We almost turned back, but 2 mi. later we joined a far better road, unpaved but broad and well kept.

We were now within the Habitat Management Area, a strip of land a mile or more wide on the floor of a broad, scenic valley. The area was acquired as a winter range for mule deer. Along the valley are several small lakes. The Department of Game maintains a number of primitive campgrounds, most of them beside lakes: level sites, modern latrines, no water. They are not listed in popular directories. We judged them unusually attractive, but in midsummer no one else was camping. A few people were fishing, swimming, and boating. Traffic along the valley road seemed to be about one car per hour. We had a pleasant feeling of discovery.

Terrain in the much larger Multiple Use Area is more dramatic: strangely shaped hills; massive stone mountains deeply scored by canyons, coulees, and ravines; great slides of black talus; and such oddities as Whitestone Mountain, really white, between Tonasket and Loomis. Highest point, in the N, is over 7,800 ft., the lowest almost 6,000 ft. less.

Plants: A typical valley has three vegetation zones. A S-facing slope may have few if any trees on its upper portion. Nearer the valley floor are larch, Douglas-fir, and ponderosa pine in open stands. The N-facing slope has a dense stand of Douglas-fir, larch, and spruce. In many valleys, beaver dams have formed ponds and marshes with typical wetland vegetation. In the most northern, and highest, part of the area, stunted whitebark pine and juniper occur on the ridges, thick stands of lodgepole pine and true fir just below. Wildflowers are those typical of the North Cascades.

Birds: No checklist is available. Species are much the same as those occurring in the adjacent Pasayten Wilderness (see entry, Okanogan National Forest).

Mammals: Include mule deer, black bear, mountain lion, coyote, porcupine, raccoon, weasel, and other species found in the adjoining National Forest. Moose have been seen infrequently in the North Fork of Toats Coulee drainage, near the Canadian border. Mountain goats on Chopaka. Bighorn sheep were reintroduced in the Habitat Management Area and on Aeneas Mountain.

Roads into and through the Multiple Use Area are best shown on the site leaflet and the Okanogan National Forest map, not highway maps. Some are paved, some unpaved but maintained. Not all—we saw one warning sign: "Travel at your own risk. 10 mph," to which someone had added: "You're crazy if you do!" No less disquieting was the warning that logging is going on and log trucks have the right-of-way—on roads barely wide enough for one vehicle. Such roads are best avoided. Most roads are passable and nonthreatening.

ACTIVITIES

Camping: In the Multiple Use Area, 7 campgrounds, 72 sites. We have no count for the Habitat Management Area. However, except in hunting season and early in the fishing season finding a campsite should be no problem. Facilities are primitive.

Hiking: This is something of a problem in the Multiple Use Area. According to the DNR, there was an extensive trail system before present roads were built. Trails are no longer mapped or maintained. Trails exist, used by hunters, fishermen, and cattlemen, but you have to find them. We hiked on some old logging roads not in current use.

Hunting: Mule deer hunting is big here, attracting great numbers of hunters.

Fishing: Reduced limit fly fishing for trout in Aeneas and Chopaka lakes. Trout in Leader Lake, other lakes.

Swimming: Fish Lake, Blue Lake, perhaps elsewhere. No beaches. At your own risk.

Boating: Chopaka, Leader, and Conconully lakes. Lakes are small, best suited to canoes and car-toppers.

ORV's are permitted on all roads, unless posted. Snowmobiles may not travel on county roads. Cross-country travel is prohibited.

PUBLICATION: Multiple Use Area leaflet.

HEADQUARTERS: Department of Natural Resources, Northeast Area Office, P.O. Box 190, Colville, WA 99114; (509) 684-5201. Department of Game, Regional Office, P.O. Box 1237, Ephrata, WA 98823; (509) 754-4624.

OKANOGAN NATIONAL FOREST
U.S. Forest Service
1,706,160 acres.

N and S of SR 20, adjoining North Cascades National Park on the W and SW. Several disconnected blocks are E of US 97, adjoining Colville National Forest.

The Okanogan bridges the gap between the high, rugged North Cascades and the gentler mountains of E Washington. Until the late 1960s no road crossed these mountains, because of the difficult terrain. SR 20, the North Cascades Highway, finally made it, but snow closes the route for about half of the year. Half a million acres are in the Pasayten Wilderness, a roadless area on the Canadian border. The Forest has 1,200 mi. of roads, including primitive tracks requiring 4-wheel drive. Even so, while the Pasayten is the largest roadless area, there are several others large enough for backcountry adventuring.

The highest peaks, over 8,000 ft., are in the W and N, but peaks over 1 mi. high can be found in almost every part of the Forest, including the detached blocks in the E. The rain shadow effect is conspicuous on the E slope of the Cascades. Precipitation there decreases sharply with decreasing elevation. Annual precipitation near a ridgetop may be more than 90 in., but little more than 20 in. in the valley below. Much of this precipitation falls as snow in winter, about 400 in. at the summits, about 75 in. at the 2,000-ft. elevation.

The North Cascades Highway, SR 20, eastbound, enters the Forest about a mile beyond the end of Ross Lake. In 2 mi. it turns SE, and it is here at its closest point to the Wilderness. For the next 17 mi. it parallels the North Cascades National Park boundary, then crosses the Pacific Crest Trail and turns NE, soon crossing over Washington Pass. At the Early Winters Information Station, it meets the Methow River and turns SE in a long corridor of private land that penetrates the Forest to the NW. The all-weather road along this corridor is one of the principal approach routes to the Wilderness. On and near it are a number of Forest campgrounds.

Other all-weather roads, routes to campgrounds, the Wilderness, and other roadless areas, lead N from Winthrop on SR 20 and NW from Omak. These and other roads are shown on the Forest map, not on highway maps. Studying the Forest map for a few minutes will enable you to identify the areas that are popular and thus likely to be crowded at times, and areas offering more solitude. The disconnected pieces of the Forest to the E should not be ignored. One of them contains over 55,000 acres and a number of attractive lakes.

These and several other lakes at lower elevations can be reached by auto, and one can camp near the shores. Many high mountain lakes can be reached only by trail. The Forest map shows hundreds of small streams that gather in rivers flowing to the Columbia.

A few of the campgrounds are accessible as early as April 15. Most are open by June 1, but a few at higher elevations not until July 1. Most are snowed in by Nov. 15. One can camp in the Forest at any season.

Plants: 85% of the area is forested. The remainder consists chiefly of meadows and rocky slopes above timberline. Principal tree species are Douglas-fir, ponderosa pine, Engelmann spruce, subalpine fir. Much of the forest is open, parklike, brush-free, with grassy floor. Old growth remains at all elevations, occurs extensively in the wilderness. Many wildflowers, over 500 species recorded, various seasons and habitats, including Indian paintbrush, lavender penstemon, wood trillium, false Solomon's seal, wild lily-of-the-valley, vanillaleaf, littleflower collinsia, narrow-leaved montia, vernal draba, autumn willowweed, shining chickweed, western yarrow, yellow salsify, arrowleaf balsamroot, sagebrush buttercup, low pussytoes, slender fringecup. Blooming season at high altitudes peaks in mid-July.

Birds: Checklist available. Common species (resident or seasonal) include western, eared, and pied-billed grebes; great blue heron, Canada goose, mallard, pintail, American wigeon, shoveler; blue winged, green-winged, and cinnamon teals; redhead, bufflehead; Cooper's, sharp-shinned, marsh, rough-legged, red-tailed, and Swainson's hawks; golden eagle, kestrel; blue, spruce, and ruffed grouse; white-tailed ptarmigan, California quail; screech, great horned, long-eared, saw-whet, and pygmy owls; calliope and rufous hummingbirds; common flicker, hairy and downy woodpeckers, eastern and western kingbirds; willow, Hammond's, dusky, and olive-sided flycatchers; barn, cliff, violet-green, tree, bank, and rough-winged swallows. Also black-capped, mountain, and chestnut-backed chickadees; dipper; white-breasted, red-breasted, and pygmy nuthatches; house, winter, rock, and long-billed marsh wrens; Bohemian and cedar waxwings. Warblers include orange-crowned, yellow, Audubon's, Townsend's, black-throated gray, MacGillivray's.

Mammals: Checklist available. Common species include vagrant, dusky, and northern water shrews; little brown and big brown bats, Yuma and California myotis, pika, snowshoe hare, yellow-bellied and hoary marmots, Columbian ground squirrel, golden-mantled squirrel, yellow pine chipmunk, red squirrel, northern flying squirrel, beaver, deer mouse, heather vole, porcupine, black bear, raccoon, short-tailed and long-tailed weasels, mink, badger, striped skunk, coyote, mountain lion, bobcat, mule and white-tailed deer. Elk are uncommon, moose occasional.

FEATURES

Pasayten Wilderness, 505,524 acres, partly in Mount Baker–Snoqualmie National Forest but administered by Okanogan. About 40 mi. W–E, 20 mi. N–S. Roadless, old-growth forest unbroken except by peaks and high meadows. Wide range of topography, elevations, forest types, 94 mountain lakes, most stocked. Many streams; largest is the Pasayten River flowing to Canada and E to the Okanogan River.

Much of the area is rugged, difficult going for the hiker. Part of it has been kept free of trails, and this is for the experienced outdoorsman. However, several auto routes lead close to the Wilderness boundaries, and several trails, following watercourses, have easy grades and are well maintained. The popularity of the Pasayten and the fragility of the alpine and subalpine environments have made some restrictions essential. Permits to enter are required and group size is limited. Some areas are closed to horses. Camping at several popular sites is rationed; reservations should be made well in advance, especially for Sept., when a special deer hunt occurs. The Pasayten Wilderness map shows the locations of trailheads and the routes of numbered trails. We suggest you visit a Ranger District to get advice on routes.

Tiffany roadless area, 25,200 acres. By Forest Roads 364 and 370 from Conconully. Two Forest campgrounds are on the road. Tiffany Lake, one of three lakes in the area, is reached by a short trail. Seven peaks in the area exceed 7,000 ft. All the high peaks have alpine characteristics, supporting only grass and heather. At slightly lower elevations, whitebark pine, lodgepole pine; Engelmann spruce in moister areas. N-facing slopes have dense timber stands; S-facing slopes are more open. Tiffany Lake, elevation 6,500 ft., has excellent fishing.

Long Draw roadless area, 8,600 acres. A mile-wide strip extending S from the Canadian border between the Pasayten Wilderness and the Forest boundary. Elevations 4,400 ft. to 7,408 ft. Separated from Long Swamp roadless area (see next entry) by Iron Gate Road. S exposures have grass, shrubs; N slopes have shrubs and timber. Marshy bottoms in NE portion have abundant wildlife, including some waterfowl.

Long Swamp roadless area, 10,200 acres. N of Toats Coulee Rd. Eastern portion (about 3/4 of the area) has broad, high ridges. W portion plunges down to steep-walled Chewack River Canyon. Elevations from 3,600 ft. on the Chewack to 7,800 ft. atop Windy Peak. Pasayten Wilderness borders the area on the N and W. Most of the area is in the subalpine zone. Extensive lodgepole forests. Douglas-fir, larch, ponderosa pine, and aspen are more common at lower elevations. Between the Middle Fork of Toats Coulee Creek and Hodges Horse Pasture, hardwoods with many small openings, fine wildlife habitat. Excellent summer mule deer range.

Liberty Bell roadless area, 112,430 acres. On the S boundary of the Pasayten Wilderness, just W of Harts Pass. Steep, rugged mountains, sharp or knife-edged ridges. Glaciated valleys. Elevations from 1,800 ft. on Ruby Creek to 8,806 ft. on Golden Horn's Peak. Pacific Crest Trail passes through the area. Most of the area is in the alpine or subalpine zone. Stunted, widely-scattered trees, grass, huckleberry, heather. Some old-growth Douglas-fir stands on Ruby Creek. Diverse wildlife habitats. Fishing in Ruby, Granite, and Canyon creeks.

Sawtooth roadless area, 230,900 acres. Along the S boundary of the Forest, from North Cascades Highway near Ruby Creek to the Gold Creek Road. Includes large portions of the Wolf Creek and Cedar Creek drainages. Elevations from 2,400 ft. to the nearly 9,000-ft. summit of Gardner Mountain. Rugged terrain. Deep valleys. The S ridge has more lakes, meadows, gentler slopes. Trails travel through most of the S drainages; few cross the rugged N part. Open meadows and rocky slopes at high elevations. Mountain Forest Zone is lower, but with great differences in vegetation. Avalanche paths into valleys become a tangle of alder, shrubs, broken trees. Large areas of lodgepole pine in the S cover both Mountain Forest and Subalpine Zones. A number of cirque lakes in the high country, many with trout.

Goat Wall, rising 2,000 ft. above the Methow Valley, is often likened to the rock walls of Yosemite Valley.

Harts Pass, about 14 mi. beyond Goat Wall, is on an all-weather road, steep and narrow, closed to all trailers. Three campgrounds are clustered in this area. The Pacific Crest Trail passes through. A spur road leads to Slate Peak, 7,500 ft., offering a breathtaking view of the North Cascades, a seemingly unlimited array of snowy peaks. This road is not for large RV's, requires extreme caution.

Buttermilk Butte, 5,474 ft., SW of Twisp, reached by Forest road, offers a limited view of the Methow Valley and the Sawtooth Ridge. Blackpine Lake and campground are nearby.

Washington Pass Overlook, on the North Cascades Highway, SR 20, is another scenic point, looking out to Liberty Bell Mountain and Early Winters Spires. Interpretive exhibit. 400-ft. wheelchair trail.

Rainy Pass, on SR 20. Trail for 0.8-mi. paved wheelchair trail to Rainy Lake. Accessible by July 15 until early Nov.

Lost River Canyon, near the S boundary of the Pasayten Wilderness, is an outstanding geological area. Called a "challenging hike," it is approached from a trailhead in the Methow Valley near the Lost River Airstrip, but there is no trail in most of the gorge itself. Not suitable for rafting or kayaking. Look out for rattlesnakes.

Sweetgrass Butte, 6,109 ft., is the high spot of a 27-mi. scenic loop route that begins at Winthrop. Stop at the Winthrop Ranger District for a leaflet describing the route and check the route numbers: those on the leaflet don't entirely agree with those on the Forest map. Splendid views of peaks to the N in the Pasayten Wilderness, W to Sawtooth River.

Cedar Falls, one of the Forest's more spectacular falls. From the North Cascades Highway about 3 mi. W of Early Winters Campground, turn S on Sandy Butte/Cedar Creek Rd. Look for trailhead in 1/2 mi. Easy 45-minute hike to the falls. The hiking trail continues beyond.

Bonaparte Lake, Lost Lake, Beaver Lake are in one of the detached blocks of Forest land E of US 97. From Tonasket, 20 mi. E on SR 20, then N on Forest Road 396. Several other small lakes are in this block. It's a resort area with some roadside commercial development and some lakefront residences. However, a substantial part of the block is roadless, with good cross-country hiking opportunities. The Big Tree Botanical Area is between Bonaparte and Lost lakes; 2/3-mi. trail passing exceptionally large trees, the largest of them larches.

Lyman Lake and *Crawfish Lake* are in a detached block on the N border of the Colville Indian Reservation. Take SR 20 E for 13 mi., then SE on Aeneas Valley Rd. to Lyman Lake. The Forest map shows a loop route into the Reservation, then NW on Haden Creek Rd. Three Forest campgrounds on the route.

INTERPRETATION

Information station at Early Winters, where SR 20, from the W, enters the Methow Valley. Open early June to Sept.

Evening programs at Lost Lake Campground, in summer. Notices posted.

ACTIVITIES

Camping: 59 campgrounds; 490 sites. A few are accessible as early as Apr. 15, most by May 15 or June 1, a few not until July.

Hiking, backpacking: 1,200 mi. of trails (about 1,000 in the Pasayten Wilderness), plus opportunities for cross-country hiking and hiking on little-used logging roads. Trail information is available at headquarters and each Ranger District.

Hunting: Deer, black bear, mountain goat.

Fishing: Lakes and streams. Said to be excellent. Rainbow, cutthroat, Dolly Varden, brook trout.

Swimming: Chiefly in Bonaparte and Lost lakes, and in other lakes in E portions of the Forest.

Boating: Mostly on Bonaparte, Lost, other lakes in E portions of the Forest.

Horse riding: 7 improved campgrounds have pack and saddle stock facilities. 6 of these are just outside the Pasayten Wilderness. Outfitter-Guide sheet lists outfitters for pack trips, horse rentals. Inquire at Ranger Districts for trails suitable for horse travel, regulations. In some areas all feed must be carried in.

Skiing: Loup Loup Ski Area on SR 20 E of Twisp.

Ski touring: Recreation Reports includes seasonal information on best locations, snow conditions.

Snowmobiling: Some trails are groomed. *Recreation Reports* includes seasonal information on best locations, snow conditions. Special Washington State parking permits are required at some trailheads to cover plowing costs.

ADJACENT OR NEARBY

Okanogan Multiple Use Area/Sinlahekin Habitat Management Area (see entry).

Conconully State Park (see entry).

Chopaka Mountain and Lake (see entry).

Pearrygin Lake State Park (see entry).

Methow Habitat Management Area (see entry).

Alta Lake State Park (see entry).

PUBLICATIONS

Forest map. $1.00.

Pasayten Wilderness map. $1.00.

Wildlife checklist.

Pasayten bird checklist.

Wilderness use rules.

Recreation Reports, issued at intervals.

Fishing Directory.

Methow in Winter, winter sports information.

Outfitter-Guide sheet.

HEADQUARTERS: P.O. Box 950, Okanogan, WA 98840; (509) 422-2704.

RANGER DISTRICTS: Conconully R.D., Post Office Bldg., Okanogan, WA 98840; (509) 422-3811. Tonasket R.D., Tonasket, WA 98855; (509) 486-2186. Winthrop R.D., Winthrop, WA 98862; (509) 996-2266. Twisp R.D., Twisp, WA 98856; (509) 997-2131.

PEARRYGIN LAKE STATE PARK
Washington Parks and Recreation Commission
578 acres.

5 mi. N of Winthrop, off SR 20.

In the Methow Valley, at the gateway to the North Cascades Highway, Okanogan National Forest, and Forest roads to the edge of the Pasayten Wilderness. 8,200 ft. of shoreline on a pleasant lake.

Camping: A popular campground. 83 sites. Reservations required.

ADJACENT: Methow Habitat Management Area (see entry).

NEARBY: Okanogan National Forest (see entry).

HEADQUARTERS: Rt. 1, Winthrop, WA 98862; (509) 996-2370.

QUILOMENE HABITAT MANAGEMENT AREA
Washington Department of Game
45,143 acres.

NW of Vantage on I-90. Access from Old Vantage Highway and from the road leading N from Vantage past the Ginkgo State Park.

Above the Columbia River Canyon, including most of the Whiskey Dick and Quilomene Creek drainages. N of the State Park, the Habitat Management Area has several miles of frontage on the river. The two sections are separated by an E–W strip about 2 mi. wide.

Desert country. Hills rolling to steep with sparse cover of sagebrush, bunchgrass, other desert vegetation. Hunting is for elk, deer, and upland birds, with some waterfowl on the river.

For the visitor who is not hunting, spring and early summer are the best times to visit. Proper conditions produce a fine wildflower display. As the weather warms, early morning hiking is enjoyable. Most of the roads into backcountry require a husky pickup or 4-wheel drive.

Many species of petrified wood occur in the area. Collecting in noncommercial quantities is permitted.

No designated campgrounds. Camp where you please, but no fires are permitted Apr. 15–Oct. 15.

Pronghorn have been introduced to the area, and hunting them is prohibited.

PUBLICATION: Map.

HEADQUARTERS: Department of Game, Regional Office, 2802 Fruitvale Blvd., Yakima, WA 98902; (509) 575-2740.

ROCKY LAKE NATURAL RECREATION AREA
Washington Department of Natural Resources
About 800 acres.

On SR 20 E of Colville, turn S on road marked for Rocky Lake. Then 3 mi. on paved road, 2 on gravel.

A small, shallow, weedy pond with rocky, forested shores. Forest is mostly ponderosa pine, larch, Douglas-fir, some trees of considerable size. Wildflowers: sticky cinquefoil, goldenrod, golden aster, woolly mullein, klamath weed, wild carrot, Oregon grape, bull thistle. A mechanical aerator keeps the lake surface from freezing in winter.

Camping: 8 sites. Primitive.

NEARBY: Little Pend Oreille Habitat Management Area (see entry).

HEADQUARTERS: DNR, Northeast Area Office, Box 190, Colville, WA 99114; (509) 684-5201.

SHERMAN CREEK HABITAT MANAGEMENT AREA
Washington Department of Game
8,070 acres.

On SR 20 at Franklin D. Roosevelt Lake (Columbia River), W side. 5 mi. W of Kettle Falls.

The main portion of the site is about 6 mi. square, SR 20 crossing its lower third. Some roads once open to vehicles are now closed. Several parking areas along the road. Rather steep, ascending to the ponderosa pine forest of the Okanogan Highlands. Slopes face E and S. Elevations from 1,289 ft. at the lake to 4,208 ft. Annual precipitation is 16 to 19 in. at low elevations, to more than

30 in. at highest level. Site is bordered on the S by the lower drainage of Sherman Creek. Winter range for mule and white-tailed deer.

Plants: Ponderosa pine, widely scattered in bunchgrass areas, relatively heavy stands with Douglas-fir at 3,500 ft. Also lodgepole pine, western larch, Engelmann spruce, aspen, bitter cherry, black cottonwood. Shrubs include alder-leaved buckthorn, ceanothus, blue and white clematis, sticky currant, dogwood, blue elderberry, mountain gooseberry, kinnikinick, thimbleberry. May and June are best wildflower season, species including purple aster, heartleaf arnica, balsamroot, bluebell, camas, columbine, delphinium, lupine, mariposa lily, mullein, penstemon, pussytoes, phlox, western trillium, yarrow.

Birds: No checklist. List for Colville National Forest is applicable. Species noted include Canada goose, whistling swan, osprey, golden and bald eagles, kestrel, Cooper's hawk, Lewis's and northern three-toed woodpeckers; blue, ruffed, and spruce grouse; violet-and-green swallow, mountain chickadee, cedar waxwing, crossbills, Steller's jay.

Mammals: Shrews, bats, cottontail snowshoe hare, yellow pine chipmunk, yellow-bellied marmot, Columbian ground squirrel, golden-mantled squirrel, red squirrel, northern flying squirrel, northern pocket gopher, deer mouse, beaver, porcupine, coyote, red fox, black bear, raccoon, marten, weasel, mink, badger, striped skunk, wolverine, cougar, lynx, bobcat, mule and white-tailed deer. Occasional elk.

Reptiles and amphibians: Long-toed and northwestern tiger salamanders, northwest toad, Pacific tree frog, western leopard frog, western spotted frog, western painted turtle, wandering garter snake, western yellow-bellied racer, gopher snake, Pacific rattlesnake.

Camping: Permitted, but level sites are few. Nearby: Forest Service campground at Trout Lake, about 4 mi. up a dirt road; large Coulee Dam National Recreation Area campground across the river.

ADJACENT
Colville National Forest (see entry).
Coulee Dam National Recreation Area (see entry).

HEADQUARTERS: Department of Game, Regional Office, North 8702 Division St., Spokane, WA 99218; (509) 456-4082.

SQUILCHUCK STATE PARK
Washington Parks and Recreation Commission
286 acres.

9 mi. SW of Wenatchee. From Appleyard, just S of Wenatchee, local road along Squilchuck Creek.

In a steep-walled canyon at the edge of Wenatchee National Forest. Forested site, mostly ponderosa pine with cottonwood, quaking aspen, sumac, sagebrush.

ACTIVITIES
Camping: 20 sites.
Hiking: Trails into the National Forest.
Skiing: 2 ski tows.
Other winter sports: Sledding, tobogganing.

HEADQUARTERS: Rt. 4, Box X237, Wenatchee, WA 98801; (509) 663-7377.

STEAMBOAT ROCK STATE PARK
Washington Parks and Recreation Commission
900 acres.

From Grand Coulee, 12 mi. SW on SR 155.

On Banks Lake, a narrow reservoir 27 mi. long, between high basalt cliffs. Steamboat Rock is a flat-topped butte rising 1,000 ft. above the lake surface, at the tip of a peninsula of rolling land. Adjacent land is the Banks Lake Habitat Management Area (see entry). The Park has over 5 mi. of shorefront.

The developed portion of the Park is a popular, neatly barbered recreation area. Hiking trail to the top of the butte, which is a nature area and wildflower preserve. Some tule marshes on the lakeshore. Upland areas mostly grasses and sagebrush with scattered conifers.

No published bird or mammal lists. See entry for Banks Lake Habitat Management Area. A sign warns Rattlesnake Area.

ACTIVITIES
Camping: 100 sites. All Year. Reservations required Memorial Day–Labor Day.
Hiking: 3 mi. of trails within Park.
Fishing: Lake fishing said to be good.
Swimming: Lake.
Boating: Ramp on lake.
Winter sports: Ice skating, ice fishing.

HEADQUARTERS: P.O. Box 352, Electric City, WA 99123; (509) 633-1304.

STRATFORD HABITAT MANAGEMENT AREA
Washington Department of Game
6,000 acres.

From Coulee City, S on Pinto Ridge Rd. Access to Billy Clapp Lake at
Summer Falls State Park. Or continue S to Main Canal, left to dam.

The larger of two lakes is shown on some maps as Long Lake Reservoir, on
others as Billy Clapp Lake. The smaller is sometimes Stratford Lake, otherwise Brook Lake. The site has been called Long Lake Habitat Management
Area as well as Stratford. Desert terrain. Basalt cliffs and terraces. The lakes
attract many waterfowl in migrations; geese winter and nest here.

Summer Falls State Park, 260 acres, is at the head of Billy Clapp Lake. The
entrance road passes through a ravine, and the falls appear with dramatic
suddenness, a wide rush of water dropping 30–40 ft. into the lake, sending up
great clouds of spray. The falls are active only in summer when irrigation
water is being released. Day-use area.

ACTIVITIES

Hunting: Part of the area is posted as a preserve.

Boating: A boat-access point at the State Park, still shown on the Department of Game map, has been closed as hazardous. Ramps at the S end, at
the dam.

Prospective visitors should obtain a copy of the map noted under Publications. A route can include this site as well as Banks Lake, Sun Lakes, and
other nearby sites. See the Columbia Basin area entry in zone 6.

PUBLICATION: *Columbia Basin Recreation Areas.* Department of Game, 600
N. Capitol Way, Olympia, WA 98504.

HEADQUARTERS: Department of Game, Regional Office, P.O. Box 1237,
Ephrata, WA 98823; (509) 754-4624.

SUN LAKES STATE PARK; LAKE LENORE HABITAT MANAGEMENT AREA

Washington Parks and Recreation Commission/Washington Department of
Game
4,024 acres/8,941 acres.

From Coulee City, SW along SR 17.

Highway 17 is at least as scenic as SR 155 NE of Coulee City (see entry for
Banks Lake Habitat Management Area). Both run through valleys framed by

towering basalt cliffs, but this 27-mi.-long valley has a chain of lakes and marshes on the desert floor. Near Coulee City, the road is high, providing fine views of the meandering stream below. Then it drops to the valley floor, skirting pothole lakes that are populated by waterfowl in season.

This is the Grand Coulee, a unique geological area called "channeled scablands"—huge, dry, deeply cut channels in basalt. One of the most conspicuous features is Dry Falls (see description later in entry). Typical vegetation on the desert floor: big sagebrush, bluebunch wheatgrass, Idaho fescue, and western yarrow, with a variety of flowering annuals. Cattail marshes.

Birds: The Habitat Management Area is managed for waterfowl. It is an important link in migration route of the lesser Canada goose. Ring-billed and California gulls nest. Reported species include Forster's tern, long-billed dowitcher, avocet, blue-winged and cinnamon teals, Barrow's goldeneye, eared grebe, Wilson's phalarope. Many ducks. Also red-winged and yellow-headed blackbirds, cliff swallow, white-throated swift, Say's phoebe, magpie, rock wren, lazuli bunting, western tanager, lark sparrow, northern oriole, various warblers.

FEATURES

Dry Falls, a 3-mi.-wide, 400-ft.-high ancient waterfall, long dry. A National Natural Landmark. A handsome interpretive center overlooks the falls, houses exhibits, information counter; open May 15–Sept. 30.

Sun Lakes State Park includes Dry Falls and Lake Lenore Caves. The major Park development is on Park Lake: campground, marina, gas station, other facilities. Park Lake is heavily used by water skiers, other boaters.

Lake Lenore Caves are high on the cliff wall, carved by glacial meltwater, later used as shelters by Indians. A trail at the N end of the lake leads to several of the caves. Day use only.

Lake Lenore Habitat Management Area is an irregularly shaped strip of land extending from N of Park Lake to the S end of Lenore, generally adjoining State Park lands. Habitat Management Area boundary signs are posted along the highway. At Lenore, several dirt tracks lead to parking at the lakeshore. This area is closed after 10 P.M., and camping is banned.

ACTIVITIES

Camping: At Park Lake. 224 sites. All year.

Hiking: Mostly on informal trails, on the valley floor, skirting lakes and stream.

Hunting: In the Habitat Management Area. Chukar, some waterfowl.

Swimming: Supervised, at Park Lake. June 20–Labor Day.

Boating: Most boating activity is on Park Lake. One can canoe the length of the chain, 12 mi., with 3 portages, one of them over 1/2 mi. No motors on Lake Lenore.

Fishing: Lake Lenore stocked with alkaline-resistant Lahontan cutthroat trout. Special regulations.

PUBLICATIONS
Sun Lakes State Park leaflet.
Dry Falls leaflet.

HEADQUARTERS: Sun Lakes State Park, Star Rt. 1, Box 136, Coulee City, WA 99115; (509) 632-5583. Department of Game, Regional Office, P.O. Box 1237, Ephrata, WA 99823; (509) 754-4624.

TURNBULL NATIONAL WILDLIFE REFUGE
U.S. Fish and Wildlife Service
15,565 acres.

From Spokane, about 9 mi. SW on I-90. Left on SR 904 6 mi. to Cheney, then left on Cheney Plaza Road to entrance.

Managed for waterfowl on the Pacific Flyway. The original lakes and marshes of this area were almost entirely drained by the 1920s. Farming was not successful, and land for the Refuge was acquired in 1937. Lakes and marshes were then restored. Waterfowl numbers reach as high as 50,000 here in the fall migration.

Gently rolling to flat terrain. Ponds, cattail marshes, meadows, groves of ponderosa pine. Only about 1/5 of the site is open to public use. The entrance road leads to HQ past a display pool. Near HQ is the beginning of an auto tour route. Leaflet and bird checklist are available at the beginning of the route. The tour passes several impoundments. Visitors can park and walk to or around the impoundments, or, if they wish, can walk the entire route.

Birds: Over 200 species recorded. Checklist available. Species nesting include horned, eared, and pied-billed grebes; great blue heron, American bittern, western Canada goose, mallard, gadwall, pintail; green-winged, blue-winged, and cinnamon teals; American wigeon, shoveler, wood duck, redhead, ring-necked duck, canvasback, lesser scaup, bufflehead, ruddy duck, hooded merganser. Seasonally common species include red-tailed and marsh hawks, kestrel, California quail, killdeer, Wilson's phalarope, black tern, great horned owl, red-shafted flicker, downy woodpecker, eastern kingbird, willow flycatcher, western wood pewee; tree, bank, barn, and cliff swallows, magpie, black-capped and mountain chickadees, white-breasted and pygmy nuthatches, long-billed marsh wren, robin, western and mountain bluebirds, water pipit, northern shrike. Warblers include yellow, yellow-rumped, yellowthroat. Also western meadowlark; yellow-headed, red-winged and Brewer's blackbirds; American goldfinch; savannah, vesper, chipping, white-crowned, and song sparrows. The Refuge is attempting to establish a population of trumpeter swans translocated from Montana.

Mammals: Include white-tailed deer, coyote, beaver, raccoon, badger, muskrat, mink, porcupine, chipmunk, red squirrel, Columbian ground squirrel.

PUBLICATIONS
Leaflet with map.
Bird checklist.
Environmental education leaflet.
Young People's Bird and Animal Checklist.

HEADQUARTERS: Route 3, Box 385, Cheney, WA 99004; (509) 235-4723.

TWENTY-FIVE-MILE CREEK STATE PARK
Washington Parks and Recreation Commission
235 acres.

From Chelan, 18 mi. N along the lakeshore, off US 97.

Most of the lakeshore from Chelan to this Park is privately owned. The shore road ends here. Beyond is the Wenatchee National Forest and, at the head of the lake, the Lake Chelan National Recreation Area of the North Cascades National Park (see entry, zone 3), reached only by boat, float plane, or on foot.

The Park has 1,500 ft. of waterfront. A forest road leads inland, past a number of forest campgrounds, eventually connecting with a paved forest road along the Entiat River.

ACTIVITIES
Camping: 73 sites.
Swimming: Unsupervised.
Boating: Ramp and marina.

NEARBY: Lake Chelan State Park (see entry).

HEADQUARTERS: c/o Lake Chelan State Park, Rt. 1, Box 90, Chelan, WA 98816; (509) 687-3710.

WENATCHEE NATIONAL FOREST
U.S. Forest Service
1,618,287 acres (1,902,515 acres within boundaries).

Central WA. Roughly bisected E–W by US 2. Generally N of I-90, W of US 97.

The Forest extends from the crest of the Cascades E to the Columbia River, part of a huge block of federal land occupying the mountains from Canada to Oregon and beyond. The highest country is in the W portion. Here annual precipitation and snowfall are heavy. Snow remains until early July, and early season snow often falls before the end of August. Much of the Forest is in the rain shadow of the Cascades, however, and precipitation declines with decreasing altitude to semiarid conditions at the Columbia River.

The Forest includes parts of three wilderness areas, open only to foot and horse travel. However, much of the Forest is readily accessible by car, and more than a million visitors yearly accept the invitation.

A striking feature of the Forest is the extraordinary number of lakes, 237 named and listed, 156 of them 10 acres or more in area. Largest is Lake Chelan, 55 mi. long, second deepest lake in North America, maximum depth about 1,500 ft. The largest lakes have some inholdings, privately owned land, on their shores, and these are popular resorts. Many of the smaller lakes are in high country, including roadless areas.

Elevations in the Forest range from 700 to 9,511 ft. Conditions differ so much from place to place and season to season that visitors require some planning. Recreation reports are issued frequently describing road and trail conditions, which campgrounds are open, and snow cover. In 1980, a few campgrounds at low elevations opened in April. Some trails were then snow-free but muddy. Unpaved Forest roads were muddy, too, and motorists were urged to inquire before driving. Ski touring and snowmobiling were still going on at higher elevations.

More areas were open in early June, but much road and trail maintenance had yet to be done. A few of the open campgrounds did not yet have water or maintenance. High lakes were still frozen. In the first week of July, the snow line was up to 4,500 ft. on N-facing slopes, 6,000 ft. on slopes facing S. Wherever snow had recently melted, muddy conditions prevailed and road and trail maintenance were just beginning.

Plants: Mostly forested, chiefly ponderosa pine with Douglas-fir, Engelmann spruce, subalpine fir. Alpine meadows at higher elevations. Much of the forest is open, parklike. Willow, aspen, and alder along streams. Little old-growth timber remains. Many wildflowers. Blooming season begins in the low country in April, prominent species including balsamroot, trillium, spring beauty, yellow bell, glacier lily. Blooming follows the receding snow line. June display includes wild garlic, avalanche lily, phlox, currant. In the high country, July is the peak blooming time. Among the species visitors are likely to see around campgrounds: American brooklime, dwarf waterleaf, blue penstemon, forget-me-not, lupine, blue vetch, wood anemone, meadow rue, pipsissewa, snowberry, twinbells, columbine, Oregon grape, ocean spray, oxeye daisy, ceanothus, thimbleberry.

Birds: Checklist available. Species recorded include pintail, northern shoveler; blue-winged, green-winged, and cinnamon teals; mallard, gadwall, Canada and white-fronted geese, lesser scaup, redhead, canvasback, common and Barrow's goldeneyes, bufflehead, great horned owl, golden eagle, Cooper's and sharp-shinned hawks, goshawk, great blue heron, American bittern, cedar and Bohemian waxwings, chukar, spruce and sage grouse, blue and Steller's jays, dipper; Cassin's, house, and purple finches; hermit and Swainson's thrushes, common flicker; white-headed, northern three-toed, downy, hairy, and black-backed three-toed woodpeckers; mountain, chestnut-backed, and black-capped chickadees; magpie, pine grosbeak, red- and white-winged crossbills, mountain and western bluebirds; red-breasted, white-breasted, and pygmy nuthatches; warbling, red-eyed, and solitary vireos; white-throated, golden-crowned, white-crowned, and Harris's sparrows.

Mammals: Checklist available. Species listed include desert pallid bat, porcupine; yellow pine, least, and Townsend's chipmunks; aplodontia, beaver, northern flying squirrel, hoary and yellow-bellied marmots, marten, fisher, striped skunk, muskrat, raccoon, badger, black bear, red fox, coyote, lynx, bobcat, mountain lion, wolverine, moose, elk, mule and white-tailed deer, mountain goat, bighorn sheep.

FEATURES

Glacier Peak Wilderness, 464,219 acres, about half in the Mount Baker–Snoqualmie National Forest. In the N Cascade Range, the Wilderness is an area of heavily forested stream courses, steep-sided valleys, and peaks with glaciers, more active glaciers than any other range in the Lower 48. Climate is moist on the W side of the range, producing verdant forests and deep snows. Vegetation is more open and parklike on the drier E side.

Glacier Peak is the dominant feature, at 10,541 ft. More than 30 other major peaks, three of them over 9,000 ft. The snowfields and glaciers are the sources of hundreds of streams with many cascades, falls, and pools. Many high mountain lakes.

The Wilderness boundary comes close to the upper end of Lake Chelan, where the Forest adjoins the Lake Chelan National Recreation Area. Its general course is then SW, irregularly, because the line was drawn to exclude existing roads. The ends of several of these roads are Wilderness trailheads.

Fish and game are plentiful, attracting many hunters and fishermen, on foot and horseback. The principal visitor activity is backpacking. The Pacific Crest Trail crosses the area. Many hikers choose less-traveled routes. The area has 350 mi. of trails as well as large areas where off-trail hiking is practical for the experienced.

Commercial outfitters are located on the principal approaches. Ask Forest HQ for addresses. Not all trails are suitable for horses. Trails that have much horse traffic in hunting season are likely to be in bad condition for hiking, at least temporarily. Inquire at Ranger District.

Wilderness permits are required.

The *Alpine Lakes Area* includes a core wilderness of 303,508 acres, of which about 120,000 acres are in the Mount Baker–Snoqualmie National Forest. Congress authorized the Forest Service to acquire the private inholdings within an additional 88,050 acres. A peripheral management unit includes about 520,000 acres. I-90 is close to the Wilderness boundary where it enters the Forest at Snoqualmie Pass. The Wilderness lies to the N and E of the Pass, N of Lakes Keechelus, Kachess, and Cle Elum. The terrain is rugged, but less so than in the Glacier Peak Wilderness. Many peaks are over 4,000 ft., a few over 7,000. The area is best known for its lakes, more than 700 of them including those as small as an acre. The largest is about 1 1/2 mi. long, three others close to a mile.

The Enchantments Area is about 3,500 acres in the heart of the Wilderness, a unique and fragile ecosystem. High elevations, rugged granite relief, snow remaining until midsummer. Glaciers. Several small lakes. Special rules protect this delicate area; inquire before entering. Foot travel only.

Trails in the Wilderness generally follow drainages. Some are easy going, destination lakes only 2–3 mi. from trailheads.

Goat Rocks Wilderness, 82,680 acres. 22,940 acres of this Wilderness are within the Mount Baker–Snoqualmie National Forest but administered by the Wenatchee National Forest. The larger portion is in the Gifford Pinchot National Forest (see entry, zone 2). The Wenatchee portion is in the SW part of the Tieton Ranger District, S of US 12, SW of Rimrock Lake. An all-weather road SW from Rimrock Lake along the North Fork of the Tieton River leads to one of several trailheads.

Terrain is mountainous, elevations from 3,000 ft. to 8,201-ft. Gilbert Peak. Much of the central area is above timberline. Summer is short in the Goat Rocks. In July the snow covering the meadows is rapidly replaced by the white blossoms of avalanche fawnlily and elkslip marsh-marigold. Other alpine flowers, as the short season progresses, are lupine, Indian paintbrush, scarlet and magenta paintedcup, red mountainheath, with spreading phlox on drier, rocky soils.

Flinty peaks rise from snowfields. Streams meander through meadows, cascade down hillsides. The Tieton and Klickitat River systems drain the E side of the Wilderness.

The Wilderness has 95 mi. of hiking trails, including part of the Pacific Crest Trail. Trails are usually open by July 15, but some snow may persist into Aug. 85 mi. of trail are suitable for horse travel. (Horse travelers must carry feed or pelletized grain.) Wildlife is abundant, including mountain goat. Many streams and lakes are stocked.

In winter, visitors can enter the area by the White Pass Chairlift and ski to Hogback Mountain.

Wilderness permit is required.

Lake Chelan, 55 mi. long, 1/2 to 2 mi. wide, lies between steep-sided mountains with peaks to 8,000 ft. on both sides. About 15 mi. at the S end are within privately owned land. At the N, about 5 mi. are within the Lake Chelan National Recreation Area. All the shoreline between, except for a few small inholdings, is National Forest. Beyond Twenty-Five-Mile Creek, the lakeshore is inaccessible for car. Campgrounds on the shore are patronized chiefly by boaters, although a few visitors hike in.

The National Recreation Area also has no road access. Most visitors come by the daily boat from Chelan. The N end of the lake also provides a close approach to the Glacier Peak Wilderness. For about 10 mi. S of the NRA boundary, a trail follows the lakeshore. Otherwise the map shows no shoreline trails, and only a few follow drainages back from the shore.

Lake Wenatchee, N of Leavenworth, about 5 mi. long, is a popular resort, much of the shoreline privately owned. Two Forest campgrounds and a State Park are on the shore. Forest roads beyond the lake lead to camps and trailheads near the Glacier Peak Wilderness boundary.

Lakes Keechelus, Kachess, and *Cle Elum,* 5 to 7 mi. long, roughly parallel, are in a part of the Forest checkerboarded with inholdings. I-90 is near the E shore of Keechelus. Lake elevations are between 2,200 and 2,500 ft. All three are busy resort areas. From Cle Elum Lake, a Forest road follows the Cle Elum River to several Forest campgrounds and the Pacific Crest Trail.

Naches and *Tieton Ranger Districts,* technically part of the Gifford Pinchot National Forest, are administered by Wenatchee. Adjoining Mount Rainier National Park. Not shown on the Wenatchee Forest map, but a special map is available. Tieton is crossed by US 12, Naches by SR 410. A busy recreation area lies along US 12, beside the Tieton River. River canyon is deep, narrow. Dense forest on N-facing slope, sparse on S. Bulletin board at Tieton Ranger District has useful map of the area. Many campgrounds along the route. Rimrock Lake, about 7 mi. long, is heavily used. Many trails lead into backcountry, including nearby Goat Rocks Wilderness. Ski area at White Pass. Naches Ranger District includes Bumping Lake, about 4 mi. long; several small lakes; Bumping, American, and Naches rivers. Numerous campgrounds. Popular but no area as heavily used as that along US 12.

ACTIVITIES

Camping: 147 campgrounds, including campgrounds accessible by boat only, not including those reached only by foot or horse. 1,937 sites. Earliest opening Apr. 15, latest about July 15. Earliest closing Oct. 1, latest Nov. 15.

Hiking, backpacking: 2,584 mi. of trails. All but about 300 are also open to horse travel, only about 1,000 open to ORV's. Most trails are shown on the Forest map, but not in sufficient detail to indicate more than location and destination. Hiking season begins at low elevations in May. July–Aug. is the season in high country. Each Ranger District issues mimeographed trail guides giving trail names and numbers, destinations, mileages, types of use, and comments on trail conditions and hazards. Frequent recreation reports describe current trail conditions.

Hunting: Deer, bear, elk, bighorn, grouse. Some hunters use guides and pack animals for backcountry hunting.

Fishing: Said to be excellent. Many out-of-the-way lakes and streams. Rainbow, cutthroat, brook, and Dolly Varden trout; steelhead. Bass and perch in Fish Lake.

Swimming: Chiefly in the lakes at low elevations.

Boating: On the larger lakes.

Canoeing, kayaking: Wenatchee River from Lake Wenatchee to Tumwater Campground; 19 mi., some class II rapids. A 4-mi. run from Fish Lake to Cle Elum Lake on the Cle Elum River with class II rapids, including a slalom course.

Horse riding: Many hunters and summer travelers use pack and saddle stock for wilderness visits. Commercial packers operate on several approach routes. Names and addresses from Forest HQ. Unless you are using a guide, check with a Ranger District for trail conditions and restrictions, need to carry feed, etc.

Skiing: Ski areas at Echo Valley, Entiat Valley, Hyak, Leavenworth, Mission Ridge, Ski Acres, Snoqualmie Summit, Stevens Pass. Consult Ranger District for details and current snow conditions.

Ski touring, snowshoeing, snowmobiling: Winter travel in the Forest is increasingly popular. Recreation reports and Ranger Districts provide information on snow conditions and best current locations.

ADJACENT OR NEARBY

Mount Baker–Snoqualmie National Forest (see entry, zone 4).
Okanogan National Forest (see entry, zone 5).
Gifford Pinchot National Forest (see entry, zone 2).
North Cascades National Park (see entry, zone 3).
Mount Rainier National Park (see entry, zone 4).
State Parks: Alta Lake (zone 5), Lake Chelan (zone 5), Twenty-Five-Mile Creek (zone 5), Lake Wenatchee (zone 5), Squilchuck (zone 5). See entries.

PUBLICATIONS

Forest map. $1.00.
Glacier Peak Wilderness map. $1.00.
Goat Rocks Wilderness map. $1.00.
Alpine Lakes Area map.
Enchantments Area map.
Ranger District trail guides (mimeo):
    Chelan R.D.
    Entiat R.D.
    Cle Elum R.D.

Ellensburg R.D.
Lake Wenatchee R.D.
Leavenworth R.D.
Naches R.D.
Tieton R.D.
List of lakes (size, location).
List of mountains (elevation, location).
Winter Recreation Guide.
Winter Trips & Information.
Lady of the Lake (Chelan boat schedule).
Flowers of Nason Creek and Glacier View Campgrounds.

HEADQUARTERS: Wenatchee, WA 98801; (509) 662-4335.

RANGER DISTRICTS: Chelan R.D., Chelan, WA 98816; (509) 682-2576. Cle
Elum R.D., Cle Elum, WA 98922; (509) 674-4411. Ellensburg R.D.,
Ellensburg, WA 98926; (509) 962-9813. Entiat R.D., Entiat, WA 98822;
(509) 784-1511. Lake Wenatchee R.D., Lake Wenatchee, Star Rt., Leav-
enworth, WA 98826; (509) 763-3103. Leavenworth R.D., Leavenworth,
WA 98826; (509) 782-1413. Naches R.D., 16680 Highway 410, Naches,
WA 98937; (509) 658-2435. Tieton R.D., Star Route, Box 189, Naches,
WA 98937; (509) 672-4101.

WILLIAMS LAKE
Washington Department of Natural Resources
About 600 acres.

From US 395 about 1 mi. NW of Colville, about 13 mi. N on Echo County
Rd. (also known as Williams Lake Rd.).

A small, shallow lake in an attractive forested setting. The road from Colville
offers a quiet drive through a farming valley. Part of the shoreline is marshy.
A meadow near the campsite has many wildflowers. Mechanical aerator
keeps the lake ice-free in winter.

Camping: 10 primitive sites. Hand water pump.

HEADQUARTERS: Department of Natural Resources, Box 190, Colville, WA
99114; (509) 684-5201.

YAKIMA CANYON SCENIC HIGHWAY
U.S. Bureau of Land Management/Washington Department of Game

SR 821 between Ellensburg and Yakima.

The canyon, about 20 mi. long, is a scenic recreation area. The Highway, broad and well paved, is sometimes close to the river, sometimes 100 ft. above. Dry hills on either side, sparsely covered with sagebrush and bunchgrass. Along the stream, some large ponderosas, as well as cottonwood, alder, shrubs. The river is about 50 ft. wide, swift-moving, popular with rafters and canoeists.

Many turnouts are along the route, and there seems to be no prohibition against camping. The BLM and the Department of Game jointly manage three larger turnouts, good riverside campgrounds without facilities. At two of these, footbridges cross the river into the L. T. Murray Habitat Management Area (see entry), a quick entry into good backpacking country.

The third area is just above Roza Dam. This draws the largest crowds, because the pool is large enough for boats with motors and pleasant for swimming.

ZONE 6

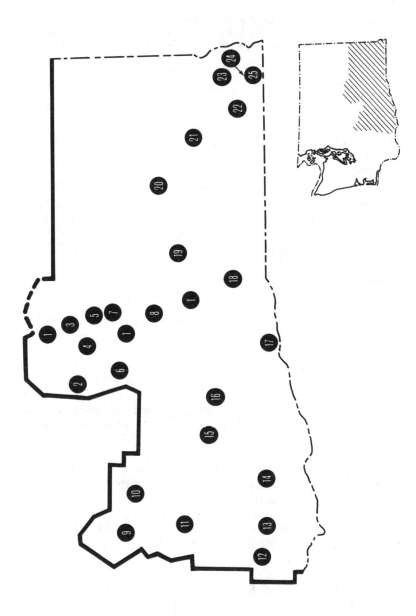

ZONE 6

Includes these counties:

Grant (except N tip)	Klickitat	Columbia
Adams	Benton	Garfield
Whitman	Franklin	Asotin
Yakima	Walla Walla	

The NW corner of this zone is mountainous, a part of the Cascade Range just E of Mount Rainier National Park. A bit to the S, a part of the Goat Rocks Wilderness extends into the zone. Still further S, Mt. Adams lies on the zone boundary. In the far SE, the Blue Mountains and the Umatilla National Forest project into the zone from Oregon.

Except for these areas, the zone is predominantly semiarid to arid. However, it includes much of the basins of the Columbia, Yakima, Snake, and lesser rivers. Almost all these rivers have been dammed, and the zone has many irrigation reservoirs. These and associated works have produced many interesting wetlands, waterways, and seep lakes. The contrasts between wetlands and surrounding desert are often dramatic. For example, driving through a dry canyon, one turns a corner and is confronted by a fine waterfall. The many wetland areas attract large numbers of waterfowl, shorebirds, and other fauna.

Many of the larger reservoirs have heavy water-based recreational use: boating, water skiing, sailing. We include such sites only if they are in natural settings. Usually this means that a significant portion of shoreline is within a wildlife area or undeveloped park.

The Columbia Basin has a remarkable array of these wetland areas, extending from Grand Coulee in zone 5 to the Oregon border. See the Columbia Basin Recreation Areas entry for a list of sites.

One of the least-known parts of Washington is the extreme SE corner, along the canyons of the Snake and Grande Ronde rivers and in the Wenaha-Tucannon Wilderness of the Umatilla National Forest.

AHTANUM MULTIPLE USE AREA
Washington Department of Natural Resources
39,000 acres.

From Yakima, S on I-82 and US 12 about 2 mi. to Union Gap, exit 36. W 1 mi. to First St., then right 1/4 mi. and left on West Washington. In 6 1/2 mi., left on 64th St. about 0.7 mi., right on Ahtanum Rd. to Tampico. There take North Fork into the Multiple Use Area. Total from Yakima, 28 mi.

About 8 mi. beyond Tampico on the North Fork Road, one enters the Multiple Use Area. The road divides again at the Ahtanum Campground. Turn left to travel a 27-mi. loop, including Darland Mountain, back to the fork. The MUA map shows Headquarters at this point; what one actually sees is a gate marked Private Residences. In fact, it's a DNR work center.

Justice Douglas said Darland Mountain has "the most commanding view in the Cascades." 6,981 ft. high, it's the second highest point in Washington to which one can drive. At least that's what their leaflet says. The road is quite satisfactory as far as Eagle Nest vista. Beyond that we consider it unsuitable for large RV's.

The auto tour route follows stream valleys, often in narrow, steep-walled canyons, sometimes through broader valleys. Within a few miles the route makes a transition from near-desert through mountain forests to alpine meadows.

The Multiple Use Area's N and W boundaries adjoin the Tieton Ranger District, administered by Wenatchee National Forest (see entry). The Goat Rocks Wilderness is 6 mi. W of Darland Mountain. Trails from the MUA lead to the Wilderness and to the Rimrock Lake area of the Ranger District. The Oak Creek Habitat Management Area (see entry) is on the NE.

The DNR is under mandate to manage its lands for timber production and income to the trusts of the state-owned Trust Lands. Other land uses are subordinated under present laws.

Plants: Ponderosa pine forest in the valleys. On forested slopes, pine with Douglas-fir, spruce, larch, and hemlock. Much of the forest is relatively open, the understory including some low shrubs. Transition to subalpine vegetation on Darland Mountain. The area is noted for its wildflower displays May–Aug. In Aug. many hillsides were carpeted with yellow aster. Also seen then: scarlet gilia, purple monkeyflower, devil's club, sneezeweed, larkspur, sunflower, Queen Anne's lace, fireweed.

Wildlife: No checklists available. Area is noted for a large herd of elk that migrate through. Few mule deer. Beaver, skunk, muskrat, marmot, chickaree, golden-mantled squirrel, chipmunk. Little information on birds, but species should be much the same as in the Okanogan National Forest. A few mallard, wood duck, and teal nest along Ahtanum Creek. Chukar, ruffed grouse, pheasant, and California quail are principal game birds.

FEATURES

Darland Mountain Viewpoint. The mountain is on the National Forest boundary.

Eagle Nest Viewpoint is less dramatic but offers a good view of a valley within the Multiple Use Area.

Diamond and *Cirque Lakes* are on the SW boundary at 5,600 ft. elevation. *Blue* and *Green Lakes* are higher, smaller. Only Green Lake is accessible by car; it has a campground. Blue Lake can be reached with a 4-wheel-drive vehicle.

Interpretive signs are placed at intervals along the auto route.

ACTIVITIES

Camping: 7 campgrounds, 70 sites. Primitive. Only 2 campgrounds have drinking water. DNR campgrounds are not listed in popular directories. Use is heavy in hunting season. Otherwise most visitors are local, but sites may be full on fine weekends.

Hiking, backpacking: The Ahtanum Trail is used by horses and motorcycles as well as hikers. The 13-mi. Gray Rock Trail, also multiple use, was constructed in 1981. We saw abandoned logging roads that can be hiked, and the forest is sufficiently open to make bushwhacking feasible. Most backpackers would cross into the National Forest.

Hunting: Game birds. Elk in a restricted area.

Fishing: Ahtanum Creek and some lakes stocked. Rainbow, cutthroat, whitefish.

Horse riding: Some camps have stanchions, other facilities. When we visited, horses could be rented at Soda Springs, between Tampico and the Multiple Use Area.

Snowmobiling: On unplowed roads and trails.

PUBLICATION: Leaflet.

HEADQUARTERS: Department of Natural Resources, Southeast Area Office, 713 E. Bowers Rd., Ellensburg, WA 98926; (509) 925-6131.

ASOTIN CREEK HABITAT MANAGEMENT AREA
Washington Department of Game
8,725 acres.

From Clarkston on US 95, on the Idaho border, 6 mi. S on SR 129 to Asotin, then 13 mi. SW along Asotin Creek.

Here is an opportunity for a quiet, pleasant adventure in an out-of-the-way corner of Washington. The road passes through a scenic canyon, dry slopes with rock outcrops, talus, rimrock, sparse vegetation. Scattered trees along the valley floor, mostly ponderosa pine with cottonwood, willow. Spring is the best time to visit, for there is then a fine wildflower display. Summers are dry, and the area is best left to hunters in the fall.

The road continues into the NE corner of the Umatilla National Forest, in Oregon, higher country with many streams, campgrounds, and trails into the Wenaha-Tucannon Wilderness.

ACTIVITIES
Camping: Informal; no designated sites.
Hunting: Chukar, elk.
Fishing: Creek. Best in early summer.

HEADQUARTERS: Department of Game, Regional Office, North 8702 Division St., Spokane, WA 99218; (509) 456-4082.

BROOKS MEMORIAL STATE PARK
Washington Parks and Recreation Commission
701 acres.

On US 97, 15 mi. N of Goldendale.

Traveling S on US 97, one leaves dry sagebrush country on the climb to Satus Pass, 3,149 ft., in the Simcoe Mountains; scenic, forested. The road passes through an Indian reservation, closed to public use.

The Park is forested: ponderosa, Douglas-fir, spruce. Some Oregon white oak. Cottonwood, willow, and aspen in the draws.

ACTIVITIES
Camping: 45 sites.
Hiking: 6 mi. of trails. 1 1/2-mi. nature trail.
Snowmobiling: 3-mi. trail.

NEARBY: Toppenish National Wildlife Refuge (see entry).

HEADQUARTERS: Rt. 1, Box 136, Goldendale, WA 98620; (509) 773-4611.

CHIEF JOSEPH HABITAT MANAGEMENT AREA
Washington Department of Game
9,176 acres.

From Clarkston on US 95 at the Idaho border, S 6 mi. to Asotin, then S about 25 mi. on local road following the Snake River Canyon. Beyond Rogersburg and the Grande Ronde River, the Habitat Management Area is on both sides of the road.

In the far SE corner of Washington, a lightly traveled area. The Habitat Management Area is known to hunters for big game and upland birds. Out of hunting season, and especially in spring and early summer, it's a quiet, scenic area for undisturbed camping, hiking, and fishing. Between Rogersburg and SR 129 no road follows the twisting canyon of the Grande Ronde River. From SR 129, County Road 100 follows the canyon into Oregon, and this drive is well worth while, although it requires a bit of backtracking from the HMA. NW of Clarkston the Snake River Canyon is 2,000 ft. deep, and is accessible by road.

Except for a dirt road to headquarters, the Habitat Management Area is practically roadless. However, the terrain is dry and open, making for easy cross-country hikes, pleasant rather than challenging for the backpacker.

ACTIVITIES
Camping: Informal. No designated sites.
Fishing: Smallmouth bass, trout, steelhead.

HEADQUARTERS: Department of Game, Regional Office, North 8702 Division St., Spokane, WA 99218; (509) 456-4082.

COLUMBIA BASIN RECREATION AREAS
Washington Department of Game/Washington Parks and Recreation Commission/U.S. Fish and Wildlife Service

From Grand Coulee Dam to the OR border, along and E of the Columbia River. W of US 395 and SR 21. Crossed by US 2, I-90, several SRs.

The Washington Department of Game and U.S. Department of the Interior have published an excellent map with brief descriptions of the state and federal recreation sites in the Columbia Basin area. With this map, one can plan a visit combining a number of sites and activities.

The region is predominantly arid: mountains, canyons, bluffs, mesas, channeled scablands, rolling hills, low dunes, sagebrush flats, as well as irrigated cropland. Almost all the recreation sites are based on water: reservoirs, streams, marshes, seep lakes, waterways. Thus they attract much wildlife.

The following are sites for which we have entries:*
In zone 5: Banks Lake Habitat Management Area, Lake Lenore Habitat Management Area, Steamboat Rock State Park, Stratford Habitat Manage-

---

*Department of Game sites were known as Wildlife Recreation Areas. In 1980 they were renamed Habitat Management Areas. The former title appears on many maps and in other references.

ment Area, Sun Lakes State Park. *In zone 6:* Columbia National Wildlife Refuge, Crab Creek Habitat Management Area, Desert Habitat Management Area, Gloyd Seeps Habitat Management Area, McNary National Wildlife Refuge, McNary Habitat Management Area, Potholes State Park, Quincy Habitat Management Area, Wahluke Habitat Management Area.

PUBLICATION: *Columbia Basin Recreation Areas.* Department of Game, 600 N. Capitol Way, Olympia, WA 98501.

COLUMBIA NATIONAL WILDLIFE REFUGE
U.S. Fish and Wildlife Service
28,952 acres.

From I-90 at Moses Lake, SE about 2 1/2 mi. on SR 17, then S 5 mi. on Sullivan Rd. Across bridge, turn right and look for Refuge sign on left. *Open:* Daylight hours.

A visit here should include the Potholes Habitat Management Area, adjacent, the Gloyd Seeps Habitat Management Area to the N (see entry), and perhaps the Sun Lakes area further N on SR 17 (see entry, zone 5). Better still, get the Department of Game folder, *Columbia Basin Recreation Areas,* which shows these and other sites as well as the network of secondary roads.

This is an area of the Columbia Basin called "channeled scablands." A great lava field was slightly tilted, then scoured by torrents released by the melting of gigantic Ice Age dams. Until recently this was desert, waterless except for a few alkali ponds. Building O'Sullivan Dam, creating an irrigation reservoir, made a great change. Seepage created many marshes, sloughs, and lakes, as well as numerous water-filled potholes. Indeed, when we visited in 1980, many of the Refuge roads had been closed because of flood damage caused by release of water from the reservoir.

Now the Refuge provides nesting, feeding, and wintering grounds for over 100,000 ducks and geese. Irrigated croplands produce browse and grain. Fishing is popular in the several lakes.

The Drumheller Channels at the north end of the Refuge is a spectacular complex of buttes, basins, and abandoned cataracts.

Elevations range from 600 to 1,200 ft. Annual precipitation is a mere 8 to 9 in.

Nov.–Jan. is best time for waterfowl observation, Sept. for shorebirds.

Plants: Several plant communities, depending on moisture conditions: cattail-bulrush marsh, sedge meadow, saltgrass meadow, greasewood, sagebrush, and grassland. Wildflowers include aster, phlox, lupine, balsamroot.

Birds: Checklist available. Nesting species include pied-billed grebe, mallard, gadwall, pintail, blue-winged and cinnamon teals, American wigeon, northern shoveler, ruddy duck, red-tailed and marsh hawks, prairie falcon, American kestrel, California quail, pheasant, chukar, Virginia rail, long-billed curlew; great horned, burrowing, and short-eared owls; Say's phoebe, canyon and rock wrens, sage thrasher, common yellowthroat, yellow-breasted chat, lazuli bunting; savannah, vesper, lark, sage, Brewer's, and song sparrows.

Seasonally common shorebirds include greater yellowlegs, least sandpiper, long-billed dowitcher, western sandpiper.

Mammals: Beaver, muskrat, marmot, coyote, Townsend ground squirrel, small number of mule deer, occasional bobact.

Reptiles and amphibians: Pacific tree frog, western spadefoot, sagebrush lizard, common garter snake, Pacific gopher snake, western yellow-bellied racer, bull snake, western rattlesnake.

FEATURES: *Auto tour route,* 5 mi., self-guiding with leaflet, gives a comprehensive view of the area. A letter written in January 1981 informed us that the 1980 flood-damaged roads had been repaired.

ACTIVITIES
Camping: One campground, primitive, no fixed sites. Camping is also available at several nearby Department of Game sites and Potholes State Park.
Hunting: Waterfowl and upland birds.
Fishing: 50 seep lakes, sloughs, 15 mi. of streams and canals. Rainbow and German brown trout, largemouth bass, bluegill, black crappie, yellow perch, walleye. Special regulations.
Canoeing: Water Trails of Washington (see state bibliography) describes a canoe trail through 6 small lakes: 3 mi., 5 portages. The description errs in saying the trail is within the Refuge; it begins and ends outside Refuge boundaries. It passes through, passing the Refuge campground.

Volcanic ash was still a problem on windy days in early 1981.

PUBLICATIONS
Leaflet with map. (Maps in the hunting and fishing leaflets are much better.)
Self-guiding tour leaflet.
Bird checklist.
Hunting information.
Fishing information.

REFERENCE: *Columbia Basin Recreation Areas.* Department of Game, 600 N. Capitol Way, Olympia, WA 98501.

HEADQUARTERS: P.O. Drawer F, Othello, WA 99344; (509) 488-2668.

CONBOY LAKE NATIONAL WILDLIFE REFUGE
U.S. Fish and Wildlife Service
6,726 acres.

From Trout Lake on SR 141, take road E toward Glenwood about 8 mi.
Entrance on right.

This is a Refuge in the making. Authorized in 1965, only two-thirds of the
planned acreage has been acquired. Nor have water needs been met. Conboy
Lake was drained in 1910 by digging a canal. Blocking the canal today would
flood privately owned land within the old lakebed. Aquatic habitat now
depends on runoff exceeding the canal's capacity. Between Dec. and May
there is usually 1,000–5,000 acres of wetland, enough to attract up to 10,000
waterfowl. When we visited in summer, the lakebed was dry. Several streams,
canals, and ditches provide summer habitat for limited numbers of wood
duck, mallard, other summer residents.

The Refuge is in a small, quiet, attractive valley not far from Mt. Adams
and the Gifford Pinchot National Forest. Elevations from 1,800 to 2,000 ft.
About 2,500 acres of grassland, 2,200 of forest. Most of the forest has been
logged at least once, but a few old-growth ponderosas remain.

March and April have large migratory waterfowl concentrations, especially
whistling swans. Scenically the Refuge is at its best in the fall, usually mid-
Oct. when the aspens turn color with Mt. Adams as a backdrop.

It's a pleasant place for a two-hour hike if you happen to be driving this
way. The Klickitat Habitat Management Area (see entry) is nearby, as well
as the National Forest, and the route from Goldendale to Trout Lake is
scenic. Except in hunting season, you may be the only visitors.

Birds: Checklist available. 134 species recorded. Manager reports a nesting
pair of sandhill cranes, first in Washington since 1941. Seasonally common
species include great blue heron, Canada goose, mallard, pintail, green-
winged and cinnamon teals, wood duck, red-tailed and marsh hawks, kestrel,
ruffed grouse, common snipe, Wilson's phalarope, mourning dove, great
horned owl, rufous and calliope hummingbirds, common flicker, hairy woodpecker, eastern and western kingbirds, Say's phoebe; alder, olive-sided, and
western flycatchers; western wood pewee; violet-green, tree, bank, rough-
winged, barn, and cliff swallows; raven, crow, western and mountain bluebirds, pine siskin, American goldfinch. One to 10 bald eagle usually present
when waterfowl are abundant.

Mammals: Beaver, chipmunk, flying squirrel, golden-mantled squirrel, gopher, muskrat, porcupine, mule deer, coyote, skunk. Present but seldom seen:
river otter, elk, bobcat, badger, weasel, black bear, raccoon, pine marten.

FEATURES: *Willard Trail*, 2 mi., near headquarters, passes through variety of habitats. Beaver active.

ACTIVITIES
Hunting: Waterfowl, upland game birds, deer. Special rules; see Refuge Manager.
Fishing: Limited. Rainbow and brook trout, catfish, bullhead.

PUBLICATIONS
Leaflet.
Bird checklist.

HEADQUARTERS: Box 5, Glenwood, WA 98619; (509) 364-3410.

CRAB CREEK HABITAT MANAGEMENT AREA
Washington Department of Game
20,333 acres.

From Beverly on SR 243, beside the Columbia River, E about 1 mi. toward Smyrna and Corfu. The Habitat Management Area is between Beverly and Smyrna. On both sides of the road, but most of the acreage on N side.

Acreage includes Priest Rapids Habitat Management Area, a satellite, on the Columbia River just W of Mattawa. We thought the road between Beverly and Smyrna unsuitable for large RV's but we were told it is usually well maintained by the county.

The Crab Creek Habitat Management Area is about 13 mi. E–W, 3 mi. N–S, lying along Crab Creek at the foot of the Saddle Mountains. Includes the Lenice-Nunnally lake chain, managed for quality fishing. Sagebrush desert, rolling hills, cattail marshes. Good waterfowl habitat. Known chiefly to hunters and fishermen. Dunes at the W end are managed by the DNR for use by ORV's. They are prohibited in the HMA, and trespass has been a problem.

Spring and early summer are the best times to visit. The prospective visitor should obtain the Columbia Basin folder (see Reference) and include Crab Creek as a side trip from the Columbia National Wildlife Refuge, Potholes Habitat Management Area, and other sites in the region. The secondary roads, such as those between Potholes Reservoir and Crab Creek, offer good sightseeing with little or no traffic. The road from O'Sullivan Dam to Othello and Smyrna Road W from Othello pass through fenced portions of the Columbia National Wildlife Refuge. Good birding along the roadside. Beyond Corfu the road is on a shelf cut into Saddle Mountain, providing a good view of wetland and irrigated farmland below.

ACTIVITIES
Camping: Informal.
Canoeing: From bridge 5 1/2 mi. E of Beverly to Columbia River. One S-curve requires short portage.

NEARBY: See entry, Columbia Basin Recreation Areas.

REFERENCE: *Columbia Basin Recreation Areas.* Department of Game, 600 N. Capitol Way, Olympia, WA 98501.

HEADQUARTERS: Department of Game, Regional Office, P.O. Box 1237, Ephrata, WA 98823; (509) 754-4624.

DESERT HABITAT MANAGEMENT AREA
Washington Department of Game
27,719 acres.

From I-90 W of Moses Lake, S on Dodson Rd. about 3 mi., then either right or left.

The Frenchman Hills and Winchester Wasteways cut through this previously dry sandy area, developing a striking contrast of extensive wetlands amidst dry sand dunes and sagebrush. Desert, Harris, and Beda lakes are managed for trout; walk-in access only. The wasteway systems have trout and warm-water species. Many waterfowl, shorebirds. Wildlife is much the same as in the adjoining Potholes Habitat Management Area (see entry).
Good canoeing on quiet waters in spring and early summer. Two small waterfalls require portaging.
Prospective visitors should obtain a copy of the area folder noted below.

Camping: Informal, at boat-access points.

REFERENCE: *Columbia Basin Recreation Areas.* Department of Game, 600 N. Capitol Way, Olympia, WA 98501.

HEADQUARTERS: Department of Game, Regional Office, P.O. Box 1237, Ephrata, WA 98823; (509) 754-4624.

FIELDS SPRING STATE PARK
Washington Parks and Recreation Commission
456 acres.

Extreme SE WA. 30 mi. S of Clarkston, off SR 129.

Near the ID and OR borders, in the Blue Mountains. On the edge of the breaks of the Grande Ronde River Canyon, deep, winding, spectacular. Park elevations from 3,980 to 4,450 ft. Site is partly forested: ponderosa pine, grand fir, western larch, Douglas-fir. Wild rose and berry species in understory. Fine wildflower display in spring and early summer.

Wildlife forms are said to resemble those of the Rocky Mountains. Site manager says it's a fine birding area, with all of WA's woodpecker species, many hawks, owls. A bird checklist was being printed in 1981. Mammals include mule and white-tailed deer, coyote, marmot, porcupine, black bear, elk, raccoon, squirrels, chipmunk.

The Park is often crowded in hunting season, since several public hunting areas are nearby. Otherwise, it's a quiet, scenic camping spot in an out-of-the-way region with many day-trip possibilities.

SR 129 to the S descends into the gorge, crosses the river, ascends into OR. There are side roads along the river. Other roads enter the National Forest. A canyon overlook is a 1-mi. hike from the campground.

ACTIVITIES

Camping: 20 sites.

Hiking: 7 mi. of trails, including fire roads. 1-mi. trail to Puffer Butte overlook. The Umatilla National Forest map shows unpaved roads leading from the Park to Anatone Butte at the Forest boundary and Forest Road 4304.

Ski touring: Excellent area for ski touring and snowshoeing. Warming huts, covered shelters. Entry from Anatone, Asotin, or in OR.

NEARBY

Umatilla National Forest (see entry, Oregon zone 4).
Asotin Creek Habitat Management Area (see entry).

HEADQUARTERS: P.O. Box 86, Anatone, WA 99401; (509) 256-3332.

GLOYD SEEPS HABITAT MANAGEMENT AREA
Washington Department of Game
10,111 acres.

From Moses Lake on I-90, N on Stratford Rd. Public-access areas on left at Roads 9, 12, 14, 16.

Visitors should have the Columbia Basin leaflet noted in this entry. One might not plan a special trip just to Gloyd Seeps, but it can be part of an exploration of the channeled scablands.

The Habitat Management Area is about 11 mi. long, NW–SE, on Crab Creek, which has several small impoundments. Average width: a bit over 1 mi. Swampy region of saltgrass flats, marsh, extensive cattail patches surrounded by sagebrush desert. A waterfowl habitat that also supports populations of pheasant, quail, cottontail. A good birding area in spring. Popular hunting area. Homestead and Magpie lakes are managed for trout; walk-in access.

Birds: No checklist. Species generally the same as at Columbia National Wildlife Refuge (see entry). Those noted here include white pelican (in spring), blue and green herons, common snipe, green-winged teal, shoveler, Wilson's phalarope, yellow-headed blackbird, magpie, western kingbird, kingfisher.

Camping: Informal.

NEARBY: See entries, Columbia Basin Recreation Areas, zones 5 and 6.

REFERENCE: *Columbia Basin Recreation Areas.* Department of Game, 600 N. Capitol Way, Olympia, WA 98501.

HEADQUARTERS: Department of Game, Regional Office, P.O. Box 1237, Ephrata, WA 98823; (509) 754-4624.

JUNIPER FOREST
U.S. Bureau of Land Management
7,806 acres.

18 mi. NE of Pasco. From Pasco, about 20 mi. NE on Pasco-Kahlotus Rd. At Snake River Rd., turn left about 3 1/2 mi. to Blackman Ridge Rd. Left and go 2 1/2 mi. to Rypzinski Rd. Left 2 mi. to end.

The largest area of active sand dunes in Washington and the largest concentration of western juniper. Site is almost entirely sand dunes up to 300 ft. high in various stages of stabilization, active dunes in the central and NE portions. Two major groves of western juniper are within a 4,600-acre area closed to ORV's.

The site was considered for wilderness status. Those opposed were predominantly ORV enthusiasts. The BLM opposed wilderness classification but has, thus far, kept the ORV ban in the special zone.

Vegetation, aside from juniper, is scattered pockets of sagebrush, bitterbrush, rabbitbrush, wheatgrass, needlegrass, cheatgrass. Birds noted here or nearby include ferruginous, Swainson's, and red-tailed hawks; great horned, barn, short-eared, and burrowing owls; long-billed curlew, sage thrasher, sage sparrow. Mammals: Ord's kangaroo rat, a few mule deer.

HEADQUARTERS: BLM, Spokane District, Room 551, U.S. Court House, Spokane, WA 99201; (509) 456-2570.

KLICKITAT HABITAT MANAGEMENT AREA
Washington Department of Game
12,220 acres.

From Goldendale on US 97, W on SR 142 about 10 mi. to Glenwood Rd. NW toward Glenwood about 5 mi. Look for dirt roads on the left, then HQ. The more accessible public areas are beyond HQ, after the road drops down into the canyon.

The road to Glenwood and Trout Lake is scenic, lightly traveled. For some miles it passes through unbroken forest. Between the Habitat Management Area and Glenwood, look for Outlet Falls, an overlook well worth a brief stop.

The Habitat Management Area is on the meandering Klickitat River, a swift stream. Although not mentioned in any of the canoe trail books at hand, the river seemed popular with boaters. We saw rafts, kayaks, and drift boats taking out at Stinson Flat. Almost all, we were told, are steelhead anglers. Here the river is about 50 ft. wide, apparently shallow.

Some of the roads into the Habitat Management Area may require 4-wheel drive, at least in wet weather. Beyond HQ, however, the highway drops down into the river canyon, with some fine views along the way. We estimated the drop to be at least 1,500 ft. At the bottom, the road into Stinson Flat is adequate for any vehicle.

Slopes are partially forested, varying from grassy areas to moderately dense stands. Mostly ponderosa and other conifers on the slopes, deciduous trees and shrubs in the draws. At Stinson Flat is a handsome grove of oaks and several large ponderosas.

The Habitat Management Area was established as a wintering area for mule deer coming down from nearby high country, and this is still its chief purpose.

Birds: No checklist. Species noted include Merriam turkey, chukar, valley quail, band-tailed pigeon, golden eagle, prairie falcon, kingbird, mountain bluebird.

Mammals: No checklist. Species noted include black bear, deer, marmot.

ACTIVITIES

Camping: Map available at HQ shows 3 campgrounds, other camping areas. Primitive. Area is usually snow-free by Mar. Open forest offers numerous sites for informal camping.

Hiking, backpacking: No marked trails, but they're not really needed in such open country.

Hunting: Excellent deer hunting. Upland birds.

Fishing: Steelhead. Good summer-run stream. Trout, whitefish.

NEARBY: Conboy Lake National Wildlife Refuge (see entry).

HEADQUARTERS: Department of Game, Regional Office, 5405 NE Hazel Dell, Vancouver, WA 98665; (206) 696-6211.

LYONS FERRY STATE PARK
Washington Parks and Recreation Commission
1,177 acres.

SE WA, on SR 261 at the Snake River; 17 mi. SE of Washtucna.

The Park itself is not a natural area, but it offers access by boat to some interesting country. The property is leased from the U.S. Army Corps of Engineers. The Corps has 1,609 acres on the Palouse Canyon, which is managed as a natural area. The Park has 8 mi. of shoreline on the Snake River where it is joined by the Palouse River. This portion of the Snake is impounded by Lower Monumental Dam, forming a pool extending 29 mi. upriver to Little Goose Dam. The Snake River Gorge is here about 200 ft. deep, cut through a basalt plateau. Surrounding terrain is dry. Rolling hills with bluffs, lava outcrops, terraces. Vegetation is chiefly sagebrush and sparse grasses.

Birds: The impoundment is attracting increasing numbers of migratory waterfowl. No checklist. Species noted by manager: pheasant, chukar, meadowlark, killdeer, red-tailed hawk, eastern kingbird, goldfinch, great blue heron, northern shrike, Oregon junco, horned lark.

Mammals: Include yellow-bellied marmot, coyote, porcupine, cottontail, mule deer, beaver.

ACTIVITIES

Camping: 50 sites.

Hunting: Waterfowl. Not within the Park. Also upland game.

Fishing: Salmon, shad, steelhead, bass, catfish, sturgeon.

Swimming: 300-ft. supervised beach.

Boating: Ramp.

NEARBY: Palouse Falls, scenic area. Falls drop 200 ft. into a canyon with vertical walls. Best when water is at full flow, spring and early summer.

HEADQUARTERS: Box 217, Starbuck, WA 99359; (509) 525-8775, unit 3017.

MCNARY HABITAT MANAGEMENT AREA
Washington Department of Game
7,700 acres.

Just S of Burbank, off US 395.

Adjoins the McNary National Wildlife Refuge (see entry). The federal Refuge is on the inland side of US 395; the Habitat Management Area is on the other side, with about 7 mi. of river frontage. A major portion of the HMA is closed to vehicle access from Feb. 1 to mid-Oct.; entry on foot or horseback is permitted. A gravel road from Burbank extends into the HMA. A railroad embankment extends through its full length. The local HQ is near the Burbank end.

Wildlife on the Habitat Management Area includes long-billed curlew, sandhill crane, white pelican, bald and golden eagles, and most species of North American waterfowl; also deer, raccoon, coyote, mink, badger; an occasional painted turtle.

Camping is not prohibited, but there is no campground.

HEADQUARTERS: Department of Game, Regional Office, North 8702 Division St., Spokane, WA 99218; (509) 456-4082.

MCNARY NATIONAL WILDLIFE REFUGE
U.S. Fish and Wildlife Service
3,631 acres.

6 mi. S of Pasco on US 395, near Burbank.

The closing of McNary Dam submerged a number of Columbia River islands that had been important nesting habitat for Canada geese. Strawberry Island, in the Snake River just before it meets the Columbia, and the six Hanford Islands upstream from Richland in the last free-flowing section of the Columbia are a partial replacement. They are administered by the Refuge.

The mainland part of the Refuge includes 825 acres of marshes and open water, 750 acres of cropland, 1,359 acres of native grasslands. Cropland is used to produce cereal grains, corn, winter wheat, and alfalfa for waterfowl feed. Crops are also used by upland game birds.

Two public roads cross the Refuge, but there is no auto tour route. Most visitors take the 1-mi. wildlife trail, which circles the slough area.

Elevations from 330 to 500 ft. Precipitation is a scant 7 to 8 in., requiring that crops be irrigated.

Plants: Uplands: sagebrush, rabbitbrush, bluebunch wheatgrass, cheatgrass. Cattail and hardstem bulrush in marsh. A few cottonwood, willow, Russian olive.

Birds: Checklist available. Seasonally common or abundant species include great blue heron, black-crowned night heron, whistling swan, Canada goose, mallard, gadwall, pintail; green-winged, blue-winged, and cinnamon teals; American wigeon, shoveler, redhead, ring-necked duck, canvasback, lesser scaup, common and Barrow's goldeneyes, bufflehead, ruddy duck, common merganser. Also marsh hawk, ring-necked pheasant, American coot, killdeer, long-billed curlew, spotted sandpiper, avocet, Wilson's phalarope, California and ring-billed gulls, Caspian tern, mourning dove, burrowing and short-eared owls; violet-green, rough-winged, barn, bank, and cliff swallows; long-billed marsh wren, water pipit. Warblers: yellow, MacGillivray's, yellow-breasted chat, Wilson's. Yellow-headed and red-winged blackbirds.

Mammals: Include black-tailed jackrabbit, cottontail, coyote, beaver, muskrat, raccoon, mule deer, silver-haired bat. Present but seldom seen: mink, long-tailed weasel, Ord's kangaroo rat, northern pocket gopher, deer mouse, sagebrush vole, badger.

Reptiles and amphibians: Northwest fence lizard, pygmy horned lizard, tiger salamander, bullfrog, leopard frog, Great Basin spadefoot toad, painted turtle, valley garter snake, bullsnake.

ACTIVITIES

Hunting: Refuge is best known for its goose hunting. Also other waterfowl, pheasant.

Fishing: Largemouth bass, bluegill, bullhead, carp.

ADJACENT: McNary Habitat Management Area (see entry).

PUBLICATIONS
Leaflet.
Bird checklist.
Wildlife trail guide.
Hunting and fishing leaflet.

HEADQUARTERS: P.O. Box 308, Burbank, WA 99323; (509) 547-4942.

OAK CREEK HABITAT MANAGEMENT AREA
Washington Department of Game
89,023 acres.

From Yakima, NW about 23 mi. on US 12.

Between the Wenas Valley and Tieton River, bisected by the Naches River and SR 410. US 12 continues into the adjacent Tieton Ranger District of the Wenatchee National Forest (see entry), a busy resort area. Visitors should stop first at HQ, on the N side of US 12 about 2 mi. from SR 410. A good map of the Habitat Management Area is on the bulletin board. Maps are sometimes available for distribution. Even with the map, though, we had difficulty finding several of the roads. Ask at HQ for route advice and information on road conditions. Roads are usually in their best condition in summer.

The W portion of the Habitat Management Area, bordering on the National Forest, is mostly heavy ponderosa forest. To the E, trees are more scattered, open forest giving way to grasses. Slopes are moderate to steep, rising 500 to 1,500 ft. above the river valleys. Cottonwood, aspen, willow along the stream bottom. The Cowiche Unit, to the S, is on the South Fork of Cowiche Creek, along a county road. 1,440 acres. Open bunchgrass, sagebrush, rolling hills. Trout fishing; bird hunting; some deer.

The area is known for its large elk population, attracting many elk hunters. Many people visit the feeding stations at HQ, which may be used by up to 4,000 elk in severe winters.

The Tieton is a swift-moving shallow stream, popular with fishermen. US 12, following the stream, has numerous turnouts. The Oak Creek and Bethel Ridge roads, which begin near headquarters, continue into the National Forest; Oak Creek Road becomes Forest Road 140, linking with roads N of Rimrock Lake. Both are primitive roads, and checking current condition is advisable. Bethel Ridge Road was closed by washouts when we visited, is closed during winter feeding of elk.

The Habitat Management Area has several popular camping areas, but you are free to camp in almost any suitable place. Hiking is said to be good in the Cleman Mountain area, on the NE side of SR 410 but reached more easily from the Wenas Road N from Selah. In summer we'd try the Bethel Ridge area first.

Information about plants, birds, and mammals of the area is not available, but species are much the same as those mentioned in the Wenatchee National Forest entry.

In hunting season, any Habitat Management Area is best left to hunters. Spring is a good time to visit here, as soon as roads are dry enough for travel. Summer weather is a bit cooler here than in lower, drier areas to the E.

PUBLICATION: Site map, not always available.

HEADQUARTERS: Department of Game, Regional Office, 2802 Fruitvale Blvd., Yakima, WA 98902; (509) 575-2740.

POTHOLES HABITAT MANAGEMENT AREA
Washington Department of Game
38,588 acres.

From I-90 at Moses Lake, SE about 2 1/2 mi. on SR 17, then S 5 mi. on Sullivan Rd.

Obtain the *Columbia Basin Recreation Areas* map, noted in the Publications section, before coming here. The Desert Habitat Management Area and the Columbia National Wildlife Refuge (see entries) are adjacent, several other sites of interest nearby. The area, described as channeled scablands, was waterless desert until the O'Sullivan Dam formed Potholes Reservoir. Countless sand dune islands dot the N half of the reservoir, creating unique habitats. Seepage has formed countless small lakes, ponds, marshes, and sloughs, and the area is now a major nesting, resting, and feeding area for waterfowl and shorebirds. A wildlife reserve at the N end has a winter population of 20,000 to 50,000 waterfowl.

At the S end of the lake are several launching areas where RV camping is permitted. However, this end of the lake is often noisy with racing motors. If you have a canoe, the far NW end of the reservoir is quieter and more interesting. Since the reservoir is about 10 mi. long, try one of the several access points coming in from Potholes Rd. on the N. Here are many quiet channels too shallow for power boats. RV camping is possible at most boat-access points. Since the reservoir is used for irrigation, water level drops in summer.

For fauna and flora of the area, see entry for Columbia National Wildlife Refuge.

ACTIVITIES
Camping: Primitive, at boat-access points.
Hunting: Waterfowl, upland game birds.
Fishing: Largemouth bass, black crappie, yellow perch, trout, bluegill, walleye. The lake is popular with fishermen.

ADJACENT
Potholes State Park (see entry).
Columbia National Wildlife Refuge (see entry).

PUBLICATION: *Columbia Basin Recreation Areas.*

HEADQUARTERS: Department of Game, Regional Office, P.O. Box 1237, Ephrata, WA 98823; (509) 754-4624.

POTHOLES STATE PARK
Washington Parks and Recreation Commission
50 acres.

> From I-90 at Moses Lake, SE about 2 1/2 mi. on SR 17, then S 5 mi. on Sullivan Rd. Across bridge turn right and continue past dam to Park.

See entry, Columbia Basin Recreation Areas. The Park is just a convenient camping area on Potholes Reservoir, adjacent to the Potholes Habitat Management Area and Columbia National Wildlife Refuge. Many visitors prefer to park their RV's for the night at one of the many Department of Game boat-access points. Those who want a proper campground will come here.

In odd contrast with the surrounding desert, the Park is landscaped with irrigated lawns and rows of poplars. Although the site is on the reservoir and has a beach, campsites are set well back, almost out of sight of the water.

ACTIVITIES
Camping: 126 sites.
Boating: Ramp.

HEADQUARTERS: Royal Star Route, Othello, WA 99344; (509) 765-7271.

QUINCY HABITAT MANAGEMENT AREA
Washington Department of Game
13,508 acres.

> On the Columbia River, W of SR 281, N of I-90. Access from SR 28 W of Quincy by Ancient Lake Rd., from SR 281 S of Quincy by Road 5 or Base Line Rd. Signs mention Evergreen Reservoir, Quincy Lake, Stan Coffin Lake, etc., rather than the Habitat Management Area.

Several of the lakes can be reached by car over reasonably good dirt roads. But to appreciate the area fully, one must hike. Towering cliffs, sagebrush coulees, basalt pillars, and—if you hike—magnificent views from the rim of the Columbia River Canyon.

Within the Habitat Management Area, high points give a view of great expanses of sagebrush broken by large, jagged lava outcrops. Some of the lakes are surrounded by lava bluffs up to 30 ft. high.

The area is maintained for waterfowl, an important link in the Columbia Basin chain. Canada geese, whistling swans, and many species of ducks are among those stopping for a time. On a summer visit, we saw a few Canada geese, grebes, coots, great blue heron, ring-billed gull, red-tailed hawk, canyon wren, chukar.

Many of the lakes are managed for trout fishing. Very large crowds of fishermen gather during the early spring opening weekend. Both shore and boat fishing.

Hunters are busy here in the fall. For others, spring and early summer are good for visiting.

ACTIVITIES
Camping: Informal. Latrines at Evergreen.
Hunting: Waterfowl, pheasant, chukar.
Fishing: Trout, bass.

HEADQUARTERS: Department of Game, Regional Office, P.O. Box 1237, Ephrata, WA 98823; (509) 754-4624.

SUNNYSIDE HABITAT MANAGEMENT AREA
Washington Department of Game
7,604 acres.

Near Mabton on SR 22 between Toppenish and Richland. Two sections. For HQ: 4 1/2 mi. E from Mabton on SR 22; left at Bus Rd. For the larger section: N from Mabton on Mabton Rd., across the Yakima River; first left on Magee Rd., left again at Sulphur Creek.

The larger section is on the N bank of the Yakima River. It includes Griffin Lake and part of Morgan Lake. The HQ area includes the Byron Ponds. The site is managed for waterfowl and upland game birds. Both are river bottomland, typical of S central Washington. Much of the area is planted in wheat and corn for feed; multiflora rose has been planted on the nonagricultural land. The area includes some willow swamps, a grove of cottonwoods used by nesting great blue heron.

It's not a scenic area, and camping is prohibited. Birders find it interesting in spring and early summer.

HEADQUARTERS: Department of Game, Regional Office, 2802 Fruitvale Blvd., Yakima, WA 98902; (509) 575-2740.

TOPPENISH NATIONAL WILDLIFE REFUGE
U.S. Fish and Wildlife Service
1,763 acres

From Toppenish, 5 mi. S on US 97.

In the lower Yakima Valley. The Refuge has three units along Toppenish
Creek and the Yakima River. The directions above are to the HQ area. A map
available at HQ shows routes to the other areas. Brushy creek bottoms, wet
meadows, croplands, and sagebrush uplands. The Refuge is maintained for
waterfowl, and up to 200,000 ducks are present winter and spring, a dense
concentration for an area of this size. A wildlife observation point is at the
Upper Toppenish Unit.

If you plan a visit, check the Refuge schedule. We found the gate locked,
with no explanatory sign. We learned later that the sign had been removed
by a vandal. The gate was closed because the Refuge has only one regular
employee, and visitors can be accommodated only on certain days. (At present: Feb. 1–Oct. 1, open 7 A.M.–4:30 P.M., Mon.–Thurs. and Mon.–Fri. in
alternate weeks. After Oct. 1, same hours, but closed Wed.–Thurs. of each
week.)

Birds: Checklist with 148 species. Birding is said to be good at any season,
best in winter and spring. Seasonally common and abundant species include
great blue heron, Canada goose, mallard, pintail, teals, wigeon, shoveler,
wood duck; red-tailed, Swainson's, rough-legged, and marsh hawks; kestrel,
California quail, pheasant, Virginia rail, killdeer, common snipe, lesser yellowlegs, least sandpiper, Wilson's phalarope, rock and mourning doves;
screech, great horned, burrowing, and short-eared owls; common nighthawk,
common flicker, western kingbird; tree, bank, and barn swallows, magpie,
raven, common crow, long-billed marsh wren, loggerhead shrike, yellow-
rumped warbler, western meadowlark, yellow-headed and red-winged blackbirds, house finch, American goldfinch; savannah, vesper, and sage sparrows.

PUBLICATIONS
Bird checklist.
Hunting leaflet with Refuge map.

HEADQUARTERS: Route 1, Box 1300, Toppenish, WA 98948; (509) 865-2405.

UMATILLA NATIONAL FOREST
U.S. Forest Service
311,209 acres in WA; 1,088,197 acres in OR.

SE corner of WA. Access in WA by secondary roads only, chiefly from Asotin, S of Clarkston, on the ID border, and from Pomeroy and Dayton on US 12.

Forest map required.

The WA portion is in the Blue Mountains, which extend N from OR. A major part of the Wenaha-Tucannon Wilderness is in WA. Points of interest include Clearwater Lookout, 25 mi. S of Pomeroy, and Sunset Point, 30 mi. S of Pomeroy, both offering fine views. A number of Forest campgrounds are in this area. The road beyond Sunset Point goes to the edge of the wilderness area. (See entry in Oregon zone 4.)

RANGER DISTRICTS: Pomeroy, WA 99347; (509) 843-1891. Walla Walla, WA 99362; (509) 525-5500.

UMATILLA NATIONAL WILDLIFE REFUGE
U.S. Fish and Wildlife Service
14,006 acres.

On the Columbia River, bounded by SR 14, E and W of Paterson.

About half of this Refuge is in Oregon. Since the two parts are separated by the river, each is an entry.

The Refuge extends along the river for about 18 mi., with two gaps. The portion E of Paterson is open to the public all year. Lands W of Paterson to Glade Creek are closed to public use Oct. 1–Feb. 28. Closing of John Day Dam inundated much waterfowl habitat, but it also created Paterson Slough, E of Paterson, now a fine place to observe wintering or migrating waterfowl. The Refuge includes a number of islands, sandbars and sandy shores, sloughs, marsh, cultivated cropland, and bits of sagebrush upland.

Stop first at the HQ in Umatilla, OR, unless it's a weekend when the office is closed. On the Refuge in summer 1980 we found bare bulletin boards, no directional or informational signs. We have since been advised that signs are up and brochures are available.

Birds: 189 species recorded (OR and WA units). Checklist available. Seasonally abundant or common species include pied-billed grebe, double-crested cormorant, great blue heron, whistling swan, Canada goose, mallard, gadwall, pintail, teals, wigeon, shoveler, goldeneye, bufflehead. White pelican is noted as occasional in fall, uncommon in winter, but we saw two dozen on the OR side in Aug.

Also seasonally abundant or common: marsh hawk, kestrel, California quail, pheasant, coot, killdeer, greater yellowlegs, Baird's and western sandpipers, avocet, ring-billed gull, terns, rock and mourning doves, flicker, magpie, raven, crow, long-billed marsh wren, robin, cedar waxwing, house sparrow, western meadowlark, yellow-headed and red-winged blackbirds, northern oriole, cowbird, house finch, goldfinch, sparrows.

Mammals: Include black-tailed jackrabbit, cottontail, big brown bat, smallfooted myotis, opossum, porcupine, muskrat, coyote, badger, beaver, raccoon, river otter, bobcat, mule deer.

ACTIVITIES
Hunting: Waterfowl and upland game. Designated areas and special regulations, including required permit obtained by mail application.
Fishing: River. Sturgeon, bass, salmon, steelhead.

PUBLICATIONS
Leaflet for Washington side.
Bird checklist.
Hunting information and map.

HEADQUARTERS: P.O. Box 239, Umatilla, OR 97882; (503) 922-3232.

WAHLUKE SLOPE HABITAT MANAGEMENT AREA
Washington Department of Game
57,839 acres.

On both sides of SR 24, about 10 mi. S and E of Othello. From Pasco, N on Road 68 to Ringold, following signs.

This Habitat Management Area adjoins the Saddle Mountains National Wildlife Refuge, which is on Nuclear Regulatory Commission land and closed to the public. The HMA is also on NRC land, but limited public use is permitted. Regulations are posted. Day use only.

On the S slope of the Saddle Mountains, extending to the Columbia River. Seep lakes have formed from waste water, attracting waterfowl and numerous shorebirds. The area is also noted for raptors. Bald eagle often seen in winter. 50,000 to 100,000 waterfowl can be seen in winter on the river reserve.

This is the last free-flowing stretch of the Columbia River. The White Bluffs on the river provide strong visual contrast with the generally flat terrain. On the S end of the site, on the river, are abandoned farms, now a hunting area.

PUBLICATION: *Columbia Basin Recreation Areas.* Department of Game, 600 N. Capitol Way, Olympia, WA 98501.

HEADQUARTERS: Department of Game, Regional Office, P.O. Box 1237, Ephrata, WA 98823; (509) 754-4624.

W. T. WOOTEN HABITAT MANAGEMENT AREA
Washington Department of Game
11,185 acres.

From Clarkston, W on US 12 through Pomeroy. Beyond Zumwalt take left fork, SR 126, to Marengo. Then S about 15 mi. along the Tucannon River.

The road along the river is a northern entrance to the Umatilla National Forest (see entry) and the Panjab campground at the edge of the Wenaha-Tucannon Wilderness. In the spectacular Blue Mountains. Most of the Habitat Management Area is on the E side of the river. The river valley is rugged, with sharp, steep ridges, talus slopes, broad-topped tablelands. N-facing slopes are timbered, S-facing slopes open and grassy.

A local HQ is at the N edge of the Habitat Management Area. Beyond it, along the valley, are several small ponds. This is a popular fishing area in summer, and many people camp here rather than continue into the National Forest. But the HMA has enough backcountry to offer ample solitude. Tumalum Creek and Cummings Creek are possible routes.

The valley is a wintering area for elk. A few bighorn sheep may be in the Habitat Management Area. Also present: white-tailed and mule deer, black bear, snowshoe hare, cottontail, mountain lion, bobcat. Game birds include Merriam turkey, valley and mountain quail, chukar and Hungarian partridge, pheasant, dove.

HEADQUARTERS: Department of Game, Regional Office, North 8702 Division St., Spokane, WA 99218; (509) 456-4082.

INDEX

ABOUT THE AUTHORS

THE PERRYS, long residents of the Washington, D.C., area, moved to Winter Haven, Florida, soon after work on these guides began. Their desks overlook a lake well populated with great blue herons, anhingas, egrets, ospreys, gallinules, and wood ducks, plus occasional alligators and otters.

Jane, an economist, came to Washington as a congressman's secretary and thereafter held senior posts in several executive agencies and presidential commissions. John, an industrial management consultant, was for ten years assistant director of the National Zoo.

Married in 1944, they have hiked, backpacked, camped, canoed, and cruised together in all fifty states. They have written more than a dozen books and produced more than two dozen educational filmstrips, chiefly on natural history and ecology.

Both have been involved in conservation action, at home and abroad. Since 1966 John has been a member of the Survival Service Commission and the International Union for the Conservation of Nature (IUCN), with many trips—with Jane—to South America, Europe, Africa, and Asia. In Florida they are active participants in the Sierra Club and The Nature Conservancy.